尾田栄一郎

If you added "cyclone" ability to a figure skater's or ballerina's spin, they'd either fly off or go right into the ground. Well, if you could somehow install a "cyclone" in your anus so it could spin at incredible speed, it would be the answer to all of our constipation situations. *Let Cyclone Volume 77... begrugrugrugrugrunnn!!!*

–Eiichiro Oda, 2015

Eiichiro Oda began his manga career at the age of 17, when his one-shot cowboy manga **Wanted!** won second place in the coveted Tezuka manga awards. Oda went on to work as an assistant to some of the biggest manga artists in the industry, including Nobuhiro Watsuki, before winning the Hop Step Award for new artists. His pirate adventure **One Piece**, which debuted in **Weekly Shonen Jump** in 1997, quickly became one of the most popular manga in Japan.

ONE PIECE VOL. 77
NEW WORLD PART 17

SHONEN JUMP Manga Edition

STORY AND ART BY EIICHIRO ODA

Translation/Stephen Paul
Touch-up Art & Lettering/Vanessa Satone
Design/Fawn Lau
Editor/Alexis Kirsch

ONE PIECE © 1997 by Eiichiro Oda. All rights reserved.
First published in Japan in 1997 by SHUEISHA Inc., Tokyo.
English translation rights arranged by SHUEISHA Inc.

The stories, characters and incidents mentioned
in this publication are entirely fictional.

Printed in the U.S.A.

Published by VIZ Media, LLC
P.O. Box 77010
San Francisco, CA 94107

10 9 8 7 6 5 4 3 2 1
First printing, February 2016

ONE PIECE

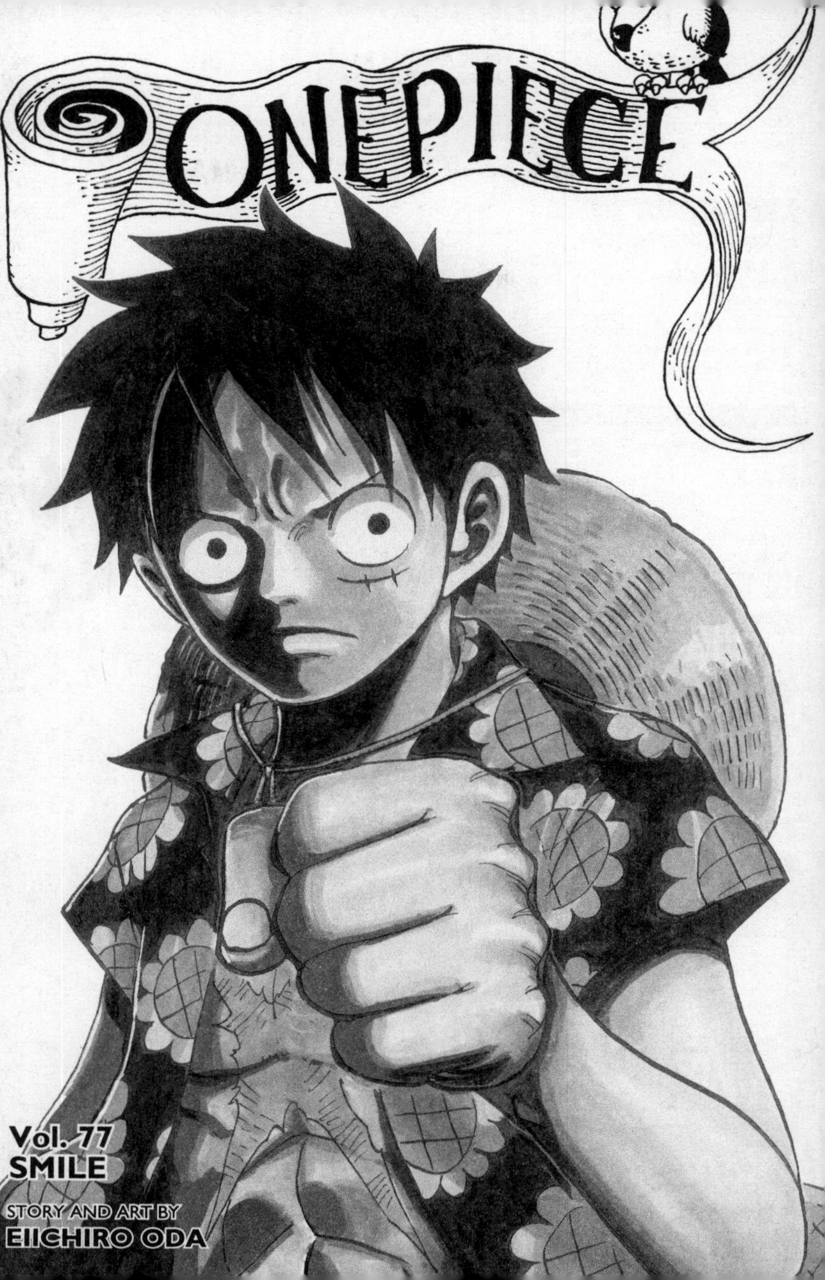

Vol. 77
SMILE

STORY AND ART BY
EIICHIRO ODA

The Straw Hat Crew

Monkey D. Luffy

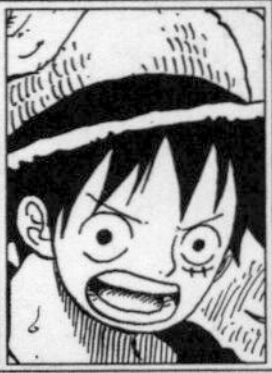

A young man who dreams of becoming the Pirate King. After training with Rayleigh, he and his crew head for the New World!

Captain, Bounty: 400 million berries

Tony Tony Chopper

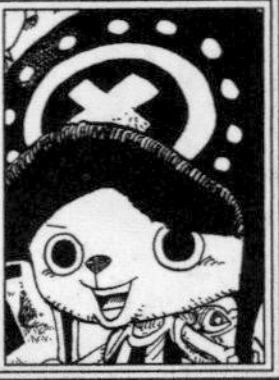

After researching powerful medicine in Birdie Kingdom, he reunites with the rest of the crew.

Ship's Doctor, Bounty: 50 berries

Roronoa Zolo

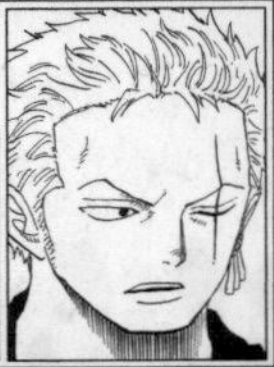

He swallowed his pride and asked to be trained by Mihawk on Gloom Island before reuniting with the rest of the crew.

Fighter, Bounty: 120 million berries

Nico Robin

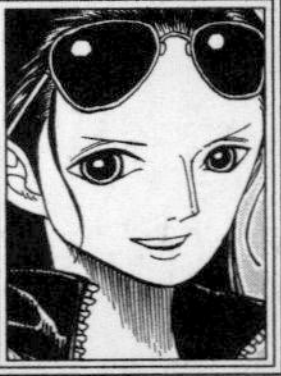

She spent her time in Baltigo with the leader of the Revolutionary Army: Luffy's father, Dragon.

Archeologist, Bounty: 80 million berries

Nami

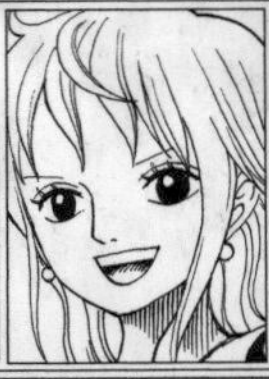

She studied the weather of the New World on the small Sky Island Weatheria, a place where weather is studied as a science.

Navigator, Bounty: 16 million berries

Franky

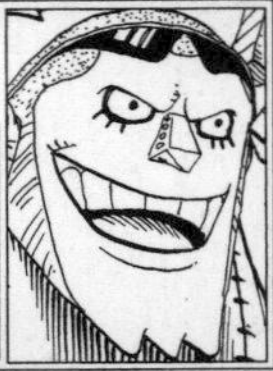

He modified himself in Future Land Baldimore and turned himself into Armored Franky before reuniting with the rest of the crew.

Shipwright, Bounty: 44 million berries

Usopp

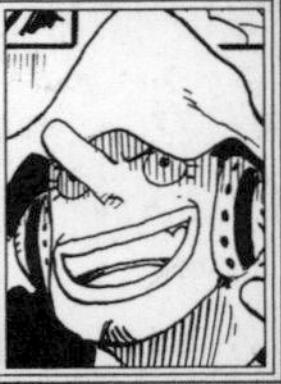

He trained under Heracles at the Bowin Islands to become the King of Snipers.

Sniper, Bounty: 30 million berries

Brook

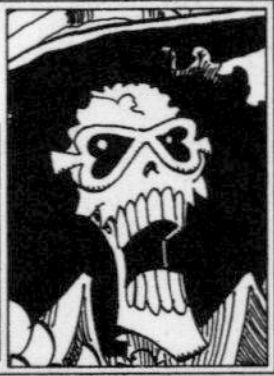

After being captured and used as a freak show by the Longarm Tribe, he became a famous rock star called "Soul King" Brook.

Musician, Bounty: 33 million berries

Sanji

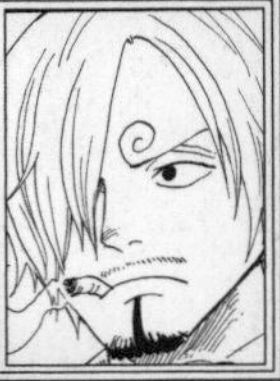

After fighting the New Kama Karate masters in the Kamabakka Kingdom, he returned to the crew.

Cook, Bounty: 77 million berries

Shanks

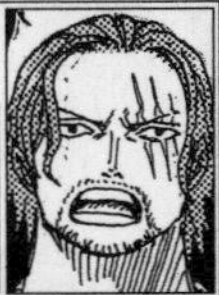

One of the Four Emperors. Waits for Luffy in the "New World," the second half of the Grand Line.

Captain of the Red-Haired Pirates

a one-legged toy soldier who informs them of the nation's hidden darkness, and they decide to help the little Tontattas in their fight for freedom. Luffy and Law head for the palace on the fourth step to face Doflamingo. Meanwhile, a collection of coliseum gladiators who are after Doflamingo's head clash with the officers of the Don Quixote family!! When Luffy and Law finally reach the fourth step, they square off in direct combat against Doflamingo!! But what secrets lie in the pasts of Law, the former officer Corazon, and Doflamingo himself?!

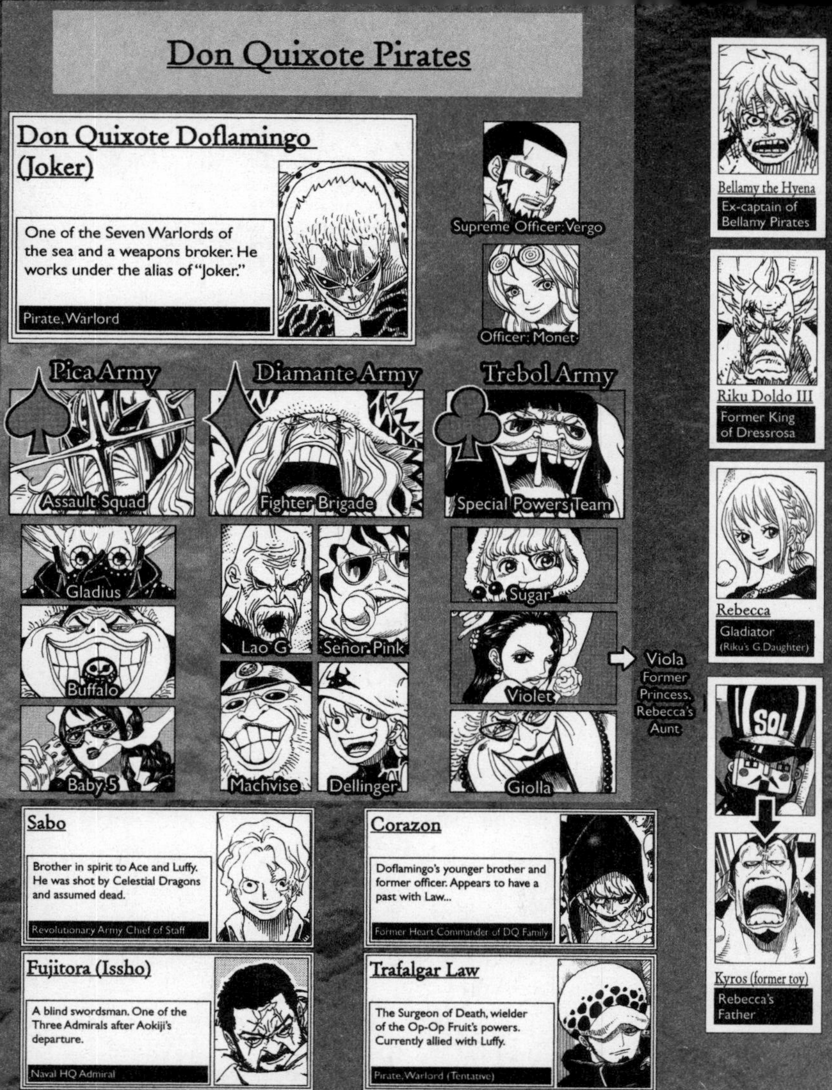
Don Quixote Pirates
Don Quixote Doflamingo (Joker)
One of the Seven Warlords of the sea and a weapons broker. He works under the alias of "Joker."
Pirate, Warlord
Supreme Officer: Vergo
Officer: Monet
Pica Army
Assault Squad
Gladius
Buffalo
Baby 5
Diamante Army
Fighter Brigade
Lao G
Señor Pink
Machvise
Dellinger
Trebol Army
Special Powers Team
Sugar
Violet
Giolla
Viola
Former Princess, Rebecca's Aunt
Bellamy the Hyena
Ex-captain of Bellamy Pirates
Riku Doldo III
Former King of Dressrosa
Rebecca
Gladiator
(Riku's G.Daughter)
SOL
Kyros (former toy)
Rebecca's Father
Sabo
Brother in spirit to Ace and Luffy. He was shot by Celestial Dragons and assumed dead.
Revolutionary Army Chief of Staff
Corazon
Doflamingo's younger brother and former officer. Appears to have a past with Law...
Former Heart Commander of DQ Family
Fujitora (Issho)
A blind swordsman. One of the Three Admirals after Aokiji's departure.
Naval HQ Admiral
Trafalgar Law
The Surgeon of Death, wielder of the Op-Op Fruit's powers. Currently allied with Luffy.
Pirate, Warlord (Tentative)

Story

After two years of hard training, the Straw Hat pirates are back together, first at the Sabaody Archipelago and then through Fish-Man Island to their next stage: the New World!!

The crew happens across Trafalgar Law on the island of Punk Hazard. At his suggestion, they form a new pirate alliance that seeks to take down one of the Four Emperors. The group infiltrates the kingdom of Dressrosa in an attempt to set up Doflamingo, but Law is abducted after falling into a trap. The rest of the crew meets

NEW WORLD

ONE PIECE

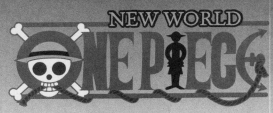

Vol. 77
Smile

CONTENTS

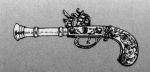

ONE PIECE

Hereafter, the 77th volume will start.

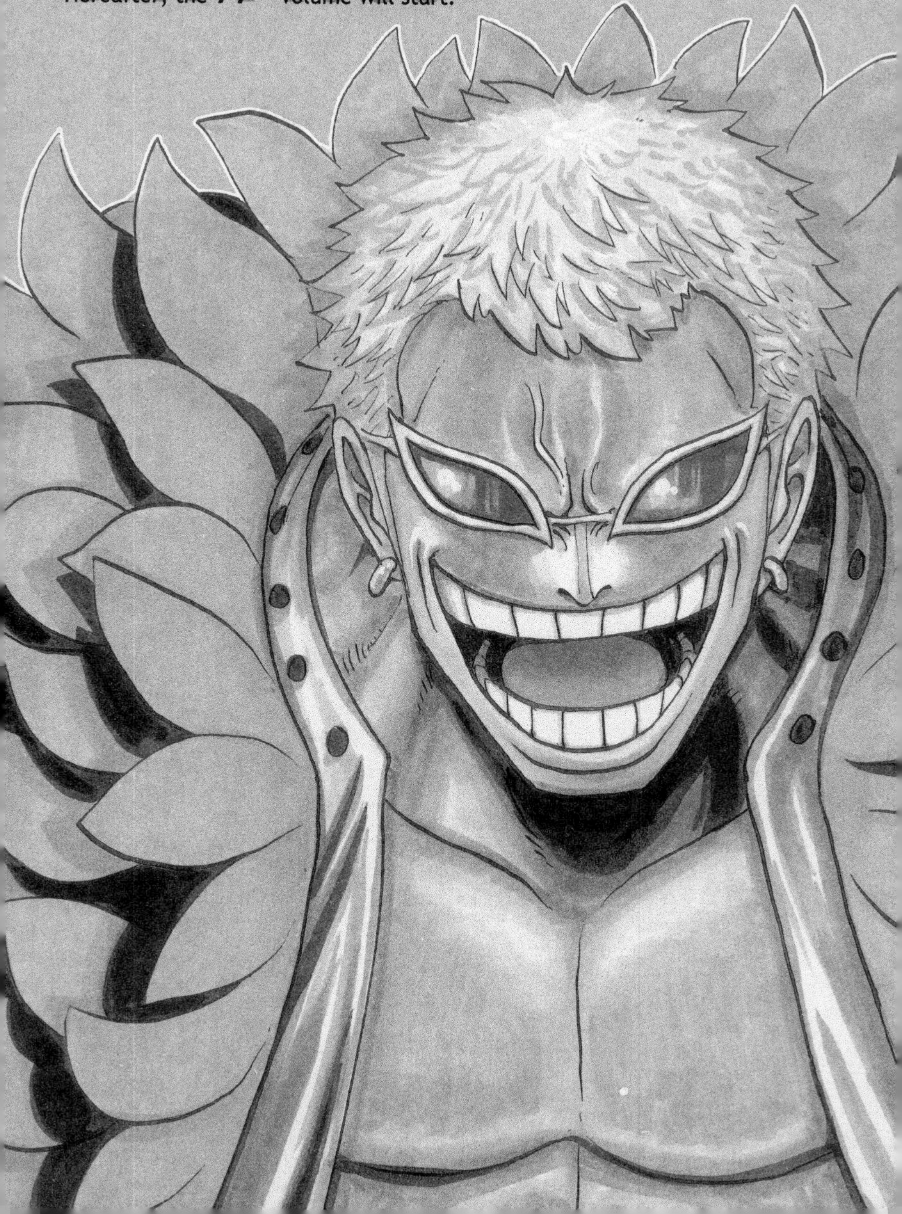

WHITE MONSTER

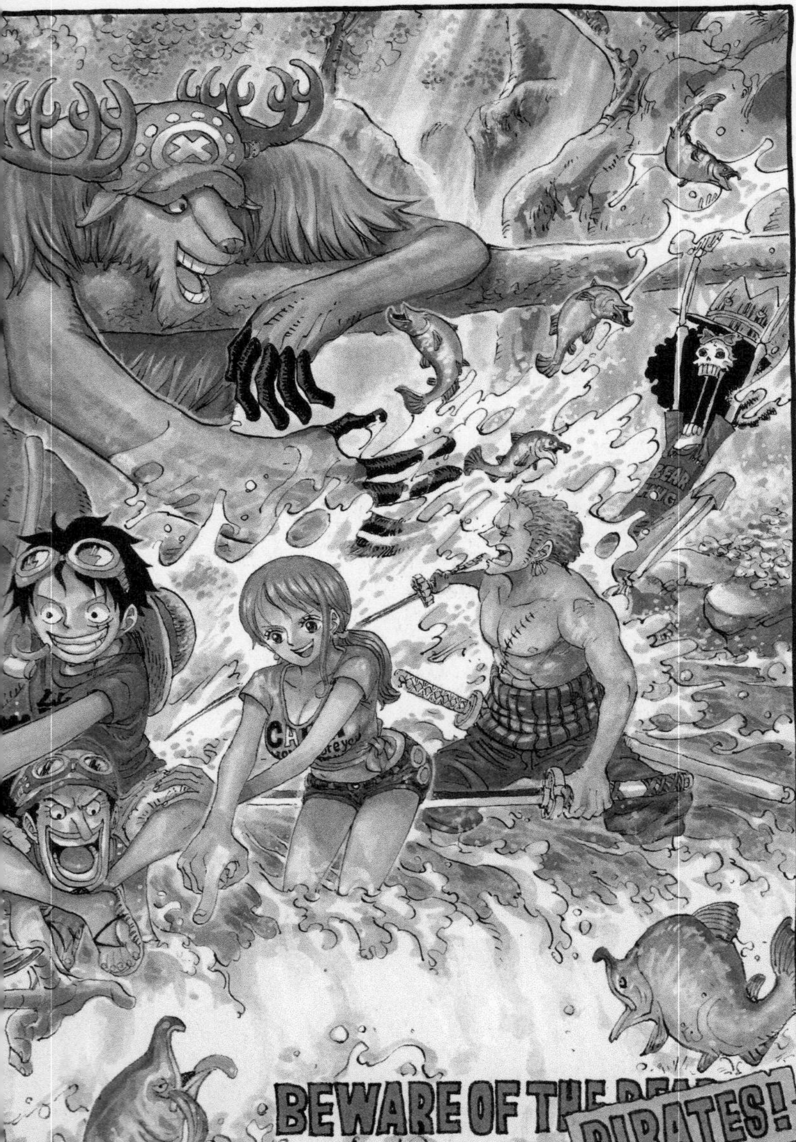
BEWARE OF TH
PIRATES!

Chapter 764:

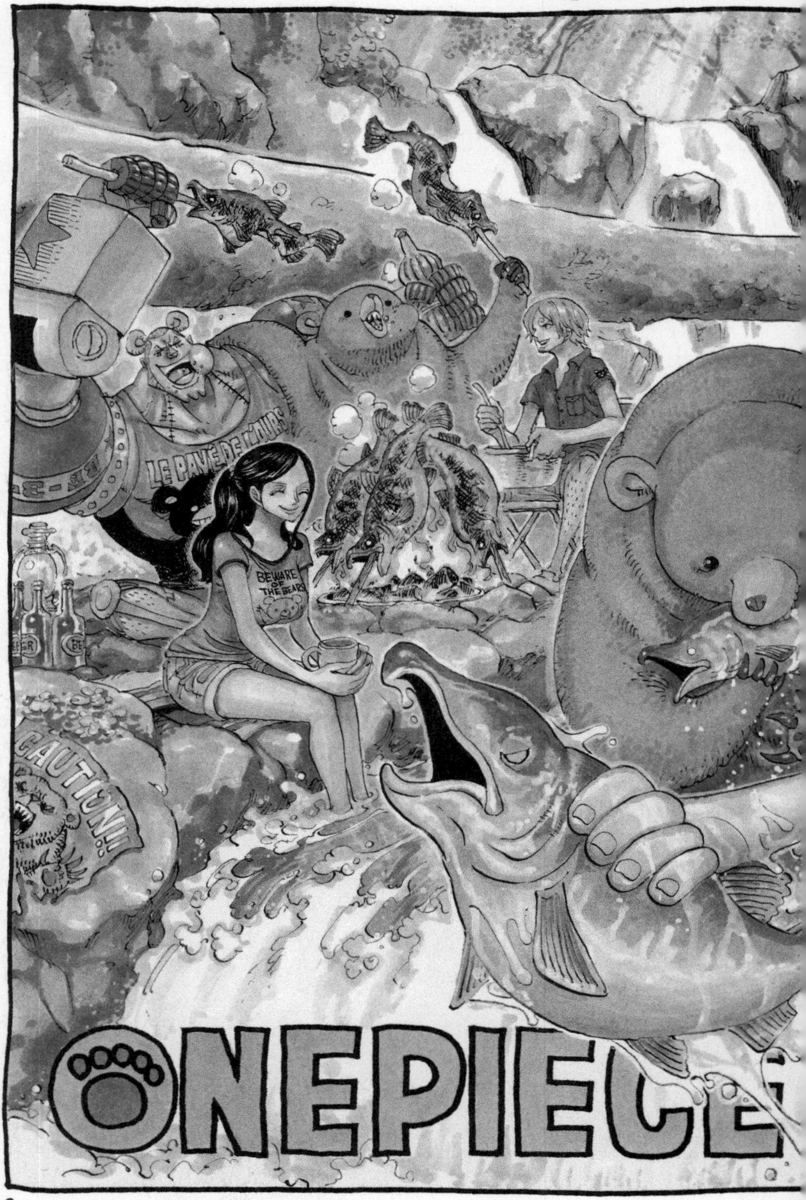
LE PAVÉ DE L'OURS
BEWARE OF THE BEARS
CAUTION!!
ONEPIECE

vol.77

ONE PIECE

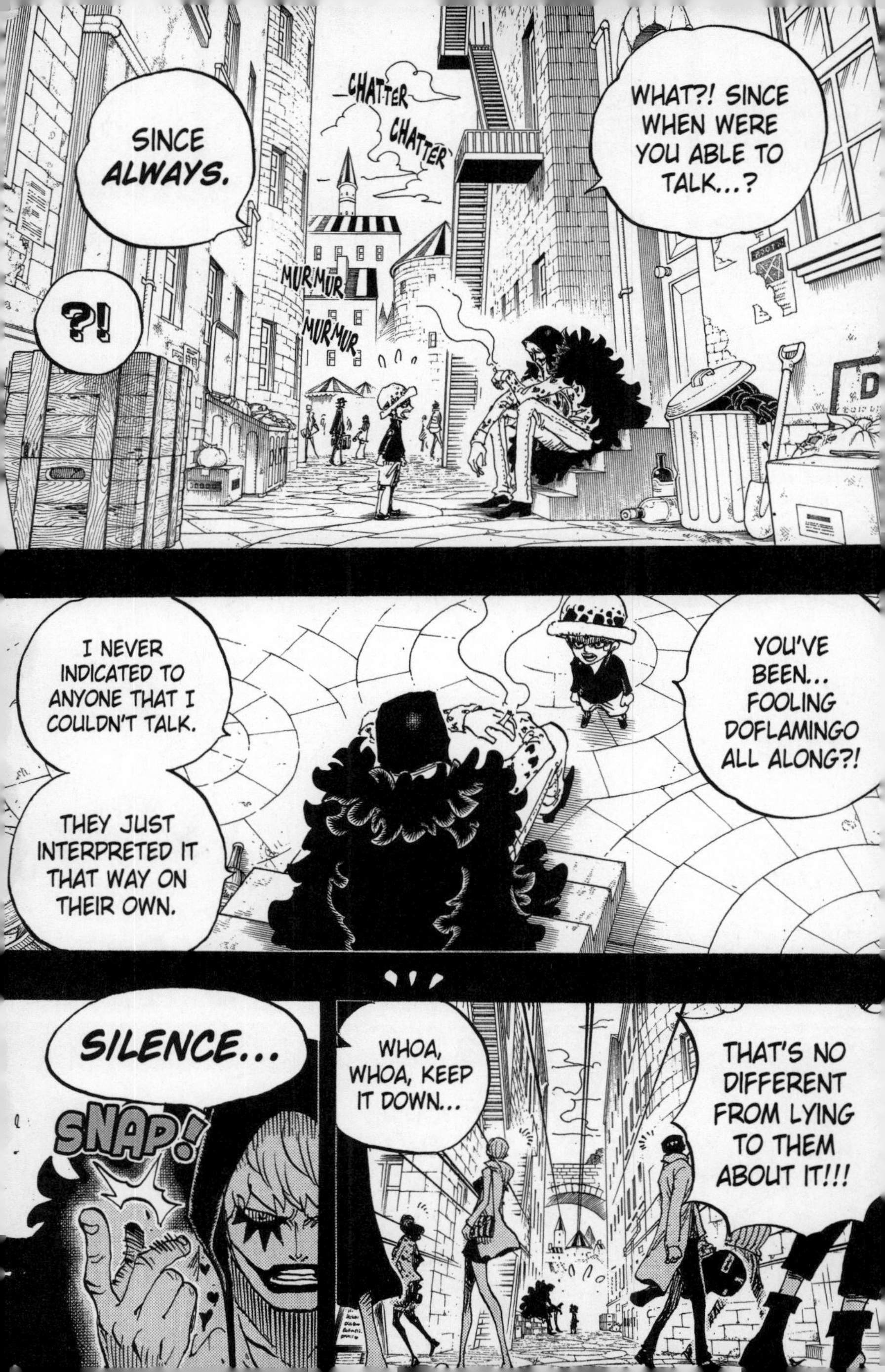
WHAT?! SINCE WHEN WERE YOU ABLE TO TALK...?
CHATTER
CHATTER
SINCE ALWAYS.
MURMUR
MURMUR
?!
YOU'VE BEEN... FOOLING DOFLAMINGO ALL ALONG?!
I NEVER INDICATED TO ANYONE THAT I COULDN'T TALK.
THEY JUST INTERPRETED IT THAT WAY ON THEIR OWN.
THAT'S NO DIFFERENT FROM LYING TO THEM ABOUT IT!!!
WHOA, WHOA, KEEP IT DOWN...
SILENCE...
SNAP!

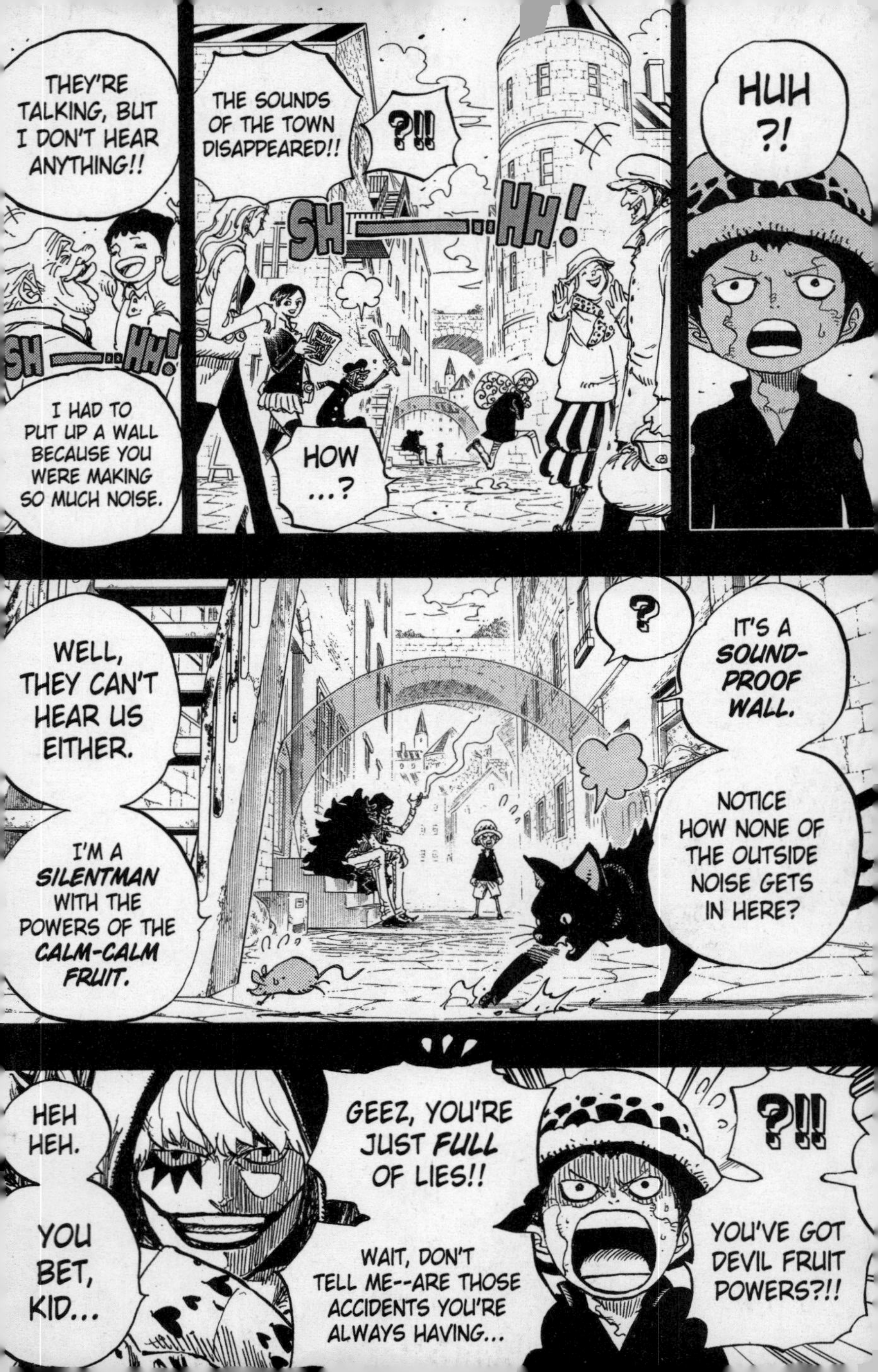
HUH ?!
?!!
THE SOUNDS OF THE TOWN DISAPPEARED!!
SH—..HH!
HOW ...?
THEY'RE TALKING, BUT I DON'T HEAR ANYTHING!!
SH—..HH!
I HAD TO PUT UP A WALL BECAUSE YOU WERE MAKING SO MUCH NOISE.
?
IT'S A *SOUND-PROOF WALL.*
NOTICE HOW NONE OF THE OUTSIDE NOISE GETS IN HERE?
WELL, THEY CAN'T HEAR US EITHER.
I'M A *SILENTMAN* WITH THE POWERS OF THE *CALM-CALM FRUIT.*
?!!
YOU'VE GOT DEVIL FRUIT POWERS?!!
GEEZ, YOU'RE JUST *FULL* OF LIES!!
WAIT, DON'T TELL ME--ARE THOSE ACCIDENTS YOU'RE ALWAYS HAVING...
HEH HEH.
YOU BET, KID...

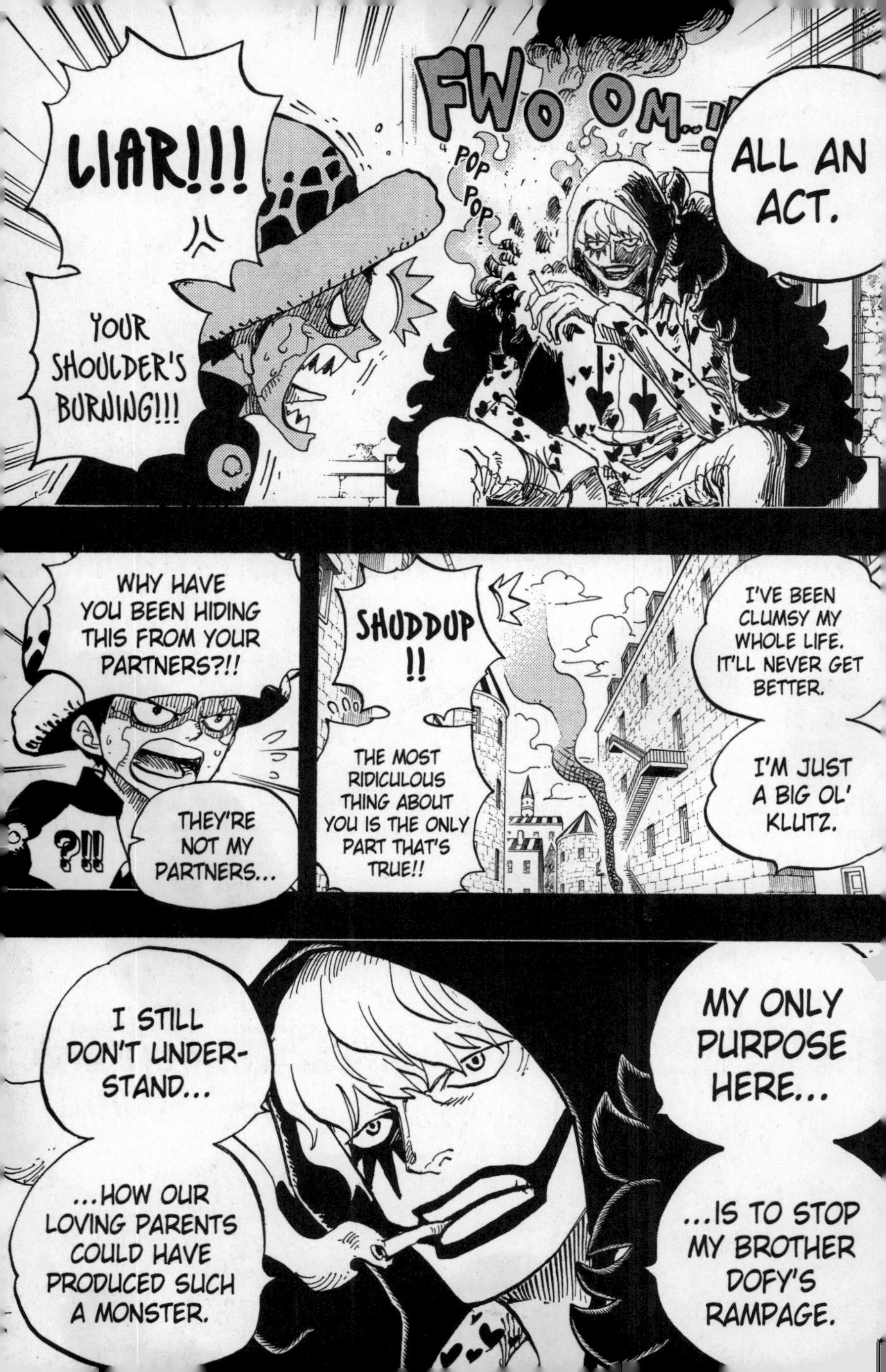
ALL AN ACT.
FWO OM..!!
POP POP POP
LIAR!!!
YOUR SHOULDER'S BURNING!!!
I'VE BEEN CLUMSY MY WHOLE LIFE. IT'LL NEVER GET BETTER.
I'M JUST A BIG OL' KLUTZ.
SHUDDUP !!
THE MOST RIDICULOUS THING ABOUT YOU IS THE ONLY PART THAT'S TRUE!!
WHY HAVE YOU BEEN HIDING THIS FROM YOUR PARTNERS?!!
THEY'RE NOT MY PARTNERS...
?!!
MY ONLY PURPOSE HERE...
...IS TO STOP MY BROTHER DOFY'S RAMPAGE.
I STILL DON'T UNDER-STAND...
...HOW OUR LOVING PARENTS COULD HAVE PRODUCED SUCH A MONSTER.

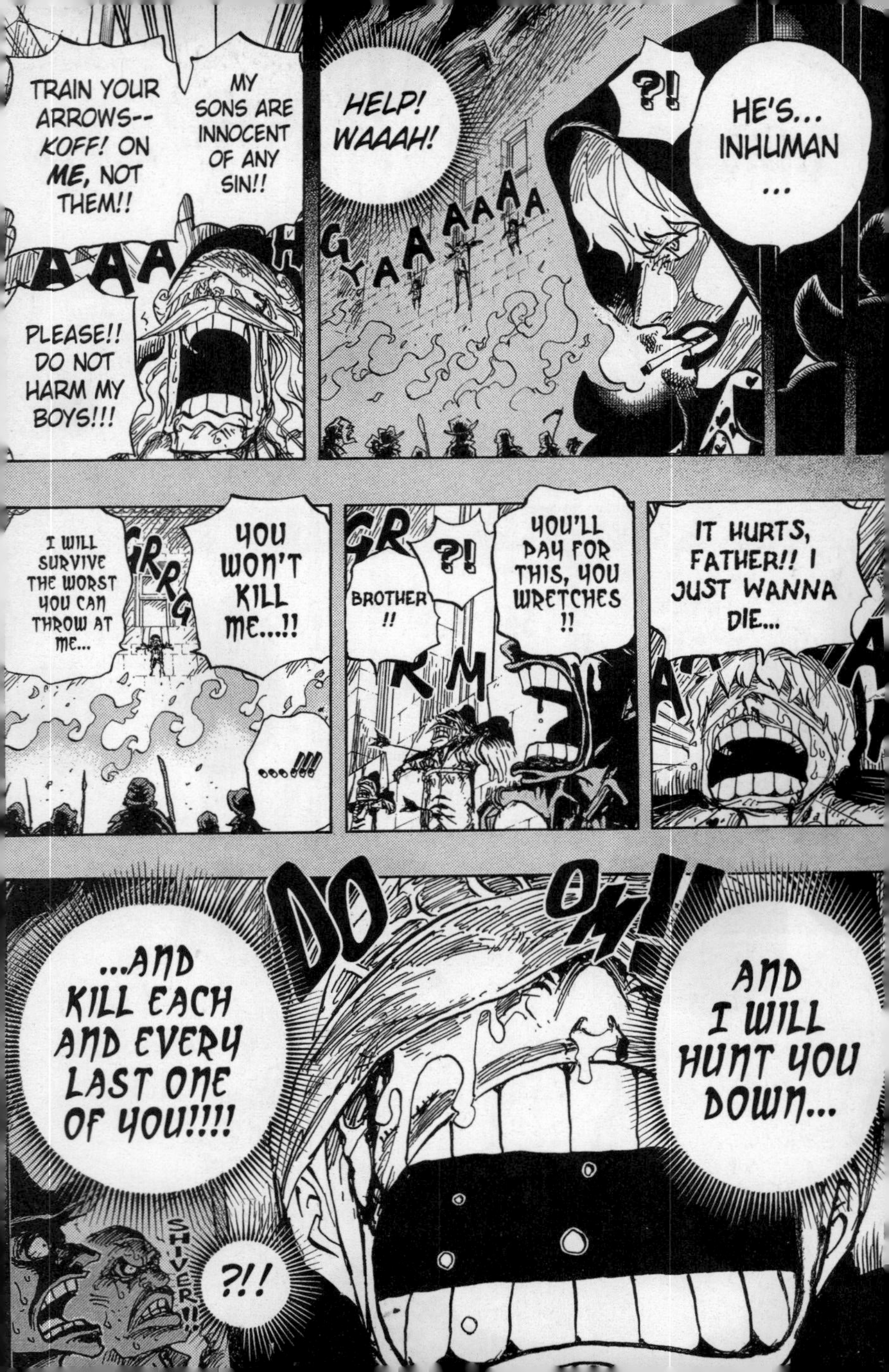
?!
HE'S... INHUMAN ...
HELP! WAAAH!
GYAAAAAAAA
MY SONS ARE INNOCENT OF ANY SIN!!
TRAIN YOUR ARROWS-- KOFF! ON ME, NOT THEM!!
AAAH
PLEASE!! DO NOT HARM MY BOYS!!!
IT HURTS, FATHER!! I JUST WANNA DIE...
YOU'LL PAY FOR THIS, YOU WRETCHES !!
?!
BROTHER !!
GRRM
YOU WON'T KILL ME...!!
I WILL SURVIVE THE WORST YOU CAN THROW AT ME...
GRRRG
...!!!
DOON!!
AND I WILL HUNT YOU DOWN...
...AND KILL EACH AND EVERY LAST ONE OF YOU!!!!!
?!!
SHIVER!!

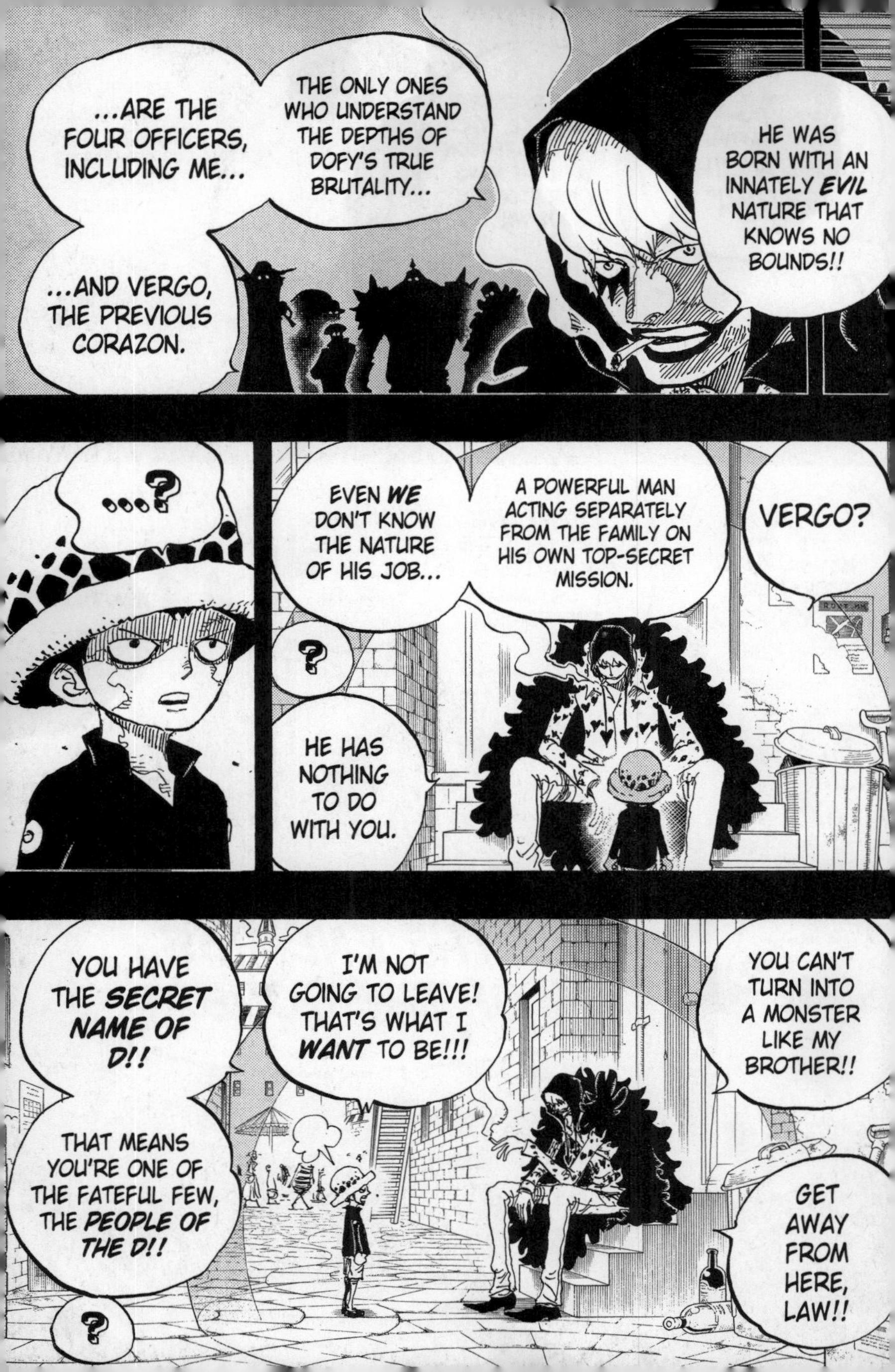
HE WAS BORN WITH AN INNATELY EVIL NATURE THAT KNOWS NO BOUNDS!!
THE ONLY ONES WHO UNDERSTAND THE DEPTHS OF DOFY'S TRUE BRUTALITY...
...ARE THE FOUR OFFICERS, INCLUDING ME...
...AND VERGO, THE PREVIOUS CORAZON.
VERGO?
A POWERFUL MAN ACTING SEPARATELY FROM THE FAMILY ON HIS OWN TOP-SECRET MISSION.
EVEN WE DON'T KNOW THE NATURE OF HIS JOB...
?
HE HAS NOTHING TO DO WITH YOU.
...?
YOU CAN'T TURN INTO A MONSTER LIKE MY BROTHER!!
GET AWAY FROM HERE, LAW!!
I'M NOT GOING TO LEAVE! THAT'S WHAT I WANT TO BE!!!
YOU HAVE THE SECRET NAME OF D!!
THAT MEANS YOU'RE ONE OF THE FATEFUL FEW, THE PEOPLE OF THE D!!
?

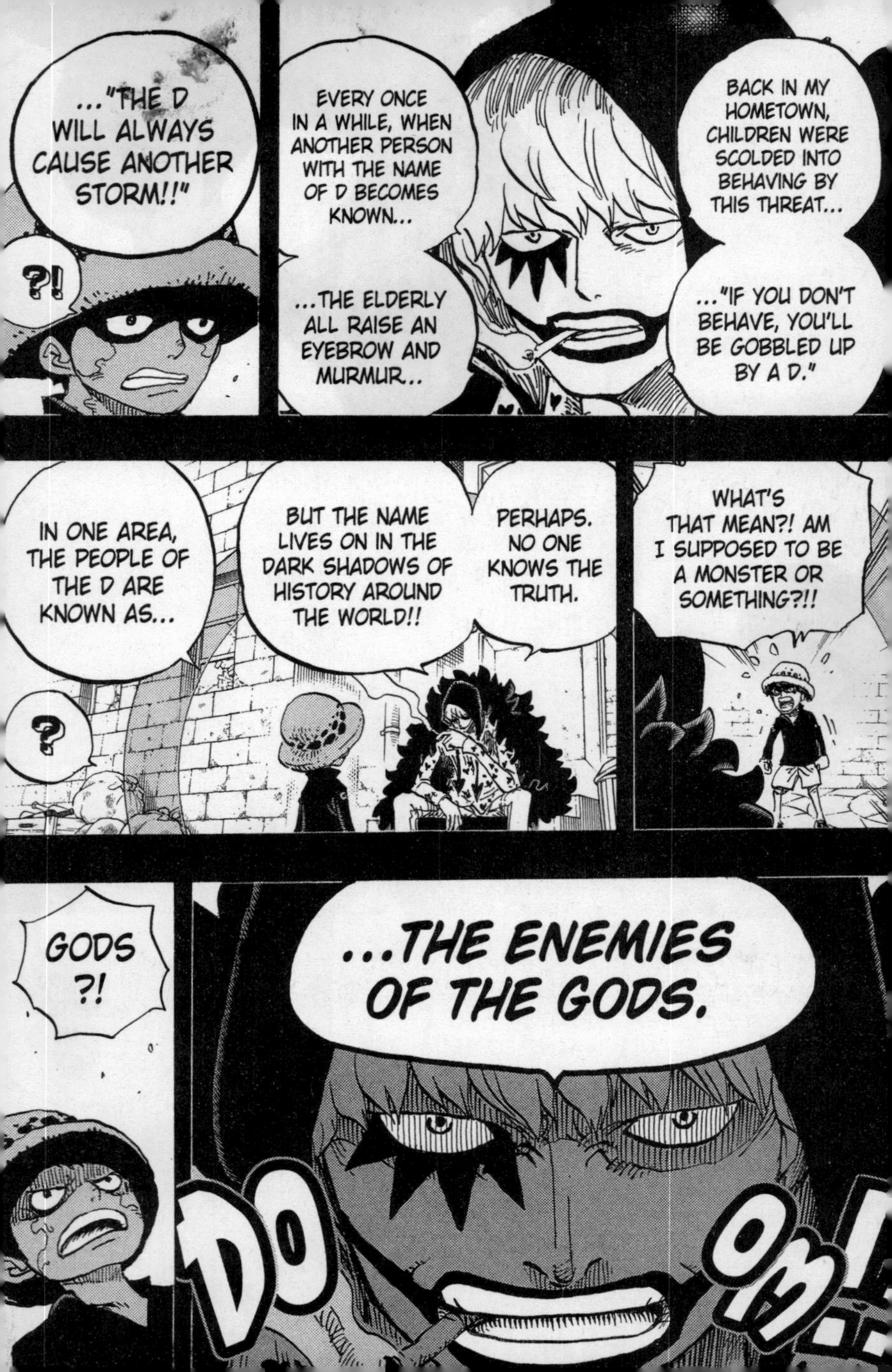
BACK IN MY HOMETOWN, CHILDREN WERE SCOLDED INTO BEHAVING BY THIS THREAT...
..."IF YOU DON'T BEHAVE, YOU'LL BE GOBBLED UP BY A D."
EVERY ONCE IN A WHILE, WHEN ANOTHER PERSON WITH THE NAME OF D BECOMES KNOWN...
...THE ELDERLY ALL RAISE AN EYEBROW AND MURMUR...
..."THE D WILL ALWAYS CAUSE ANOTHER STORM!!"
?!
WHAT'S THAT MEAN?! AM I SUPPOSED TO BE A MONSTER OR SOMETHING?!!
PERHAPS. NO ONE KNOWS THE TRUTH.
BUT THE NAME LIVES ON IN THE DARK SHADOWS OF HISTORY AROUND THE WORLD!!
IN ONE AREA, THE PEOPLE OF THE D ARE KNOWN AS...
?
...THE ENEMIES OF THE GODS.
DOOM!!
GODS ?!

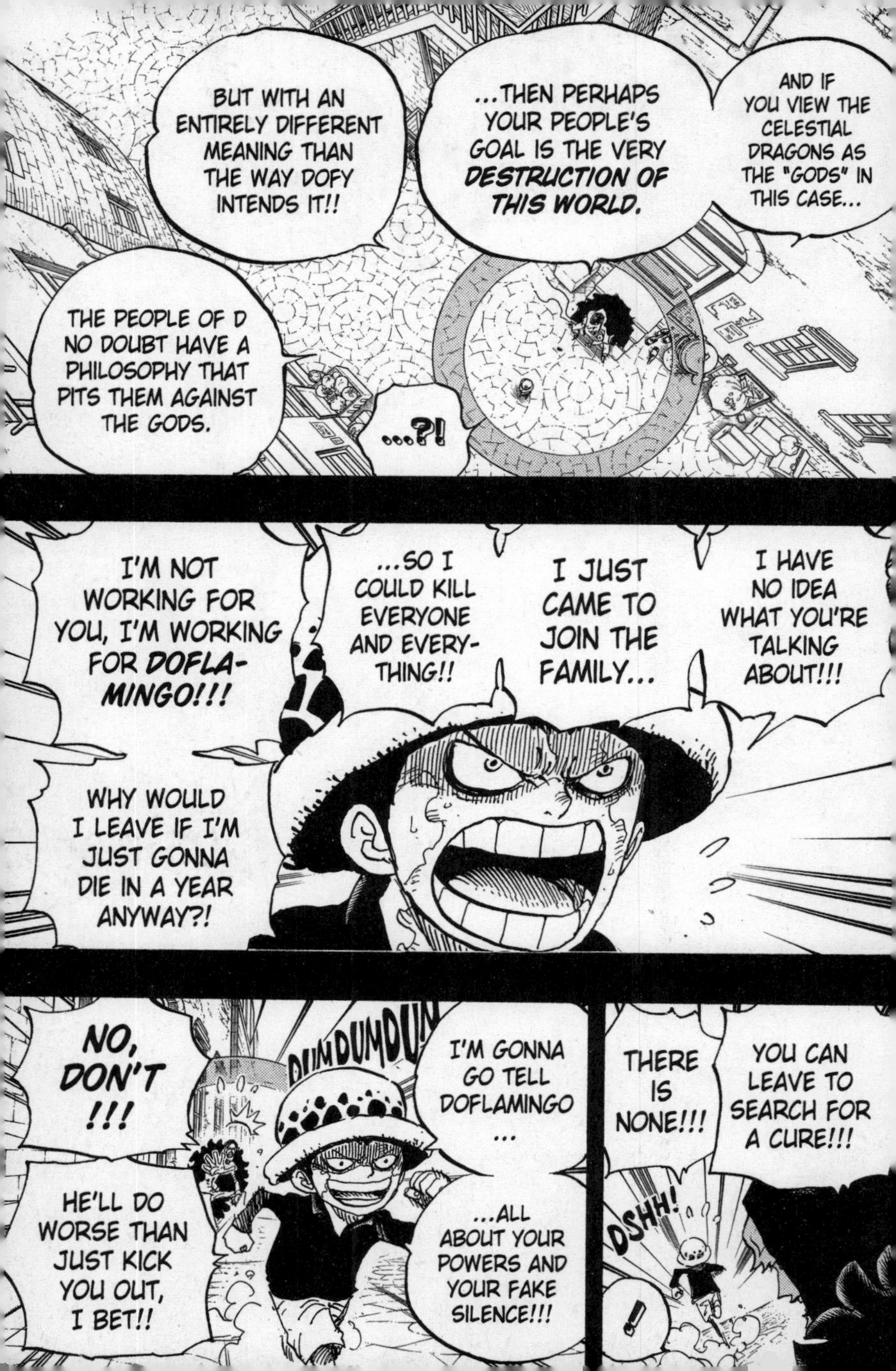

AND IF YOU VIEW THE CELESTIAL DRAGONS AS THE "GODS" IN THIS CASE...
...THEN PERHAPS YOUR PEOPLE'S GOAL IS THE VERY ***DESTRUCTION OF THIS WORLD.***
BUT WITH AN ENTIRELY DIFFERENT MEANING THAN THE WAY DOFY INTENDS IT!!
THE PEOPLE OF D NO DOUBT HAVE A PHILOSOPHY THAT PITS THEM AGAINST THE GODS.
...?!
I HAVE NO IDEA WHAT YOU'RE TALKING ABOUT!!!
I JUST CAME TO JOIN THE FAMILY...
...SO I COULD KILL EVERYONE AND EVERYTHING!!
I'M NOT WORKING FOR YOU, I'M WORKING FOR ***DOFLAMINGO!!!***
WHY WOULD I LEAVE IF I'M JUST GONNA DIE IN A YEAR ANYWAY?!
YOU CAN LEAVE TO SEARCH FOR A CURE!!!
THERE IS NONE!!!
DSHH!
!
DUMDUN
I'M GONNA GO TELL DOFLAMINGO ...
...ALL ABOUT YOUR POWERS AND YOUR FAKE SILENCE!!!
NO, DON'T!!!
HE'LL DO WORSE THAN JUST KICK YOU OUT, I BET!!

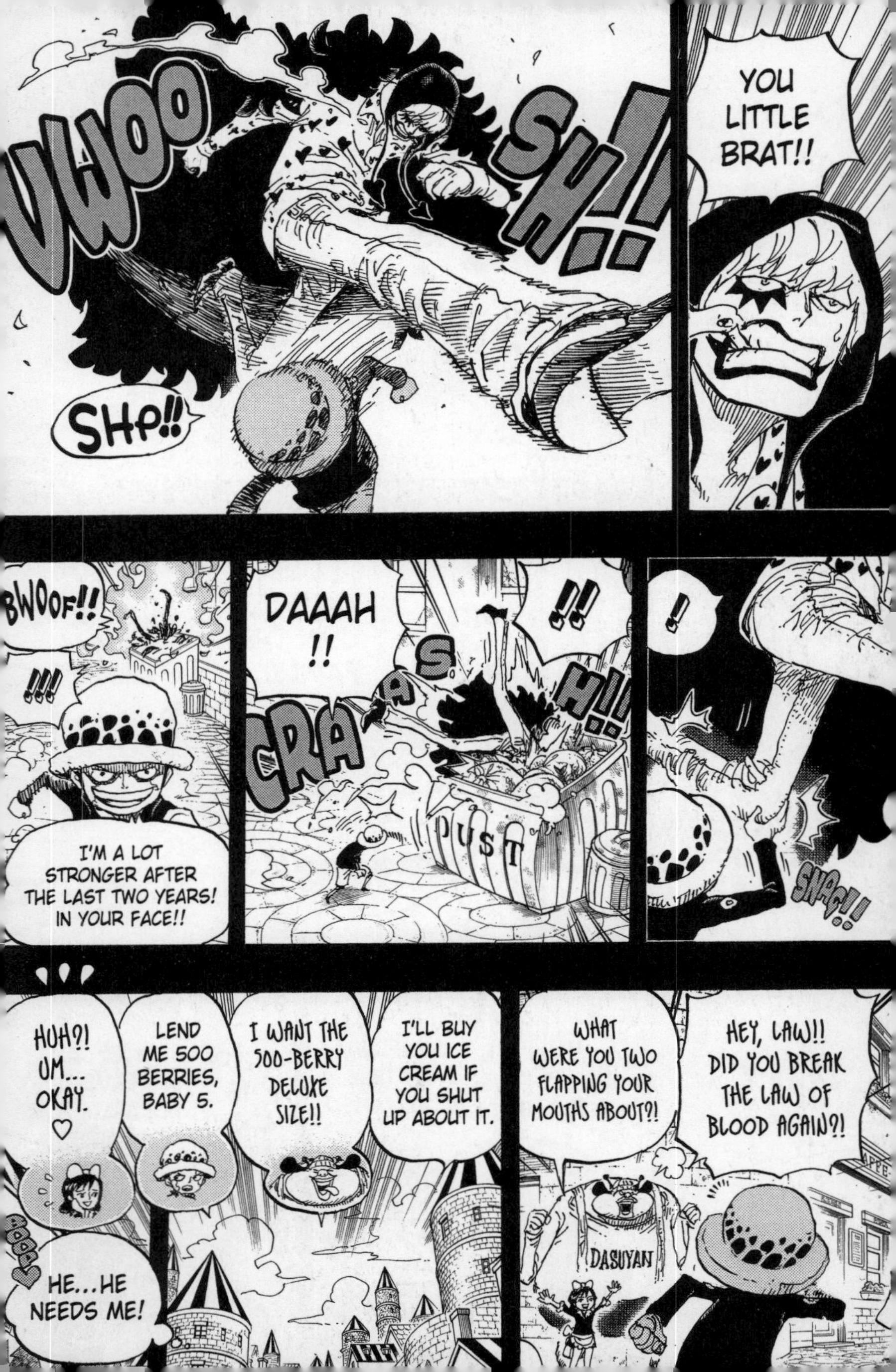
YOU LITTLE BRAT!!
VWOOOSH!!
SHP!!
!
SNAG!!
DAAAH!!
!!
CRASH!!
BWOOF!!
!!!
I'M A LOT STRONGER AFTER THE LAST TWO YEARS! IN YOUR FACE!!
...
HEY, LAW!! DID YOU BREAK THE LAW OF BLOOD AGAIN?!
WHAT WERE YOU TWO FLAPPING YOUR MOUTHS ABOUT?!
DASUYAN
I'LL BUY YOU ICE CREAM IF YOU SHUT UP ABOUT IT.
I WANT THE 500-BERRY DELUXE SIZE!!
LEND ME 500 BERRIES, BABY 5.
HUH?! UM... OKAY. ♡
HE...HE NEEDS ME!

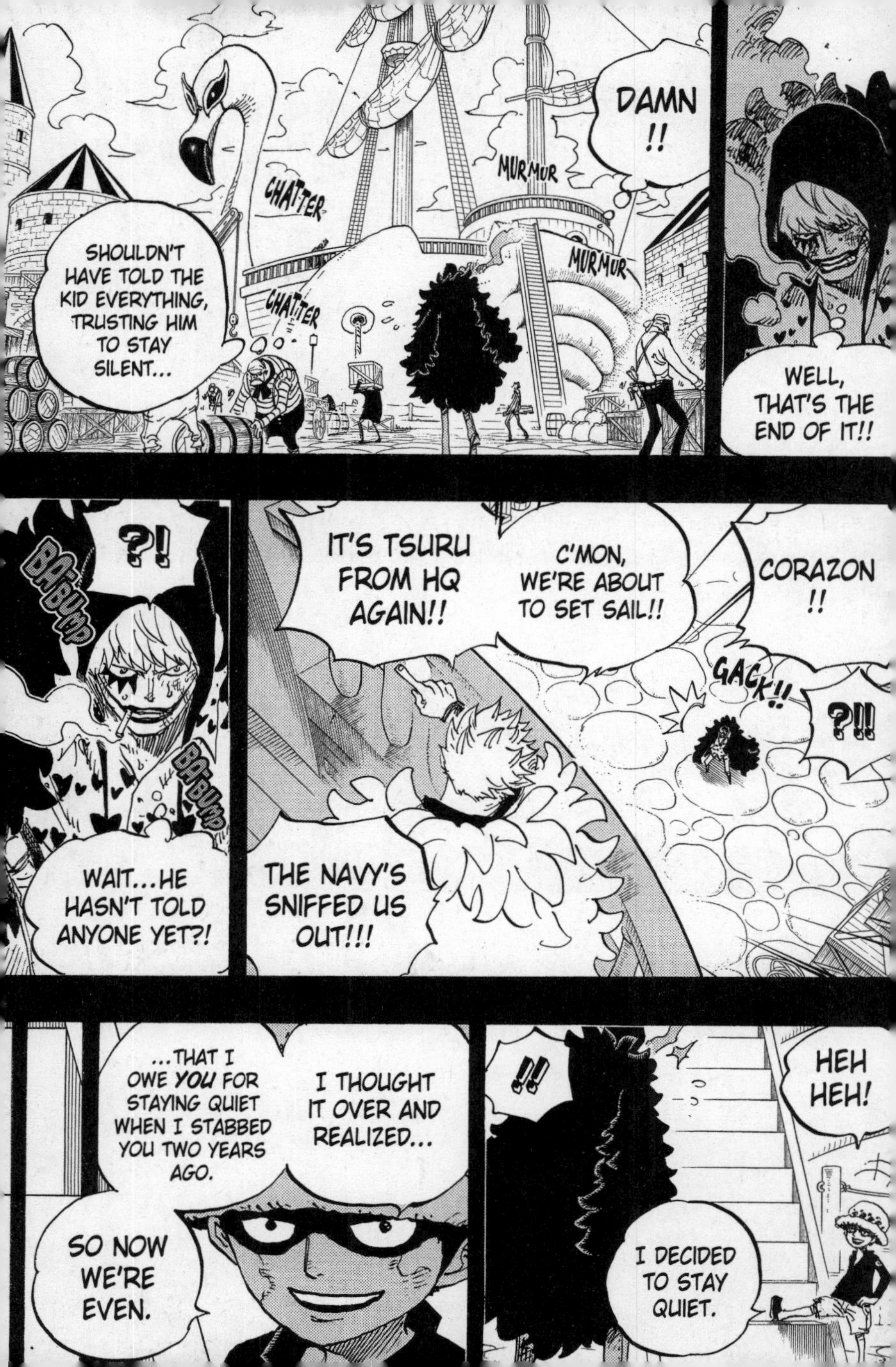
DAMN!!
WELL, THAT'S THE END OF IT!!
MURMUR
MURMUR
CHATTER
CHATTER
SHOULDN'T HAVE TOLD THE KID EVERYTHING, TRUSTING HIM TO STAY SILENT...
CORAZON!!
GACK!!
?!!
C'MON, WE'RE ABOUT TO SET SAIL!!
IT'S TSURU FROM HQ AGAIN!!
THE NAVY'S SNIFFED US OUT!!!
?!
BABUMP
BABUMP
WAIT...HE HASN'T TOLD ANYONE YET?!
HEH HEH!
!!
I DECIDED TO STAY QUIET.
I THOUGHT IT OVER AND REALIZED...
...THAT I OWE *YOU* FOR STAYING QUIET WHEN I STABBED YOU TWO YEARS AGO.
SO NOW WE'RE EVEN.

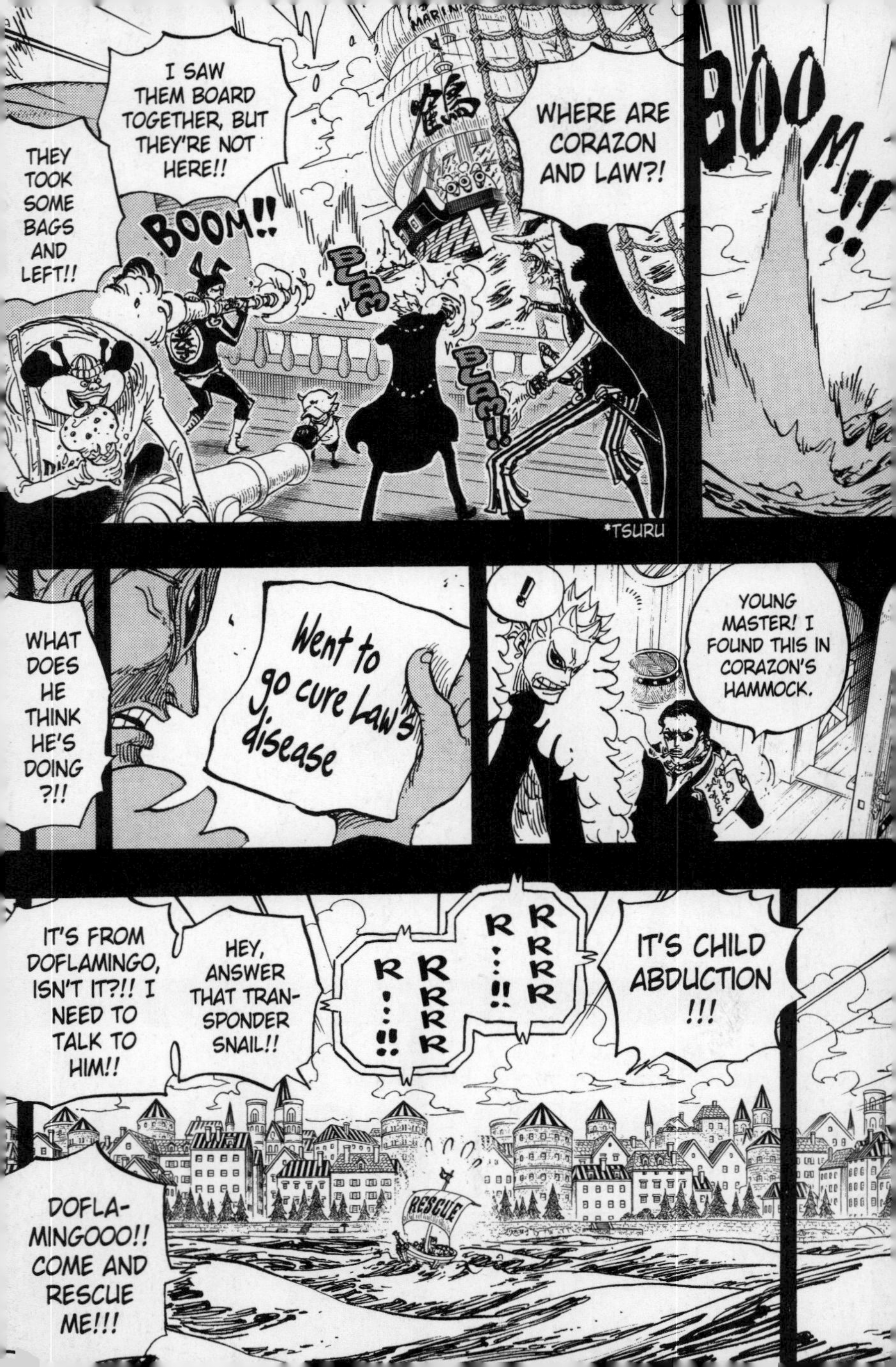
BOOM!!
MARINE
鶴
WHERE ARE CORAZON AND LAW?!
I SAW THEM BOARD TOGETHER, BUT THEY'RE NOT HERE!!
THEY TOOK SOME BAGS AND LEFT!!
BOOM!!
BLAM
BLAM!!
*TSURU
!
YOUNG MASTER! I FOUND THIS IN CORAZON'S HAMMOCK.
Went to go cure Law's disease
WHAT DOES HE THINK HE'S DOING?!!
IT'S CHILD ABDUCTION!!!
RRRR...!!
RRRR...!!
HEY, ANSWER THAT TRANSPONDER SNAIL!!
IT'S FROM DOFLAMINGO, ISN'T IT?!! I NEED TO TALK TO HIM!!
RESCUE
DOFLAMINGOOO!! COME AND RESCUE ME!!!

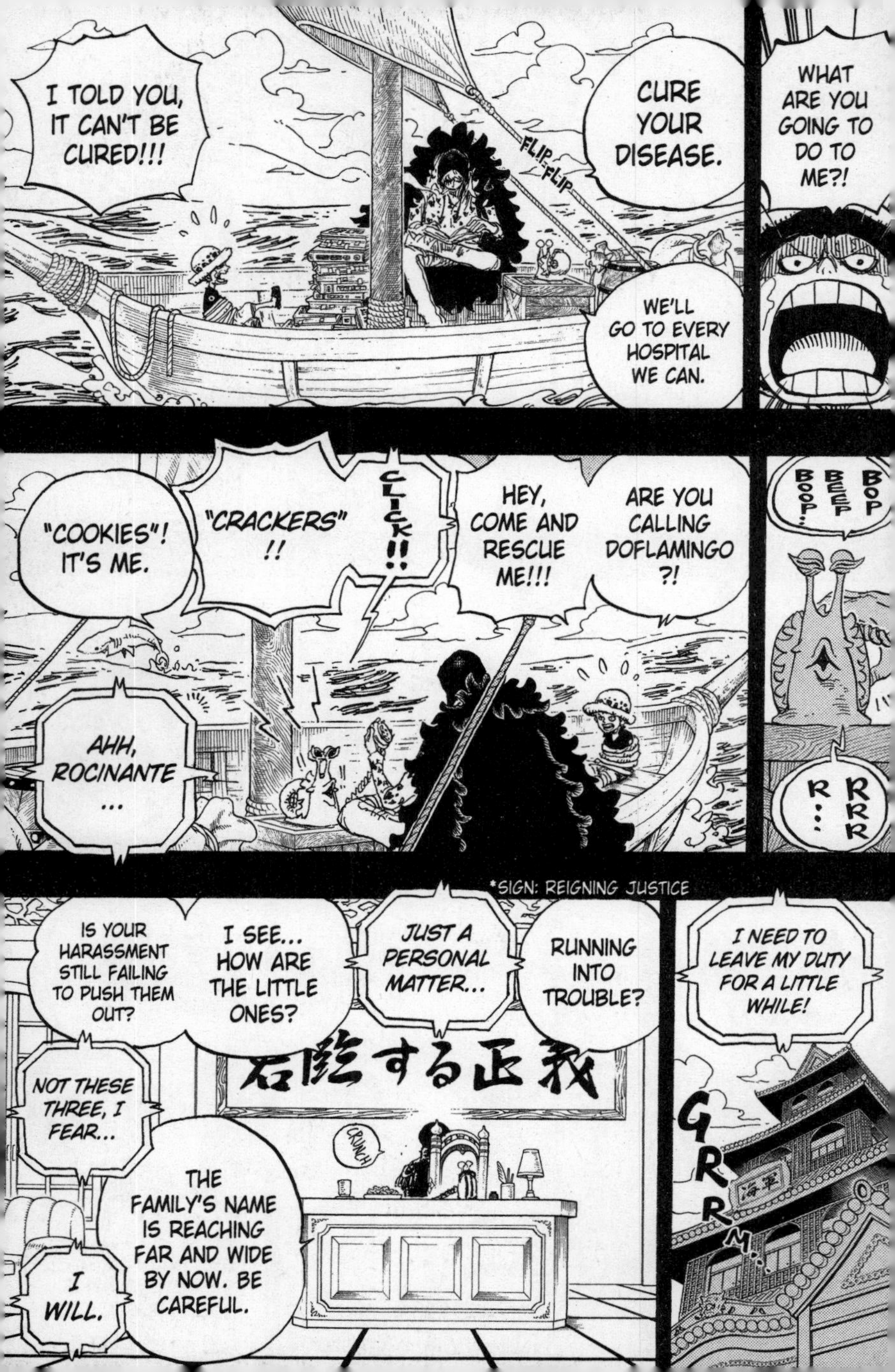

WHAT ARE YOU GOING TO DO TO ME?!
CURE YOUR DISEASE.
WE'LL GO TO EVERY HOSPITAL WE CAN.
FLIP FLIP
I TOLD YOU, IT CAN'T BE CURED!!!
BOP BEEP BOOP...
RRR R...
ARE YOU CALLING DOFLAMINGO?!
HEY, COME AND RESCUE ME!!!
CLICK!!
"CRACKERS"!!
"COOKIES"! IT'S ME.
AHH, ROCINANTE...
I NEED TO LEAVE MY DUTY FOR A LITTLE WHILE!
海軍
GRRRM...
*SIGN: REIGNING JUSTICE
RUNNING INTO TROUBLE?
JUST A PERSONAL MATTER...
I SEE... HOW ARE THE LITTLE ONES?
IS YOUR HARASSMENT STILL FAILING TO PUSH THEM OUT?
君臨する正義
NOT THESE THREE, I FEAR...
CRUNCH
THE FAMILY'S NAME IS REACHING FAR AND WIDE BY NOW. BE CAREFUL.
I WILL.

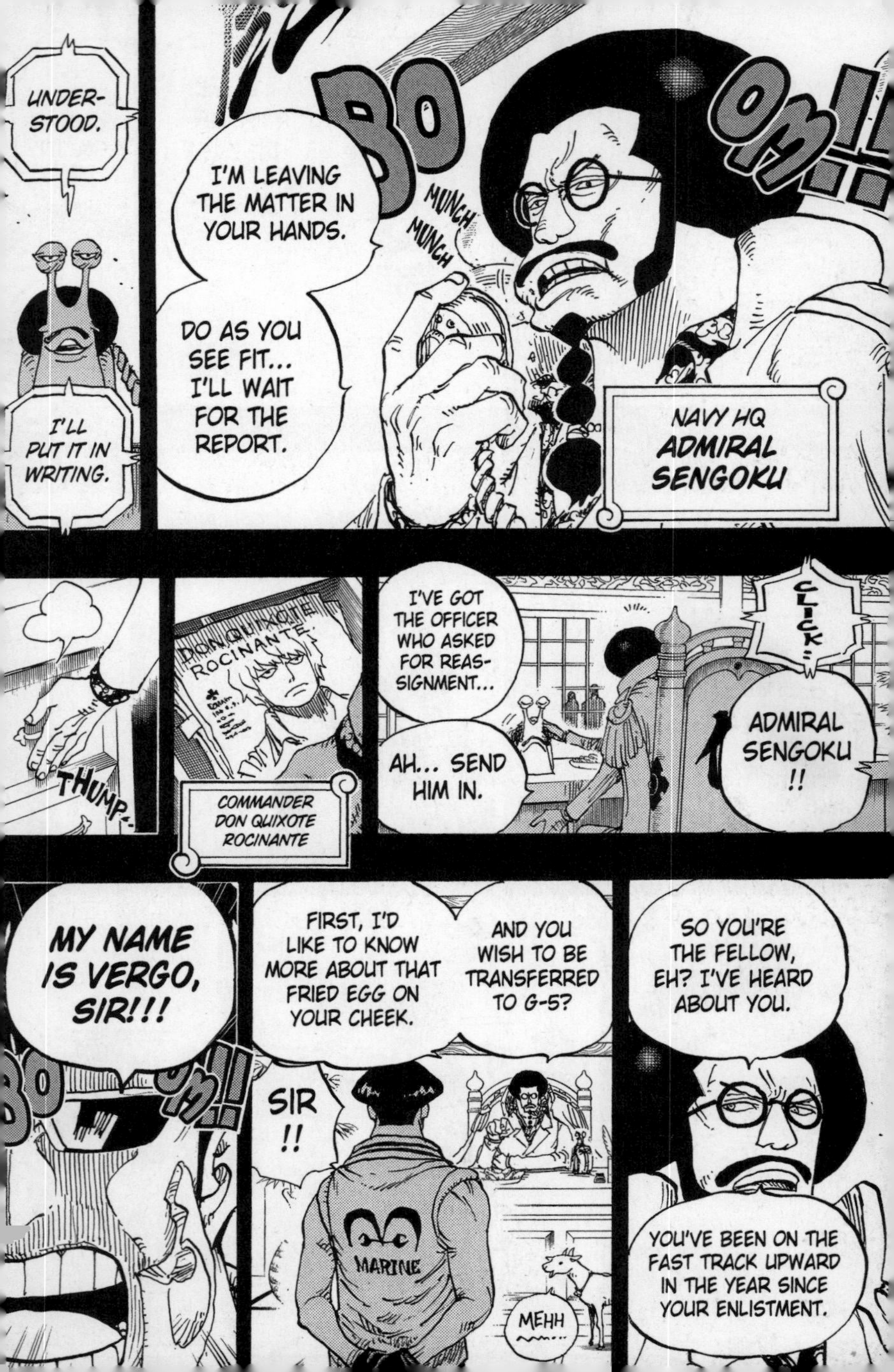
BOOM!!
I'M LEAVING THE MATTER IN YOUR HANDS.
MUNCH
MUNCH
NAVY HQ ADMIRAL SENGOKU
DO AS YOU SEE FIT... I'LL WAIT FOR THE REPORT.
UNDER-STOOD.
I'LL PUT IT IN WRITING.
CLICK!!
ADMIRAL SENGOKU!!
I'VE GOT THE OFFICER WHO ASKED FOR REAS-SIGNMENT...
AH... SEND HIM IN.
DON QUIXOTE ROCINANTE
COMMANDER DON QUIXOTE ROCINANTE
THUMP...
SO YOU'RE THE FELLOW, EH? I'VE HEARD ABOUT YOU.
YOU'VE BEEN ON THE FAST TRACK UPWARD IN THE YEAR SINCE YOUR ENLISTMENT.
AND YOU WISH TO BE TRANSFERRED TO G-5?
FIRST, I'D LIKE TO KNOW MORE ABOUT THAT FRIED EGG ON YOUR CHEEK.
SIR!!
MARINE
MEHH~...
MY NAME IS VERGO, SIR!!!
BOOM!!

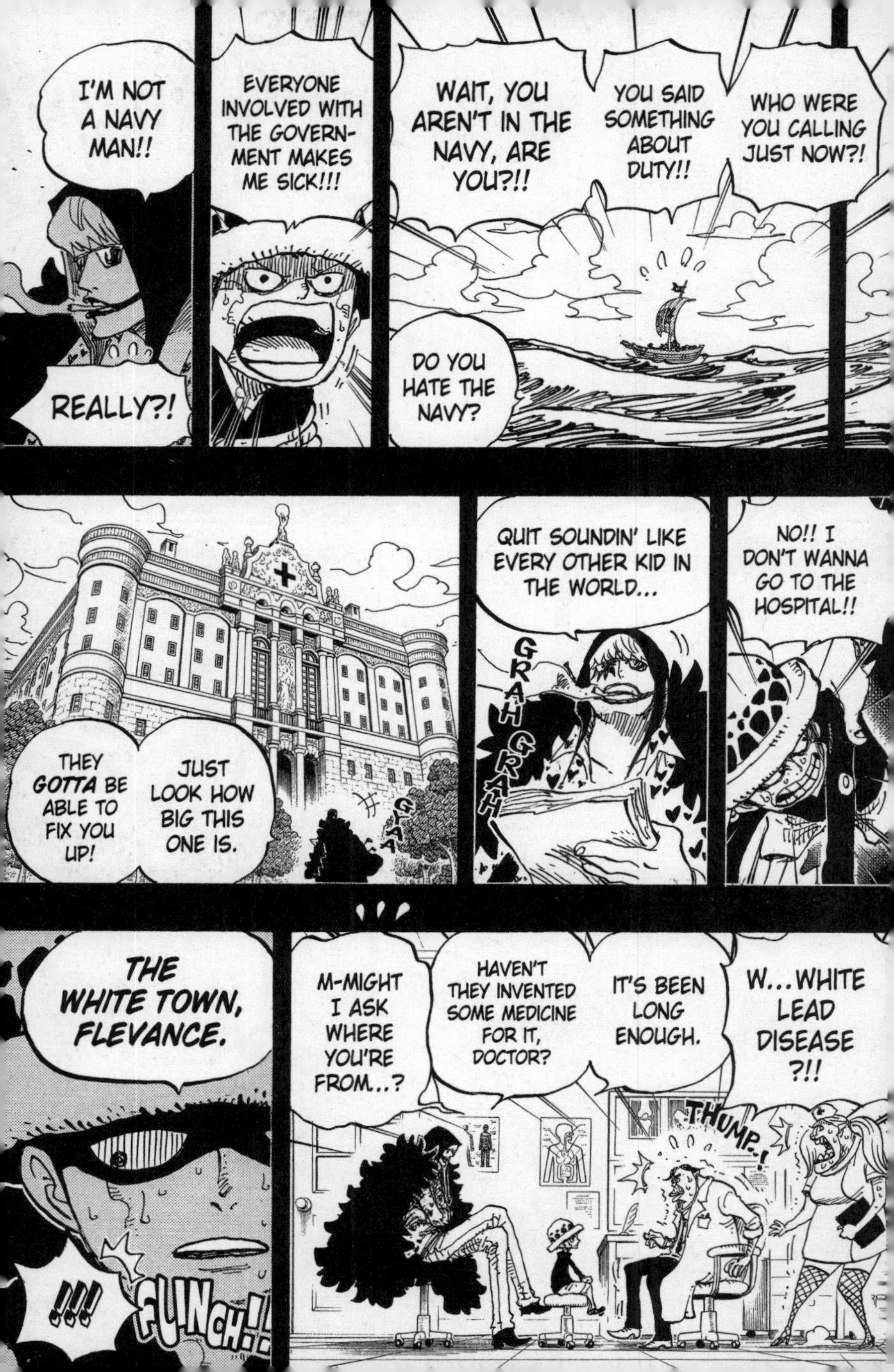
WHO WERE YOU CALLING JUST NOW?!
YOU SAID SOMETHING ABOUT DUTY!!
WAIT, YOU AREN'T IN THE NAVY, ARE YOU?!!
DO YOU HATE THE NAVY?
EVERYONE INVOLVED WITH THE GOVERN-MENT MAKES ME SICK!!!
I'M NOT A NAVY MAN!!
REALLY?!
NO!! I DON'T WANNA GO TO THE HOSPITAL!!
QUIT SOUNDIN' LIKE EVERY OTHER KID IN THE WORLD...
GRAH GRAH GRAH
JUST LOOK HOW BIG THIS ONE IS.
THEY GOTTA BE ABLE TO FIX YOU UP!
GYAA
W...WHITE LEAD DISEASE ?!!
IT'S BEEN LONG ENOUGH.
HAVEN'T THEY INVENTED SOME MEDICINE FOR IT, DOCTOR?
THUMP..!
M-MIGHT I ASK WHERE YOU'RE FROM...?
THE WHITE TOWN, FLEVANCE.
!!!
FLINCH!!

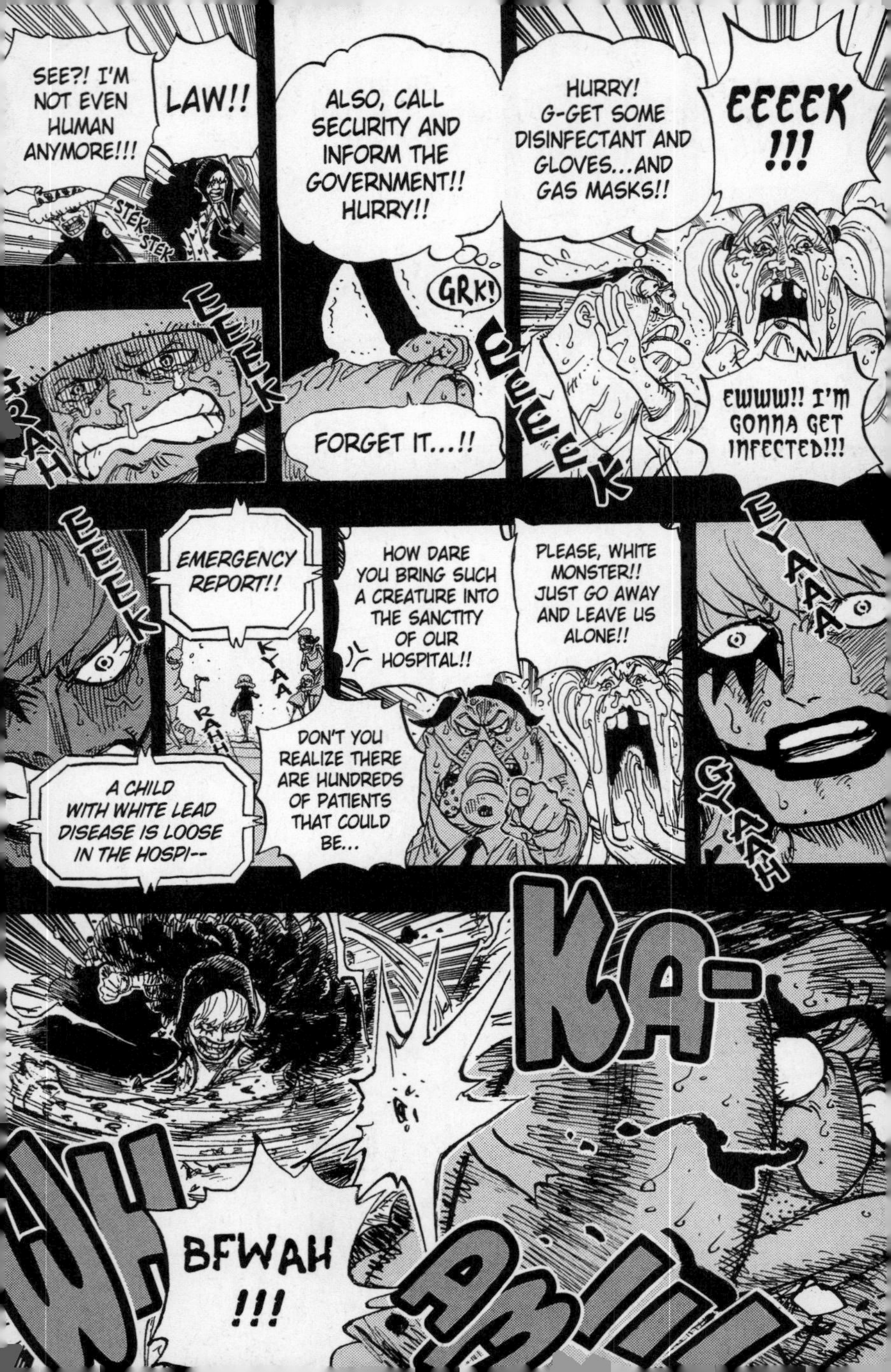
EEEEK !!!
EWWW!! I'M GONNA GET INFECTED!!!
EEEEEK
HURRY! G-GET SOME DISINFECTANT AND GLOVES...AND GAS MASKS!!
ALSO, CALL SECURITY AND INFORM THE GOVERNMENT!! HURRY!!
GRK!
FORGET IT...!!
LAW!!
SEE?! I'M NOT EVEN HUMAN ANYMORE!!!
STEK STEK
EEEEK
EYAAAA
GYAAAH
PLEASE, WHITE MONSTER!! JUST GO AWAY AND LEAVE US ALONE!!
HOW DARE YOU BRING SUCH A CREATURE INTO THE SANCTITY OF OUR HOSPITAL!!
DON'T YOU REALIZE THERE ARE HUNDREDS OF PATIENTS THAT COULD BE...
EMERGENCY REPORT!!
KYAA
RAHH
A CHILD WITH WHITE LEAD DISEASE IS LOOSE IN THE HOSPI--
EEEEK
KA-
BFWAH !!!

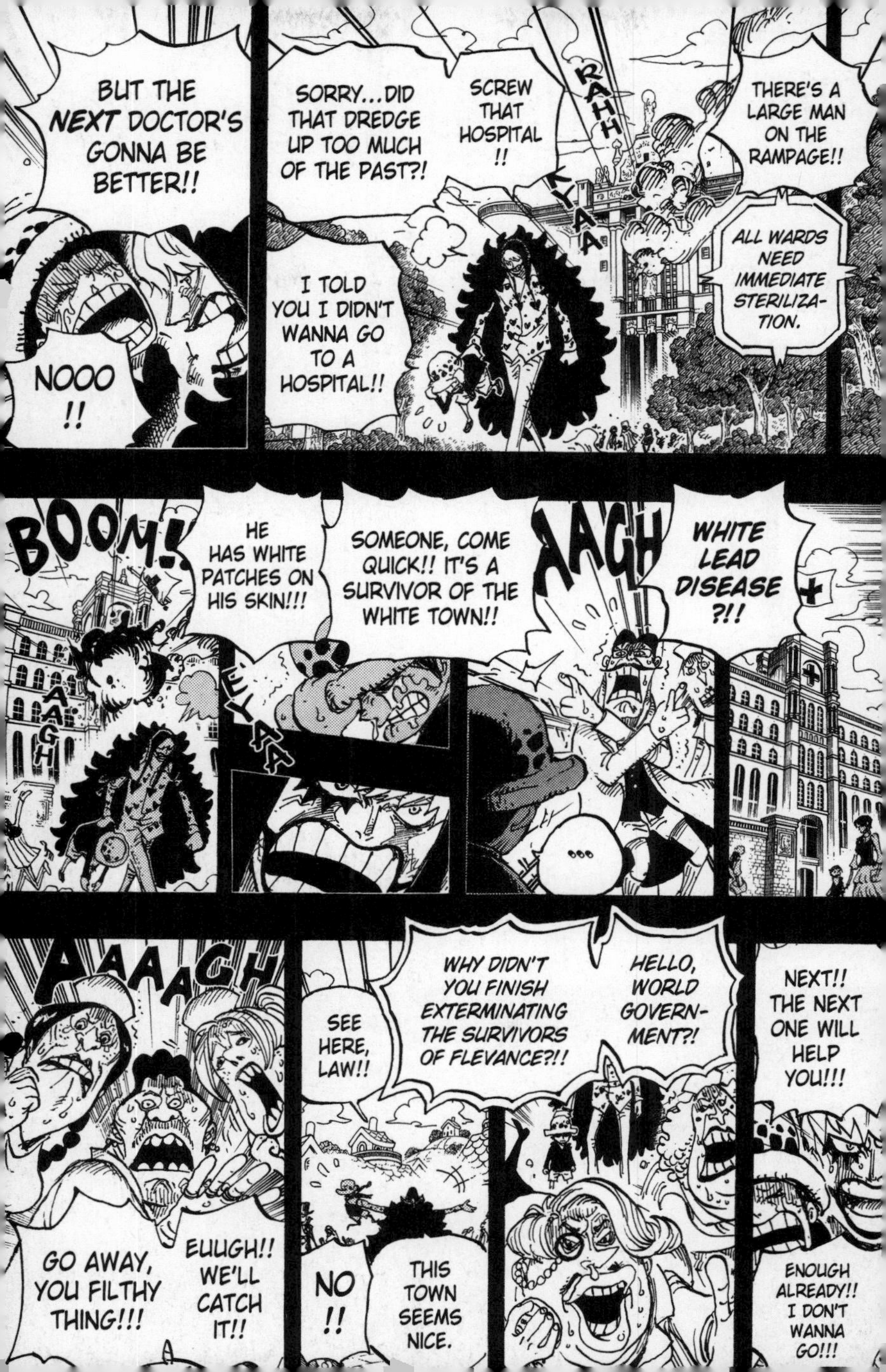
RAHH
THERE'S A LARGE MAN ON THE RAMPAGE!!
KYAA
ALL WARDS NEED IMMEDIATE STERILIZATION.
SCREW THAT HOSPITAL!!
SORRY...DID THAT DREDGE UP TOO MUCH OF THE PAST?!
I TOLD YOU I DIDN'T WANNA GO TO A HOSPITAL!!
BUT THE *NEXT* DOCTOR'S GONNA BE BETTER!!
NOOO!!
WHITE LEAD DISEASE?!!
AAGH
...
SOMEONE, COME QUICK!! IT'S A SURVIVOR OF THE WHITE TOWN!!
KYAA
HE HAS WHITE PATCHES ON HIS SKIN!!!
BOOM!
AAAGH
NEXT!! THE NEXT ONE WILL HELP YOU!!!
ENOUGH ALREADY!! I DON'T WANNA GO!!!
HELLO, WORLD GOVERNMENT?!
WHY DIDN'T YOU FINISH EXTERMINATING THE SURVIVORS OF FLEVANCE?!!
SEE HERE, LAW!!
THIS TOWN SEEMS NICE.
NO!!
AAAAGH
EUUGH!! WE'LL CATCH IT!!
GO AWAY, YOU FILTHY THING!!!

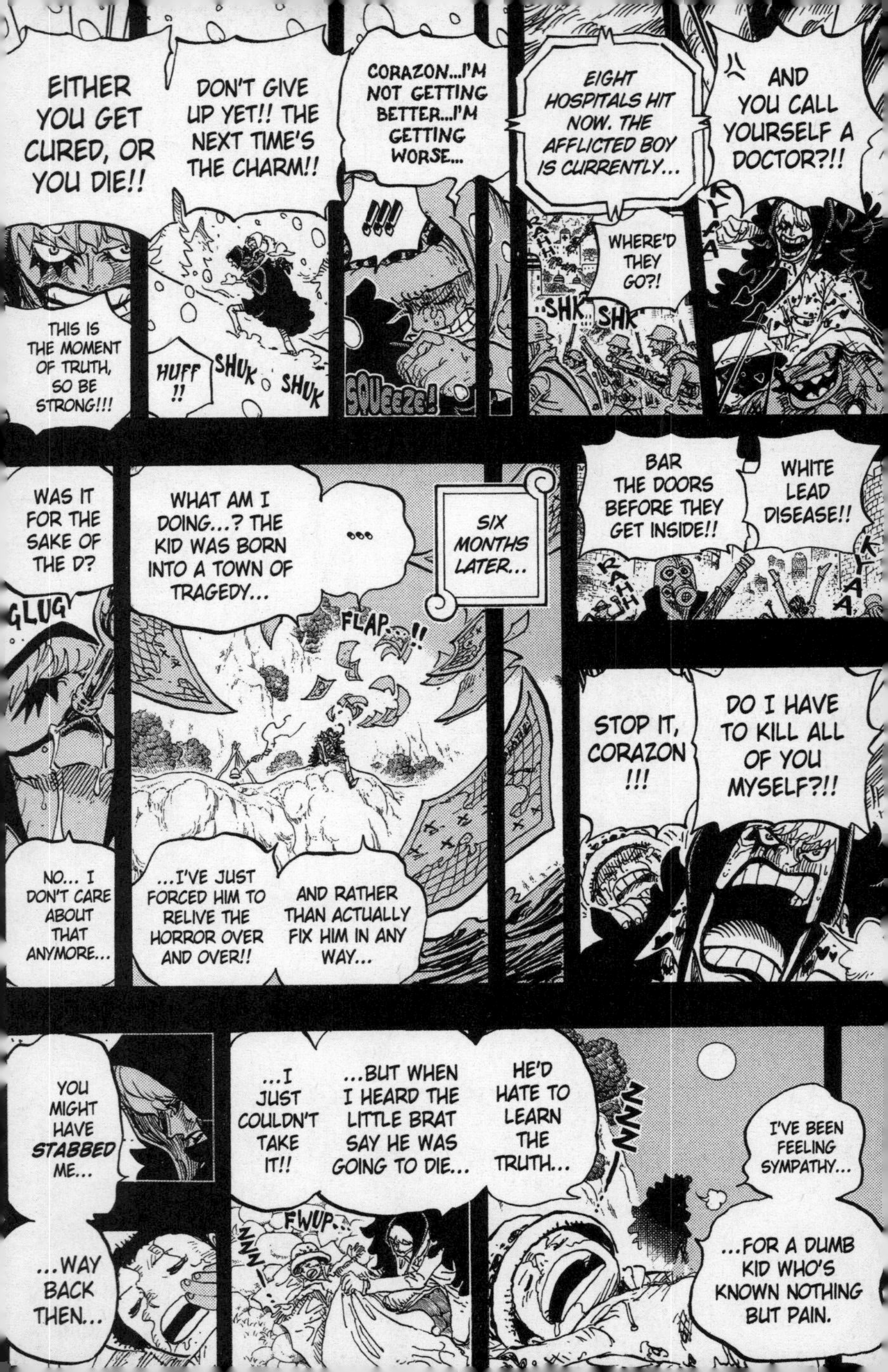
AND YOU CALL YOURSELF A DOCTOR?!!
KYAA
EIGHT HOSPITALS HIT NOW. THE AFFLICTED BOY IS CURRENTLY...
RAHH
WHERE'D THEY GO?!
SHK SHK
CORAZON...I'M NOT GETTING BETTER...I'M GETTING WORSE...
!!!
SQUEEZE!
DON'T GIVE UP YET!! THE NEXT TIME'S THE CHARM!!
HUFF!!
SHUK SHUK
EITHER YOU GET CURED, OR YOU DIE!!
THIS IS THE MOMENT OF TRUTH, SO BE STRONG!!!
WHITE LEAD DISEASE!!
BAR THE DOORS BEFORE THEY GET INSIDE!!
KYAA
RAHH
DO I HAVE TO KILL ALL OF YOU MYSELF?!!
STOP IT, CORAZON!!!
SIX MONTHS LATER...
...
FLAP!!
WHAT AM I DOING...? THE KID WAS BORN INTO A TOWN OF TRAGEDY...
AND RATHER THAN ACTUALLY FIX HIM IN ANY WAY...
...I'VE JUST FORCED HIM TO RELIVE THE HORROR OVER AND OVER!!
WAS IT FOR THE SAKE OF THE D?
GLUG
NO... I DON'T CARE ABOUT THAT ANYMORE...
I'VE BEEN FEELING SYMPATHY...
...FOR A DUMB KID WHO'S KNOWN NOTHING BUT PAIN.
NNN
HE'D HATE TO LEARN THE TRUTH...
...BUT WHEN I HEARD THE LITTLE BRAT SAY HE WAS GOING TO DIE...
...I JUST COULDN'T TAKE IT!!
FWUP
NNN
YOU MIGHT HAVE STABBED ME...
...WAY BACK THEN...

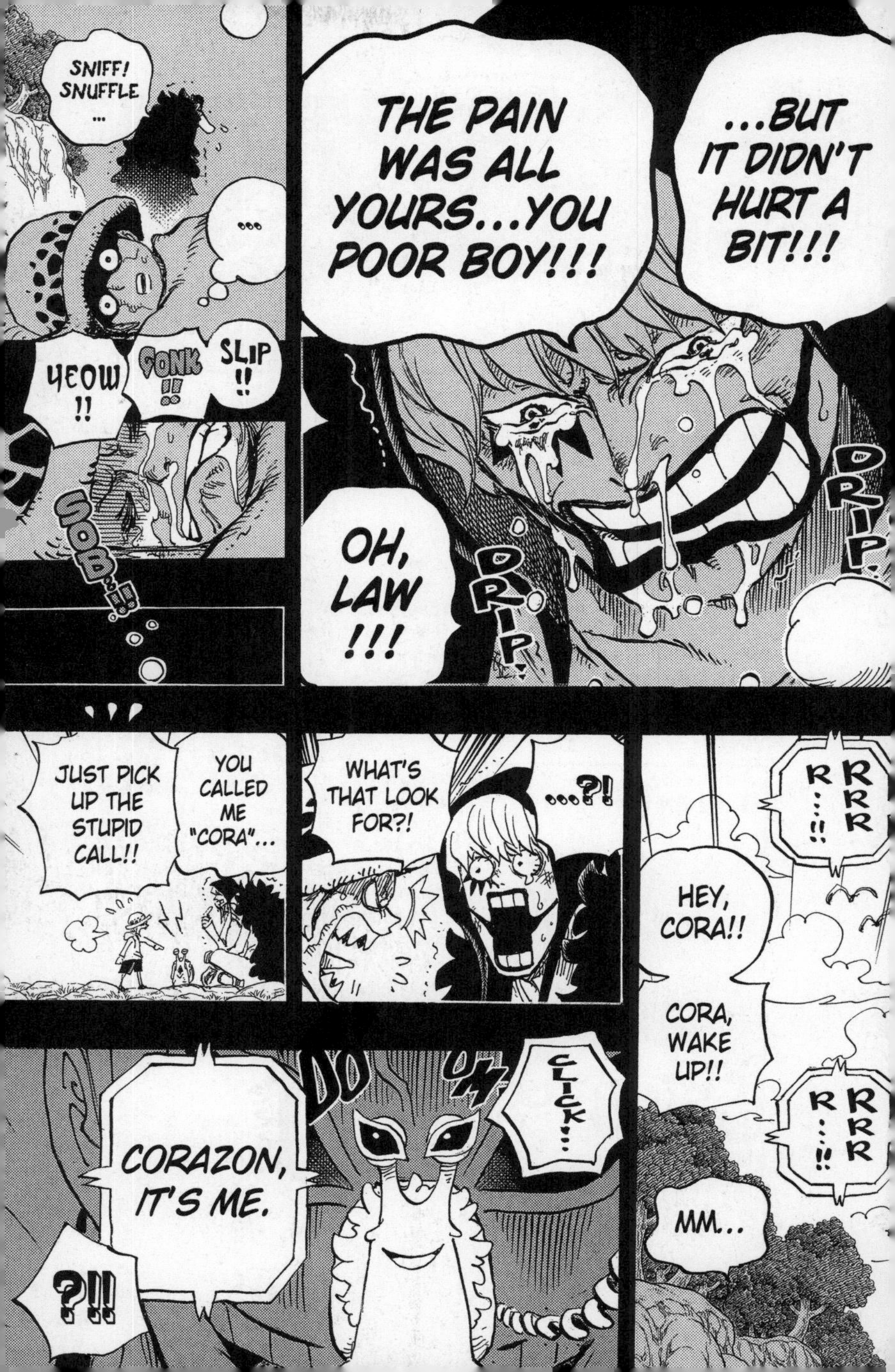
...BUT IT DIDN'T HURT A BIT!!!
THE PAIN WAS ALL YOURS...YOU POOR BOY!!!
DRIP
OH, LAW!!!
DRIP
SNIFF! SNUFFLE ...
...
SLIP!!
GONK!!
YEOW!!
SOB!!
RRRR...!!
HEY, CORA!!
CORA, WAKE UP!!
RRRR...!!
MM...
...?!
WHAT'S THAT LOOK FOR?!
YOU CALLED ME "CORA"...
JUST PICK UP THE STUPID CALL!!
CLICK...
DOOM
CORAZON, IT'S ME.
?!!

SBS Question Corner

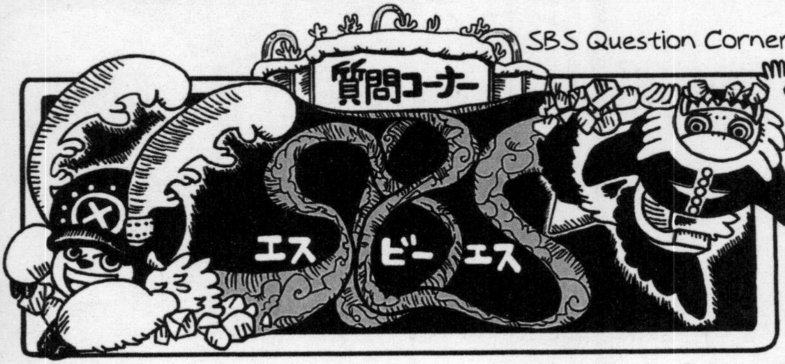
質問コーナー
エス ビー エス
(Fujima, Fukuoka)

Q: Let the SBS! Begi…!! Oh, forget it.
--Pisces Yoko the Pirate

A: What, that's it?!!
...Well, anyway, we're starting.
Listen up, everyone!! Look at this ➡
This is a piece of reader fan art that ran in Usopp's Pirate Gallery, all the way back in volume 23. Now look below, at the cover of the very popular *Shonen Jump* manga, *My Hero Academia*. Look closely at the artist's name.

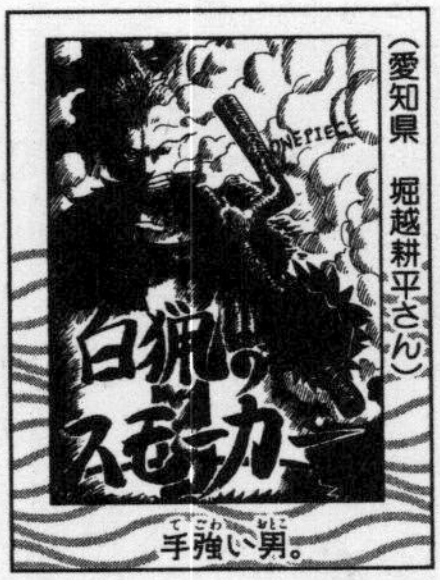
(愛知県 堀越耕平さん)
ONEPIECE
白猟のスモーカー
手強い男。

↙↗ Same guy!!!

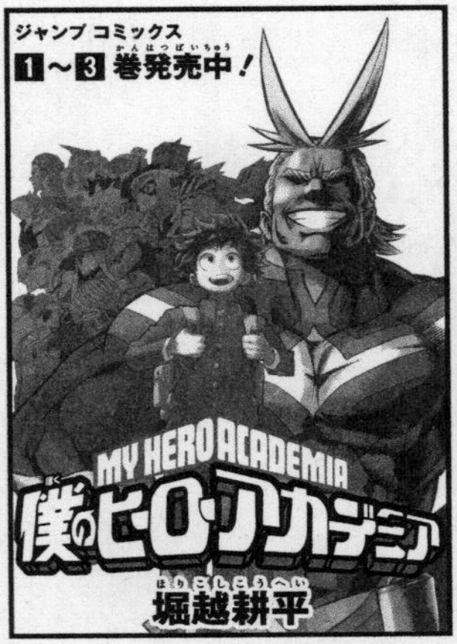
ジャンプコミックス
1~3巻発売中！
MY HERO ACADEMIA
僕のヒーローアカデミア
堀越耕平

Volume 23 was what, over ten years ago? He sent me that fan art illustration as a student, and now his career as a manga artist is blossoming before our eyes!! And not only that, it's right in the pages of *Jump* next to *One Piece*!! This is just fantastic. He told me himself at the New Year's party for *Jump* artists. You should have told me earlier, so I could cheer you on!!

So anyways, if you haven't read it yet, check out Kohei Horikoshi's *My Hero Academia*!!

Chapter 765:
MINION, THE ISLE OF FATE

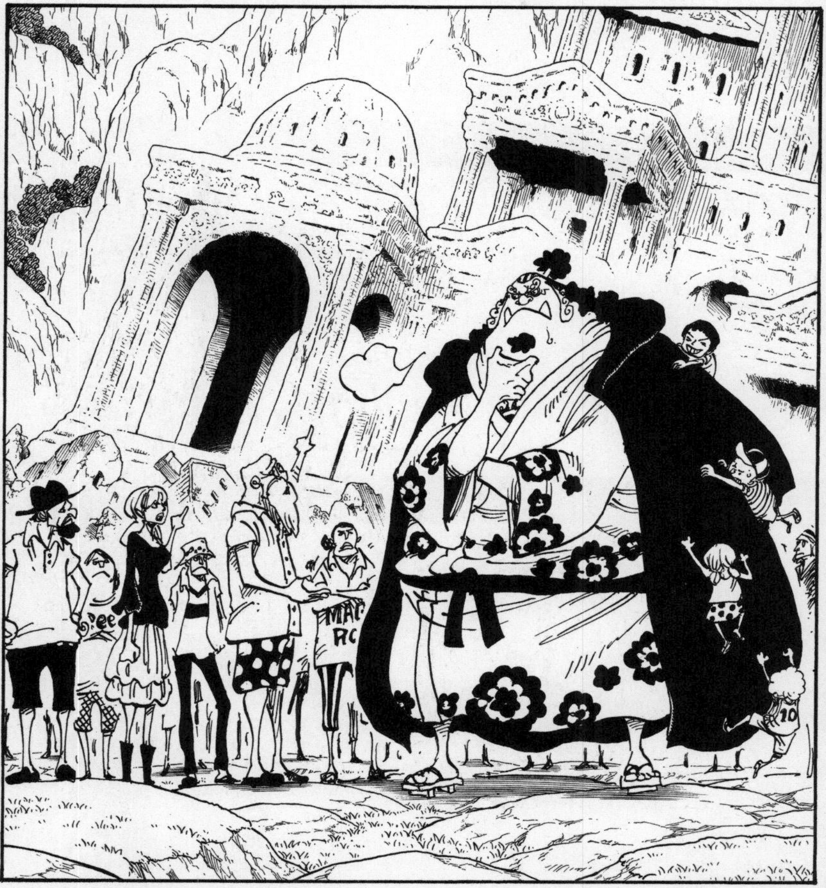

THE SOLITARY JOURNEY OF JIMBEI, FIRST SON OF THE SEA, VOL. 13:
"SUDDENLY THE RUINS DESTROYED OUR TOWN, THE CREATURES WRECKED OUR SHIPS, AND THE OFFERINGS DISAPPEARED"

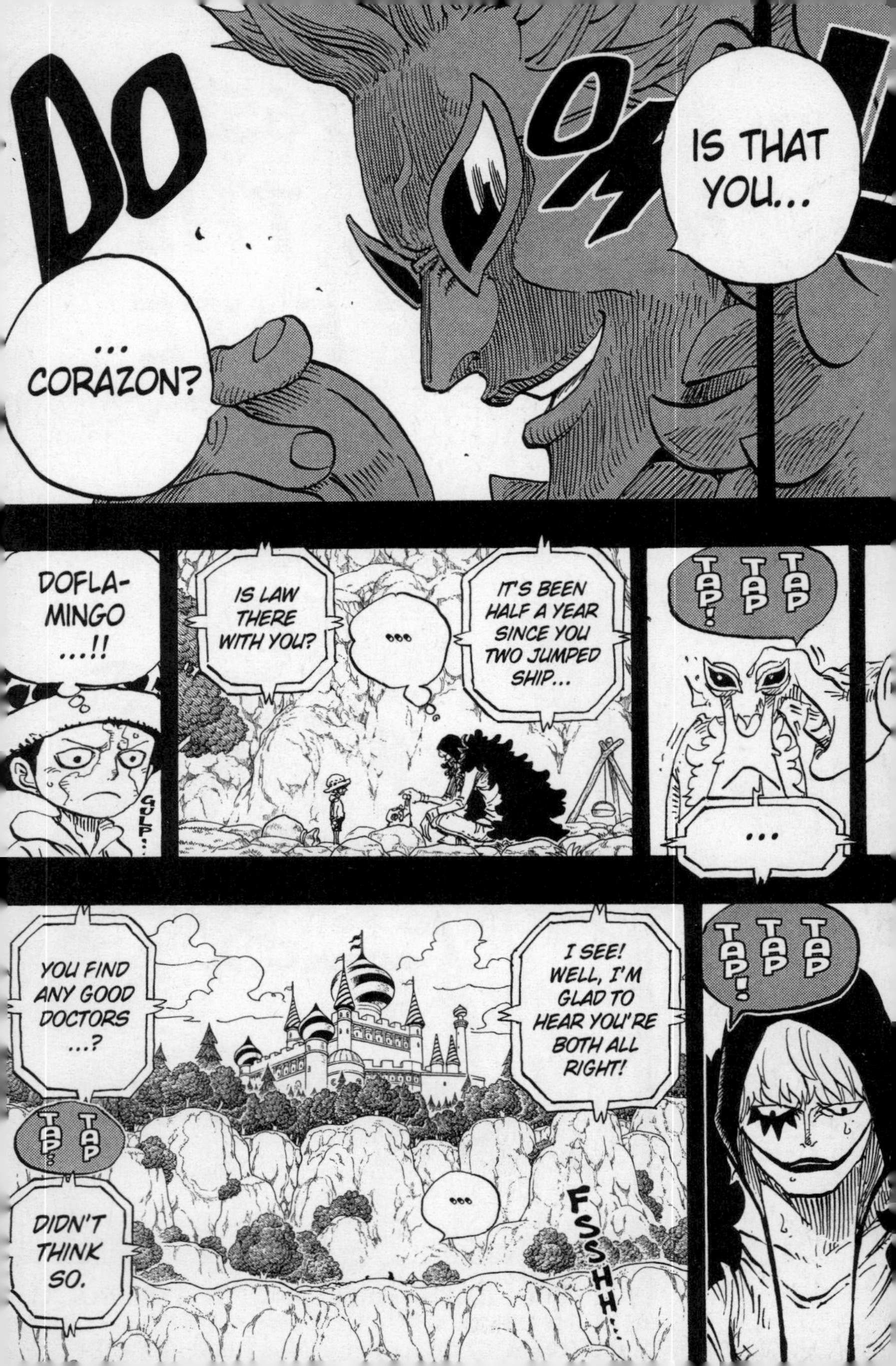
DOOM
IS THAT YOU...
... CORAZON?
TAP TAP TAP!
...
IT'S BEEN HALF A YEAR SINCE YOU TWO JUMPED SHIP...
...
IS LAW THERE WITH YOU?
DOFLA-MINGO ...!!
GULP...
TAP TAP TAP!
I SEE! WELL, I'M GLAD TO HEAR YOU'RE BOTH ALL RIGHT!
YOU FIND ANY GOOD DOCTORS ...?
...
FSSHH...
TAP TAP
DIDN'T THINK SO.

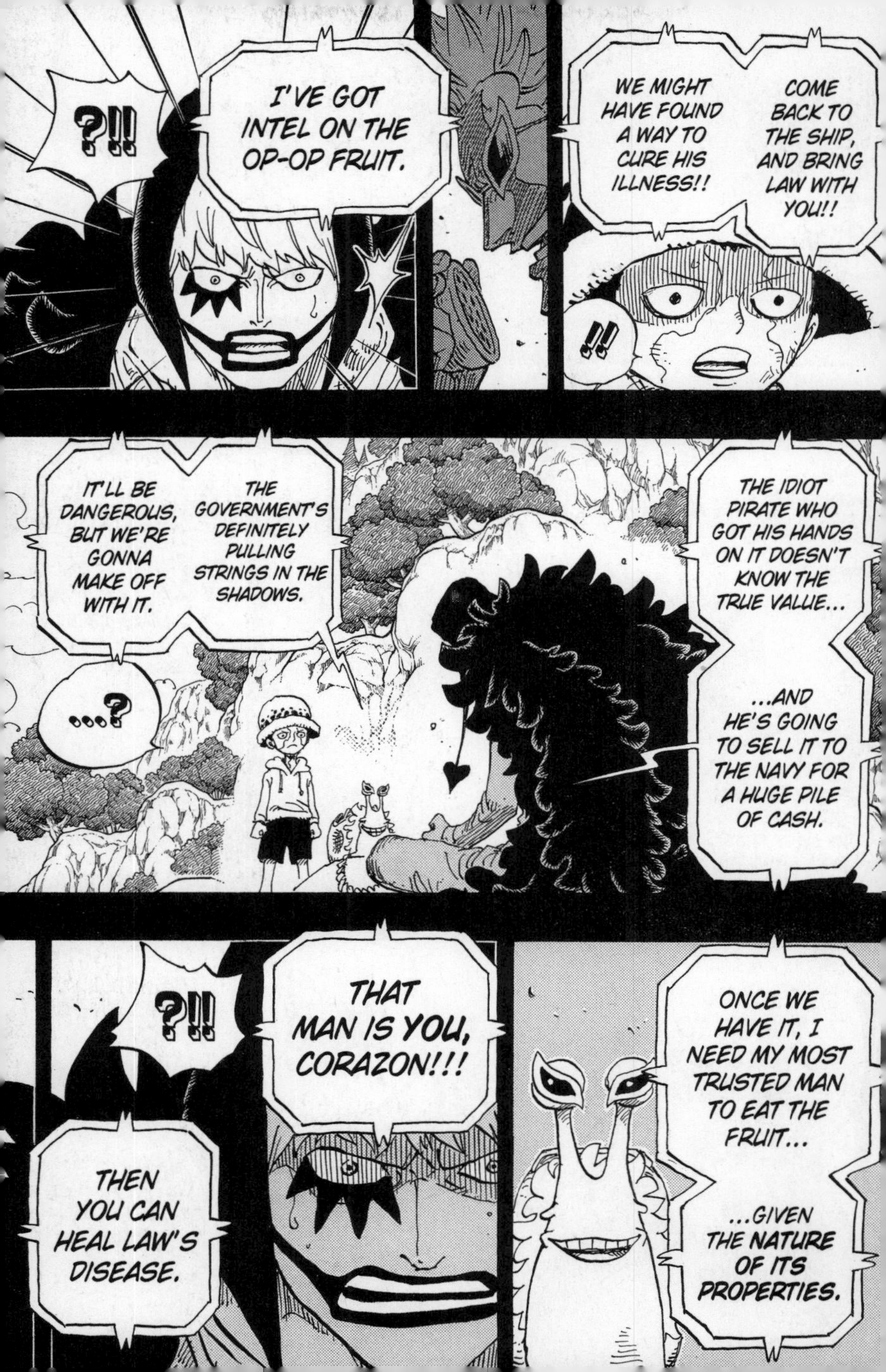
COME BACK TO THE SHIP, AND BRING LAW WITH YOU!!
WE MIGHT HAVE FOUND A WAY TO CURE HIS ILLNESS!!
!!
I'VE GOT INTEL ON THE OP-OP FRUIT.
?!!
THE IDIOT PIRATE WHO GOT HIS HANDS ON IT DOESN'T KNOW THE TRUE VALUE...
...AND HE'S GOING TO SELL IT TO THE NAVY FOR A HUGE PILE OF CASH.
THE GOVERNMENT'S DEFINITELY PULLING STRINGS IN THE SHADOWS.
IT'LL BE DANGEROUS, BUT WE'RE GONNA MAKE OFF WITH IT.
...?
ONCE WE HAVE IT, I NEED MY MOST TRUSTED MAN TO EAT THE FRUIT...
...GIVEN THE NATURE OF ITS PROPERTIES.
THAT MAN IS YOU, CORAZON!!!
?!!
THEN YOU CAN HEAL LAW'S DISEASE.

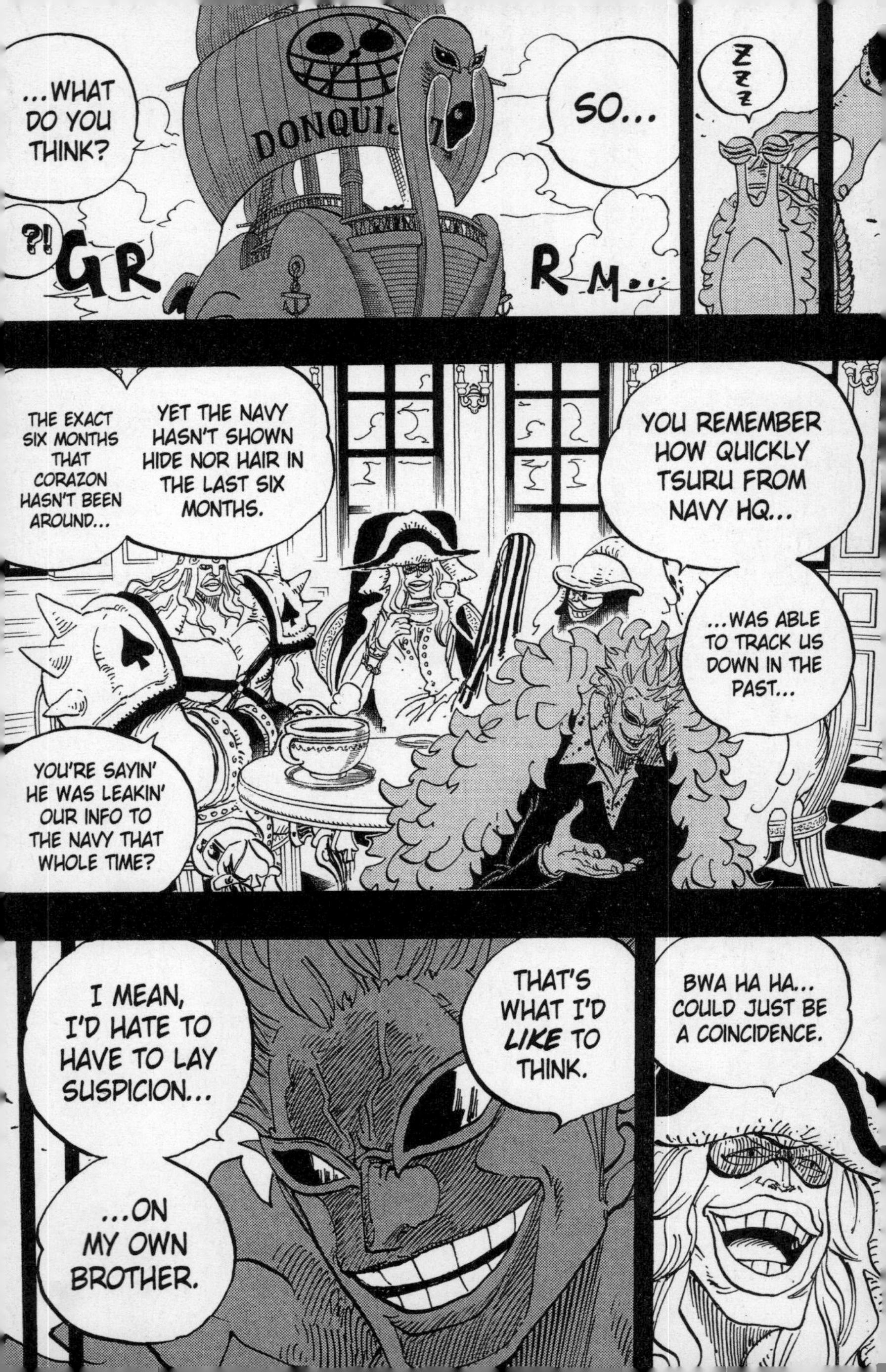
Z Z Z
SO...
...WHAT DO YOU THINK?
?!
GR RM...
DONQUI
YOU REMEMBER HOW QUICKLY TSURU FROM NAVY HQ...
...WAS ABLE TO TRACK US DOWN IN THE PAST...
YET THE NAVY HASN'T SHOWN HIDE NOR HAIR IN THE LAST SIX MONTHS.
THE EXACT SIX MONTHS THAT CORAZON HASN'T BEEN AROUND...
YOU'RE SAYIN' HE WAS LEAKIN' OUR INFO TO THE NAVY THAT WHOLE TIME?
BWA HA HA... COULD JUST BE A COINCIDENCE.
THAT'S WHAT I'D *LIKE* TO THINK.
I MEAN, I'D HATE TO HAVE TO LAY SUSPICION...
...ON MY OWN BROTHER.

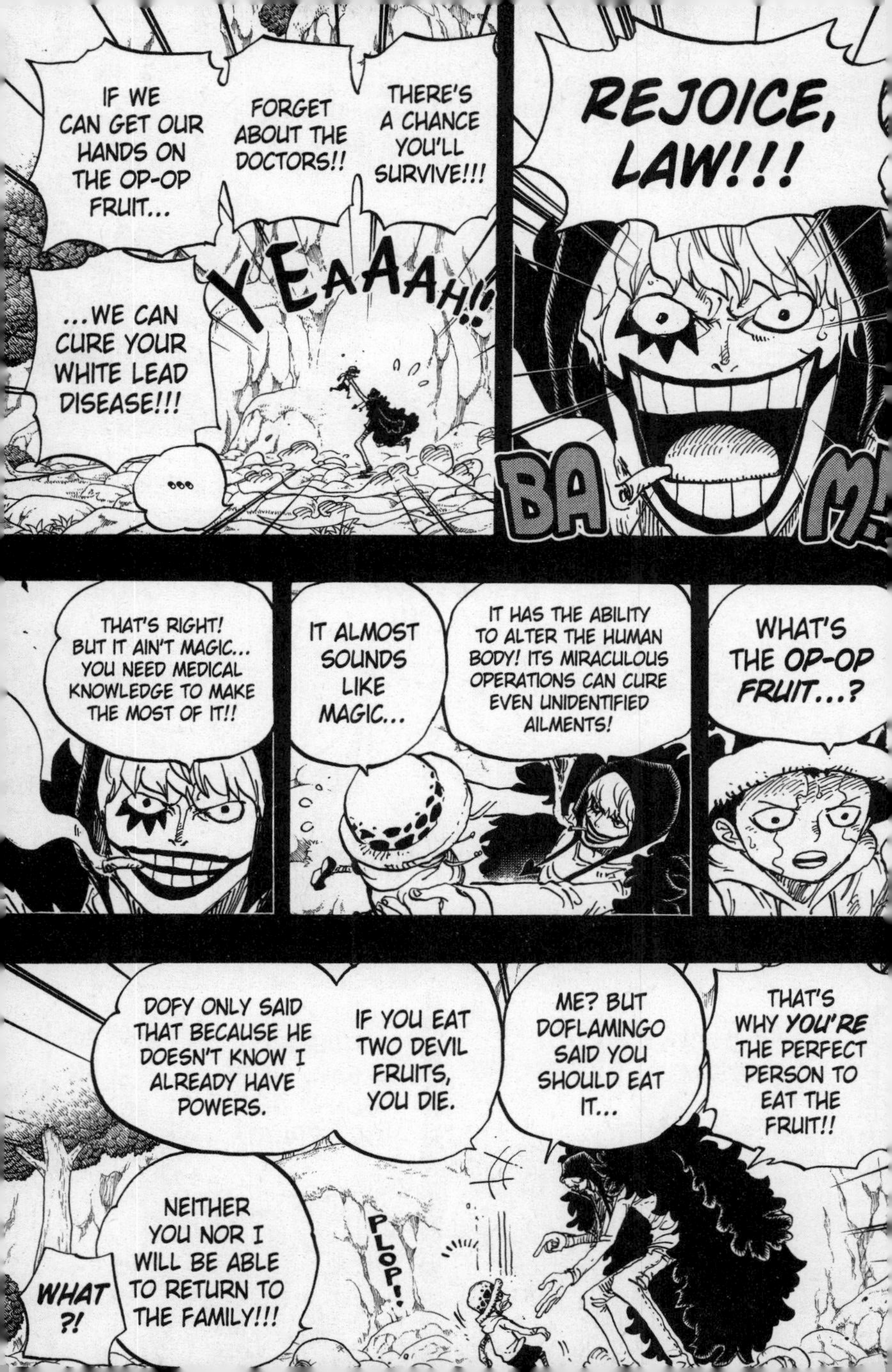
REJOICE, LAW!!!
BA M!
THERE'S A CHANCE YOU'LL SURVIVE!!!
FORGET ABOUT THE DOCTORS!!
IF WE CAN GET OUR HANDS ON THE OP-OP FRUIT...
YEAAAAH!!
...WE CAN CURE YOUR WHITE LEAD DISEASE!!!
...
WHAT'S THE OP-OP FRUIT...?
IT HAS THE ABILITY TO ALTER THE HUMAN BODY! ITS MIRACULOUS OPERATIONS CAN CURE EVEN UNIDENTIFIED AILMENTS!
IT ALMOST SOUNDS LIKE MAGIC...
THAT'S RIGHT! BUT IT AIN'T MAGIC... YOU NEED MEDICAL KNOWLEDGE TO MAKE THE MOST OF IT!!
THAT'S WHY YOU'RE THE PERFECT PERSON TO EAT THE FRUIT!!
ME? BUT DOFLAMINGO SAID YOU SHOULD EAT IT...
IF YOU EAT TWO DEVIL FRUITS, YOU DIE.
DOFY ONLY SAID THAT BECAUSE HE DOESN'T KNOW I ALREADY HAVE POWERS.
PLOP!!
NEITHER YOU NOR I WILL BE ABLE TO RETURN TO THE FAMILY!!!
WHAT ?!

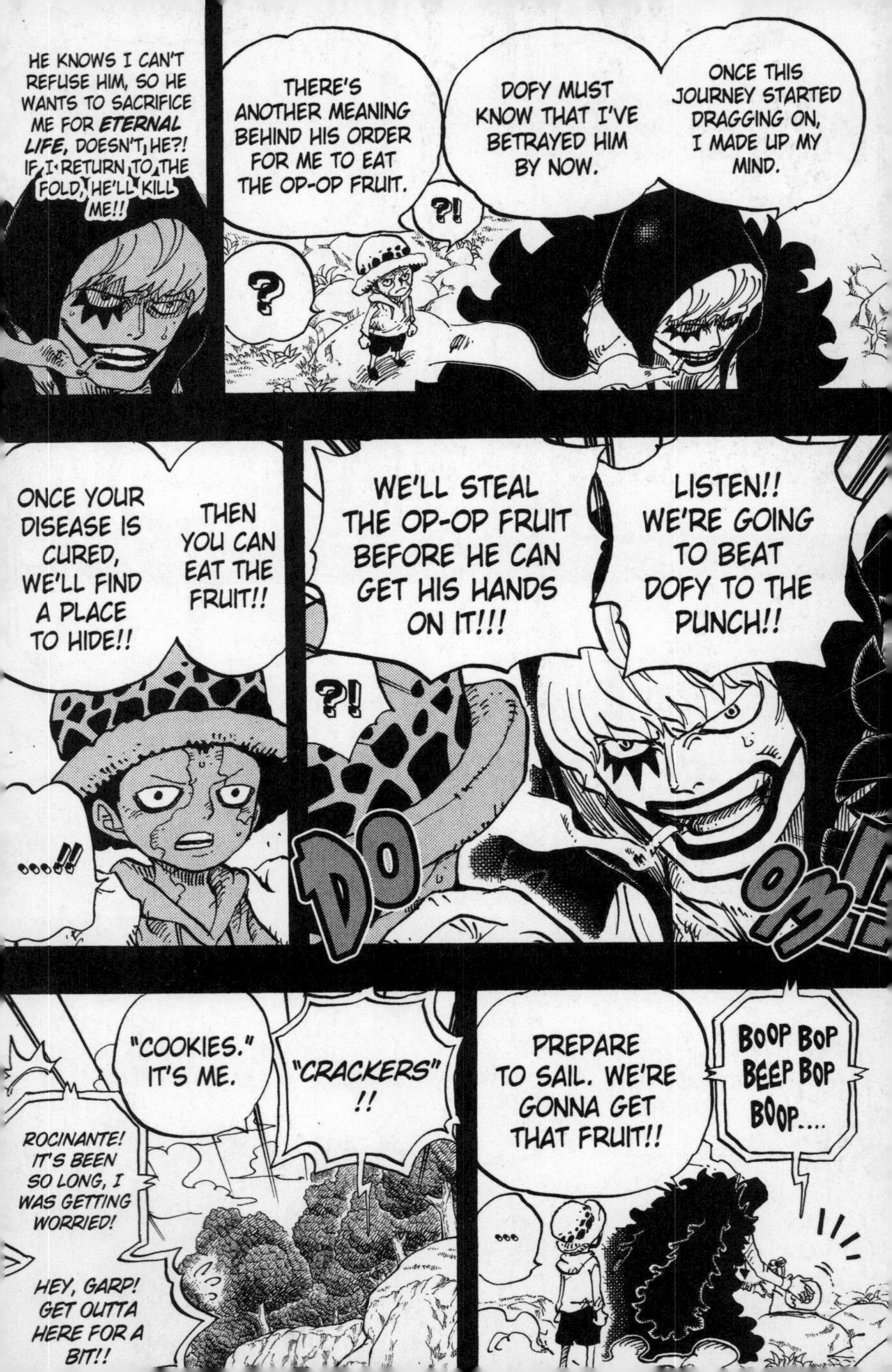

ONCE THIS JOURNEY STARTED DRAGGING ON, I MADE UP MY MIND.
DOFY MUST KNOW THAT I'VE BETRAYED HIM BY NOW.
THERE'S ANOTHER MEANING BEHIND HIS ORDER FOR ME TO EAT THE OP-OP FRUIT.
?!
?
HE KNOWS I CAN'T REFUSE HIM, SO HE WANTS TO SACRIFICE ME FOR ETERNAL LIFE, DOESN'T HE?! IF I RETURN TO THE FOLD, HE'LL KILL ME!!
LISTEN!! WE'RE GOING TO BEAT DOFY TO THE PUNCH!!
WE'LL STEAL THE OP-OP FRUIT BEFORE HE CAN GET HIS HANDS ON IT!!!
?!
DOOM!!
THEN YOU CAN EAT THE FRUIT!!
ONCE YOUR DISEASE IS CURED, WE'LL FIND A PLACE TO HIDE!!
....!!
BOOP BOP BEEP BOP BOOP....
PREPARE TO SAIL. WE'RE GONNA GET THAT FRUIT!!
...
"CRACKERS" !!
"COOKIES." IT'S ME.
ROCINANTE! IT'S BEEN SO LONG, I WAS GETTING WORRIED!
HEY, GARP! GET OUTTA HERE FOR A BIT!!

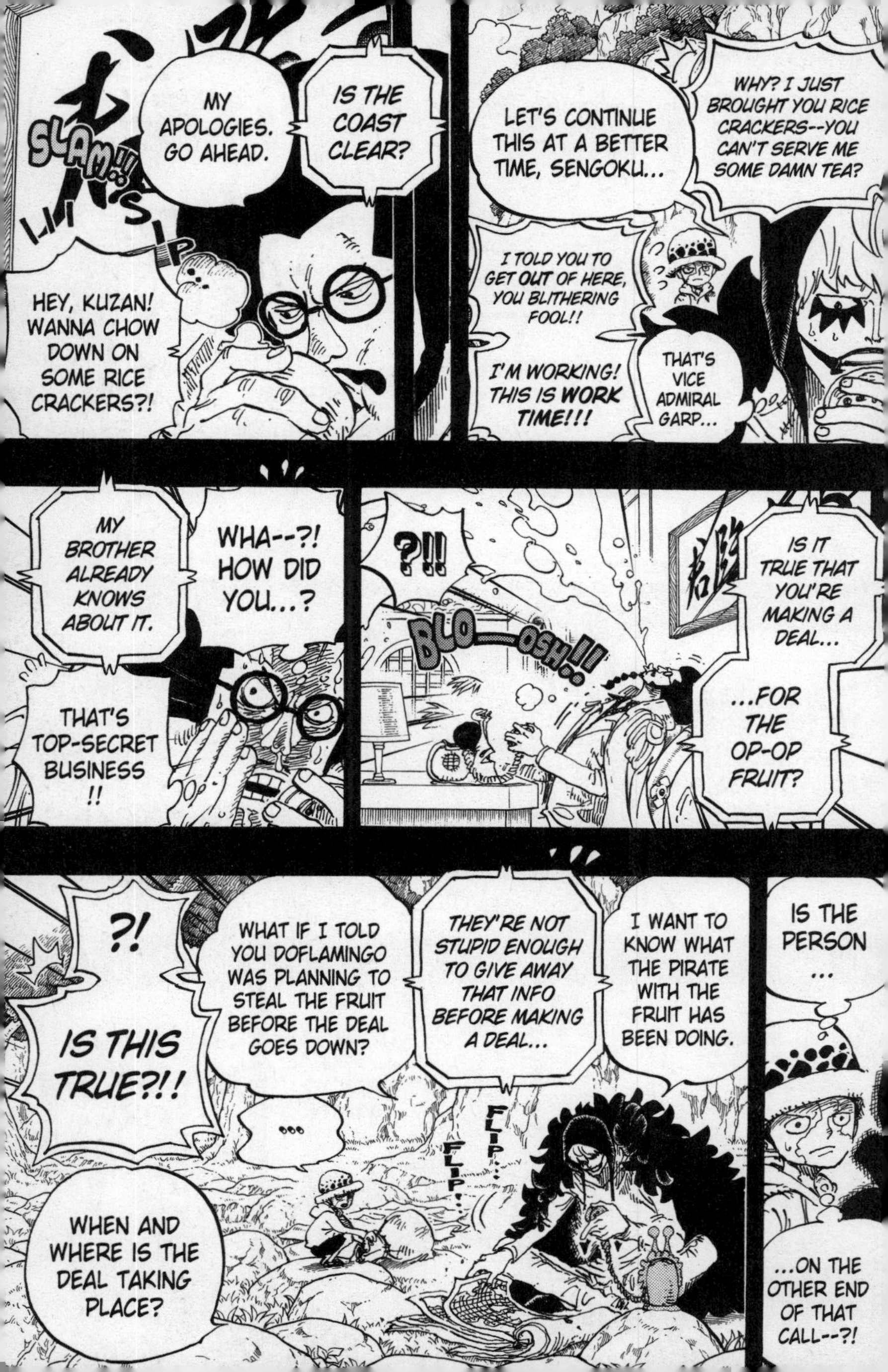
WHY? I JUST BROUGHT YOU RICE CRACKERS--YOU CAN'T SERVE ME SOME DAMN TEA?
LET'S CONTINUE THIS AT A BETTER TIME, SENGOKU...
THAT'S VICE ADMIRAL GARP...
I TOLD YOU TO GET OUT OF HERE, YOU BLITHERING FOOL!!
I'M WORKING! THIS IS WORK TIME!!!
IS THE COAST CLEAR?
MY APOLOGIES. GO AHEAD.
SLAM!!
SIP
HEY, KUZAN! WANNA CHOW DOWN ON SOME RICE CRACKERS?!
IS IT TRUE THAT YOU'RE MAKING A DEAL...
...FOR THE OP-OP FRUIT?
?!!
BLO—OSH!!
WHA--?! HOW DID YOU...?
MY BROTHER ALREADY KNOWS ABOUT IT.
THAT'S TOP-SECRET BUSINESS !!
IS THE PERSON...
...ON THE OTHER END OF THAT CALL--?!
I WANT TO KNOW WHAT THE PIRATE WITH THE FRUIT HAS BEEN DOING.
THEY'RE NOT STUPID ENOUGH TO GIVE AWAY THAT INFO BEFORE MAKING A DEAL...
WHAT IF I TOLD YOU DOFLAMINGO WAS PLANNING TO STEAL THE FRUIT BEFORE THE DEAL GOES DOWN?
?!
IS THIS TRUE?!!
FLIP...
FLIP...
...
WHEN AND WHERE IS THE DEAL TAKING PLACE?

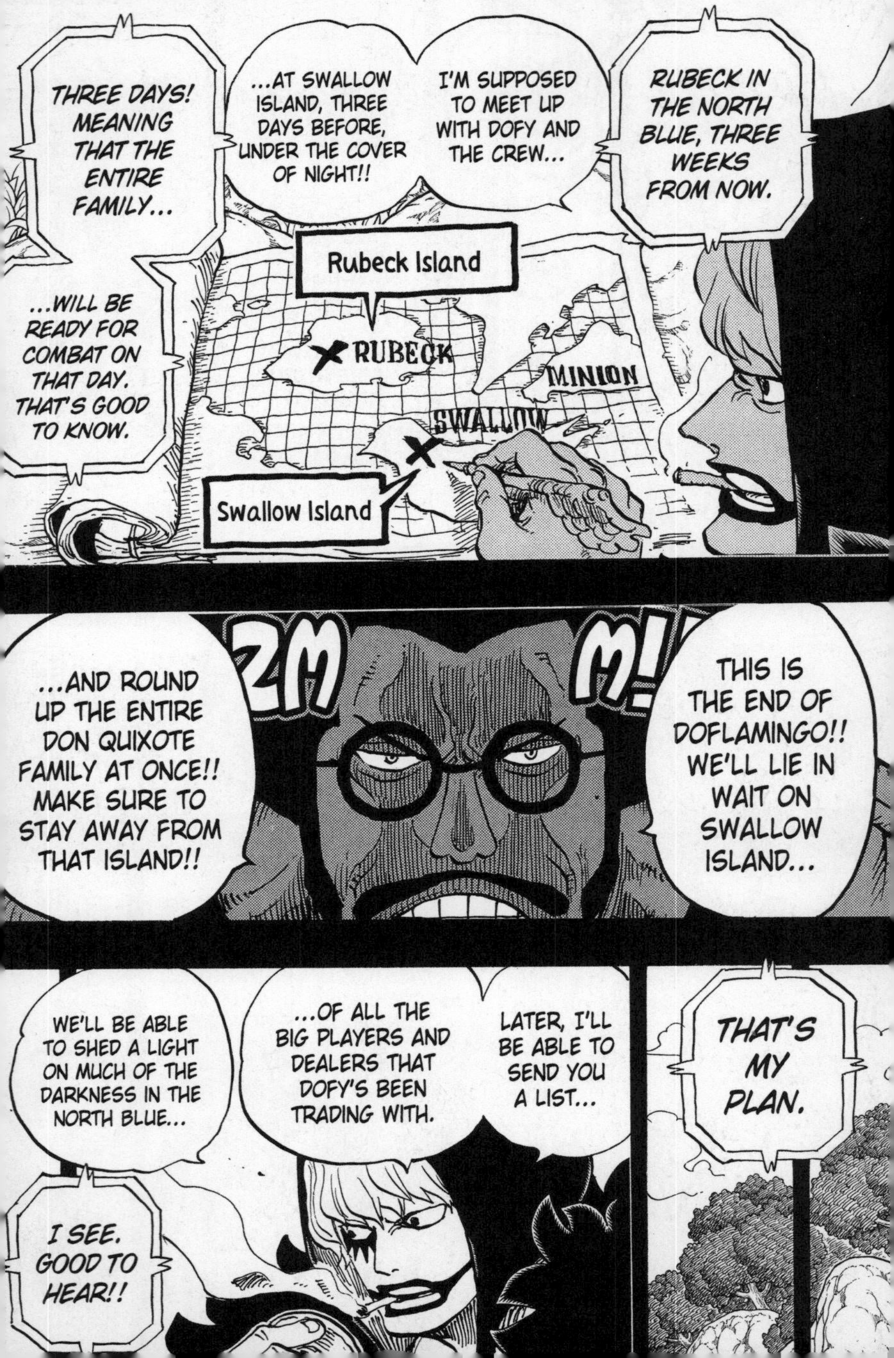
RUBECK IN THE NORTH BLUE, THREE WEEKS FROM NOW.
I'M SUPPOSED TO MEET UP WITH DOFY AND THE CREW...
...AT SWALLOW ISLAND, THREE DAYS BEFORE, UNDER THE COVER OF NIGHT!!
THREE DAYS! MEANING THAT THE ENTIRE FAMILY...
Rubeck Island
RUBECK
MINION
SWALLOW
Swallow Island
...WILL BE READY FOR COMBAT ON THAT DAY. THAT'S GOOD TO KNOW.
ZM
M!!
THIS IS THE END OF DOFLAMINGO!! WE'LL LIE IN WAIT ON SWALLOW ISLAND...
...AND ROUND UP THE ENTIRE DON QUIXOTE FAMILY AT ONCE!! MAKE SURE TO STAY AWAY FROM THAT ISLAND!!
THAT'S MY PLAN.
LATER, I'LL BE ABLE TO SEND YOU A LIST...
...OF ALL THE BIG PLAYERS AND DEALERS THAT DOFY'S BEEN TRADING WITH.
WE'LL BE ABLE TO SHED A LIGHT ON MUCH OF THE DARKNESS IN THE NORTH BLUE...
I SEE. GOOD TO HEAR!!

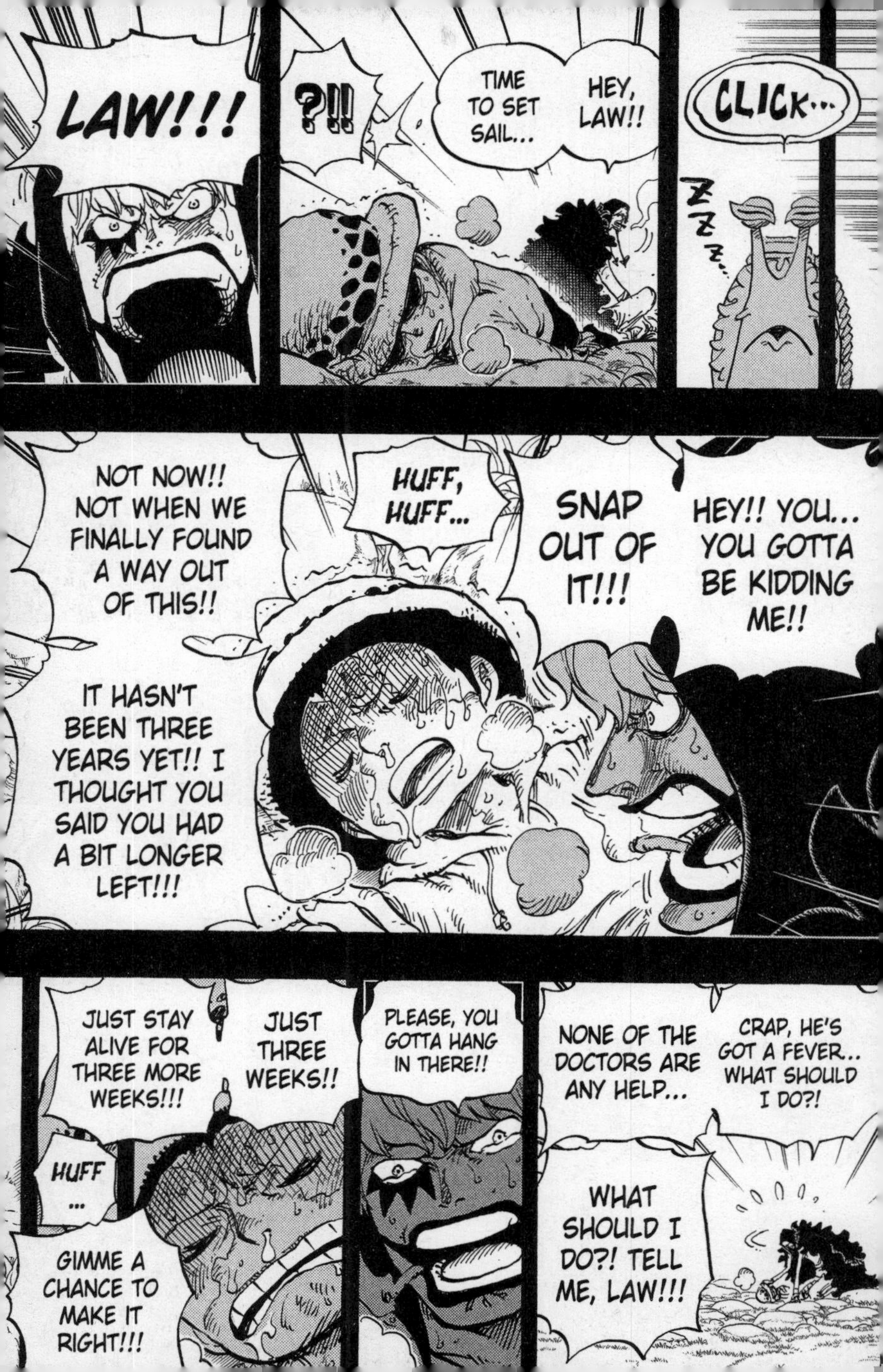
CLICK...
ZZZ...
HEY, LAW!!
TIME TO SET SAIL...
?!!
LAW!!!
HEY!! YOU... YOU GOTTA BE KIDDING ME!!
SNAP OUT OF IT!!!
HUFF, HUFF...
NOT NOW!! NOT WHEN WE FINALLY FOUND A WAY OUT OF THIS!!
IT HASN'T BEEN THREE YEARS YET!! I THOUGHT YOU SAID YOU HAD A BIT LONGER LEFT!!!
CRAP, HE'S GOT A FEVER... WHAT SHOULD I DO?!
NONE OF THE DOCTORS ARE ANY HELP...
WHAT SHOULD I DO?! TELL ME, LAW!!!
PLEASE, YOU GOTTA HANG IN THERE!!
JUST THREE WEEKS!!
JUST STAY ALIVE FOR THREE MORE WEEKS!!!
HUFF ...
GIMME A CHANCE TO MAKE IT RIGHT!!!

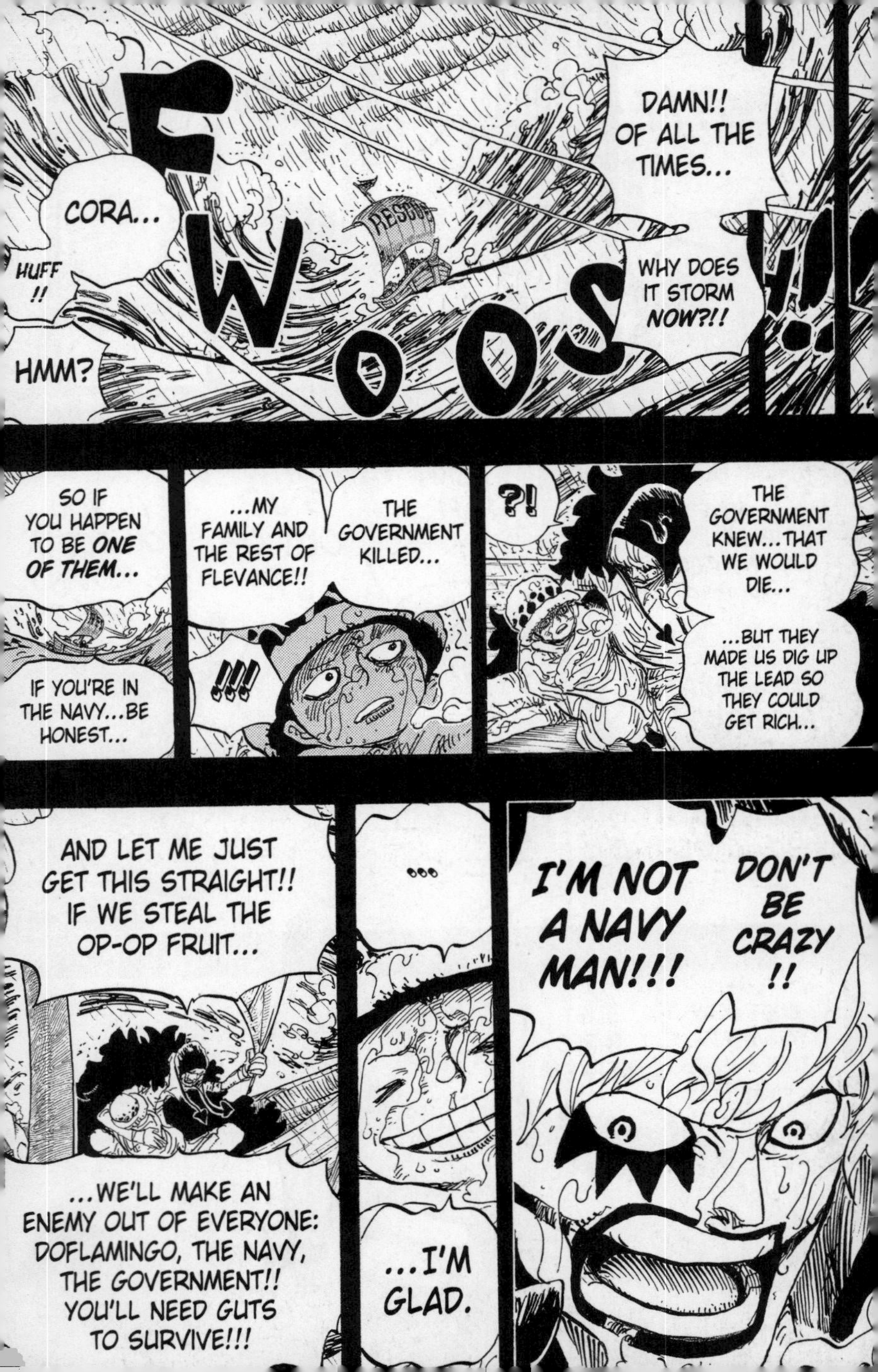
DAMN!! OF ALL THE TIMES...
WHY DOES IT STORM NOW?!!
FWOOSH
CORA...
HUFF !!
HMM?
?!
THE GOVERNMENT KNEW...THAT WE WOULD DIE...
...BUT THEY MADE US DIG UP THE LEAD SO THEY COULD GET RICH...
THE GOVERNMENT KILLED...
...MY FAMILY AND THE REST OF FLEVANCE!!
!!!
SO IF YOU HAPPEN TO BE ONE OF THEM...
IF YOU'RE IN THE NAVY...BE HONEST...
DON'T BE CRAZY !!
I'M NOT A NAVY MAN!!!
...
...I'M GLAD.
AND LET ME JUST GET THIS STRAIGHT!! IF WE STEAL THE OP-OP FRUIT...
...WE'LL MAKE AN ENEMY OUT OF EVERYONE: DOFLAMINGO, THE NAVY, THE GOVERNMENT!! YOU'LL NEED GUTS TO SURVIVE!!!

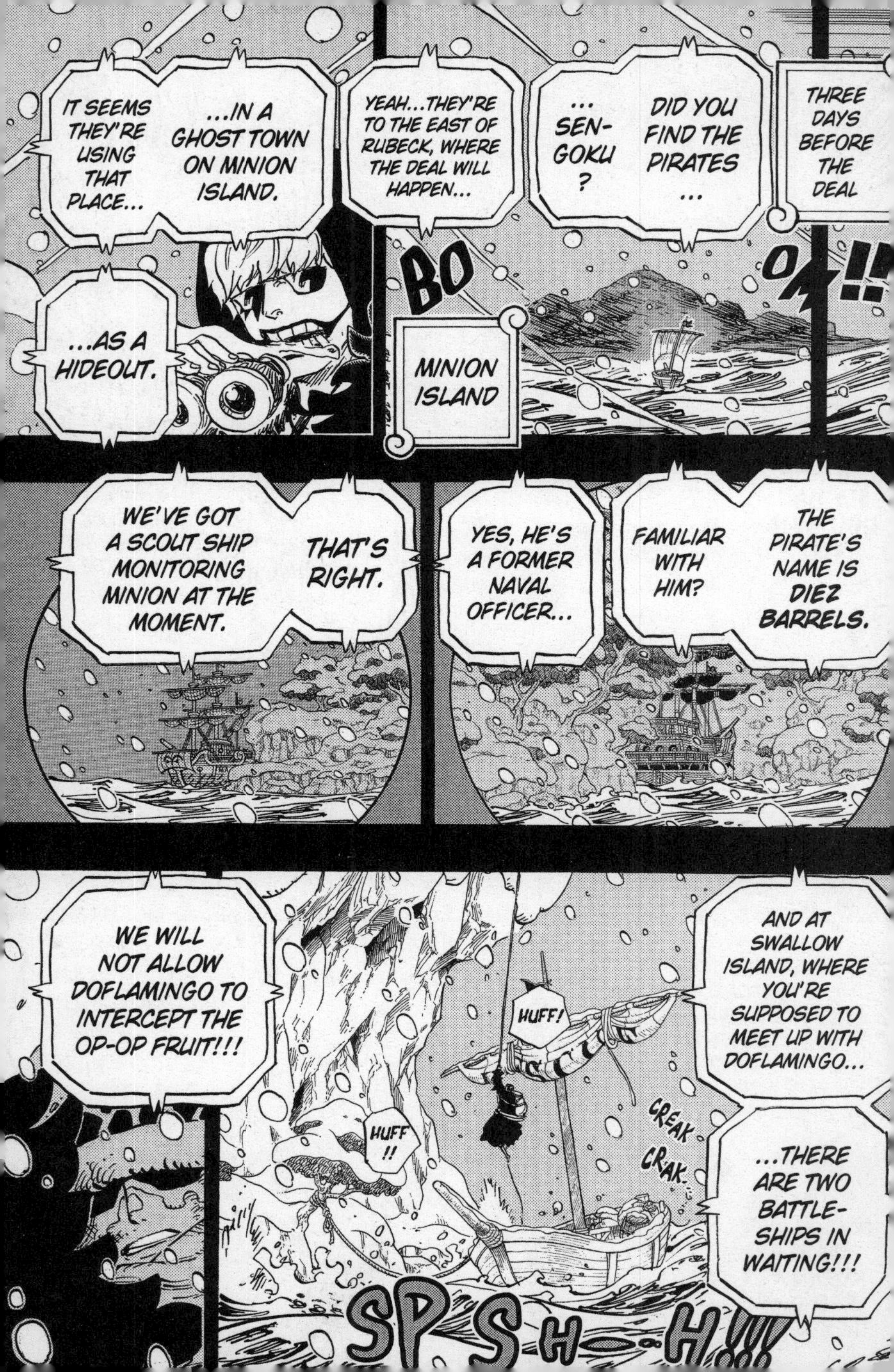
THREE DAYS BEFORE THE DEAL
DID YOU FIND THE PIRATES...
...SEN-GOKU?
YEAH...THEY'RE TO THE EAST OF RUBECK, WHERE THE DEAL WILL HAPPEN...
BO
OM!!
MINION ISLAND
...IN A GHOST TOWN ON MINION ISLAND.
IT SEEMS THEY'RE USING THAT PLACE...
...AS A HIDEOUT.
THE PIRATE'S NAME IS DIEZ BARRELS.
FAMILIAR WITH HIM?
YES, HE'S A FORMER NAVAL OFFICER...
THAT'S RIGHT.
WE'VE GOT A SCOUT SHIP MONITORING MINION AT THE MOMENT.
AND AT SWALLOW ISLAND, WHERE YOU'RE SUPPOSED TO MEET UP WITH DOFLAMINGO...
...THERE ARE TWO BATTLE-SHIPS IN WAITING!!!
CREAK
CRAK
HUFF!
HUFF!!
SPSH-H-H!!!
WE WILL NOT ALLOW DOFLAMINGO TO INTERCEPT THE OP-OP FRUIT!!!

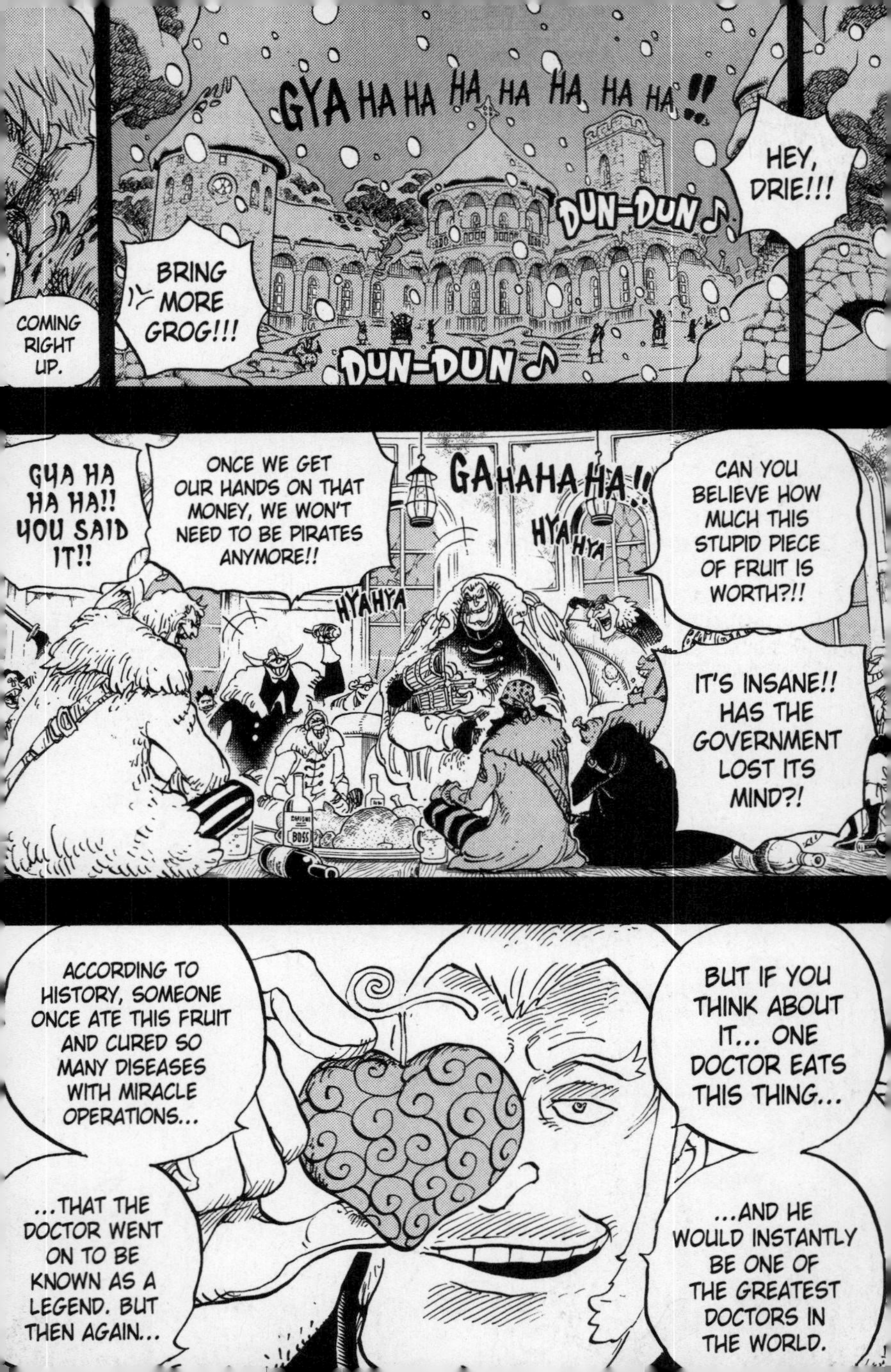
HEY, DRIE!!!
DUN-DUN♪
GYA HA HA HA HA HA HA HA!!
BRING MORE GROG!!!
COMING RIGHT UP.
DUN-DUN♪
CAN YOU BELIEVE HOW MUCH THIS STUPID PIECE OF FRUIT IS WORTH?!!
IT'S INSANE!! HAS THE GOVERNMENT LOST ITS MIND?!
GAHAHAHA!!
HYAHYA
ONCE WE GET OUR HANDS ON THAT MONEY, WE WON'T NEED TO BE PIRATES ANYMORE!!
HYAHYA
GYA HA HA HA!! YOU SAID IT!!
BUT IF YOU THINK ABOUT IT... ONE DOCTOR EATS THIS THING...
...AND HE WOULD INSTANTLY BE ONE OF THE GREATEST DOCTORS IN THE WORLD.
ACCORDING TO HISTORY, SOMEONE ONCE ATE THIS FRUIT AND CURED SO MANY DISEASES WITH MIRACLE OPERATIONS...
...THAT THE DOCTOR WENT ON TO BE KNOWN AS A LEGEND. BUT THEN AGAIN...

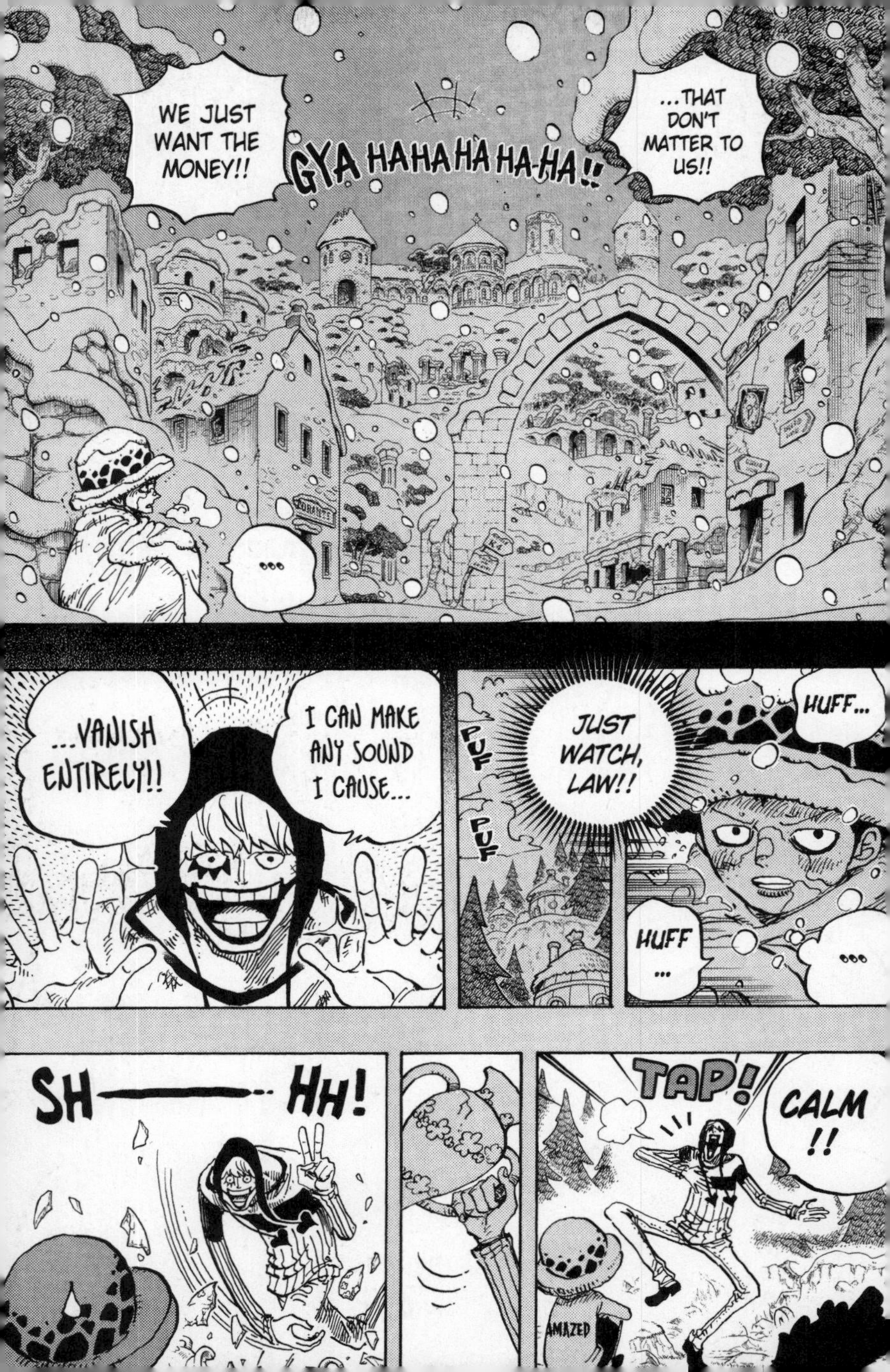
...THAT DON'T MATTER TO US!!
GYA HAHAHA HA HA-HA!!
WE JUST WANT THE MONEY!!
...
HUFF...
JUST WATCH, LAW!!
PUF
PUF
HUFF...
...
I CAN MAKE ANY SOUND I CAUSE...
...VANISH ENTIRELY!!
CALM!!
TAP!
AMAZED
SH——HH!

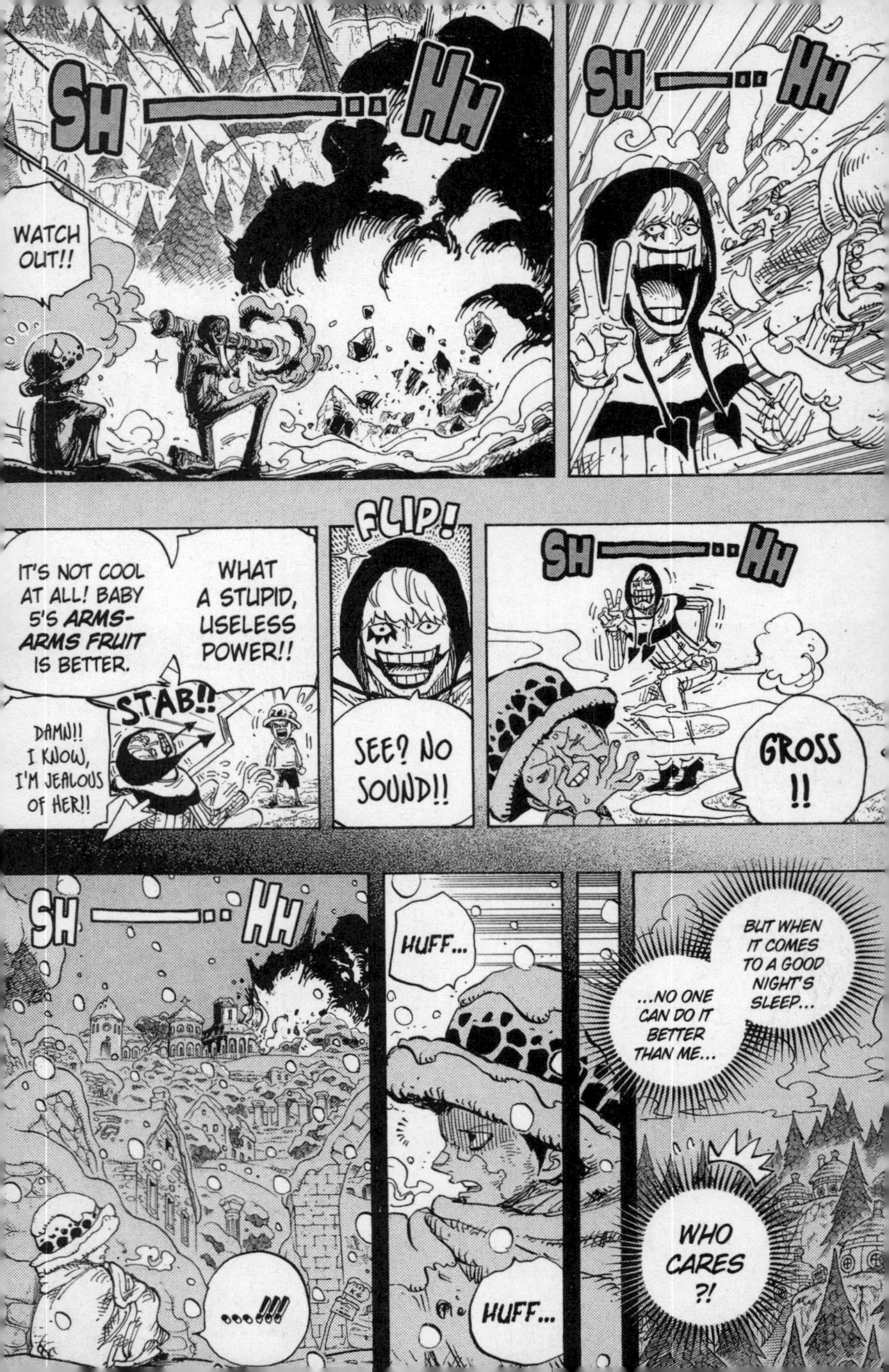
SH———..HH
SH———..HH
WATCH OUT!!
SH———..HH
GROSS!!
FLIP!
SEE? NO SOUND!!
WHAT A STUPID, USELESS POWER!!
IT'S NOT COOL AT ALL! BABY 5'S ARMS-ARMS FRUIT IS BETTER.
STAB!!
DAMN!! I KNOW, I'M JEALOUS OF HER!!
BUT WHEN IT COMES TO A GOOD NIGHT'S SLEEP...
...NO ONE CAN DO IT BETTER THAN ME...
WHO CARES ?!
HUFF...
HUFF...
SH———..HH
...!!!

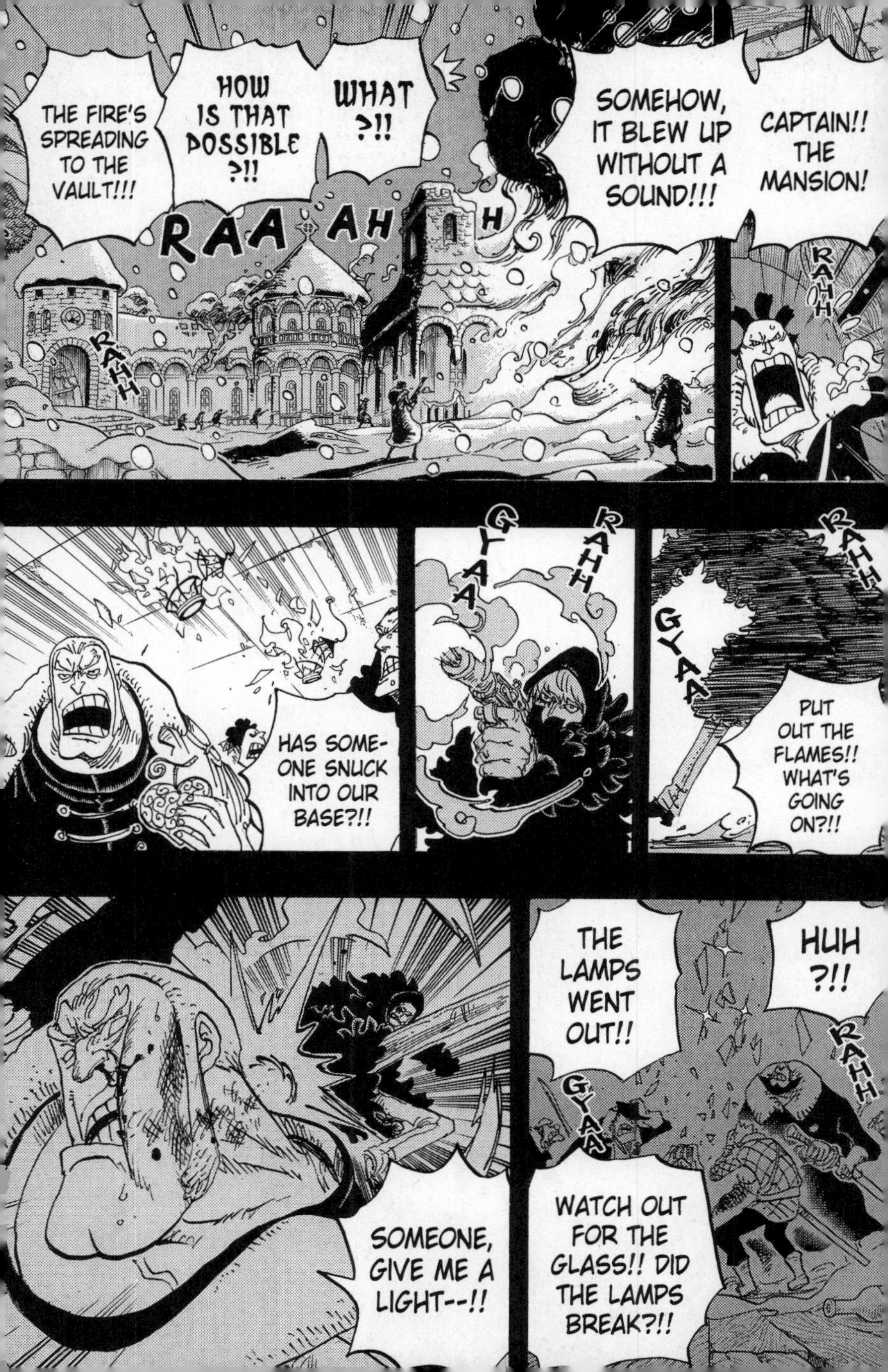
CAPTAIN!! THE MANSION!
RAHH
SOMEHOW, IT BLEW UP WITHOUT A SOUND!!!
WHAT ?!!
HOW IS THAT POSSIBLE ?!!
THE FIRE'S SPREADING TO THE VAULT!!!
RAA AH H
RAHH
RAHH
GYAA
PUT OUT THE FLAMES!! WHAT'S GOING ON?!!
RAHH
GYAAA
HAS SOME-ONE SNUCK INTO OUR BASE?!!
HUH ?!!
THE LAMPS WENT OUT!!
RAHH
GYAA
WATCH OUT FOR THE GLASS!! DID THE LAMPS BREAK?!!
SOMEONE, GIVE ME A LIGHT--!!

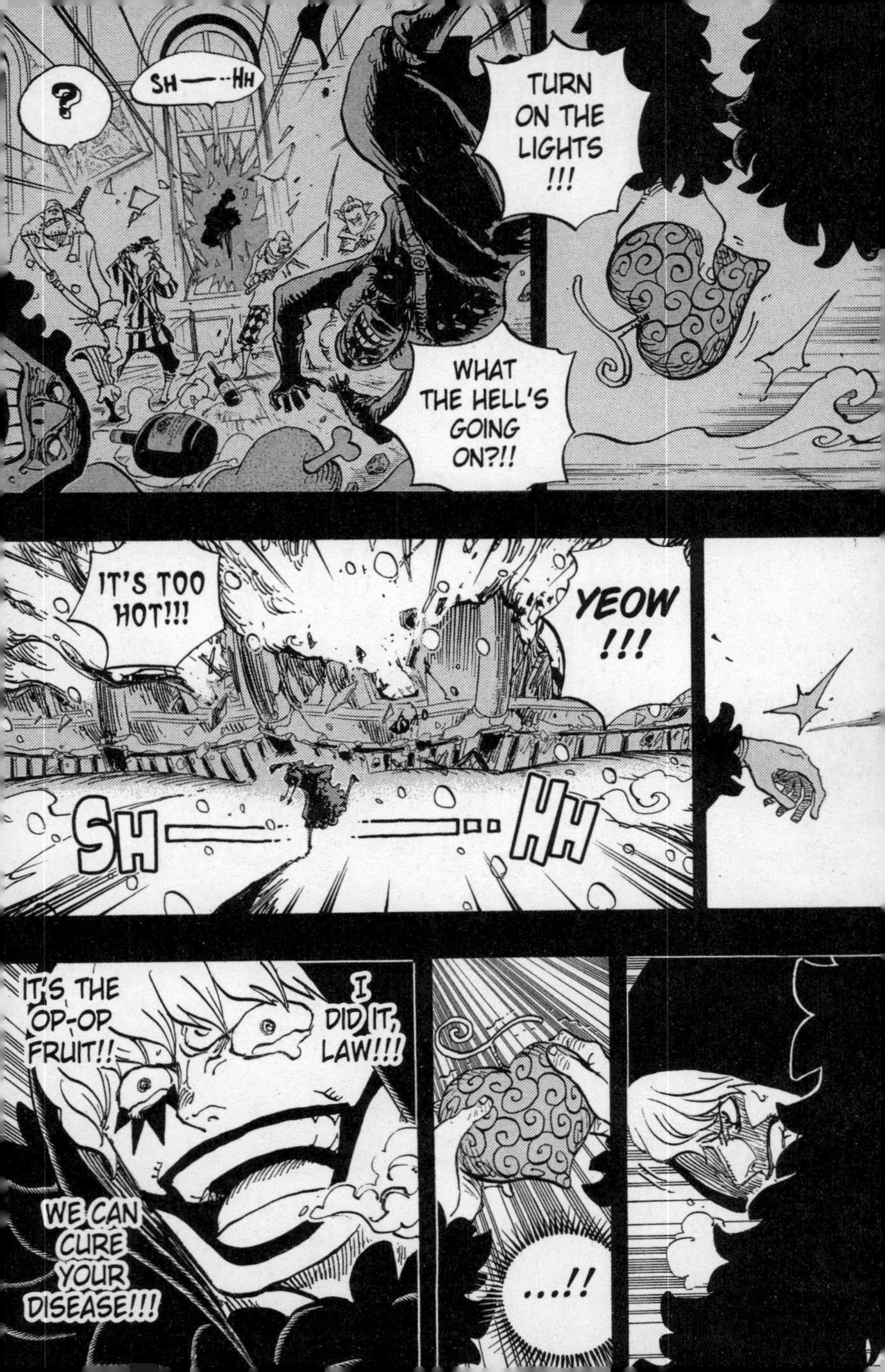
TURN ON THE LIGHTS !!!
SH—--HH
?
WHAT THE HELL'S GOING ON?!!
YEOW !!!
IT'S TOO HOT!!!
SH—-—..HH
...!!
I DID IT, LAW!!!
IT'S THE OP-OP FRUIT!!
WE CAN CURE YOUR DISEASE!!!

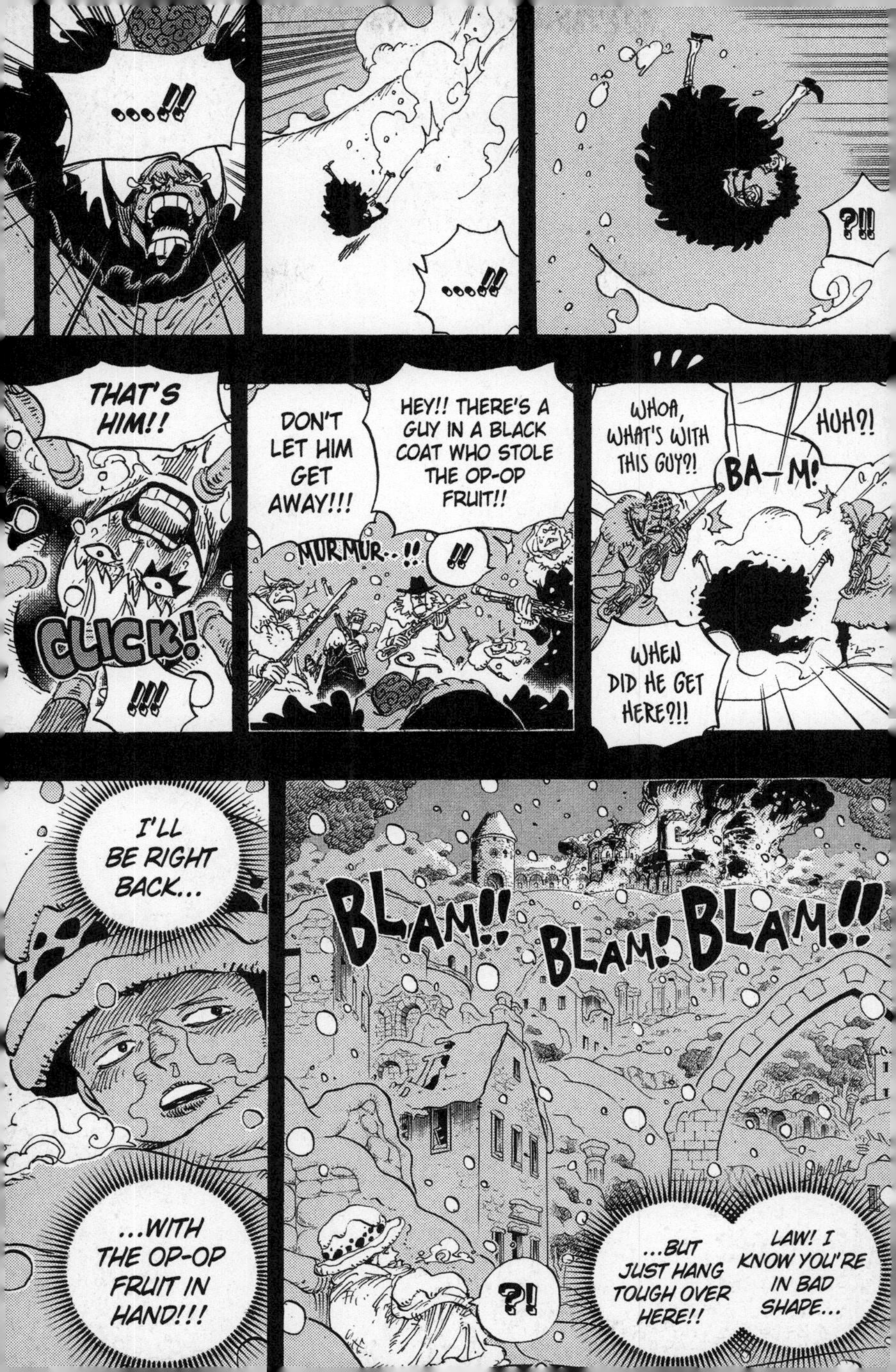
?!!
....!!
....!!
HUH?!
WHOA, WHAT'S WITH THIS GUY?!
BA—M!
WHEN DID HE GET HERE?!!
HEY!! THERE'S A GUY IN A BLACK COAT WHO STOLE THE OP-OP FRUIT!!
DON'T LET HIM GET AWAY!!!
!!
MURMUR..!!
THAT'S HIM!!
CLICK!
!!!
BLAM!!
BLAM!
BLAM!!
LAW! I KNOW YOU'RE IN BAD SHAPE...
...BUT JUST HANG TOUGH OVER HERE!!
?!
I'LL BE RIGHT BACK...
...WITH THE OP-OP FRUIT IN HAND!!!

SBS Question Corner

エス
ビー
エス
タヌキチ いったい何の呪文だ？
質問コーナー

(Ikadai, Oita)

Q: Oda Sensei, are you making Nami and Robin's boobs bigger because you ate the Perv-Perv Fruit? Please make my mom and big sister's boobs bigger too. And make my wiener bigger while you're at it.

--Boy with the Bored-Bored Fruit (age 8)

A: You know, now that you mention it, I did once have a piece of fruit for dessert that tasted like crap... And ever since, I've been like this...
What do you mean, *like this?!* How rude!!
I hope many things in your family become bigger than your bodies.

Q: Hello, Odacchi!! Look at that conversation between Kanjuro and Kin'emon on the second page of Chapter 745 in Volume 76! That's from a *rakugo* story, the traditional art of Japanese comedic storytelling! It's called the "summer doctor"! Do you enjoy rakugo, Odachi?! Which performer is your favorite?! My favorite is the 2nd Shijaku Katsura!!

--Fukutaro, age 16

A: Yes, I was hoping that those rakugo heads among us would get a chuckle from that one. There's a pun in there between the archaic word for "lettuce" and "doctor," and there's a reference to bellyaches, which is what I was secretly quoting. There's another famous story about the *nukesuzume* ("spring sparrow") painted by a **particularly talented artist** that pop out of the painting. Anyway, there are lots of rakugo storytellers I enjoy. I've been listening since elementary school! Kosanji Yanagiya, Gontaro and Kyotaro, Danshi Tatekawa and Shinosuke, Kinba San'yutei, Bunchin Katsura, Jakusaburo, Shinsho and Shincho Kokontei, and...
There's no end to them!!!
Rakugo is great! But I bet I've just gone and bored all of you. (cries)

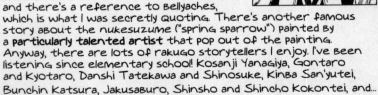

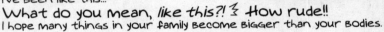

Chapter 766: SMILE

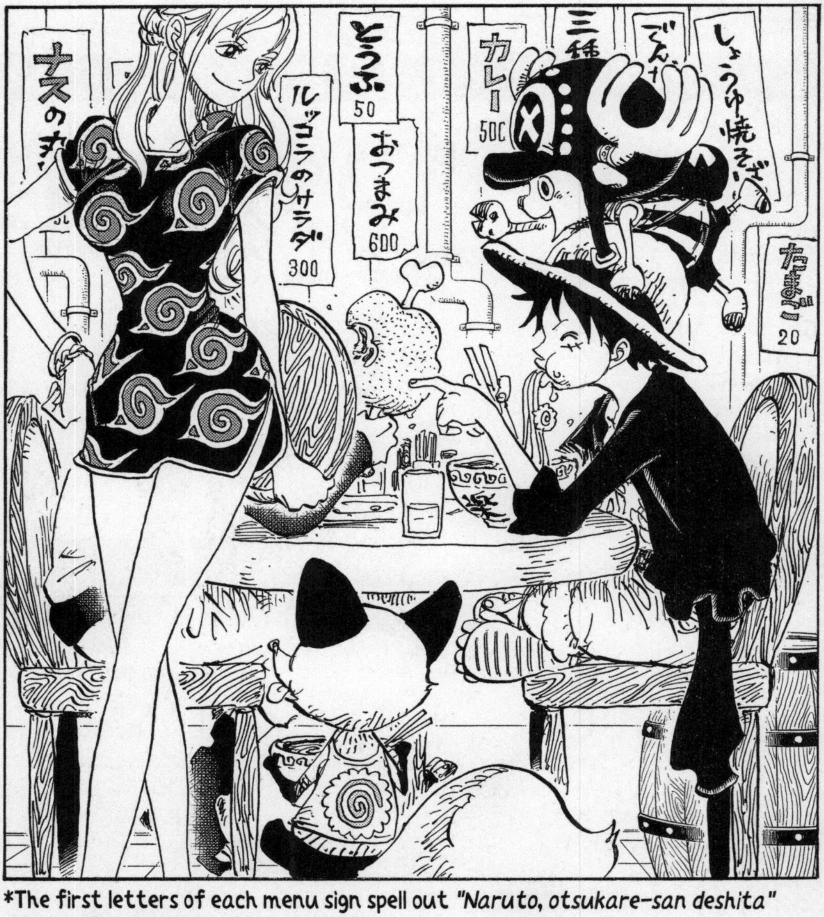

しょうゆ焼そば
たまご
20
カレー
とうふ
50
おつまみ
600
ルッコラのサラダ
300

*The first letters of each menu sign spell out "Naruto, otsukare-san deshita" (Thanks for the great run, Naruto!)

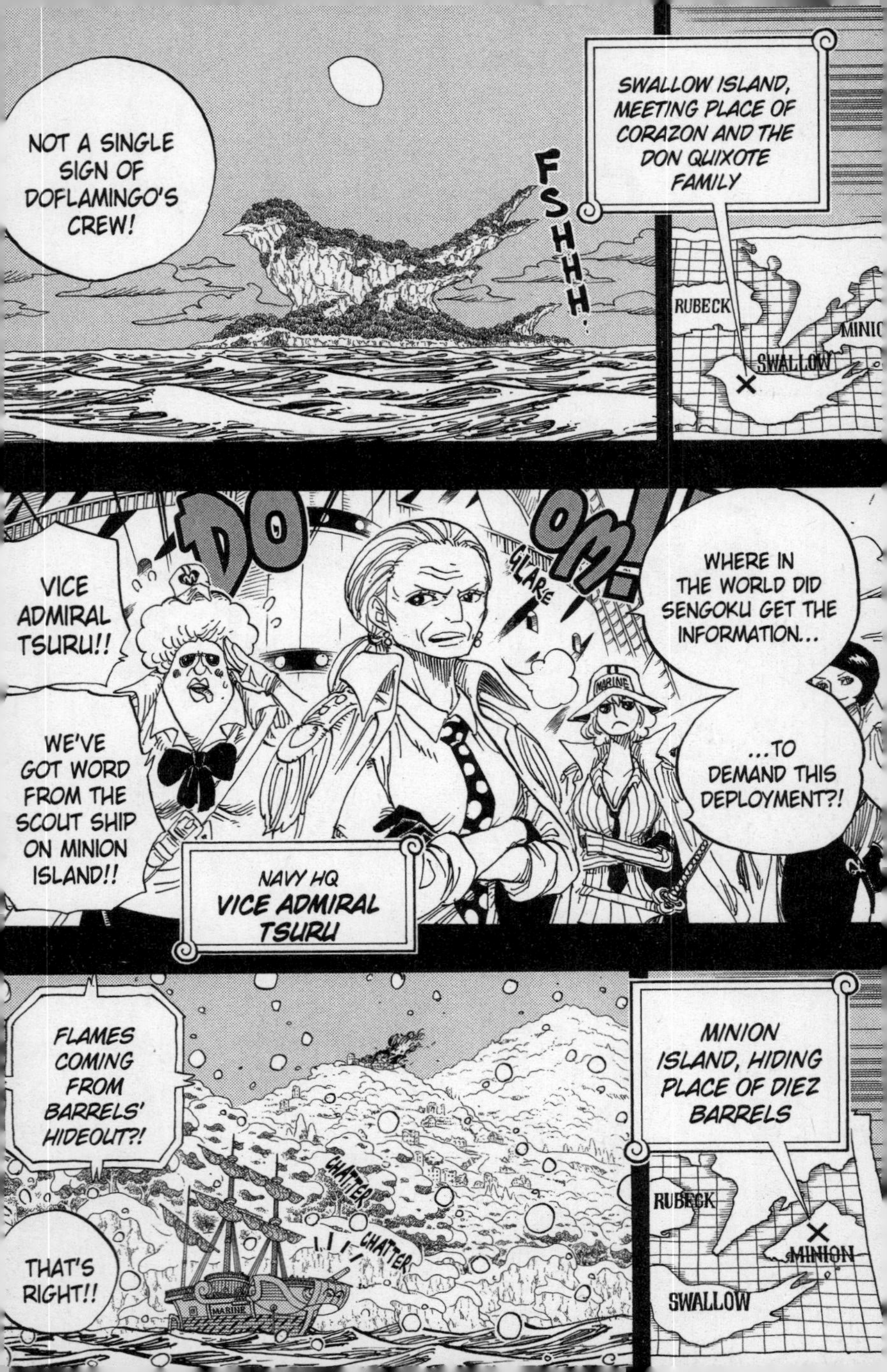
SWALLOW ISLAND, MEETING PLACE OF CORAZON AND THE DON QUIXOTE FAMILY
RUBECK
SWALLOW
FSHHH
NOT A SINGLE SIGN OF DOFLAMINGO'S CREW!
DOOM!
WHERE IN THE WORLD DID SENGOKU GET THE INFORMATION...
GLARE
VICE ADMIRAL TSURU!!
...TO DEMAND THIS DEPLOYMENT?!
MARINE
WE'VE GOT WORD FROM THE SCOUT SHIP ON MINION ISLAND!!
NAVY HQ
VICE ADMIRAL TSURU
MINION ISLAND, HIDING PLACE OF DIEZ BARRELS
RUBECK
MINION
SWALLOW
FLAMES COMING FROM BARRELS' HIDEOUT?!
CHATTER
CHATTER
THAT'S RIGHT!!
MARINE

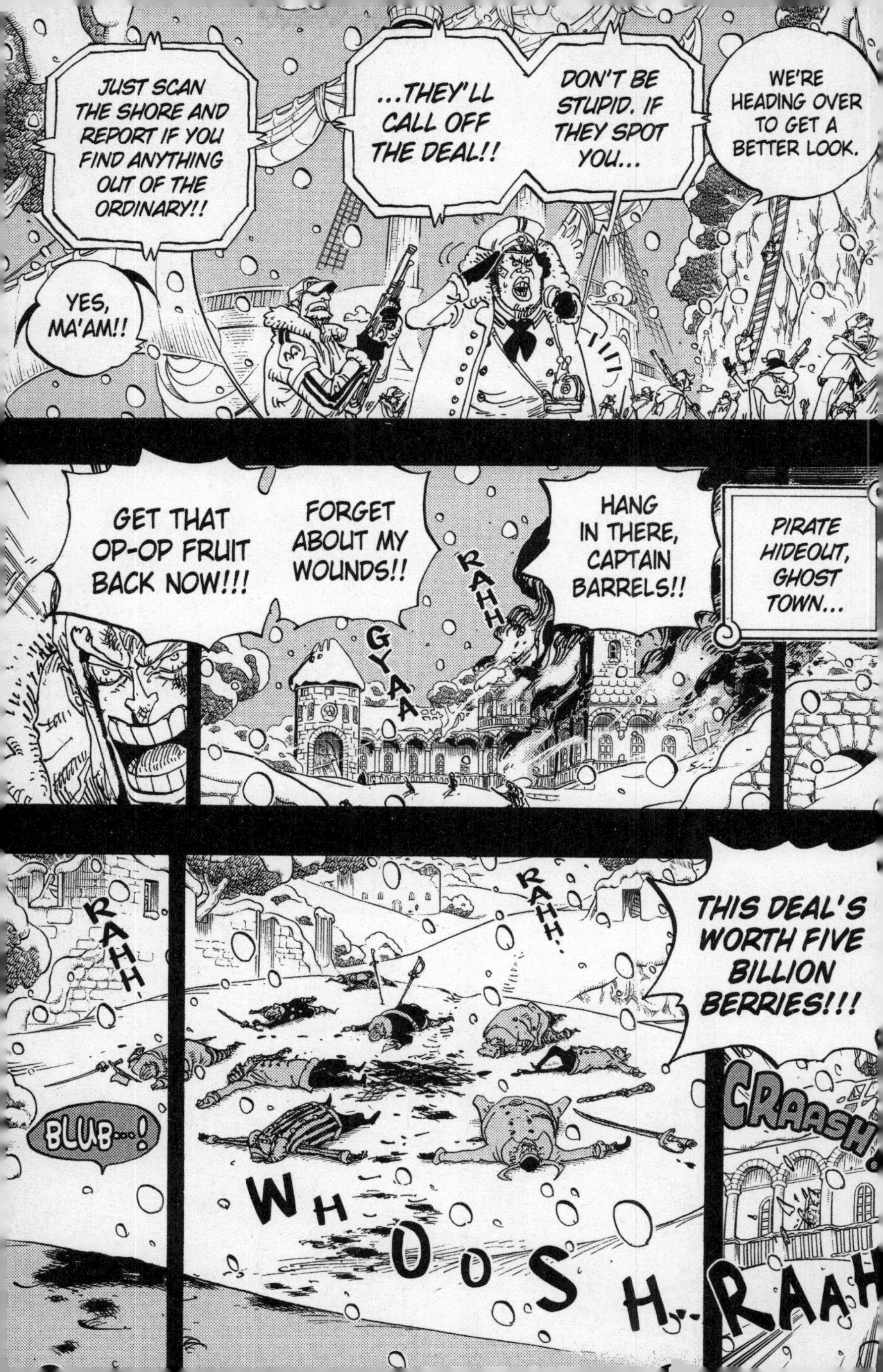
WE'RE HEADING OVER TO GET A BETTER LOOK.
DON'T BE STUPID. IF THEY SPOT YOU...
...THEY'LL CALL OFF THE DEAL!!
JUST SCAN THE SHORE AND REPORT IF YOU FIND ANYTHING OUT OF THE ORDINARY!!
YES, MA'AM!!
PIRATE HIDEOUT, GHOST TOWN...
HANG IN THERE, CAPTAIN BARRELS!!
RAHH
GYAA
FORGET ABOUT MY WOUNDS!!
GET THAT OP-OP FRUIT BACK NOW!!!
THIS DEAL'S WORTH FIVE BILLION BERRIES!!!
CRAASH
RAAH
RAHH
RAHH
BLUB...!
WHOOSH

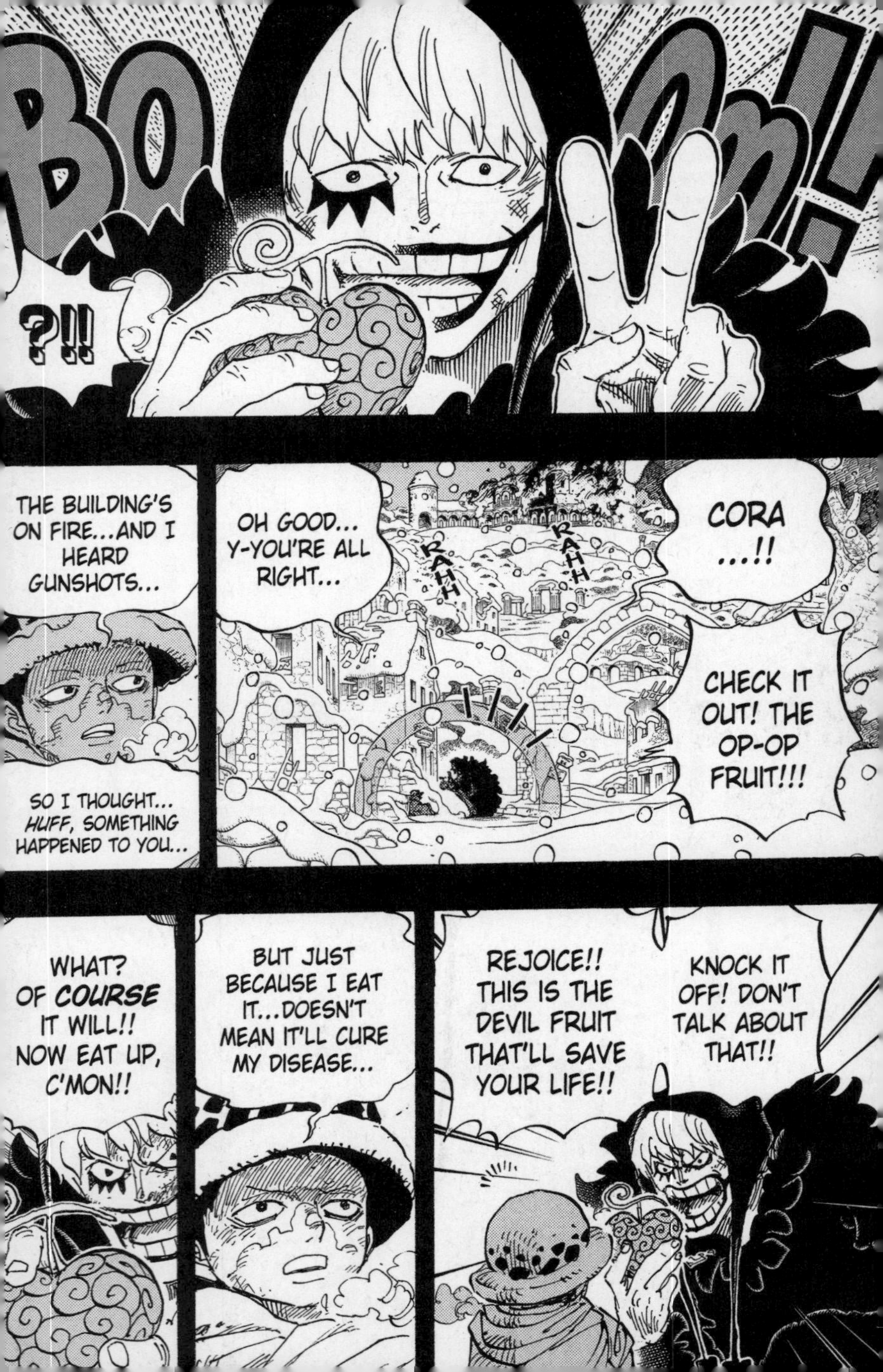

BOOM!
?!!
CORA ...!!
CHECK IT OUT! THE OP-OP FRUIT!!!
RAHH
RAHH
OH GOOD... Y-YOU'RE ALL RIGHT...
THE BUILDING'S ON FIRE...AND I HEARD GUNSHOTS...
SO I THOUGHT... *HUFF*, SOMETHING HAPPENED TO YOU...
KNOCK IT OFF! DON'T TALK ABOUT THAT!!
REJOICE!! THIS IS THE DEVIL FRUIT THAT'LL SAVE YOUR LIFE!!
BUT JUST BECAUSE I EAT IT...DOESN'T MEAN IT'LL CURE MY DISEASE...
WHAT? OF **COURSE** IT WILL!! NOW EAT UP, C'MON!!

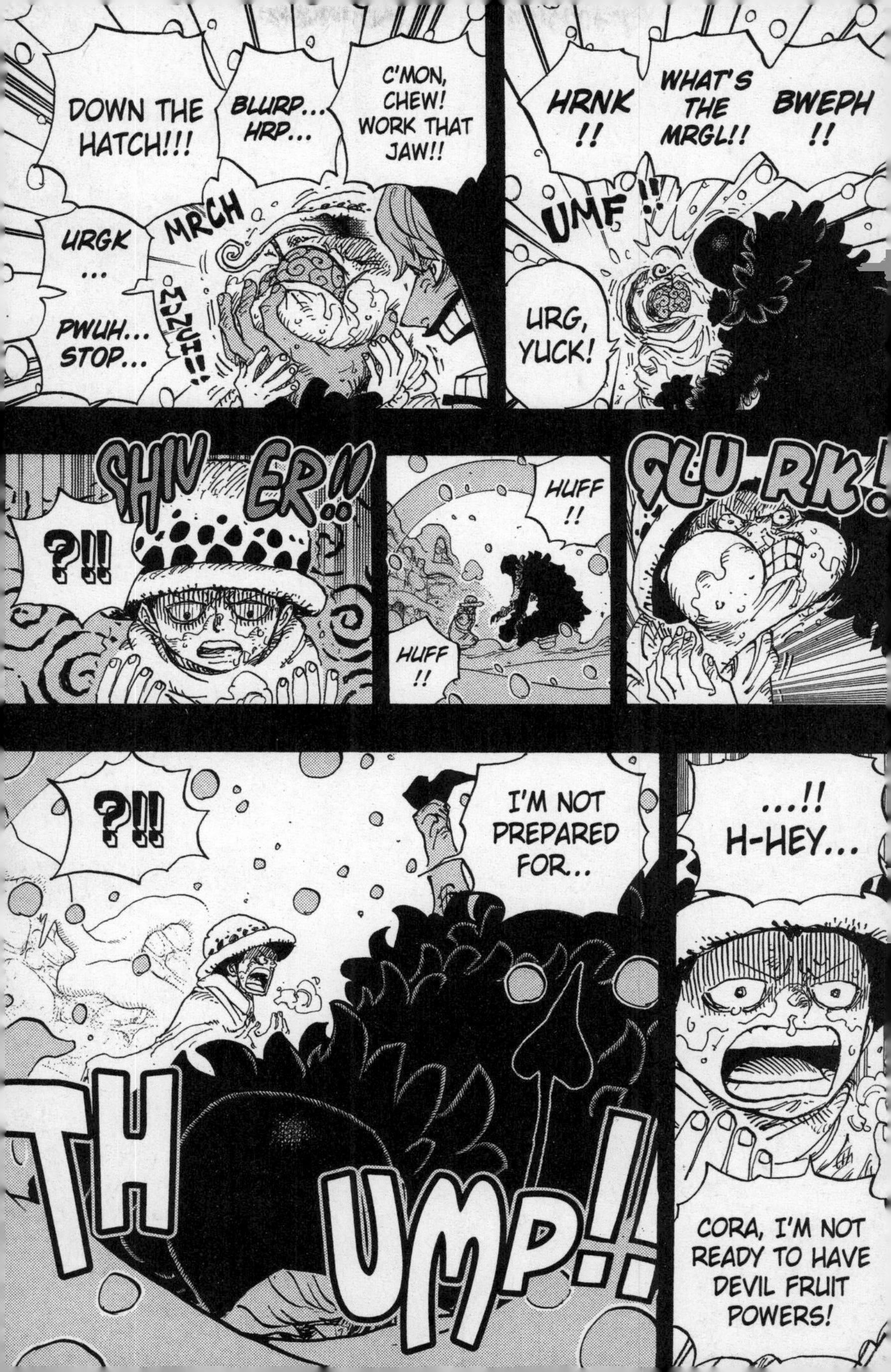

BWEPH!!
WHAT'S THE MRGL!!
HRNK!!
UMF!!
URG, YUCK!
C'MON, CHEW! WORK THAT JAW!!
BLURP... HRP...
DOWN THE HATCH!!!
MRCH
URGK...
MUNCH!!
PWUH... STOP...
GLURK!
HUFF!!
HUFF!!
SHIVER!!
?!!
...!! H-HEY...
CORA, I'M NOT READY TO HAVE DEVIL FRUIT POWERS!
I'M NOT PREPARED FOR...
?!!
THUMP!!

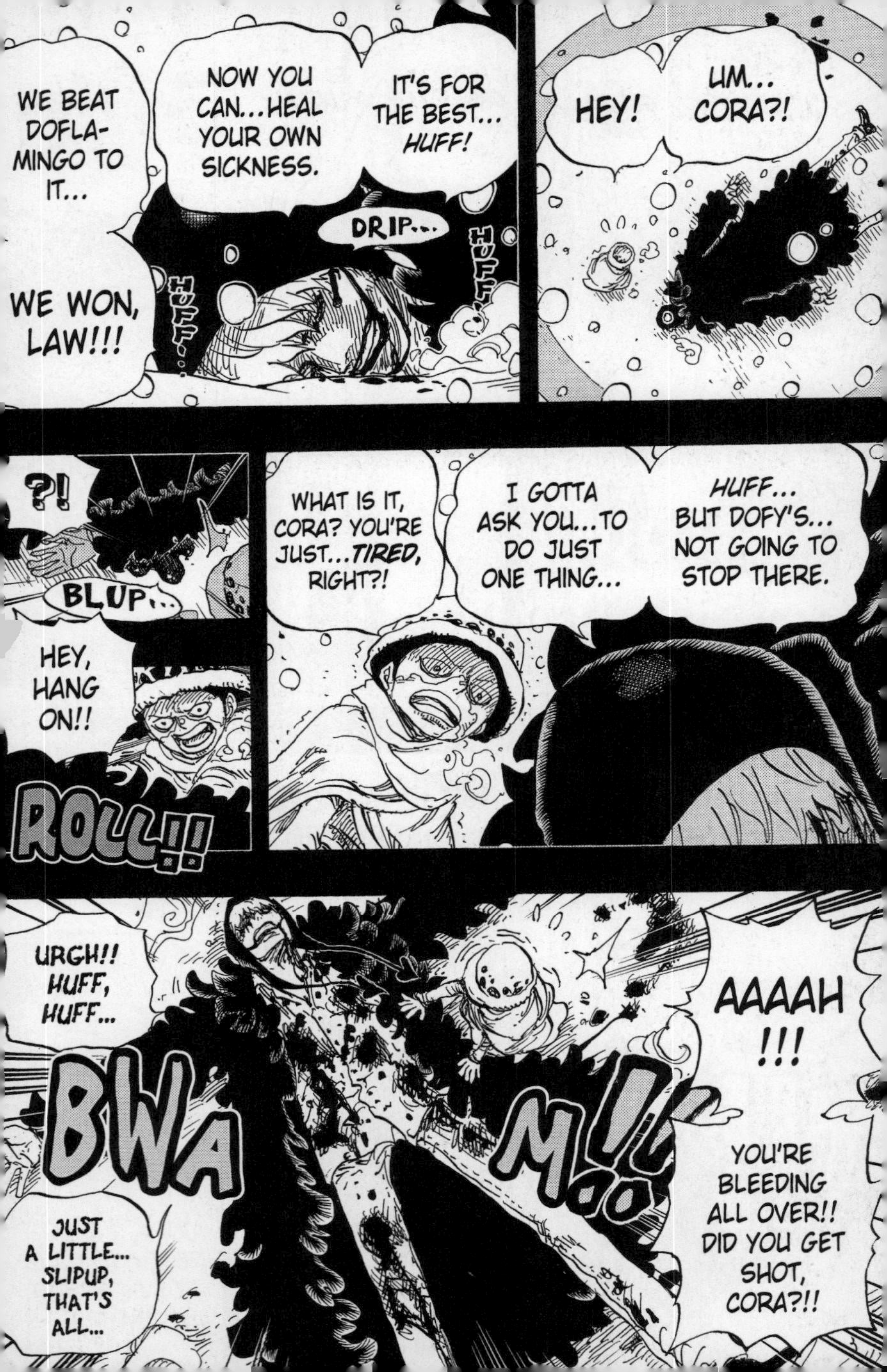
UM... CORA?!
HEY!
IT'S FOR THE BEST... HUFF!
NOW YOU CAN...HEAL YOUR OWN SICKNESS.
WE BEAT DOFLAMINGO TO IT...
DRIP...
HUFF
HUFF...
WE WON, LAW!!!
HUFF... BUT DOFY'S... NOT GOING TO STOP THERE.
I GOTTA ASK YOU...TO DO JUST ONE THING...
WHAT IS IT, CORA? YOU'RE JUST...TIRED, RIGHT?!
?!
BLUP...
HEY, HANG ON!!
ROLL!!
AAAAH!!!
YOU'RE BLEEDING ALL OVER!! DID YOU GET SHOT, CORA?!!
BWAM!!
URGH!! HUFF, HUFF...
JUST A LITTLE... SLIPUP, THAT'S ALL...

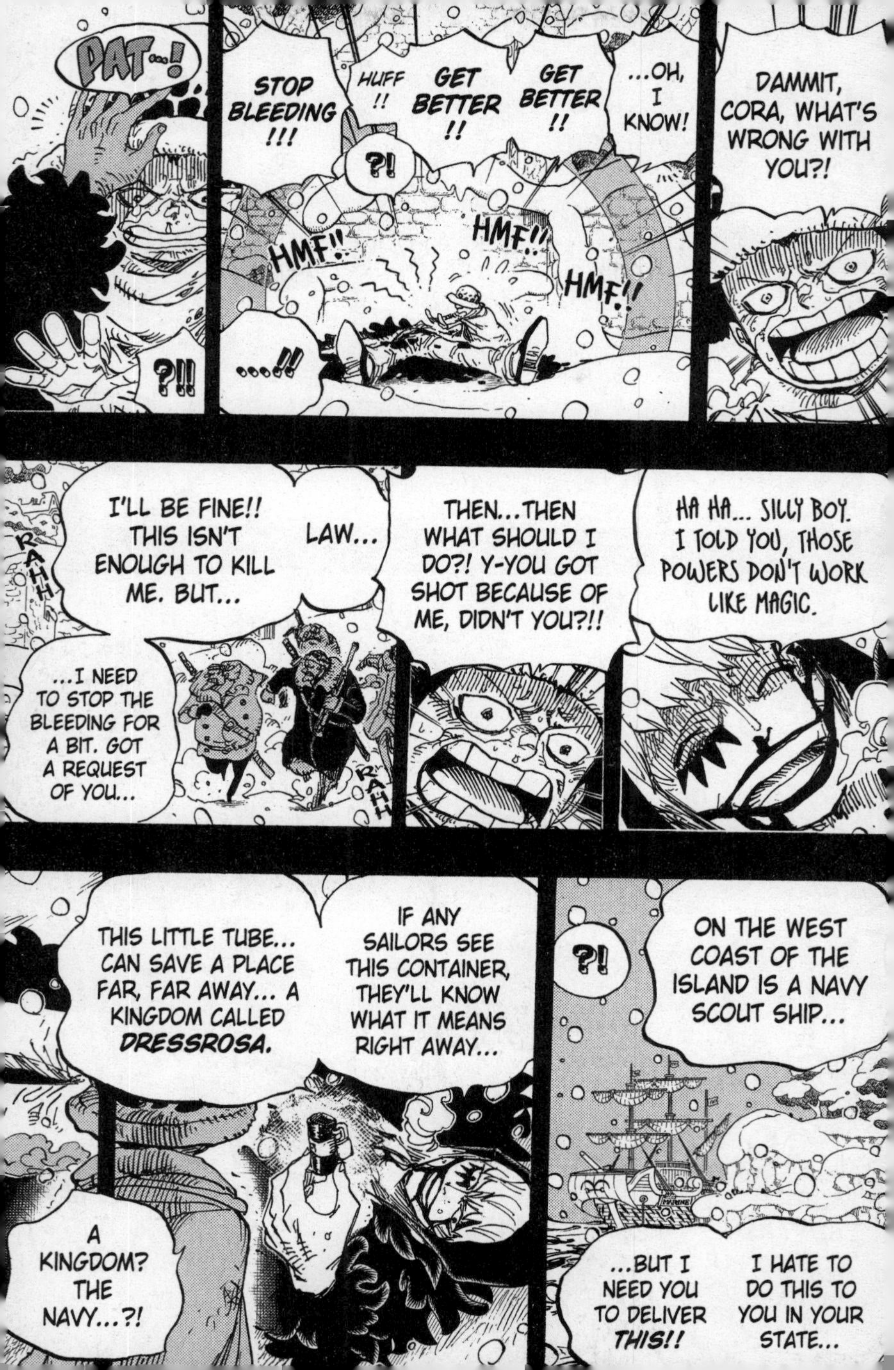
DAMMIT, CORA, WHAT'S WRONG WITH YOU?!
...OH, I KNOW!
GET BETTER !!
GET BETTER !!
HUFF !!
STOP BLEEDING !!!
?!
HMF!!
HMF!!
HMF!!
...!!
PAT...!
?!!
HA HA... SILLY BOY. I TOLD YOU, THOSE POWERS DON'T WORK LIKE MAGIC.
THEN...THEN WHAT SHOULD I DO?! Y-YOU GOT SHOT BECAUSE OF ME, DIDN'T YOU?!!
LAW...
I'LL BE FINE!! THIS ISN'T ENOUGH TO KILL ME. BUT...
RAHH
...I NEED TO STOP THE BLEEDING FOR A BIT. GOT A REQUEST OF YOU...
RAHH
ON THE WEST COAST OF THE ISLAND IS A NAVY SCOUT SHIP...
?!
I HATE TO DO THIS TO YOU IN YOUR STATE...
...BUT I NEED YOU TO DELIVER *THIS!!*
IF ANY SAILORS SEE THIS CONTAINER, THEY'LL KNOW WHAT IT MEANS RIGHT AWAY...
THIS LITTLE TUBE... CAN SAVE A PLACE FAR, FAR AWAY... A KINGDOM CALLED ***DRESSROSA.***
A KINGDOM? THE NAVY...?!

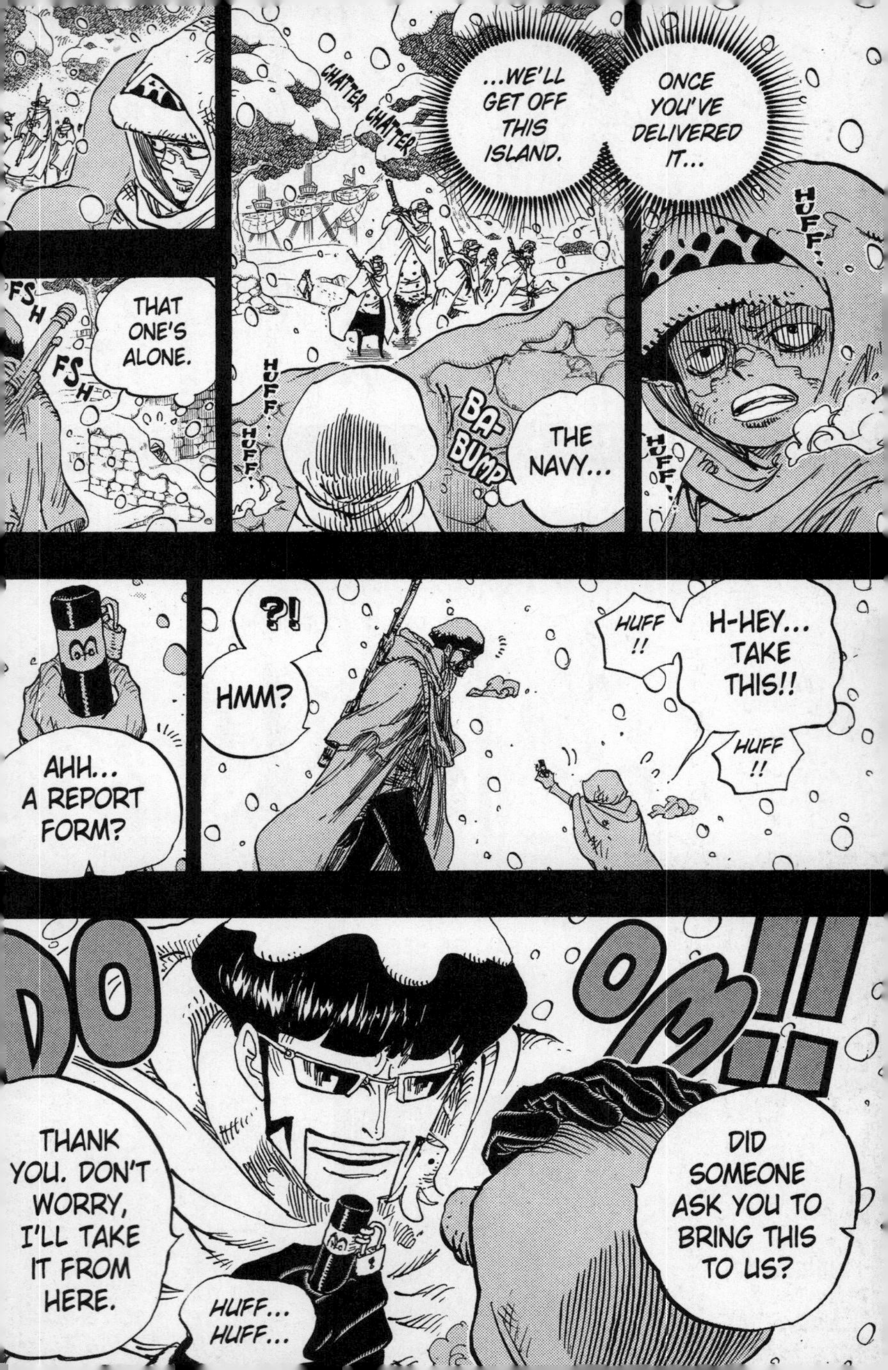
ONCE YOU'VE DELIVERED IT...
...WE'LL GET OFF THIS ISLAND.
HUFF...
HUFF...
CHATTER
CHATTER
BA-BUMP
THE NAVY...
HUFF...
HUFF...
FSH
FSH
THAT ONE'S ALONE.
HUFF!!
H-HEY... TAKE THIS!!
HUFF!!
?!
HMM?
AHH... A REPORT FORM?
DOOM!!
DID SOMEONE ASK YOU TO BRING THIS TO US?
THANK YOU. DON'T WORRY, I'LL TAKE IT FROM HERE.
HUFF... HUFF...

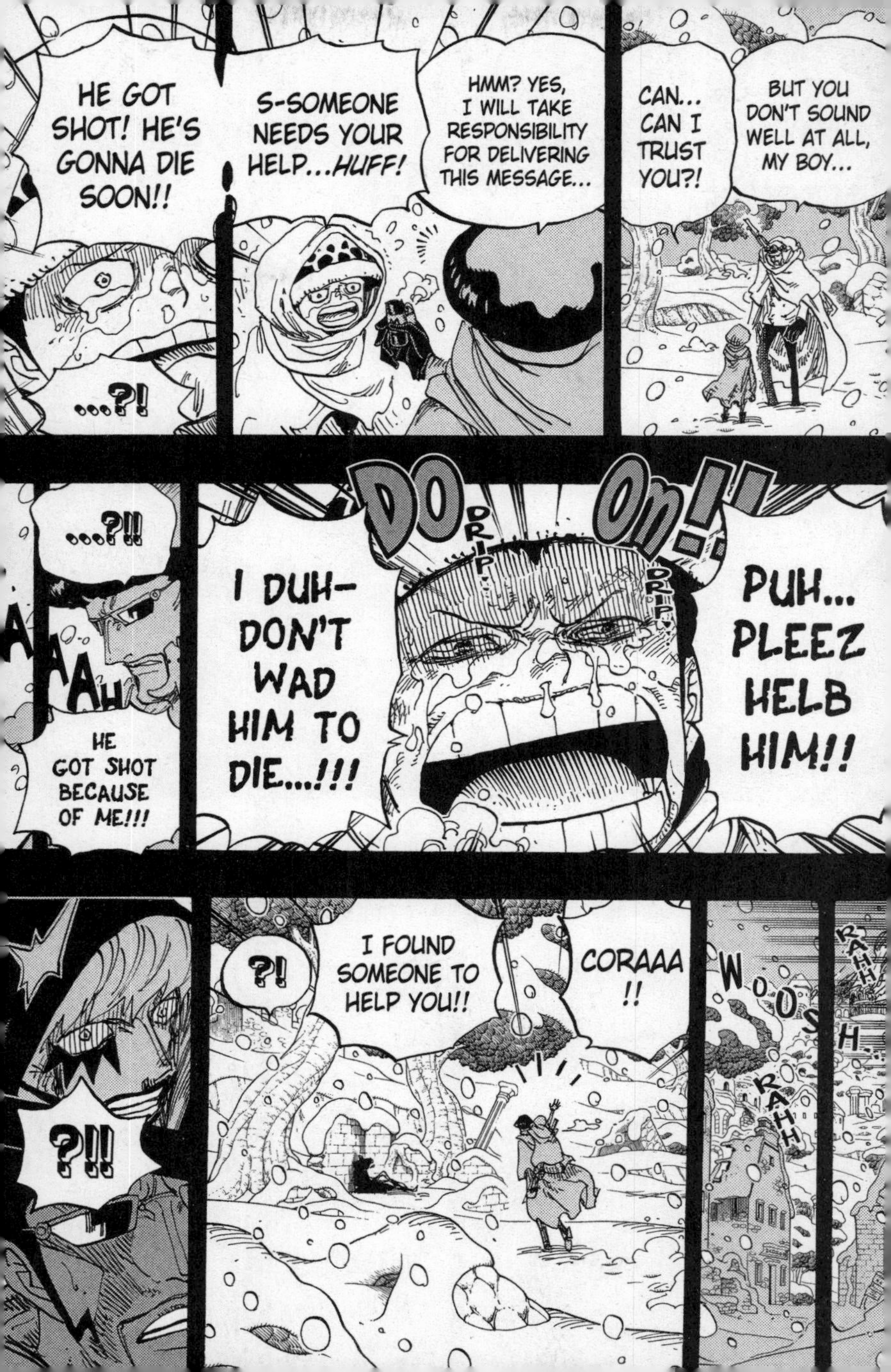
BUT YOU DON'T SOUND WELL AT ALL, MY BOY...
CAN... CAN I TRUST YOU?!
HMM? YES, I WILL TAKE RESPONSIBILITY FOR DELIVERING THIS MESSAGE...
S-SOMEONE NEEDS YOUR HELP...*HUFF!*
HE GOT SHOT! HE'S GONNA DIE SOON!!
...?!
DOOM!!
DRIP
DRIP
PUH... PLEEZ HELB HIM!!
I DUH-DON'T WAD HIM TO DIE...!!!
...?!!
AAAH
HE GOT SHOT BECAUSE OF ME!!!
RAHH
WOOSH
RAHH
CORAAA!!
I FOUND SOMEONE TO HELP YOU!!
?!
?!!

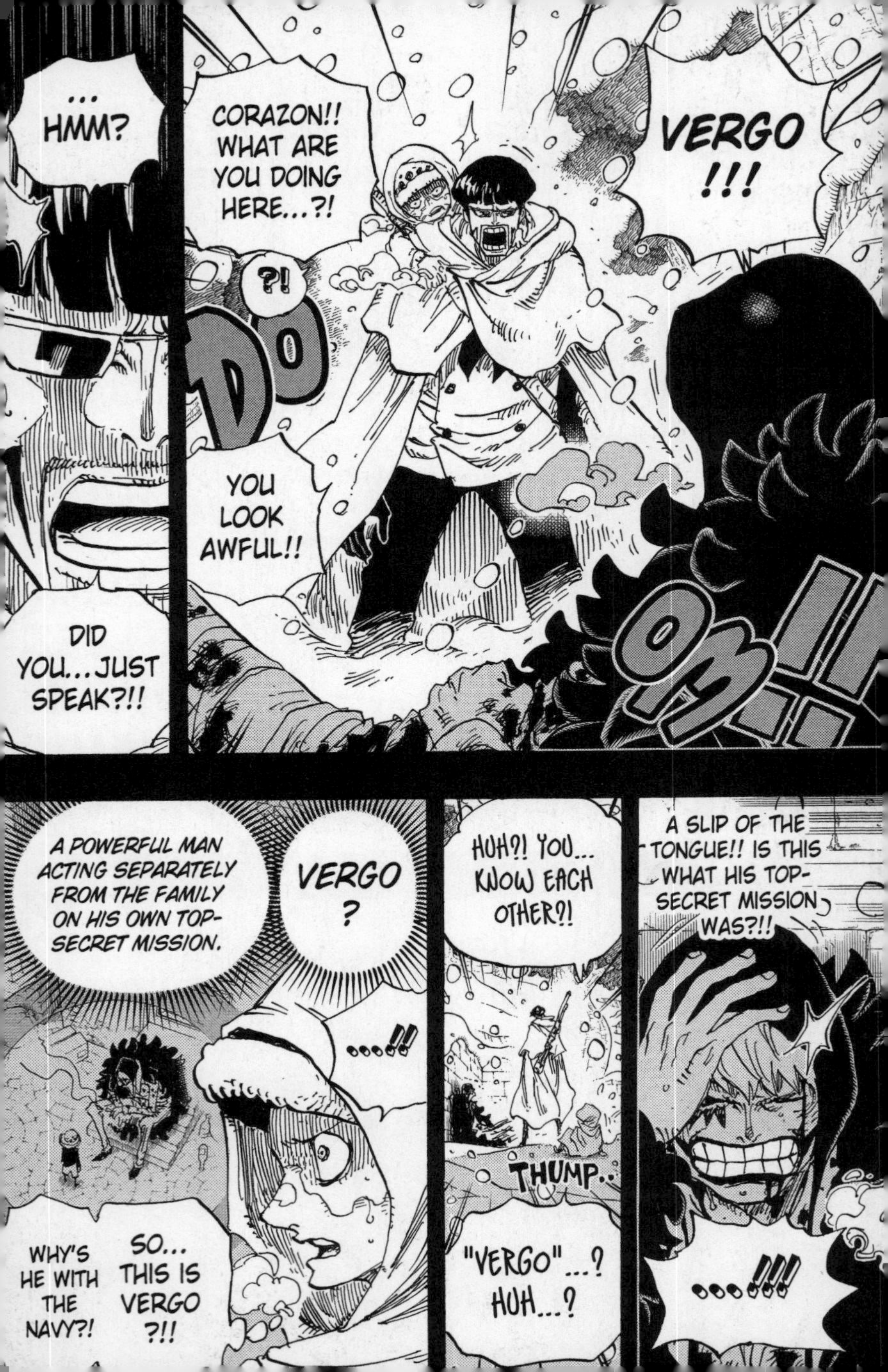
VERGO !!!
CORAZON!! WHAT ARE YOU DOING HERE...?!
?!
YOU LOOK AWFUL!!
... HMM?
DID YOU...JUST SPEAK?!!
A SLIP OF THE TONGUE!! IS THIS WHAT HIS TOP-SECRET MISSION WAS?!!
...!!!
HUH?! YOU... KNOW EACH OTHER?!
THUMP..
"VERGO"...? HUH...?
VERGO ?
...!!
A POWERFUL MAN ACTING SEPARATELY FROM THE FAMILY ON HIS OWN TOP-SECRET MISSION.
SO... THIS IS VERGO ?!!
WHY'S HE WITH THE NAVY?!

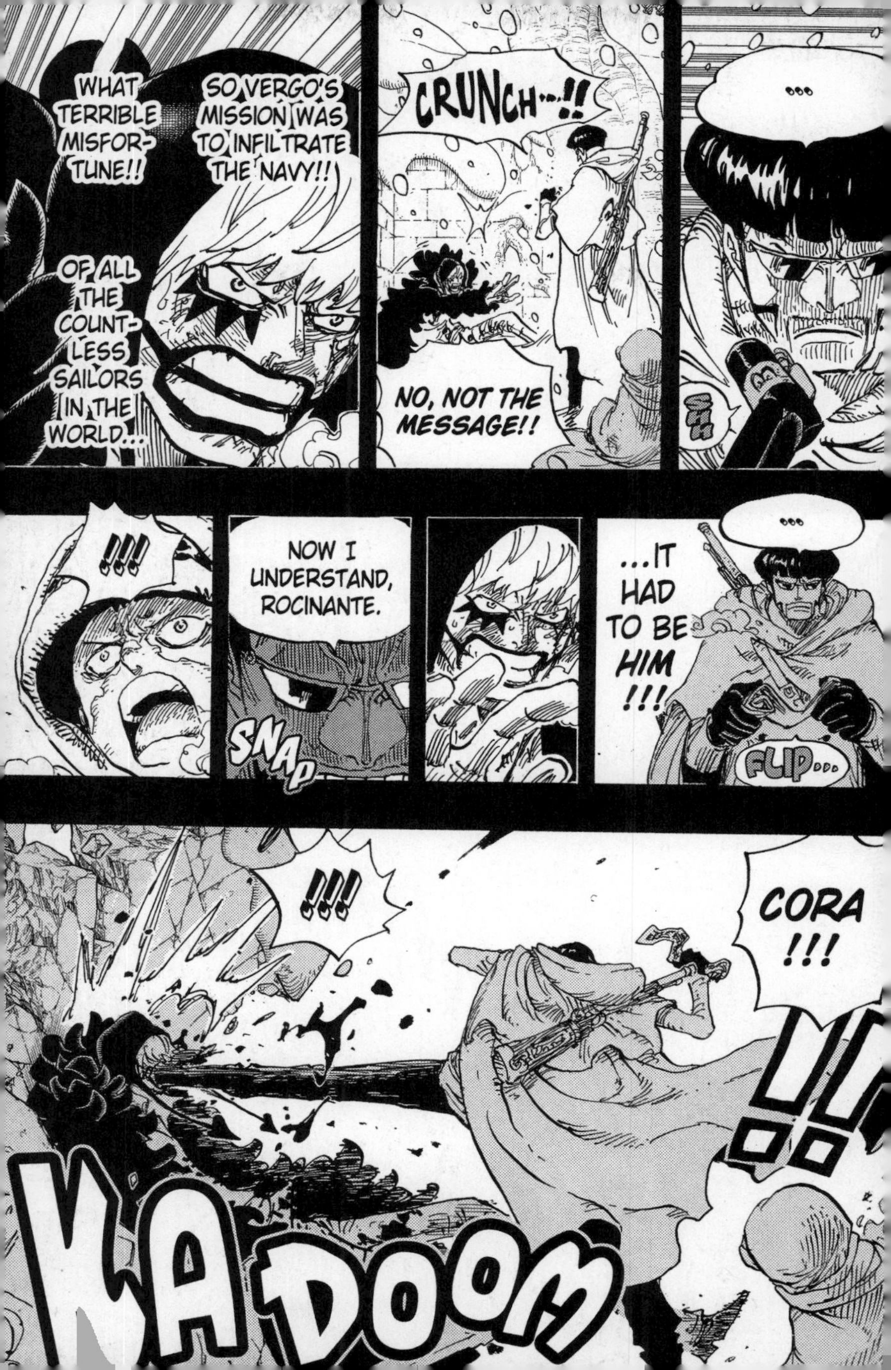
...
CRUNCH...!!
NO, NOT THE MESSAGE!!
SO VERGO'S MISSION WAS TO INFILTRATE THE NAVY!!
WHAT TERRIBLE MISFORTUNE!!
OF ALL THE COUNTLESS SAILORS IN THE WORLD...
...
...IT HAD TO BE HIM!!!
FLIP...
NOW I UNDERSTAND, ROCINANTE.
SNAP
!!!
CORA!!!
!!
!!!
KA-DOOM

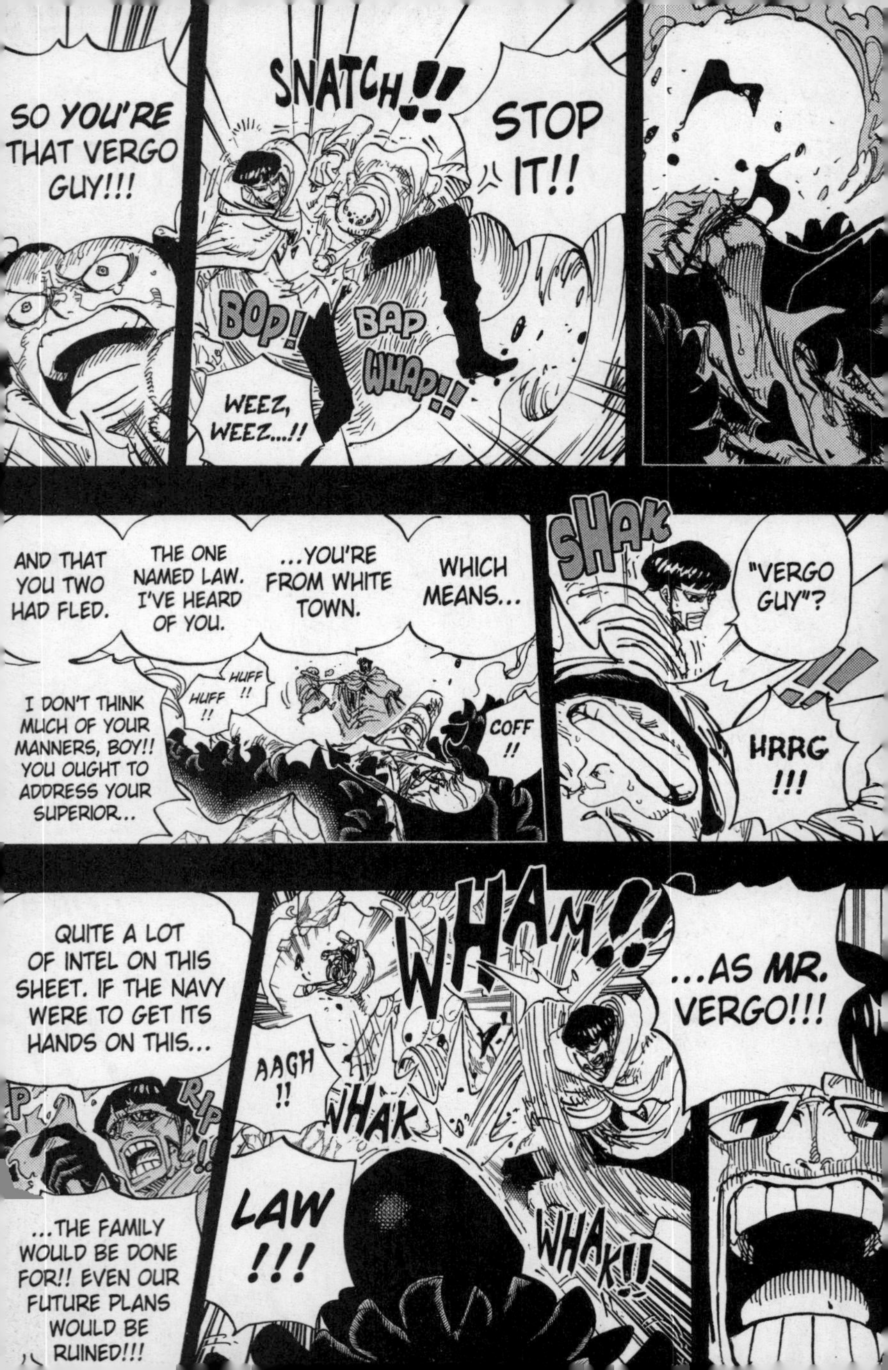
SNATCH!!
STOP IT!!
BOP!
BAP
WHAP!!
WEEZ, WEEZ...!!
SO YOU'RE THAT VERGO GUY!!!
SHAK
"VERGO GUY"?
HRRG!!!
WHICH MEANS...
...YOU'RE FROM WHITE TOWN.
THE ONE NAMED LAW. I'VE HEARD OF YOU.
AND THAT YOU TWO HAD FLED.
HUFF!!
HUFF!!
COFF!!
I DON'T THINK MUCH OF YOUR MANNERS, BOY!! YOU OUGHT TO ADDRESS YOUR SUPERIOR...
...AS MR. VERGO!!!
WHAM!!
AAGH!!
WHAK
LAW!!!
WHAK!!
QUITE A LOT OF INTEL ON THIS SHEET. IF THE NAVY WERE TO GET ITS HANDS ON THIS...
RIP!!
...THE FAMILY WOULD BE DONE FOR!! EVEN OUR FUTURE PLANS WOULD BE RUINED!!!

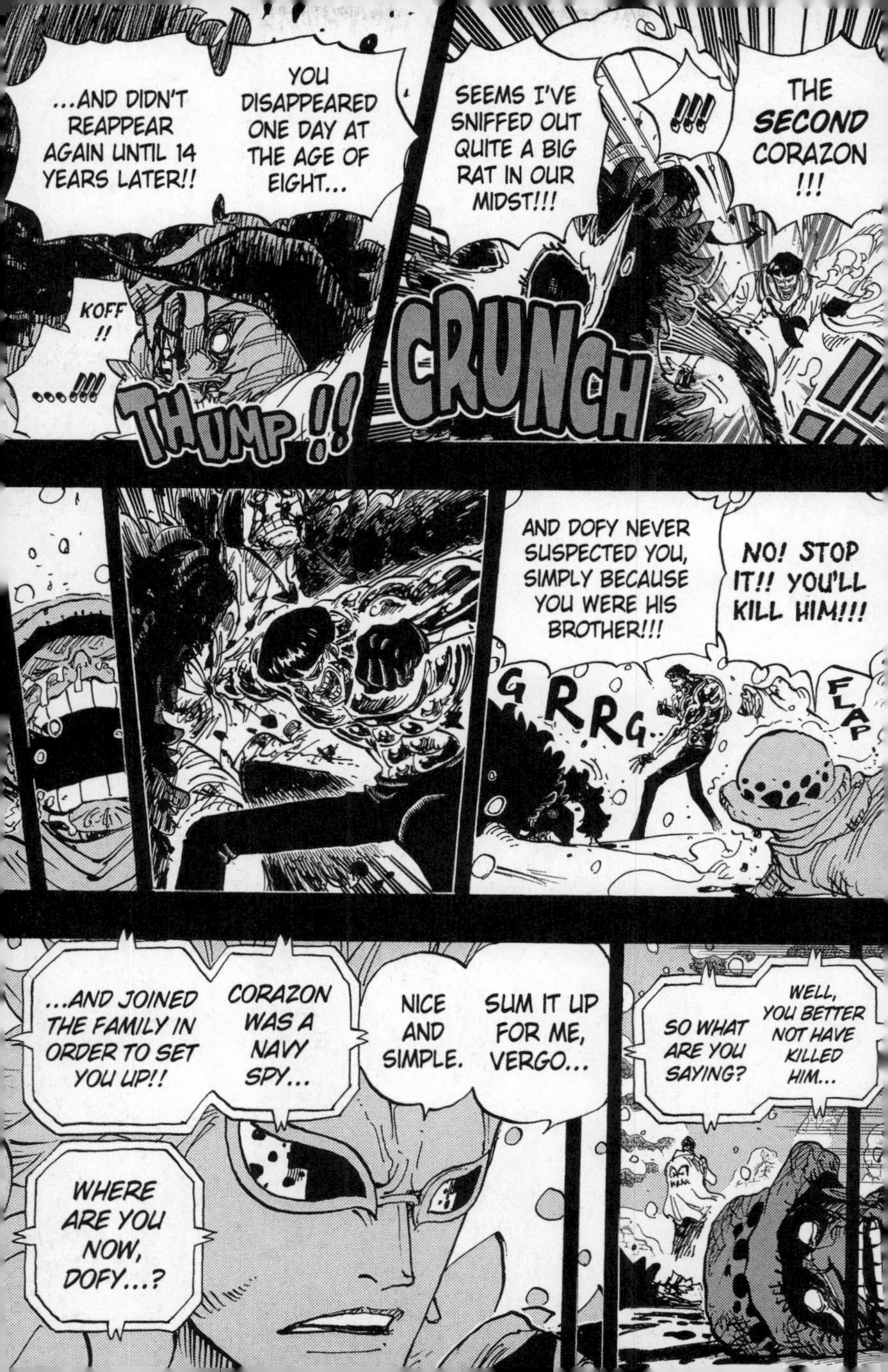
THE SECOND CORAZON!!!
!!!
SEEMS I'VE SNIFFED OUT QUITE A BIG RAT IN OUR MIDST!!!
!!
CRUNCH
YOU DISAPPEARED ONE DAY AT THE AGE OF EIGHT...
...AND DIDN'T REAPPEAR AGAIN UNTIL 14 YEARS LATER!!
KOFF!!
...!!!
THUMP!!
NO! STOP IT!! YOU'LL KILL HIM!!!
AND DOFY NEVER SUSPECTED YOU, SIMPLY BECAUSE YOU WERE HIS BROTHER!!!
FLAP
GRRRG...
WELL, YOU BETTER NOT HAVE KILLED HIM...
SO WHAT ARE YOU SAYING?
SUM IT UP FOR ME, VERGO...
NICE AND SIMPLE.
CORAZON WAS A NAVY SPY...
...AND JOINED THE FAMILY IN ORDER TO SET YOU UP!!
WHERE ARE YOU NOW, DOFY...?

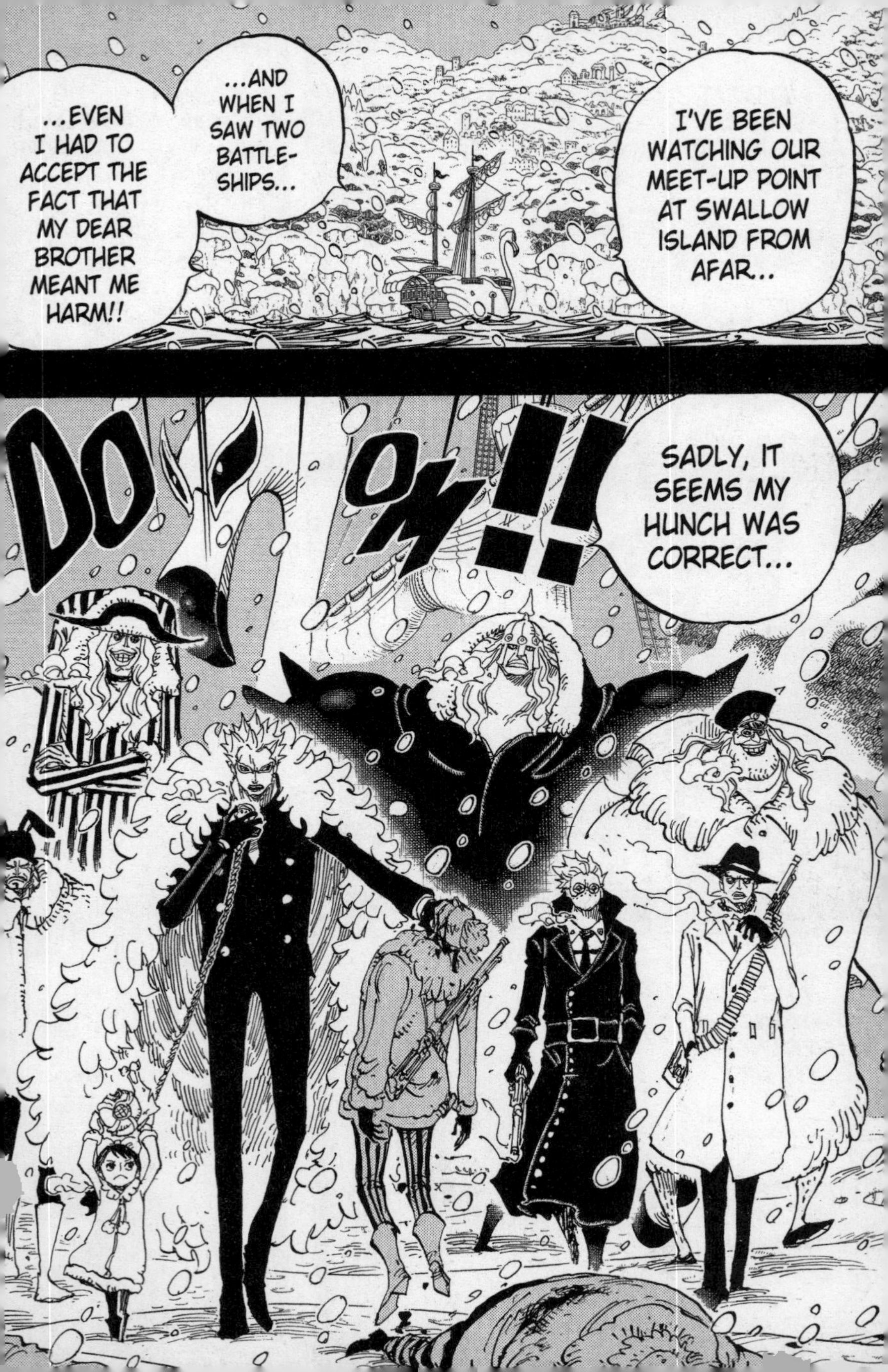
I'VE BEEN WATCHING OUR MEET-UP POINT AT SWALLOW ISLAND FROM AFAR...
...AND WHEN I SAW TWO BATTLE-SHIPS...
...EVEN I HAD TO ACCEPT THE FACT THAT MY DEAR BROTHER MEANT ME HARM!!
SADLY, IT SEEMS MY HUNCH WAS CORRECT...
DOOM!!

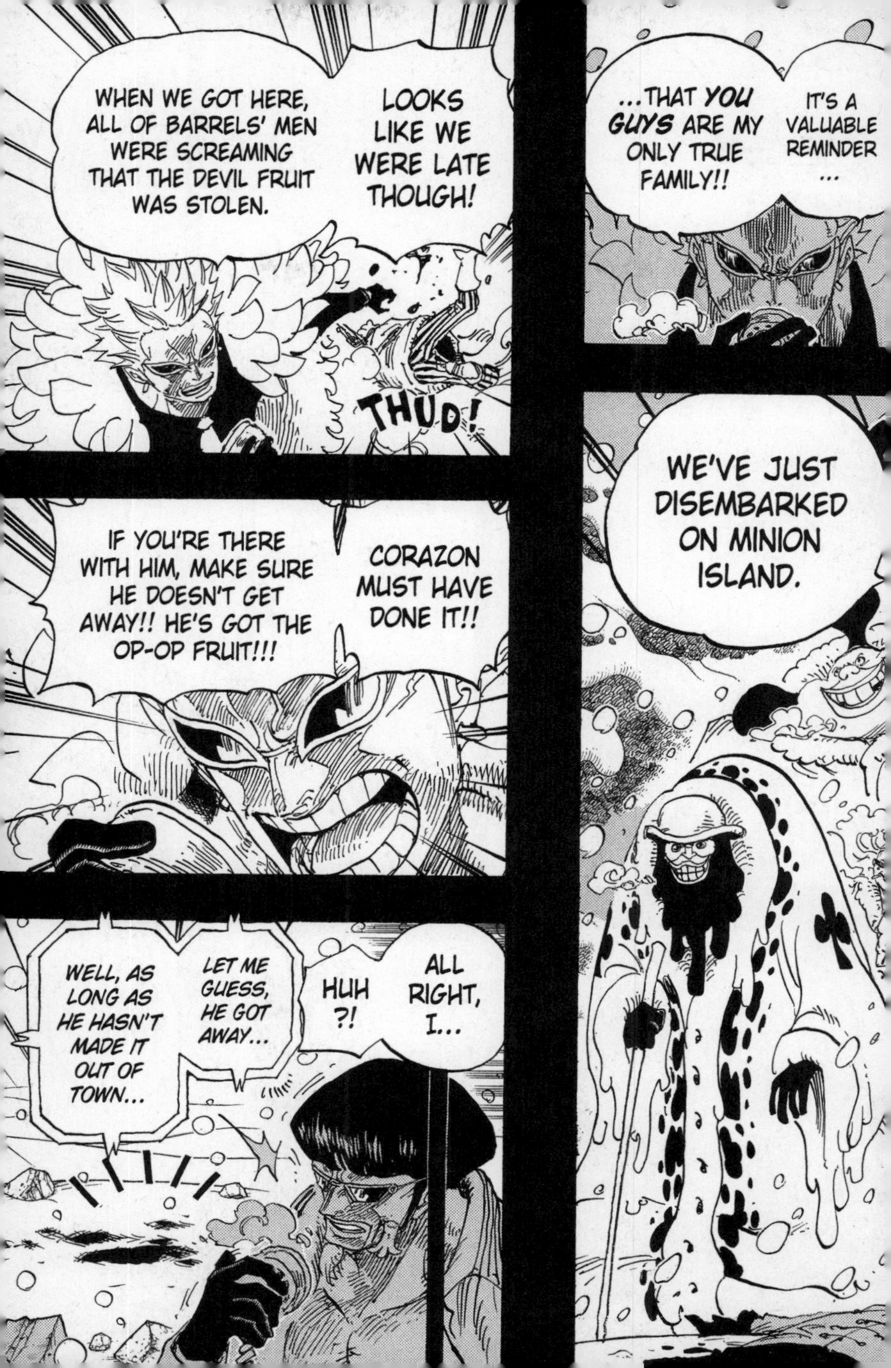
IT'S A VALUABLE REMINDER...
...THAT YOU GUYS ARE MY ONLY TRUE FAMILY!!
WE'VE JUST DISEMBARKED ON MINION ISLAND.
LOOKS LIKE WE WERE LATE THOUGH!
WHEN WE GOT HERE, ALL OF BARRELS' MEN WERE SCREAMING THAT THE DEVIL FRUIT WAS STOLEN.
THUD!
CORAZON MUST HAVE DONE IT!!
IF YOU'RE THERE WITH HIM, MAKE SURE HE DOESN'T GET AWAY!! HE'S GOT THE OP-OP FRUIT!!!
ALL RIGHT, I...
HUH ?!
LET ME GUESS, HE GOT AWAY...
WELL, AS LONG AS HE HASN'T MADE IT OUT OF TOWN...

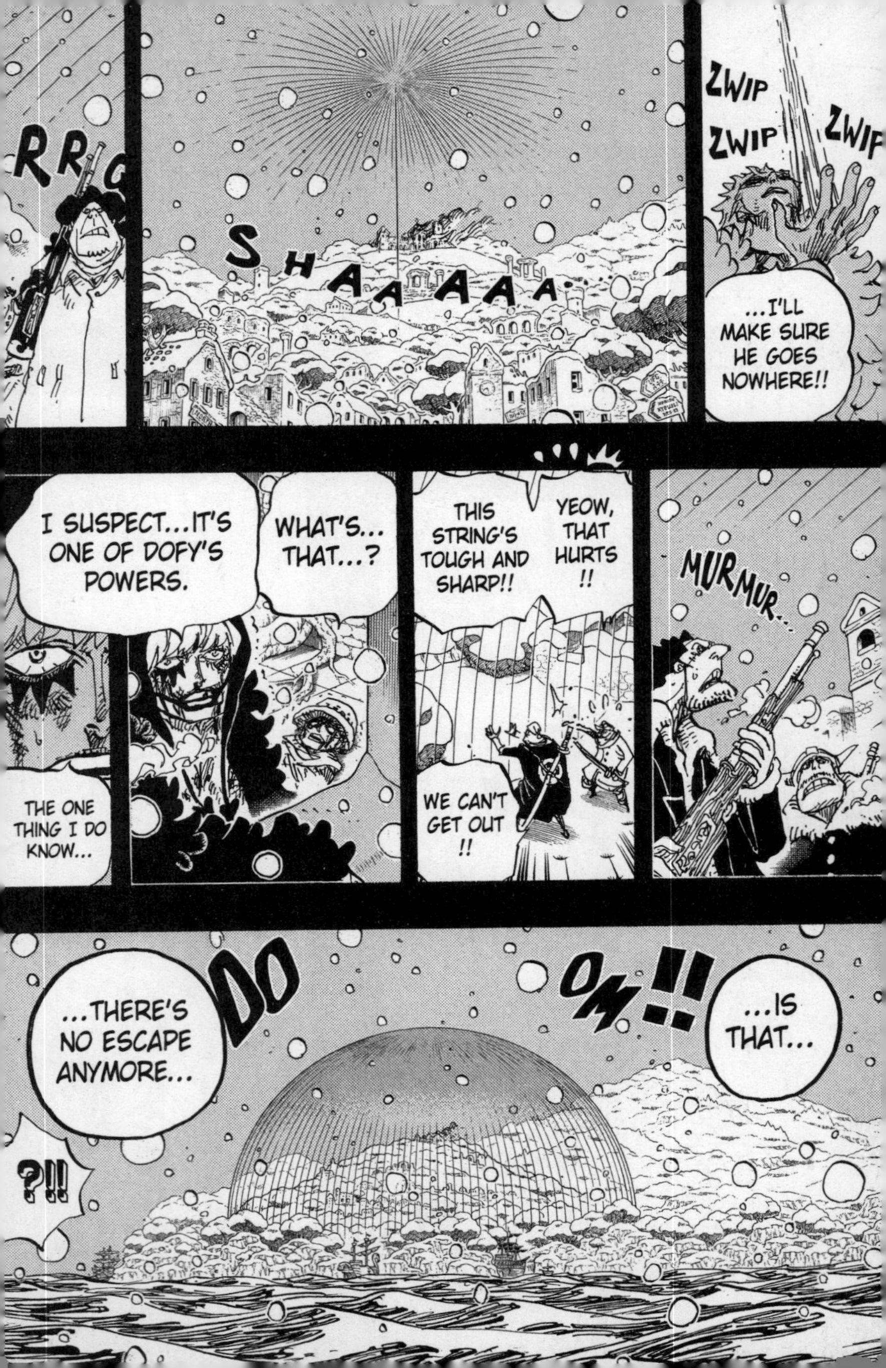
ZWIP
ZWIP
ZWIF
...I'LL MAKE SURE HE GOES NOWHERE!!
SHAAAAA
RRG
MURMUR...
YEOW, THAT HURTS!!
THIS STRING'S TOUGH AND SHARP!!
WE CAN'T GET OUT!!
WHAT'S... THAT...?
I SUSPECT...IT'S ONE OF DOFY'S POWERS.
THE ONE THING I DO KNOW...
...IS THAT...
DOOM!!
...THERE'S NO ESCAPE ANYMORE...
?!!

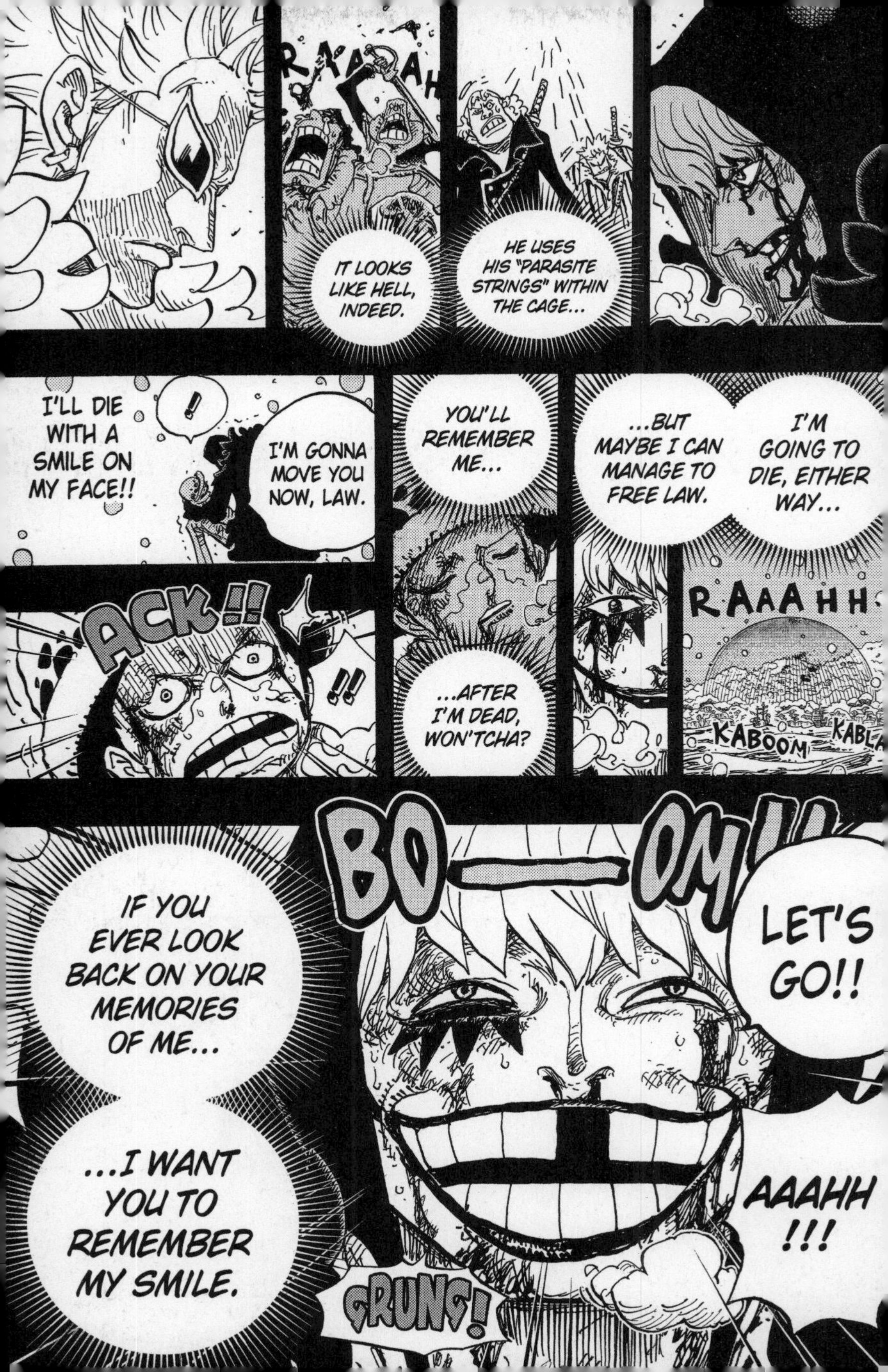
HE USES HIS "PARASITE STRINGS" WITHIN THE CAGE...
RAAAAH
IT LOOKS LIKE HELL, INDEED.
I'M GOING TO DIE, EITHER WAY...
...BUT MAYBE I CAN MANAGE TO FREE LAW.
RAAAHH
KABLA
KABOOM
YOU'LL REMEMBER ME...
...AFTER I'M DEAD, WON'TCHA?
I'M GONNA MOVE YOU NOW, LAW.
!
I'LL DIE WITH A SMILE ON MY FACE!!
!!
ACK!!
BO—OM!!
LET'S GO!!
IF YOU EVER LOOK BACK ON YOUR MEMORIES OF ME...
...I WANT YOU TO REMEMBER MY SMILE.
AAAHH!!!
GRUNG!

Chapter 767: CORA

*SIGN: SEA GOD

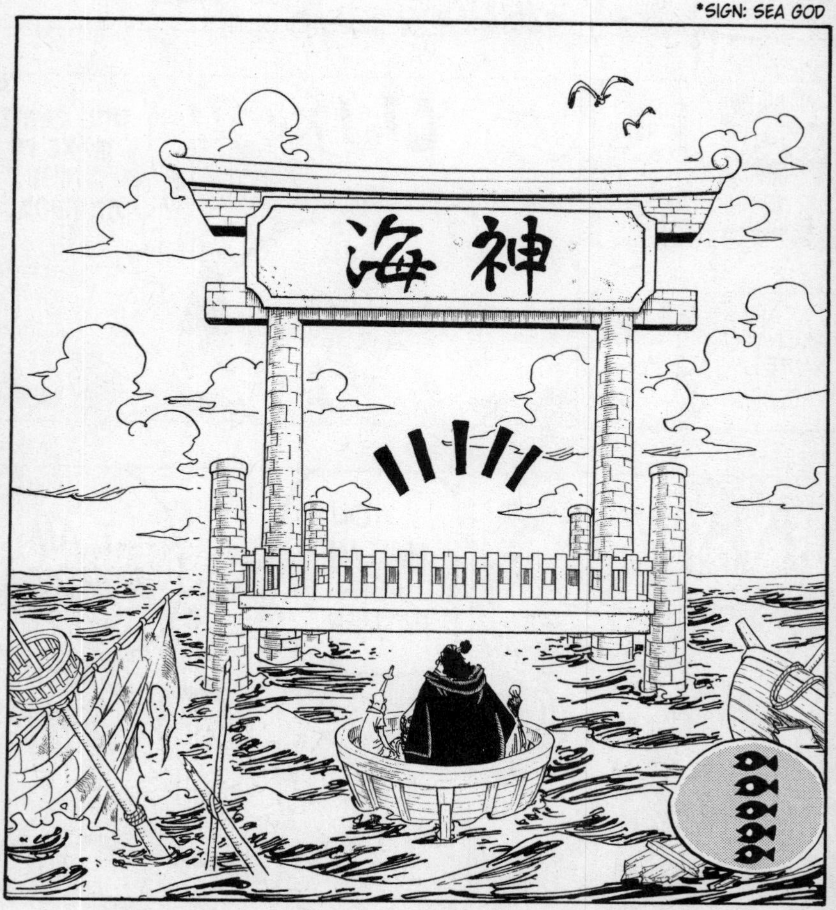
海神

THE SOLITARY JOURNEY OF JIMBEI, FIRST SON OF THE SEA, VOL. 14: "THE MOUNTAIN OF OFFERINGS, APPEARANCE OF THE RUINS, AND FURIOUS SEA CREATURES"

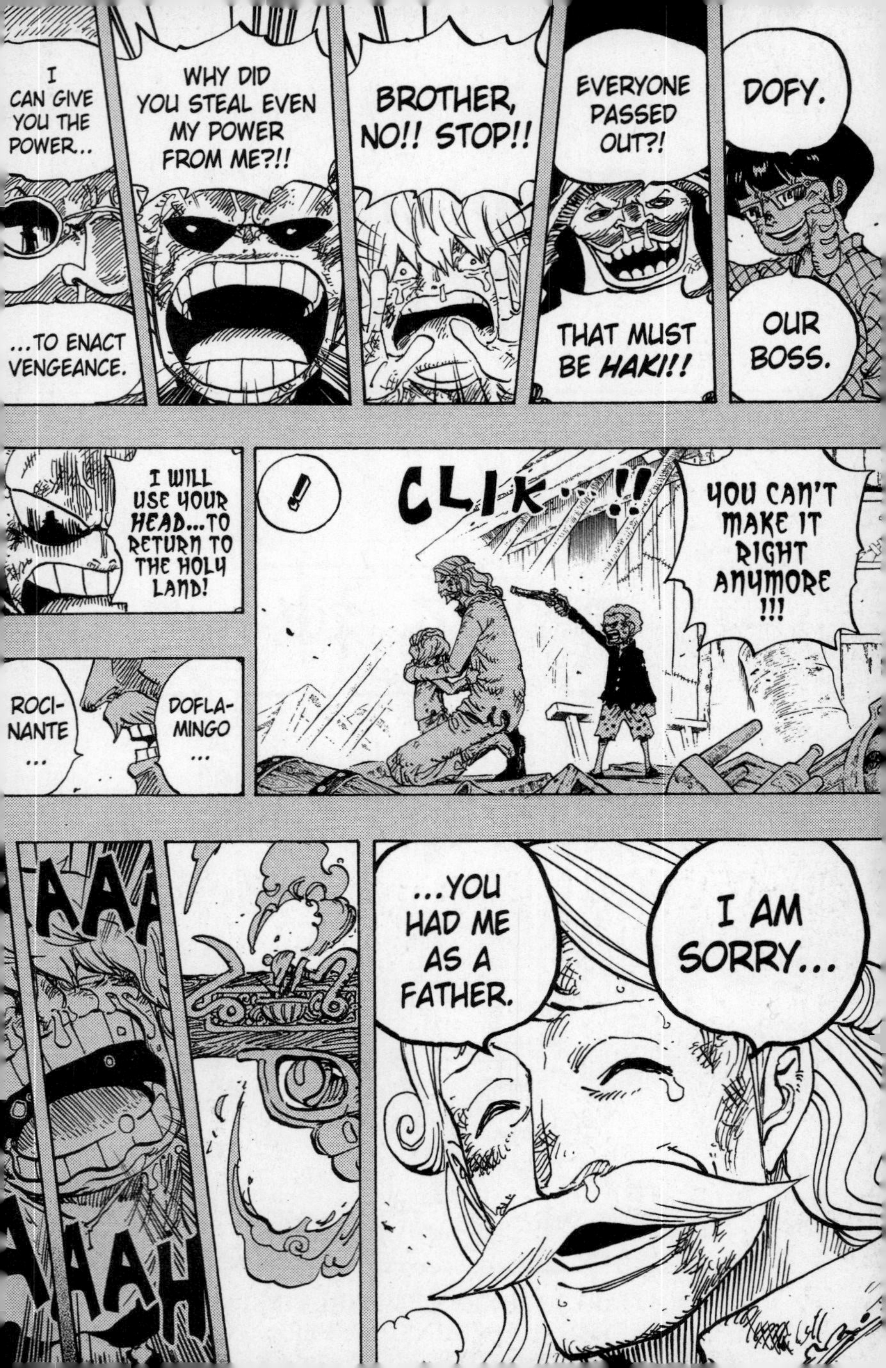
DOFY.
OUR BOSS.
EVERYONE PASSED OUT?!
THAT MUST BE HAKI!!
BROTHER, NO!! STOP!!
WHY DID YOU STEAL EVEN MY POWER FROM ME?!!
I CAN GIVE YOU THE POWER...
...TO ENACT VENGEANCE.
!
CLIK...!!
YOU CAN'T MAKE IT RIGHT ANYMORE !!!
I WILL USE YOUR HEAD...TO RETURN TO THE HOLY LAND!
DOFLAMINGO ...
ROCINANTE ...
I AM SORRY...
...YOU HAD ME AS A FATHER.
AAA
AAAH

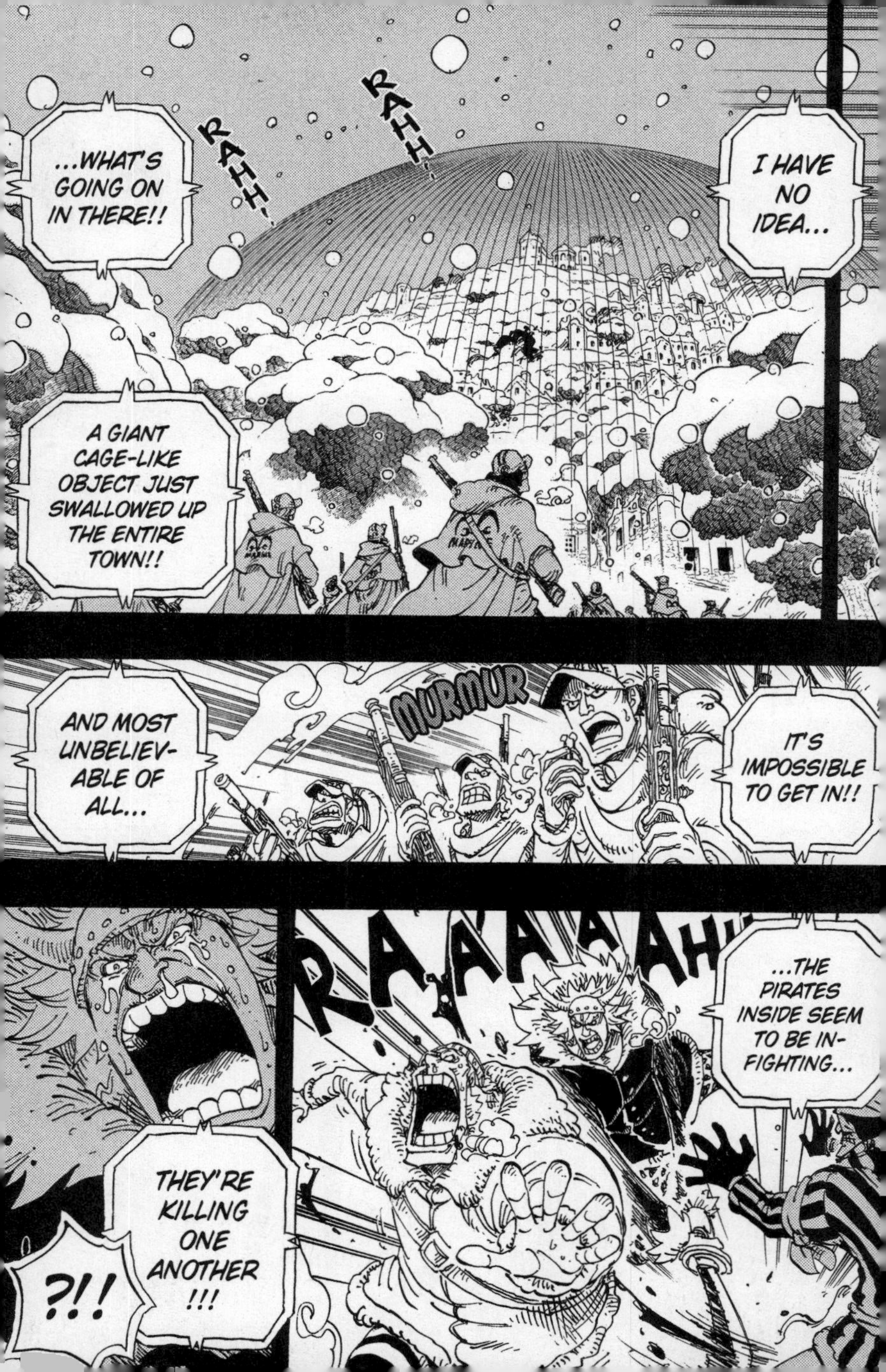
RAHH
RAHH
I HAVE NO IDEA...
...WHAT'S GOING ON IN THERE!!
A GIANT CAGE-LIKE OBJECT JUST SWALLOWED UP THE ENTIRE TOWN!!
IT'S IMPOSSIBLE TO GET IN!!
MURMUR
AND MOST UNBELIEV-ABLE OF ALL...
RAAAAAHH
...THE PIRATES INSIDE SEEM TO BE IN-FIGHTING...
THEY'RE KILLING ONE ANOTHER!!!
?!!

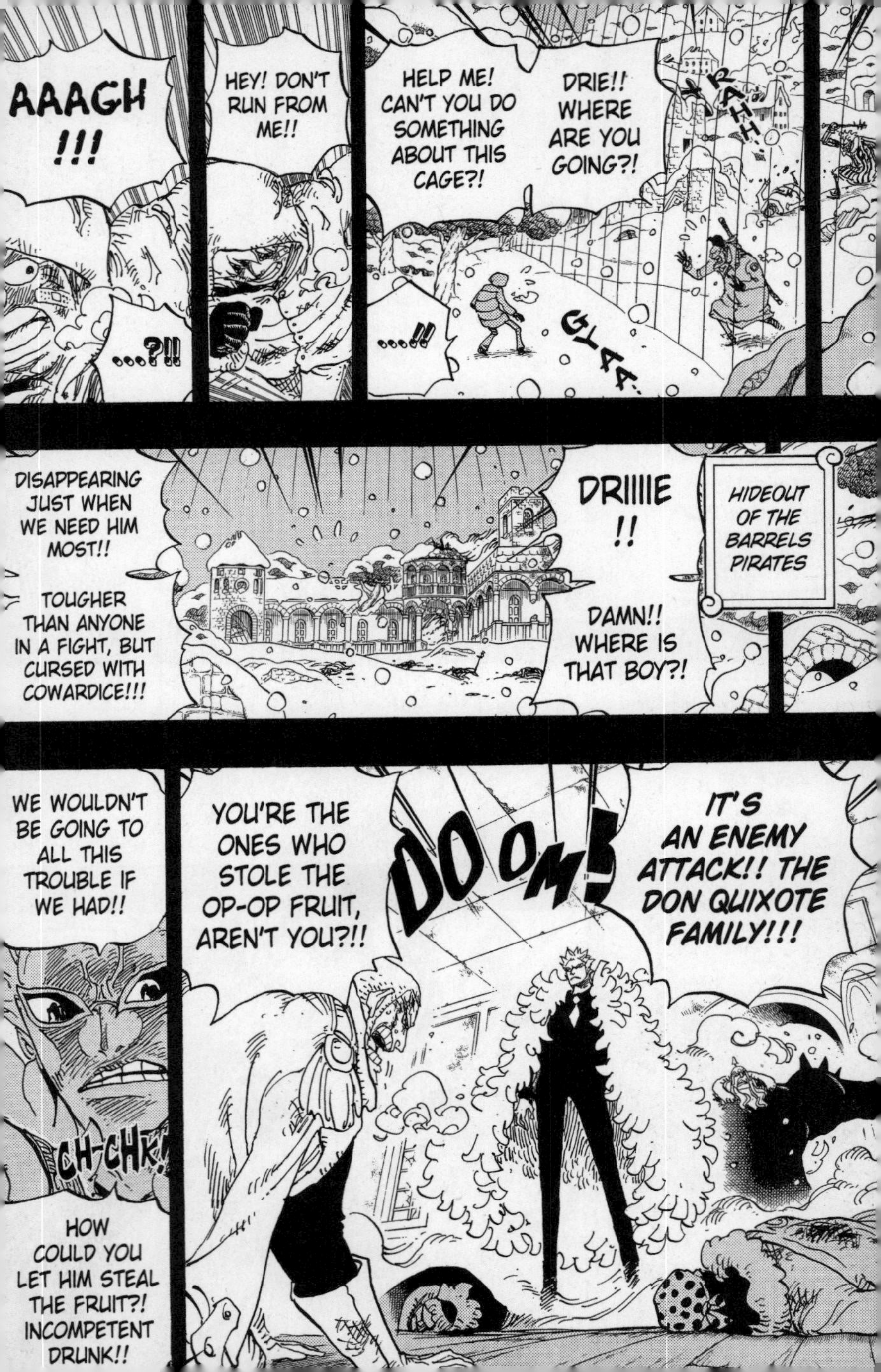
RAHH
DRIE!! WHERE ARE YOU GOING?!
HELP ME! CAN'T YOU DO SOMETHING ABOUT THIS CAGE?!
...!!
GYAA
HEY! DON'T RUN FROM ME!!
AAAGH!!!
...?!!
HIDEOUT OF THE BARRELS PIRATES
DRIIIIE!!
DAMN!! WHERE IS THAT BOY?!
DISAPPEARING JUST WHEN WE NEED HIM MOST!!
TOUGHER THAN ANYONE IN A FIGHT, BUT CURSED WITH COWARDICE!!!
IT'S AN ENEMY ATTACK!! THE DON QUIXOTE FAMILY!!!
DOOM
YOU'RE THE ONES WHO STOLE THE OP-OP FRUIT, AREN'T YOU?!!
WE WOULDN'T BE GOING TO ALL THIS TROUBLE IF WE HAD!!
CH-CHK
HOW COULD YOU LET HIM STEAL THE FRUIT?! INCOMPETENT DRUNK!!

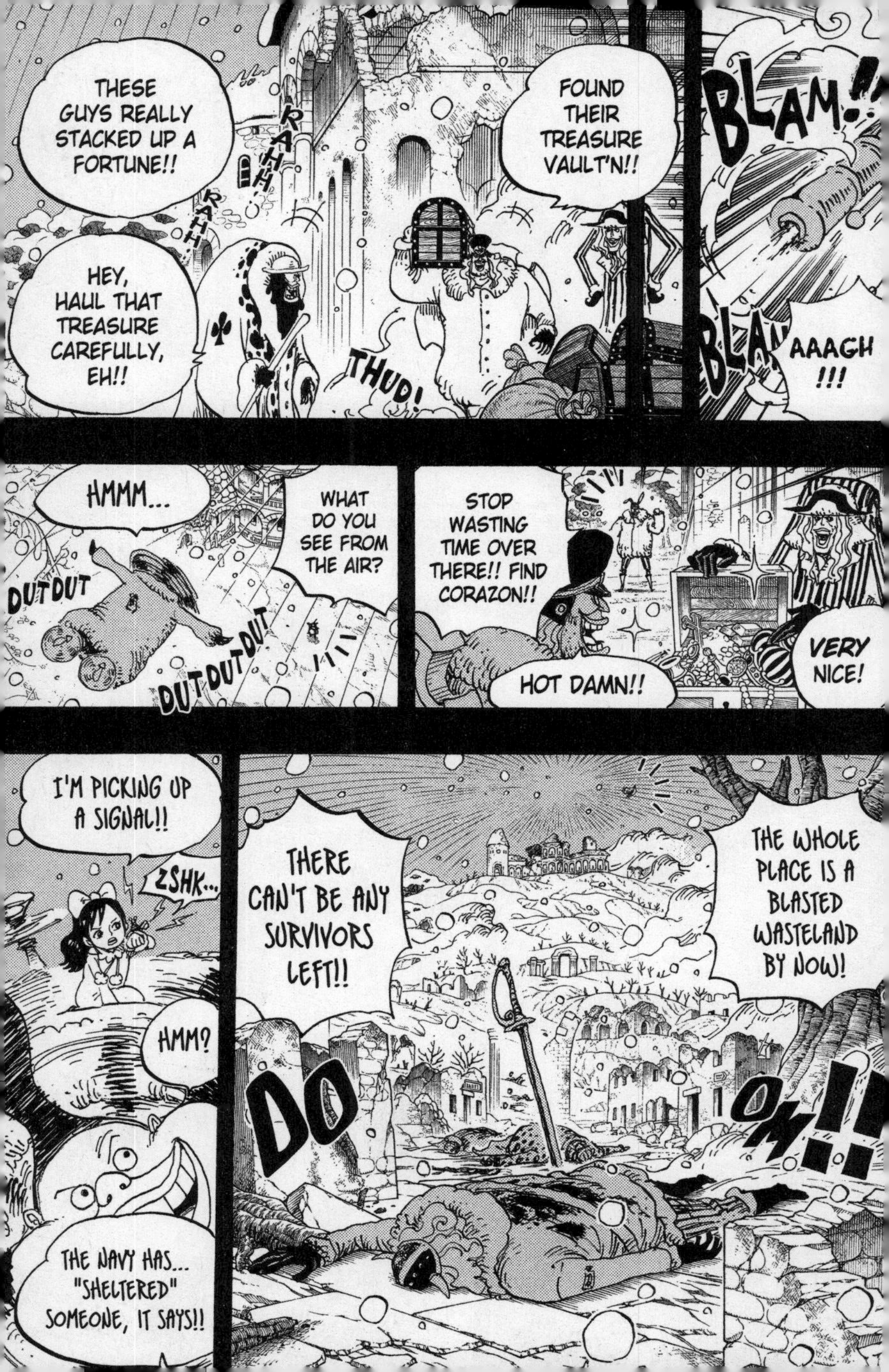
BLAM!!
BLA
AAAGH!!!
FOUND THEIR TREASURE VAULT'N!!
THESE GUYS REALLY STACKED UP A FORTUNE!!
RAHH
RAHH
HEY, HAUL THAT TREASURE CAREFULLY, EH!!
THUD!
VERY NICE!
STOP WASTING TIME OVER THERE!! FIND CORAZON!!
HOT DAMN!!
WHAT DO YOU SEE FROM THE AIR?
HMMM...
DUTDUT
DUTDUTDUT
THE WHOLE PLACE IS A BLASTED WASTELAND BY NOW!
THERE CAN'T BE ANY SURVIVORS LEFT!!
DO
OM!!
I'M PICKING UP A SIGNAL!!
ZSHK...
HMM?
THE NAVY HAS... "SHELTERED" SOMEONE, IT SAYS!!

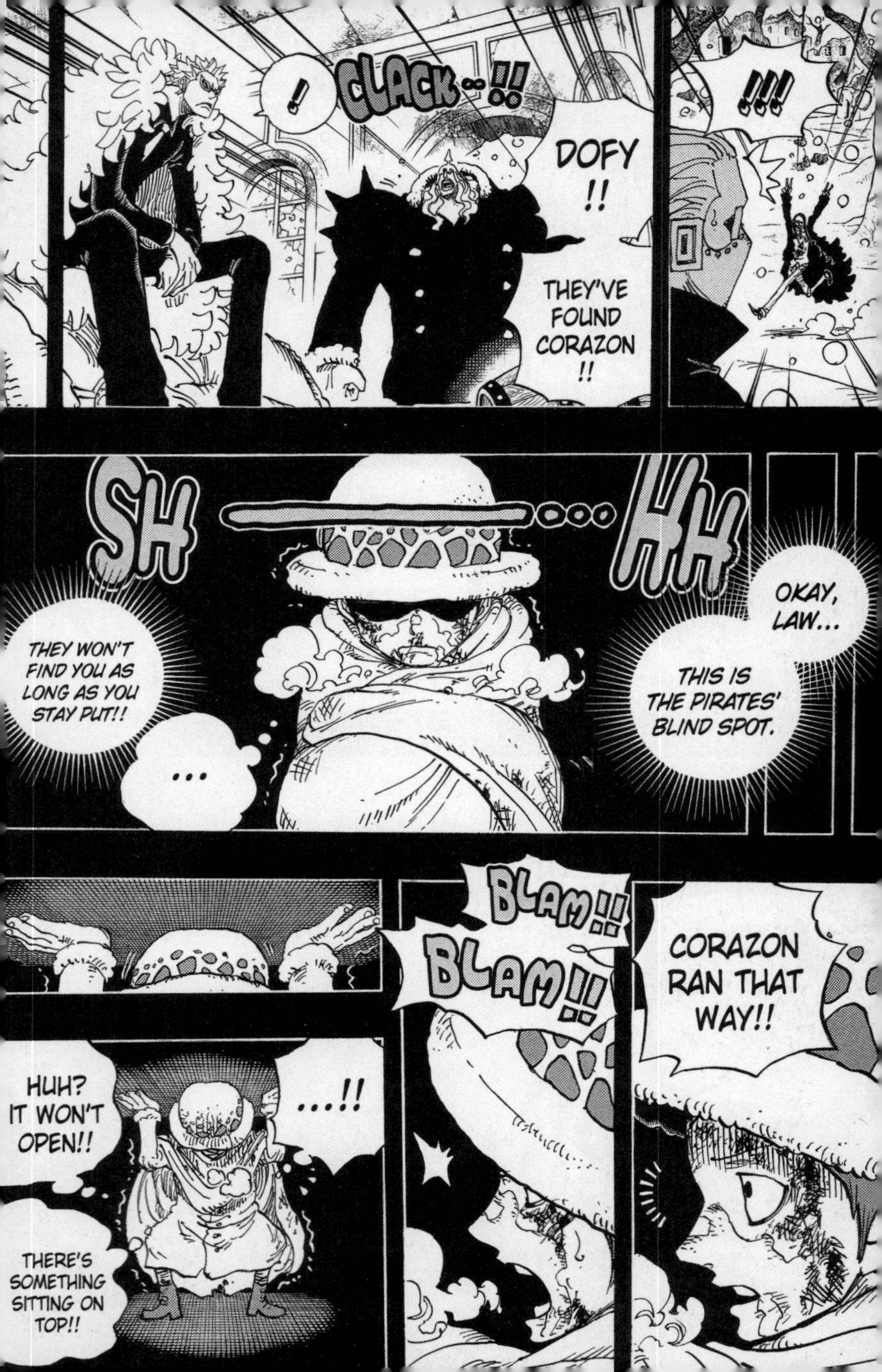
!!!
CLACK..!!
!
DOFY !!
THEY'VE FOUND CORAZON !!
SH——...HH
OKAY, LAW...
THIS IS THE PIRATES' BLIND SPOT.
THEY WON'T FIND YOU AS LONG AS YOU STAY PUT!!
...
CORAZON RAN THAT WAY!!
BLAM!!
BLAM!!
...!!
HUH? IT WON'T OPEN!!
THERE'S SOMETHING SITTING ON TOP!!

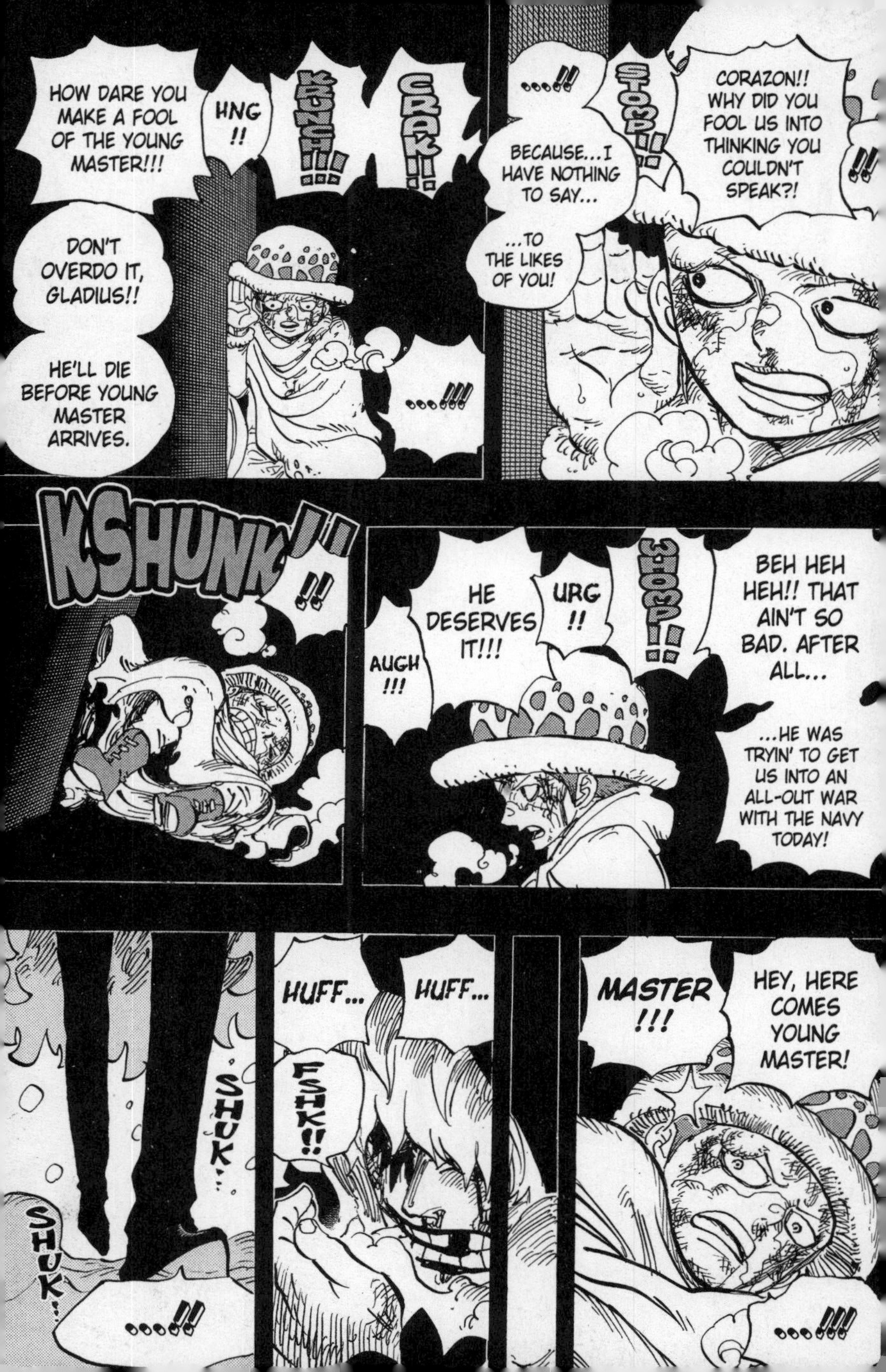
!!
CORAZON!! WHY DID YOU FOOL US INTO THINKING YOU COULDN'T SPEAK?!
STOMP!!
...!!
BECAUSE...I HAVE NOTHING TO SAY...
...TO THE LIKES OF YOU!
CRAK!!
KRUNCH!!!
HNG !!
HOW DARE YOU MAKE A FOOL OF THE YOUNG MASTER!!!
DON'T OVERDO IT, GLADIUS!!
HE'LL DIE BEFORE YOUNG MASTER ARRIVES.
...!!!
BEH HEH HEH!! THAT AIN'T SO BAD. AFTER ALL...
WHOMP!!
URG !!
HE DESERVES IT!!!
AUGH !!!
...HE WAS TRYIN' TO GET US INTO AN ALL-OUT WAR WITH THE NAVY TODAY!
KSHUNK!!
!!
HEY, HERE COMES YOUNG MASTER!
MASTER !!!
...!!!
HUFF...
HUFF...
FSHK!!
SHUK..
SHUK..
...!!

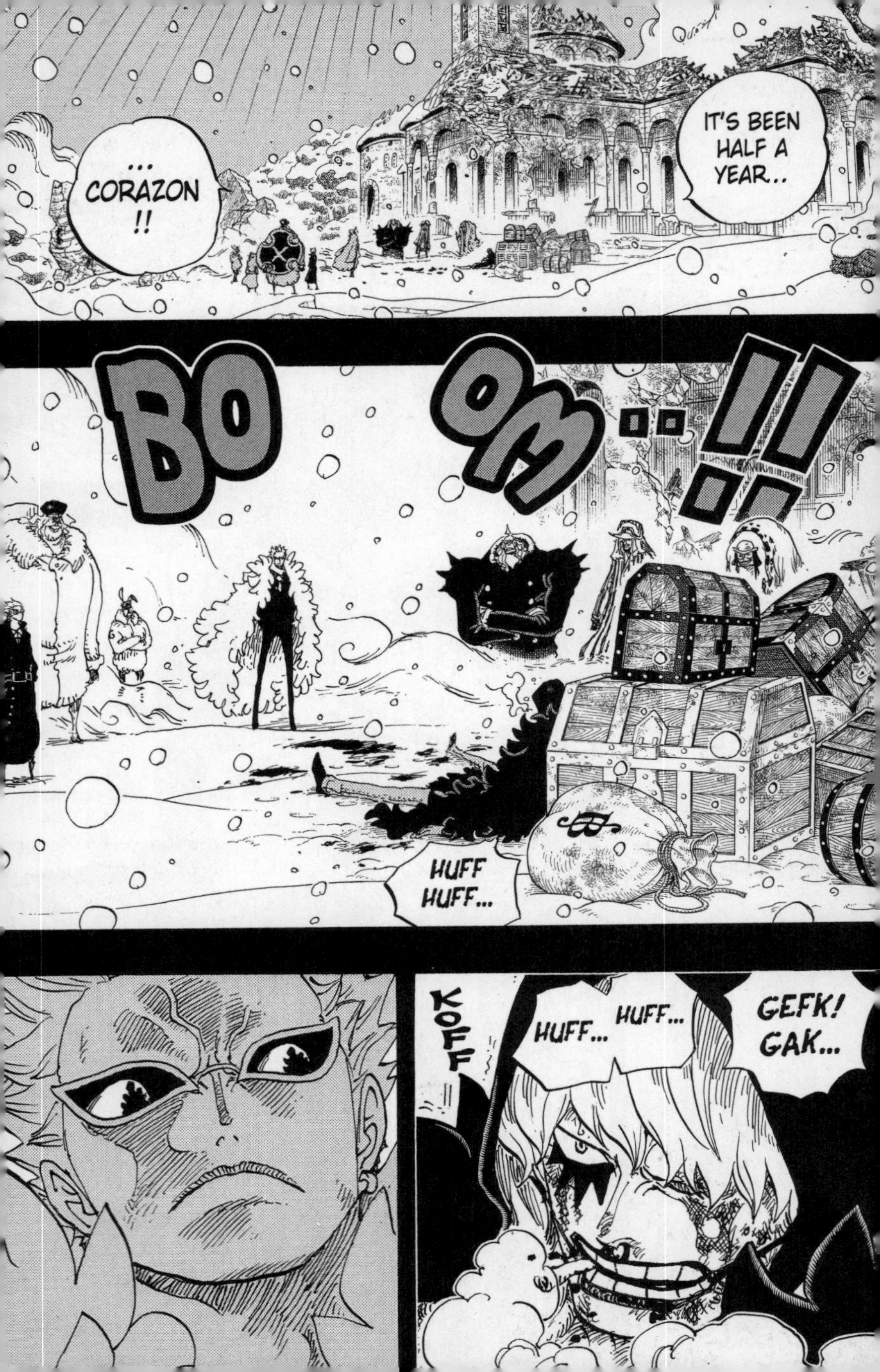
IT'S BEEN HALF A YEAR..
... CORAZON !!
BOOM..!!
HUFF HUFF...
GEFK! GAK...
HUFF... HUFF...
KOFF

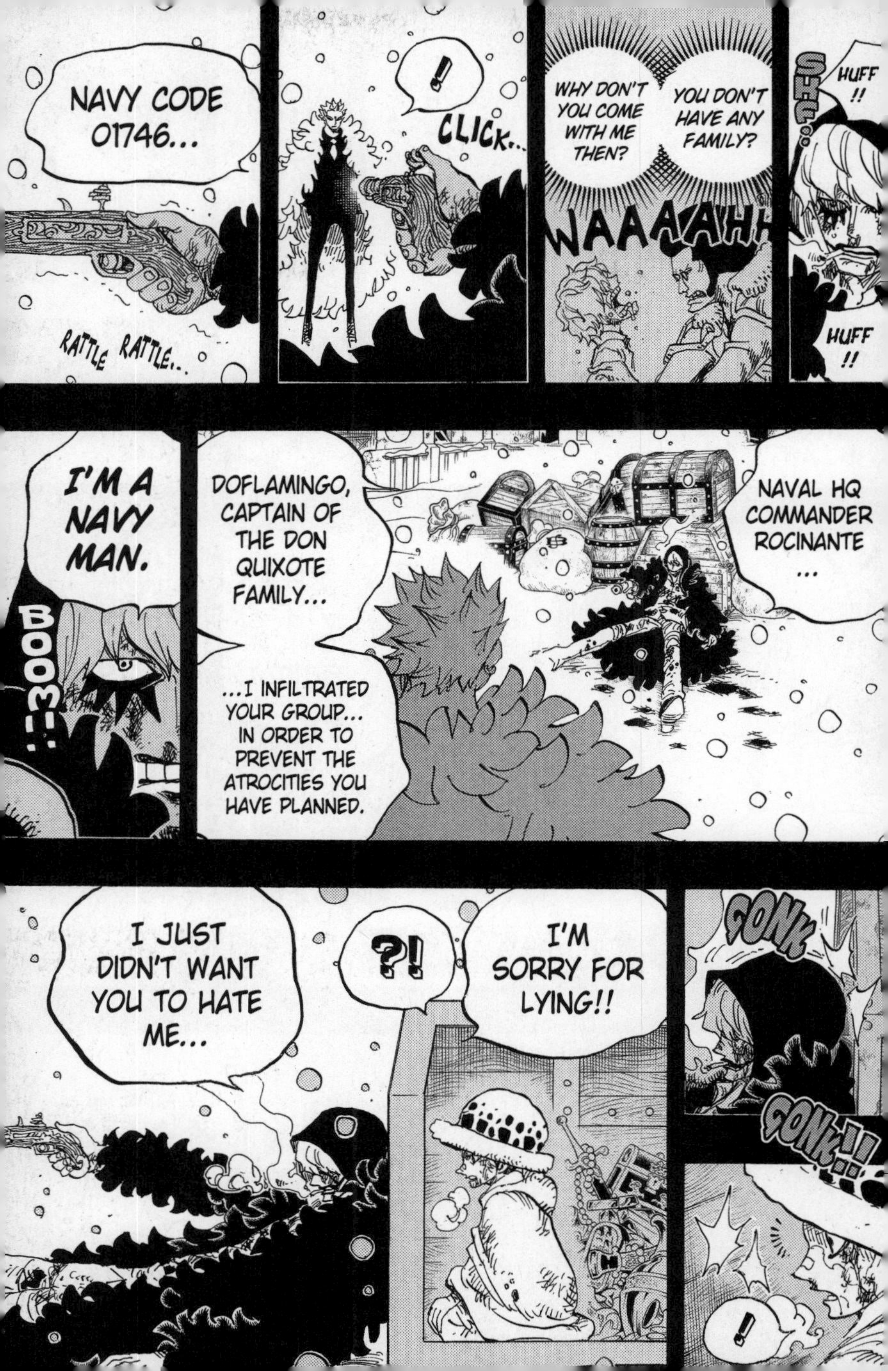
HUFF!!
SHF..
HUFF!!
YOU DON'T HAVE ANY FAMILY?
WHY DON'T YOU COME WITH ME THEN?
WAAAAAHH
!
CLICK...
NAVY CODE 01746...
RATTLE RATTLE...
NAVAL HQ COMMANDER ROCINANTE ...
DOFLAMINGO, CAPTAIN OF THE DON QUIXOTE FAMILY...
...I INFILTRATED YOUR GROUP... IN ORDER TO PREVENT THE ATROCITIES YOU HAVE PLANNED.
I'M A NAVY MAN.
BOOM!!
GONK
GONK!!
!
I'M SORRY FOR LYING!!
?!
I JUST DIDN'T WANT YOU TO HATE ME...

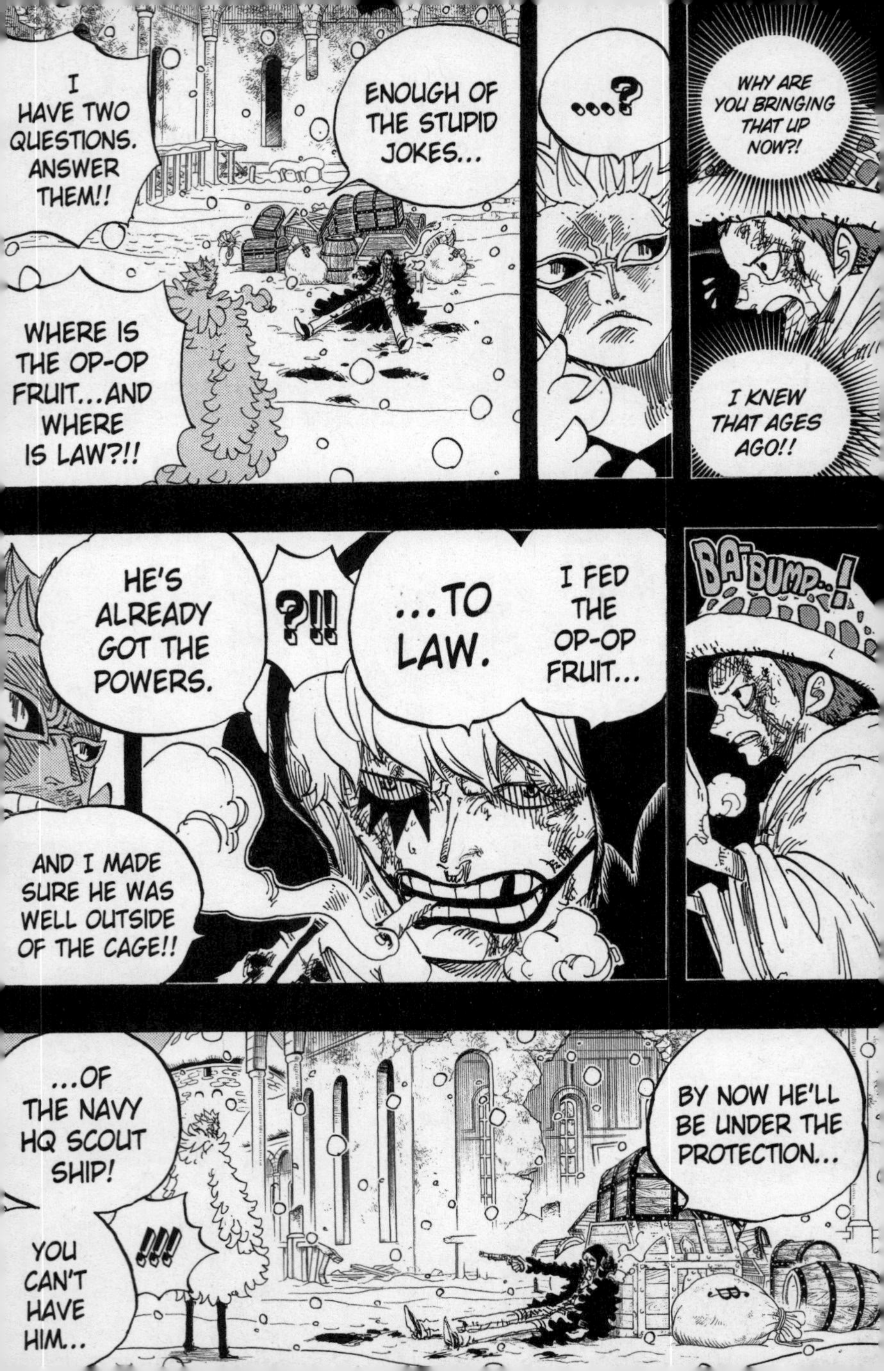
WHY ARE YOU BRINGING THAT UP NOW?!
I KNEW THAT AGES AGO!!
...?
ENOUGH OF THE STUPID JOKES...
I HAVE TWO QUESTIONS. ANSWER THEM!!
WHERE IS THE OP-OP FRUIT...AND WHERE IS LAW?!!
BA-BUMP..!
I FED THE OP-OP FRUIT...
...TO LAW.
?!!
HE'S ALREADY GOT THE POWERS.
AND I MADE SURE HE WAS WELL OUTSIDE OF THE CAGE!!
BY NOW HE'LL BE UNDER THE PROTECTION...
...OF THE NAVY HQ SCOUT SHIP!
!!!
YOU CAN'T HAVE HIM...

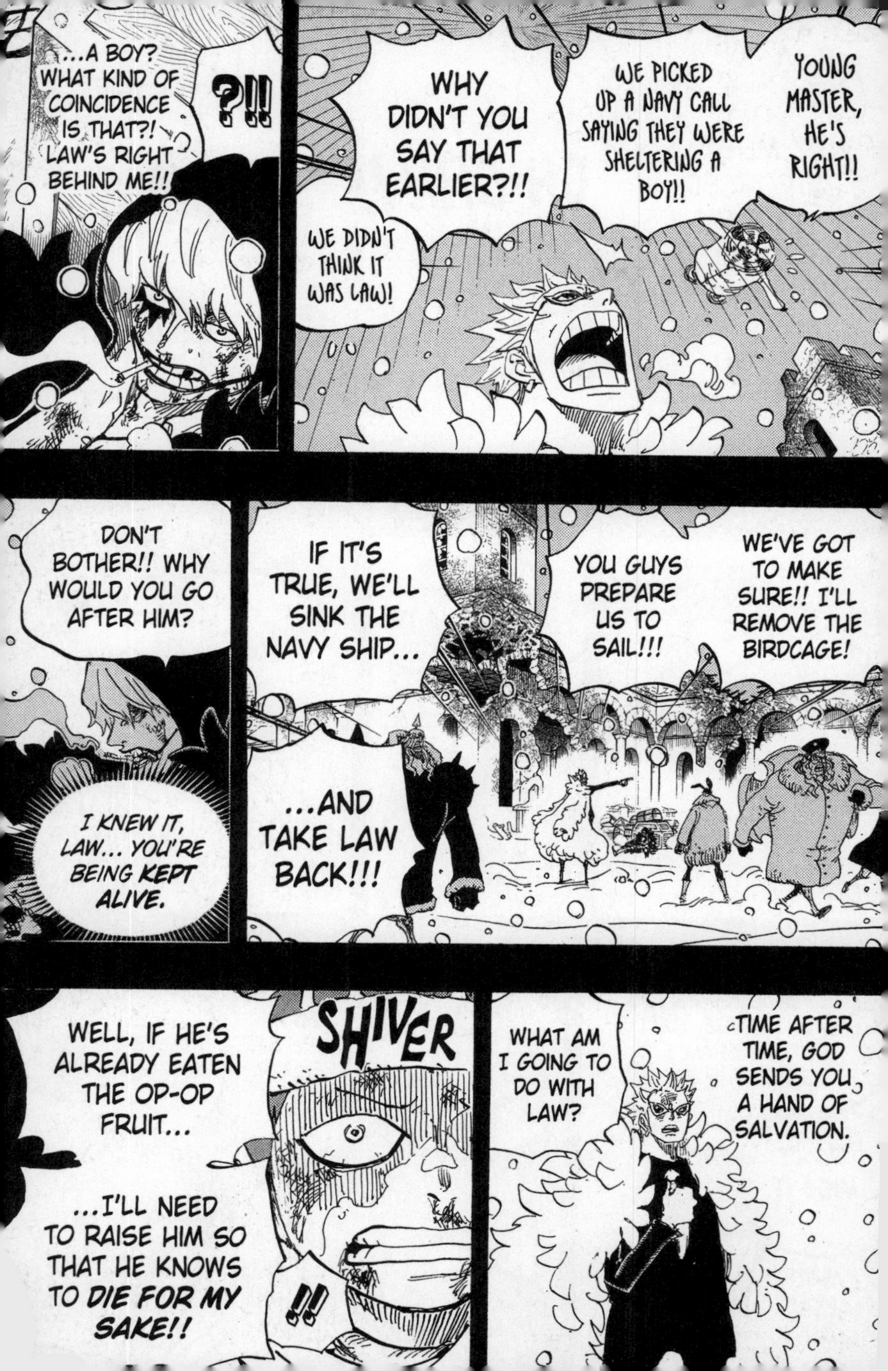
YOUNG MASTER, HE'S RIGHT!!
WE PICKED UP A NAVY CALL SAYING THEY WERE SHELTERING A BOY!!
WHY DIDN'T YOU SAY THAT EARLIER?!!
WE DIDN'T THINK IT WAS LAW!
...A BOY? WHAT KIND OF COINCIDENCE IS THAT?! LAW'S RIGHT BEHIND ME!!
?!!
WE'VE GOT TO MAKE SURE!! I'LL REMOVE THE BIRDCAGE!
YOU GUYS PREPARE US TO SAIL!!!
IF IT'S TRUE, WE'LL SINK THE NAVY SHIP...
...AND TAKE LAW BACK!!!
DON'T BOTHER!! WHY WOULD YOU GO AFTER HIM?
I KNEW IT, LAW... YOU'RE BEING KEPT ALIVE.
TIME AFTER TIME, GOD SENDS YOU A HAND OF SALVATION.
WHAT AM I GOING TO DO WITH LAW?
SHIVER
WELL, IF HE'S ALREADY EATEN THE OP-OP FRUIT...
...I'LL NEED TO RAISE HIM SO THAT HE KNOWS TO DIE FOR MY SAKE!!
!!

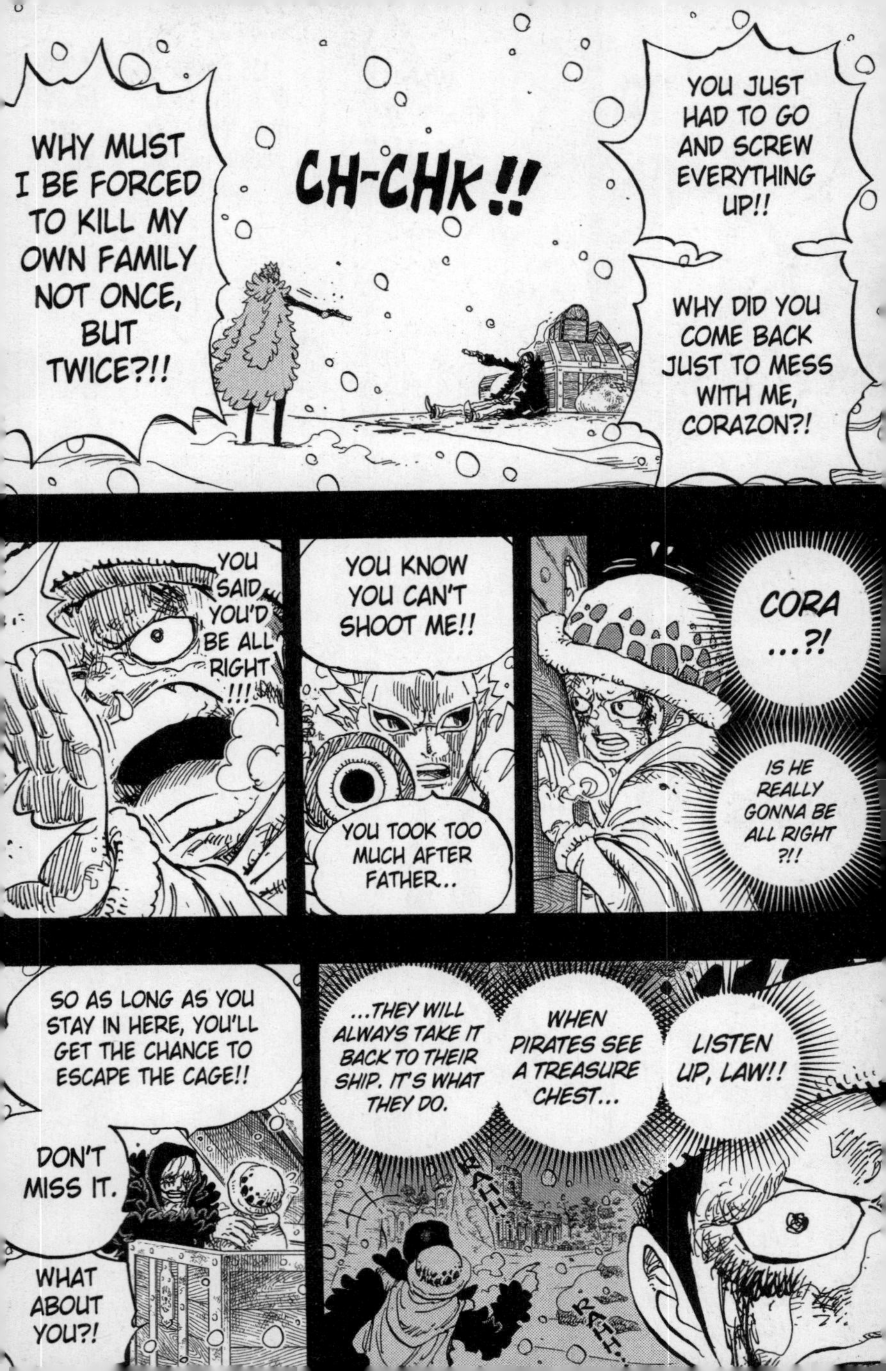
YOU JUST HAD TO GO AND SCREW EVERYTHING UP!!
WHY DID YOU COME BACK JUST TO MESS WITH ME, CORAZON?!
CH-CHK!!
WHY MUST I BE FORCED TO KILL MY OWN FAMILY NOT ONCE, BUT TWICE?!!
CORA ...?!
IS HE REALLY GONNA BE ALL RIGHT ?!!
YOU KNOW YOU CAN'T SHOOT ME!!
YOU TOOK TOO MUCH AFTER FATHER...
YOU SAID YOU'D BE ALL RIGHT !!!
LISTEN UP, LAW!!
WHEN PIRATES SEE A TREASURE CHEST...
...THEY WILL ALWAYS TAKE IT BACK TO THEIR SHIP. IT'S WHAT THEY DO.
SO AS LONG AS YOU STAY IN HERE, YOU'LL GET THE CHANCE TO ESCAPE THE CAGE!!
DON'T MISS IT.
WHAT ABOUT YOU?!

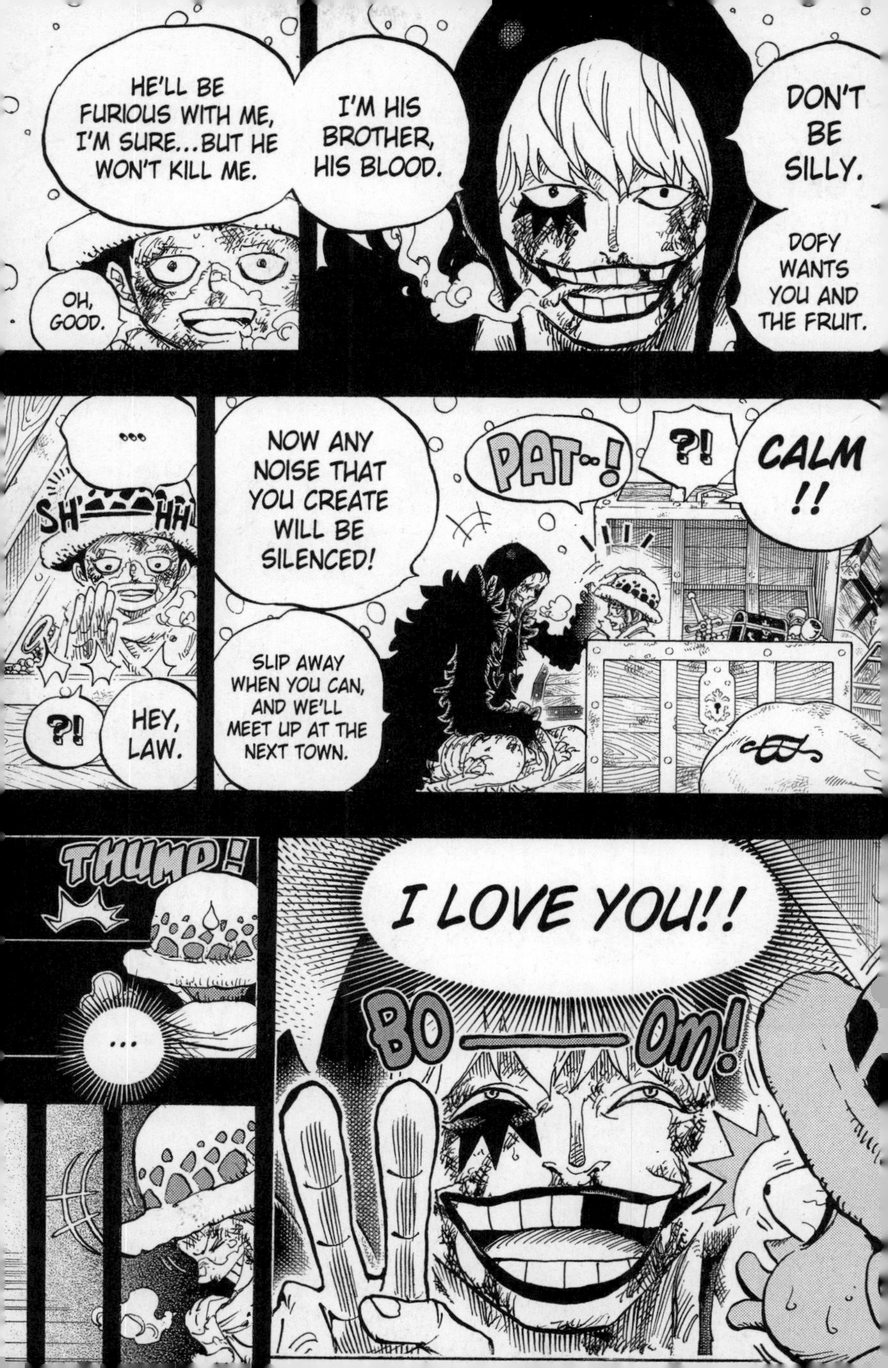
DON'T BE SILLY.
DOFY WANTS YOU AND THE FRUIT.
I'M HIS BROTHER, HIS BLOOD.
HE'LL BE FURIOUS WITH ME, I'M SURE...BUT HE WON'T KILL ME.
OH, GOOD.
CALM!!
?!
PAT..!
NOW ANY NOISE THAT YOU CREATE WILL BE SILENCED!
SLIP AWAY WHEN YOU CAN, AND WE'LL MEET UP AT THE NEXT TOWN.
...
SH—HH
HEY, LAW.
?!
I LOVE YOU!!
BO—OM!
THUMP!
...

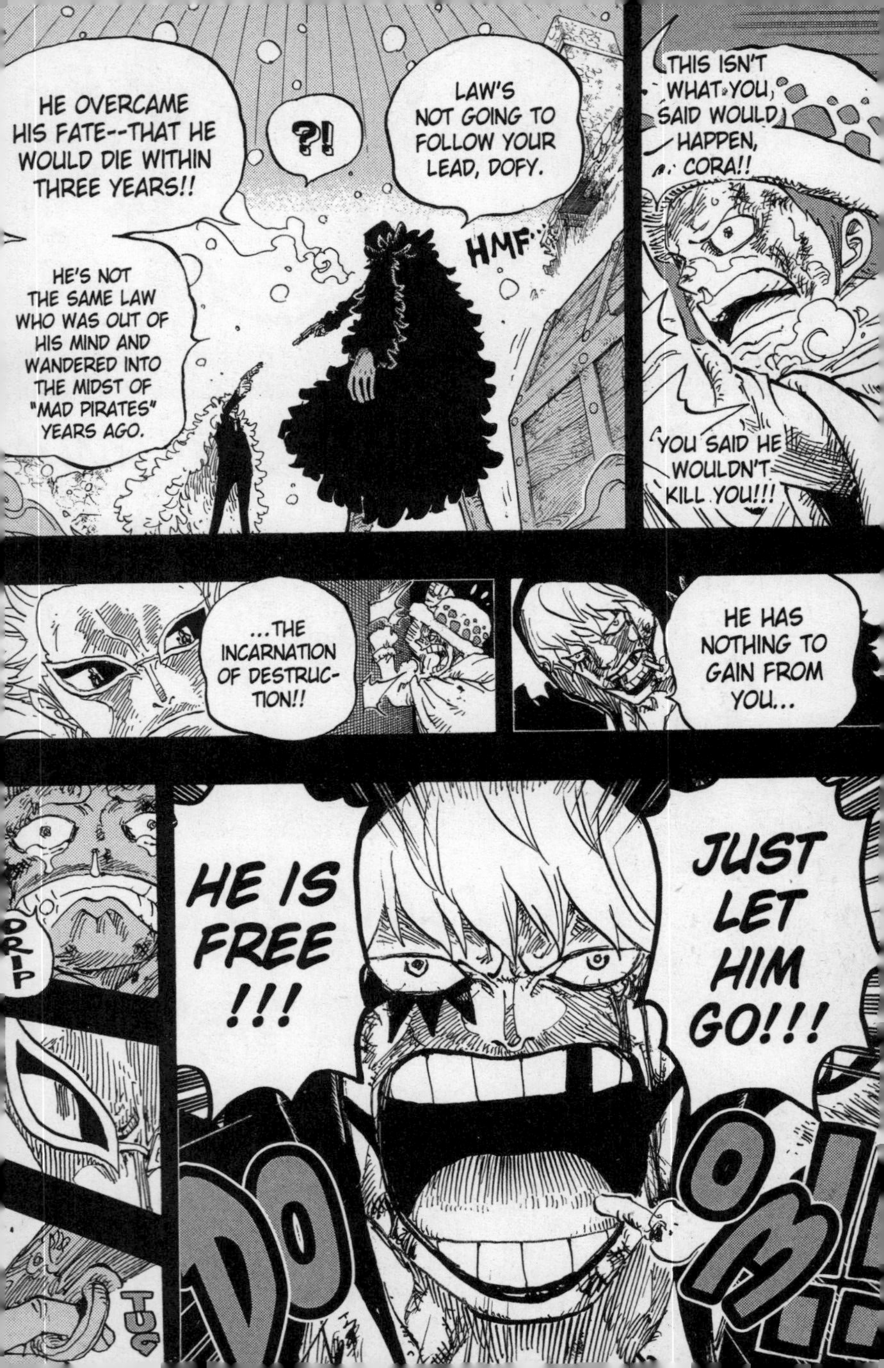
THIS ISN'T WHAT YOU SAID WOULD HAPPEN, CORA!!
YOU SAID HE WOULDN'T KILL YOU!!!
LAW'S NOT GOING TO FOLLOW YOUR LEAD, DOFY.
HMF...
?!
HE OVERCAME HIS FATE--THAT HE WOULD DIE WITHIN THREE YEARS!!
HE'S NOT THE SAME LAW WHO WAS OUT OF HIS MIND AND WANDERED INTO THE MIDST OF "MAD PIRATES" YEARS AGO.
HE HAS NOTHING TO GAIN FROM YOU...
...THE INCARNATION OF DESTRUCTION!!
JUST LET HIM GO!!!
HE IS FREE!!!
DRIP
TUG

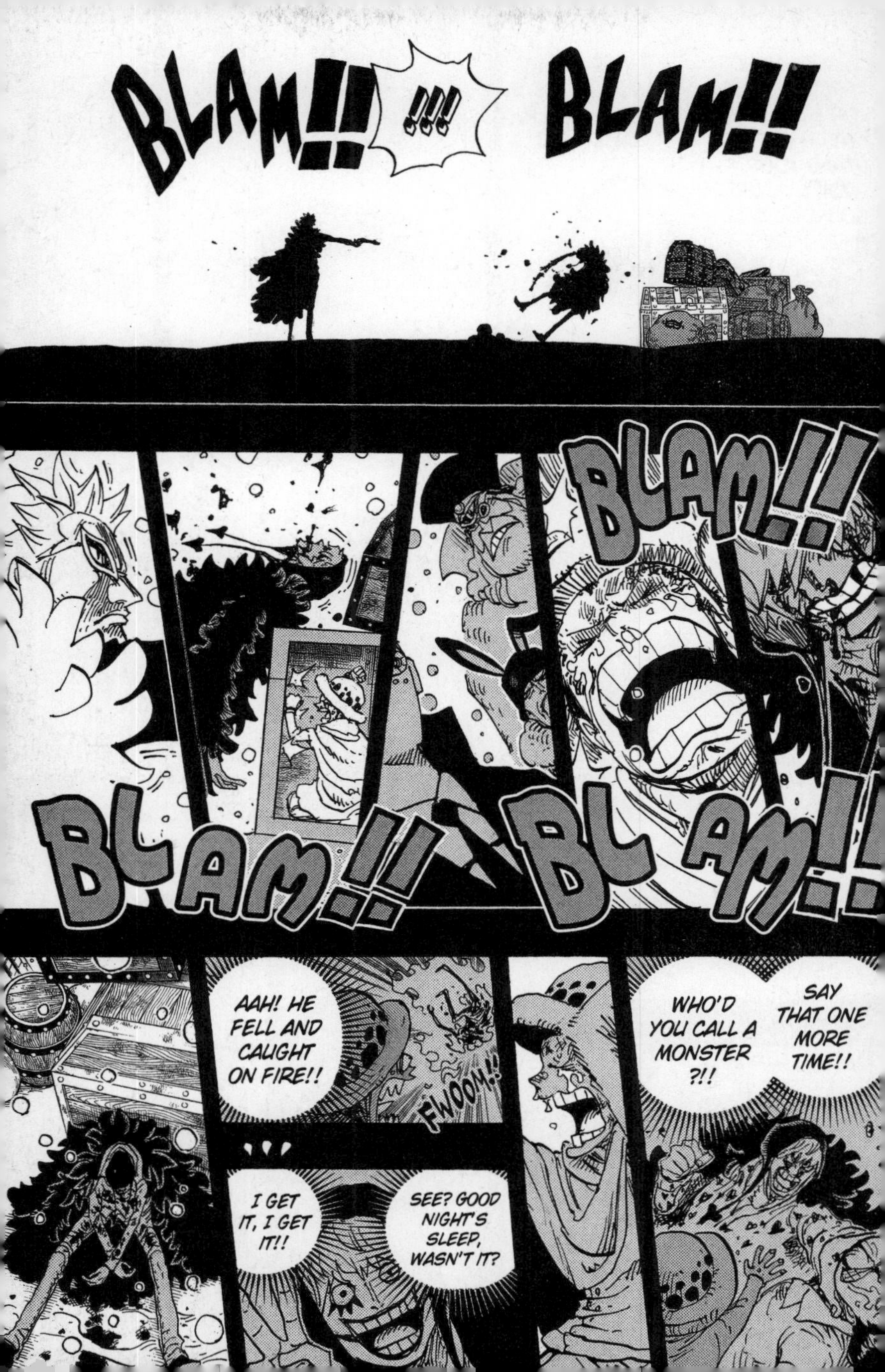

BLAM!!
!!!
BLAM!!
BLAM!!
BLAM!!
BLAM!!
SAY THAT ONE MORE TIME!!
WHO'D YOU CALL A MONSTER ?!!
AAH! HE FELL AND CAUGHT ON FIRE!!
FWOOM!!
SEE? GOOD NIGHT'S SLEEP, WASN'T IT?
I GET IT, I GET IT!!

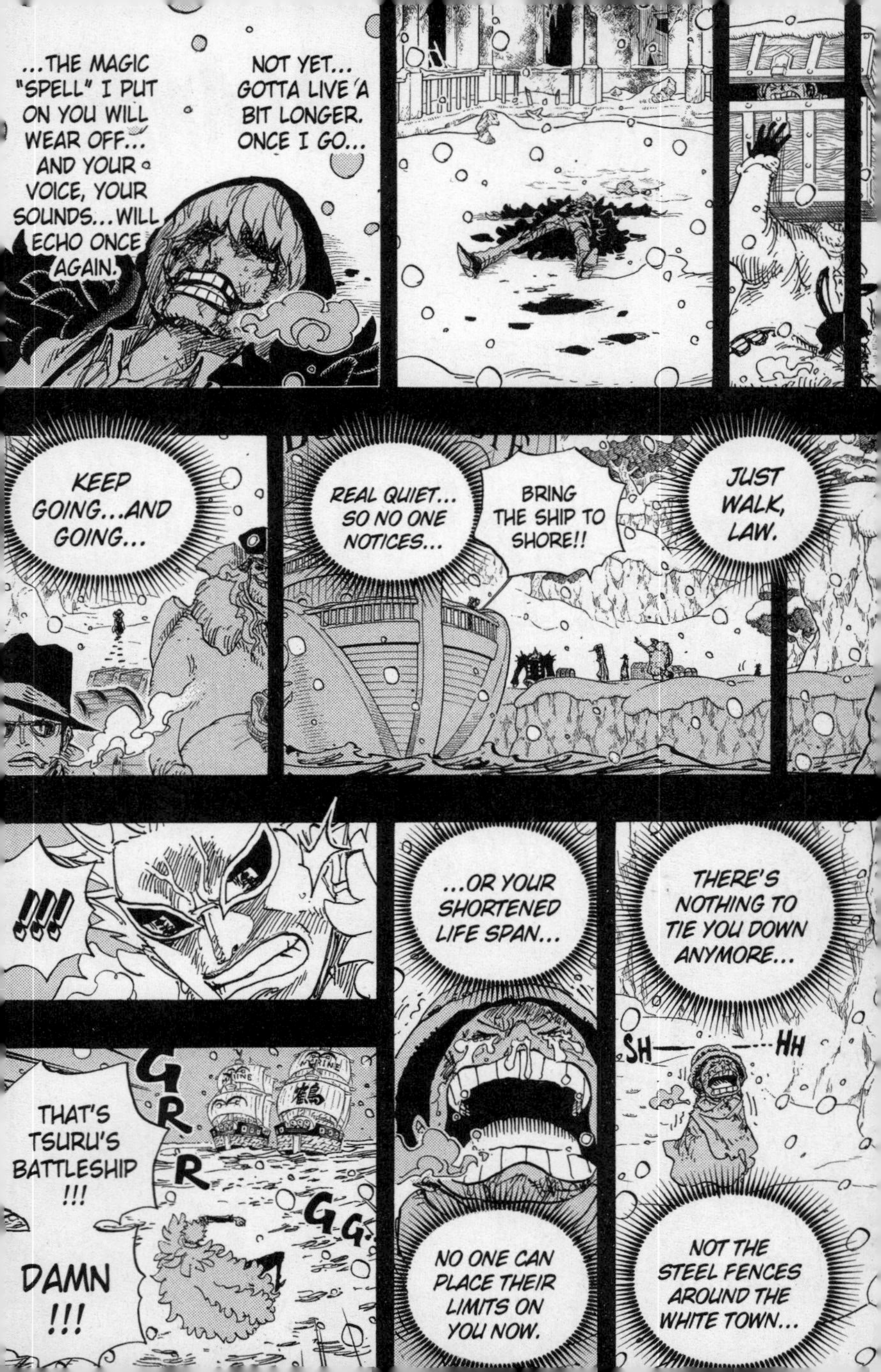
NOT YET... GOTTA LIVE A BIT LONGER. ONCE I GO...
...THE MAGIC "SPELL" I PUT ON YOU WILL WEAR OFF... AND YOUR VOICE, YOUR SOUNDS... WILL ECHO ONCE AGAIN.
JUST WALK, LAW.
BRING THE SHIP TO SHORE!!
REAL QUIET... SO NO ONE NOTICES...
KEEP GOING...AND GOING...
THERE'S NOTHING TO TIE YOU DOWN ANYMORE...
SH——HH
NOT THE STEEL FENCES AROUND THE WHITE TOWN...
...OR YOUR SHORTENED LIFE SPAN...
NO ONE CAN PLACE THEIR LIMITS ON YOU NOW.
!!!
GRRGG
THAT'S TSURU'S BATTLESHIP!!!
DAMN!!!

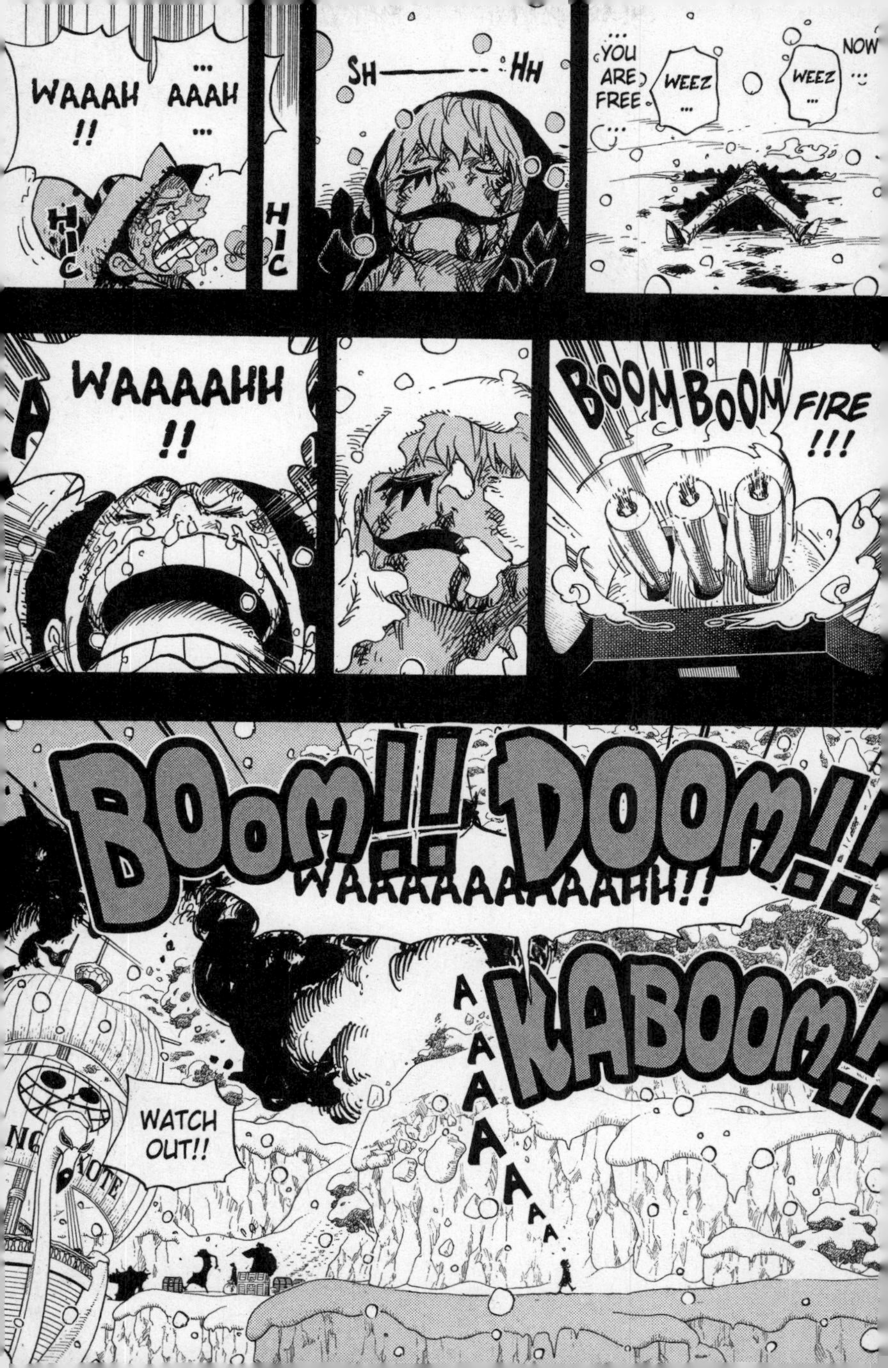
NOW ...
WEEZ ...
WEEZ ...
... YOU ARE FREE ...
SH———HH
HIC
... AAAH ...
WAAAH !!
HIC
BOOM BOOM FIRE !!!
WAAAAHH !!
BOOM!! DOOM!!
WAAAAAAAAAAAHH!!
KABOOM!!
AAAAAAAAA
WATCH OUT!!

Chapter 768:

THE TRIGGER THAT DAY

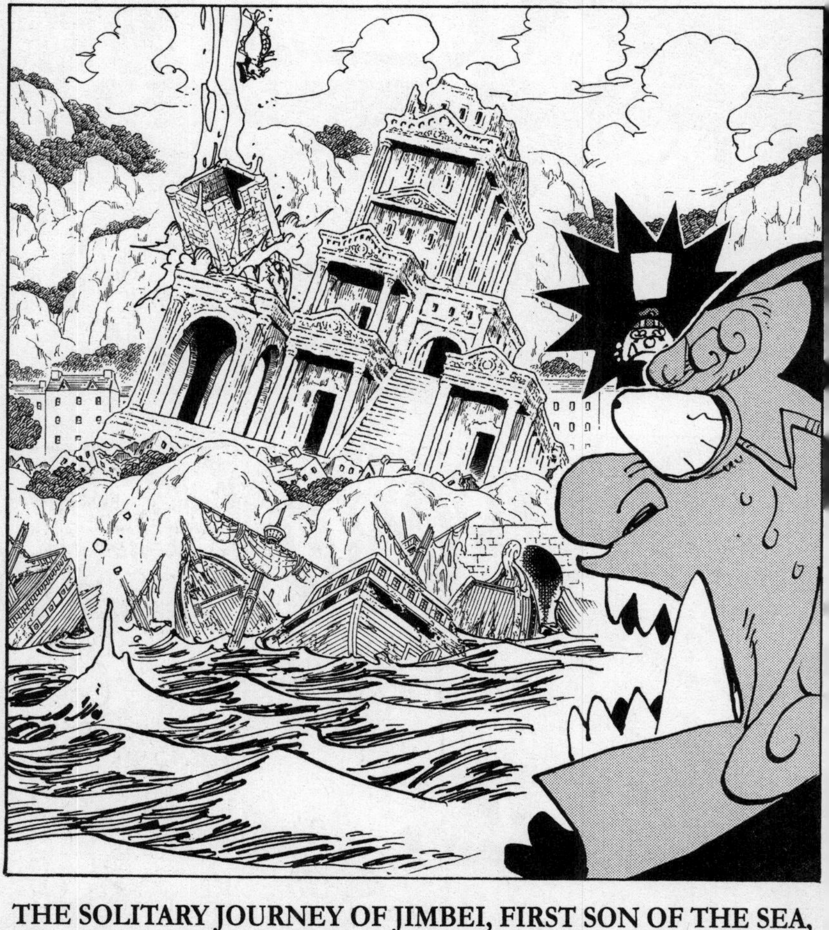

THE SOLITARY JOURNEY OF JIMBEI, FIRST SON OF THE SEA,
VOL. 15: "I DEFINITELY SAW THAT RUIN FALL JUST NOW"

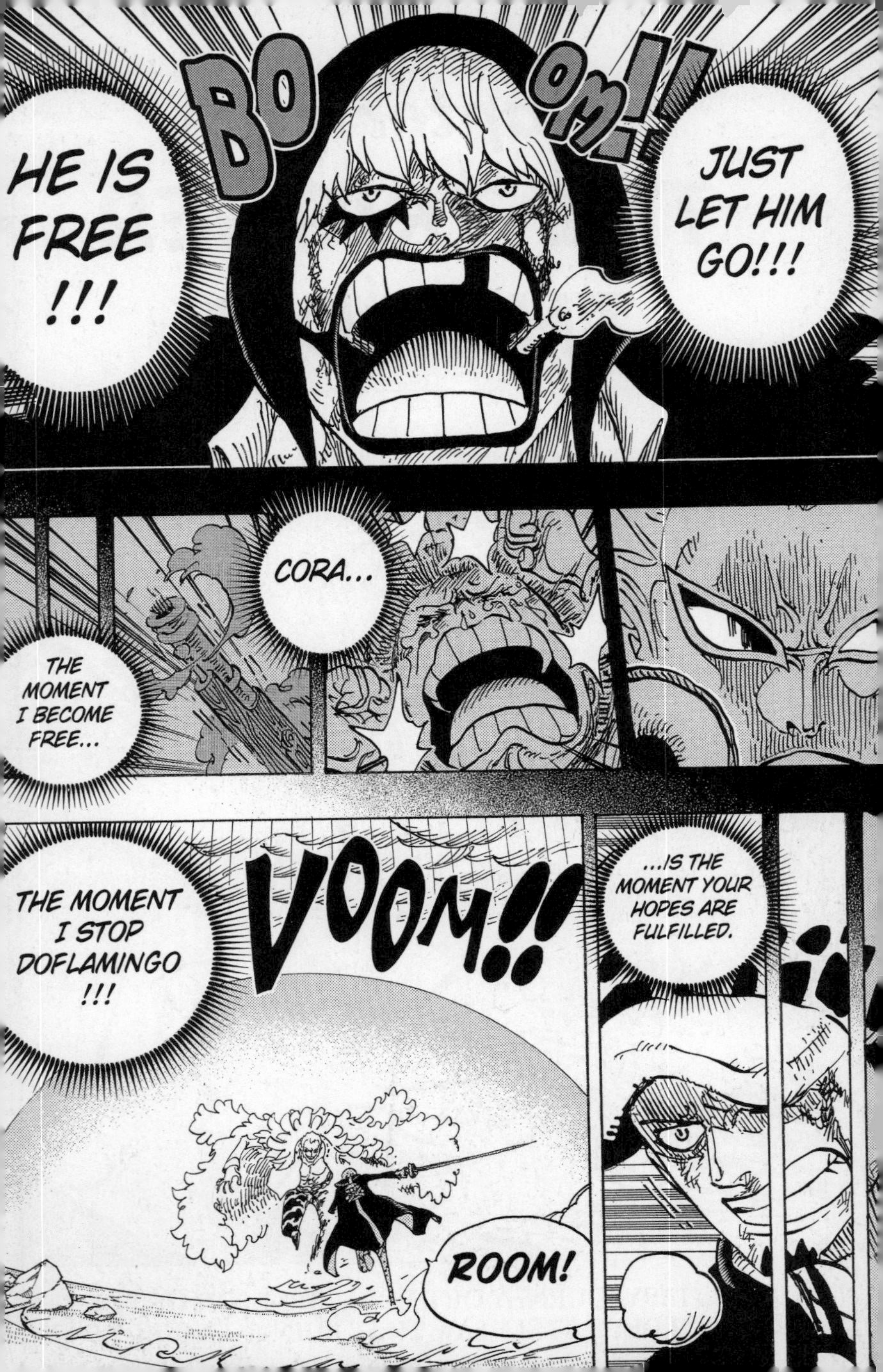
BOOM!!
JUST LET HIM GO!!!
HE IS FREE!!!
CORA...
THE MOMENT I BECOME FREE...
...IS THE MOMENT YOUR HOPES ARE FULFILLED.
VOOM!!
THE MOMENT I STOP DOFLAMINGO!!!
ROOM!

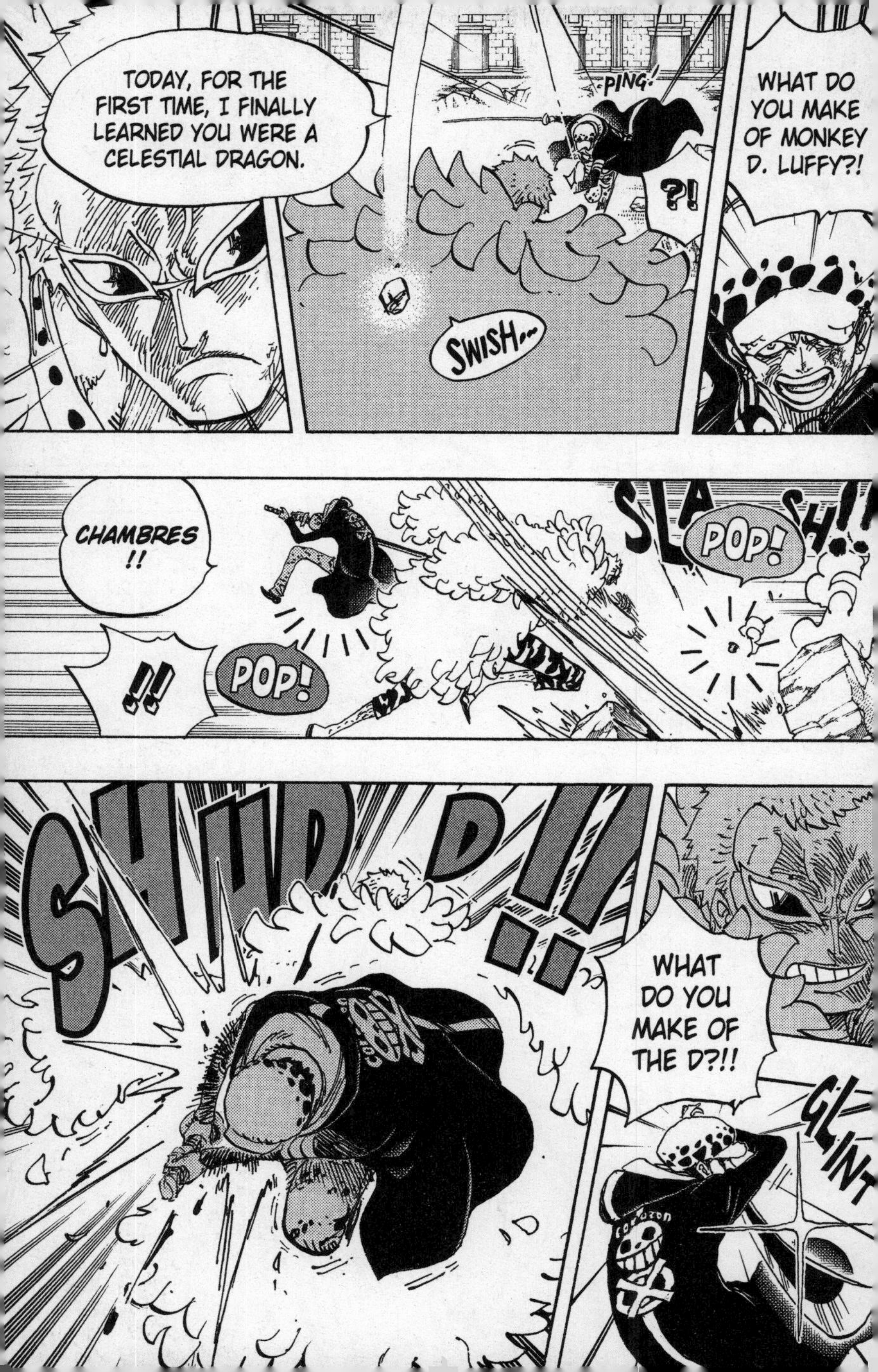
WHAT DO YOU MAKE OF MONKEY D. LUFFY?!
PING!
?!
SWISH...
TODAY, FOR THE FIRST TIME, I FINALLY LEARNED YOU WERE A CELESTIAL DRAGON.
SLASH!!
POP!
CHAMBRES !!
!!
POP!
WHAT DO YOU MAKE OF THE D?!!
GLINT
SHUDD!!

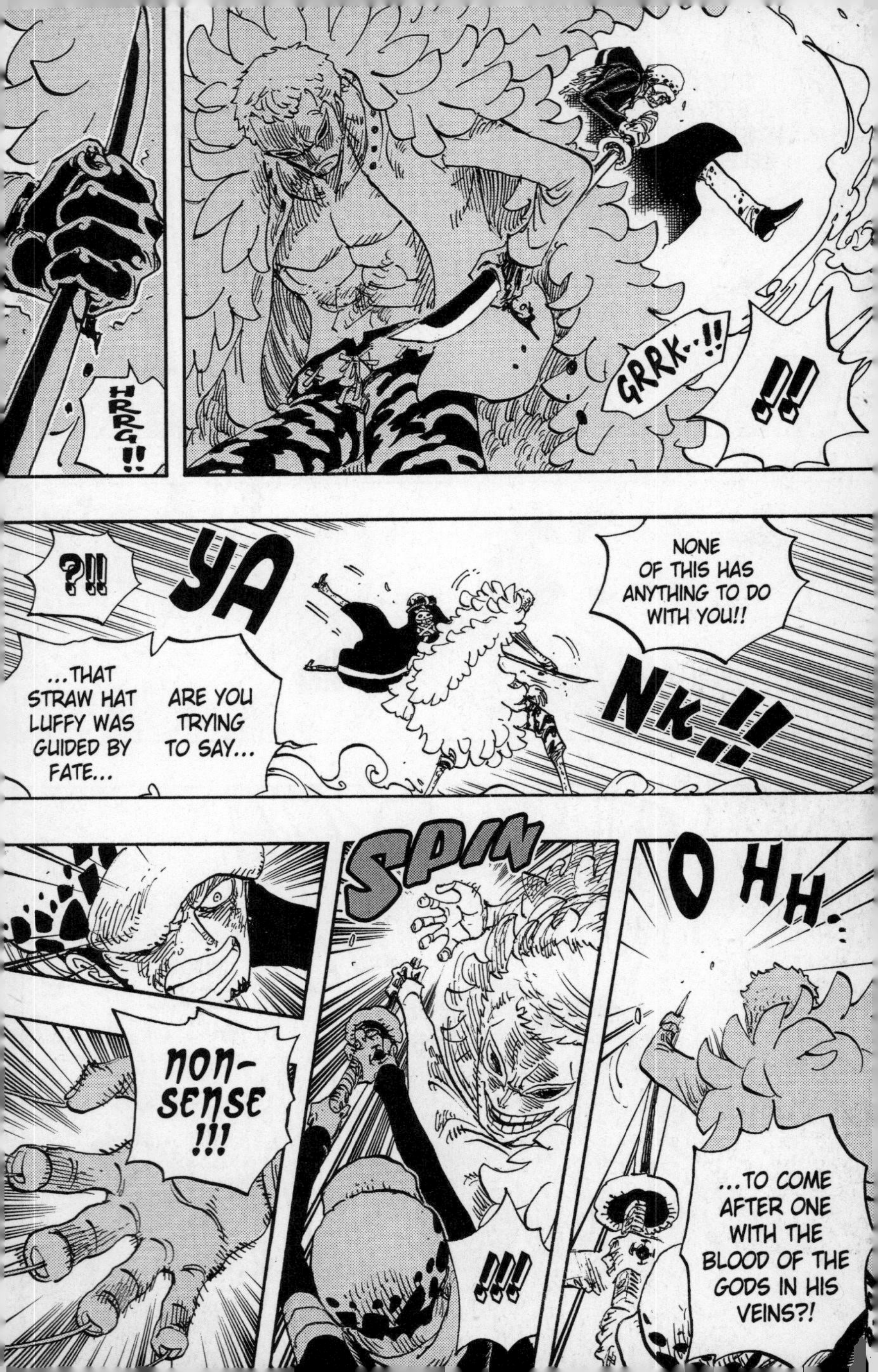
!!
GRRK..!!
HRRG!!
NONE OF THIS HAS ANYTHING TO DO WITH YOU!!
Nk!!
YA
?!!
ARE YOU TRYING TO SAY...
...THAT STRAW HAT LUFFY WAS GUIDED BY FATE...
OHH
...TO COME AFTER ONE WITH THE BLOOD OF THE GODS IN HIS VEINS?!
SPIN
!!!
non-sense!!!

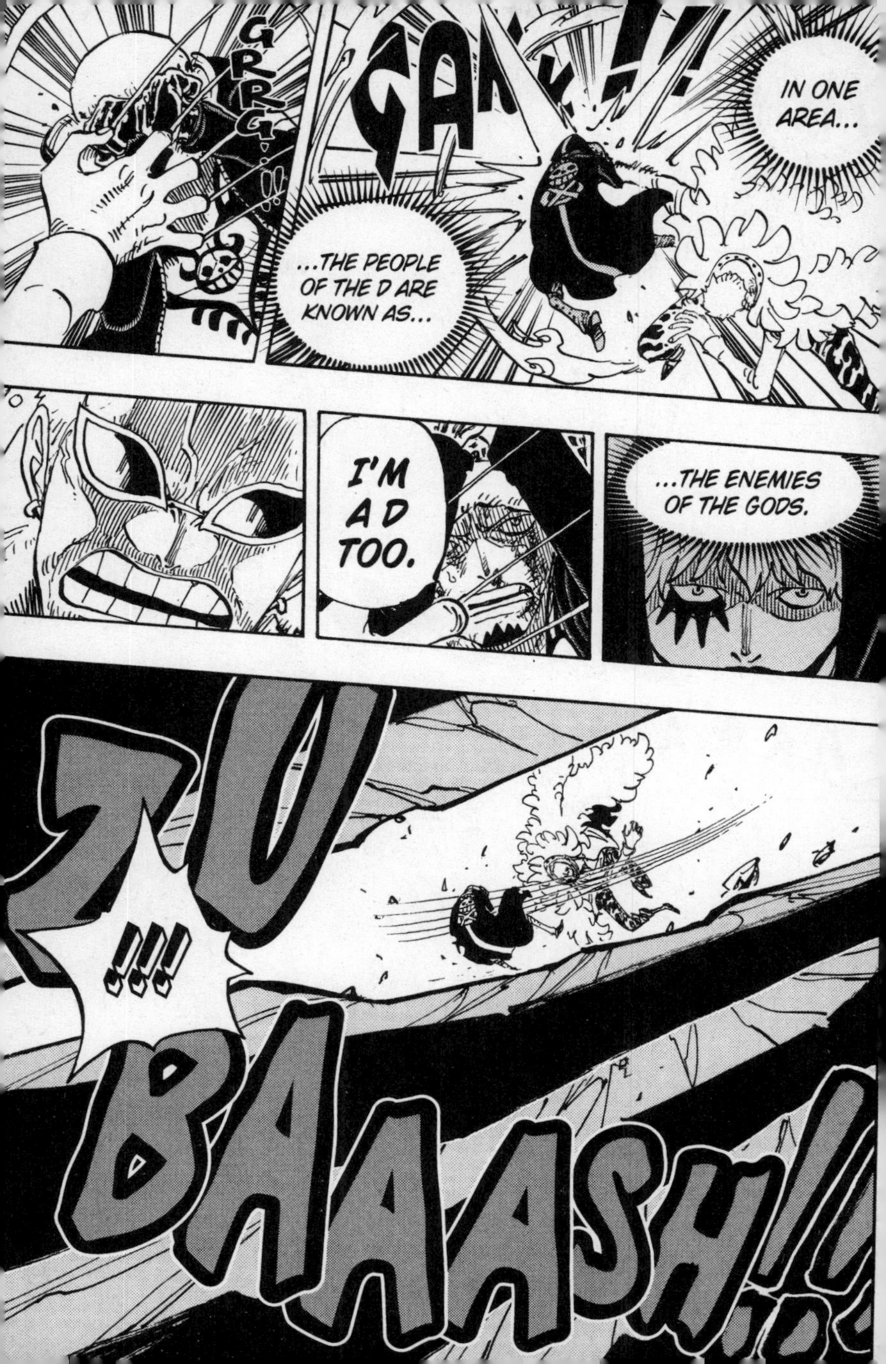
IN ONE AREA…
…THE PEOPLE OF THE D ARE KNOWN AS…
GRRG…!!
…THE ENEMIES OF THE GODS.
I'M A D TOO.
ZU!!!
BAAASH!!

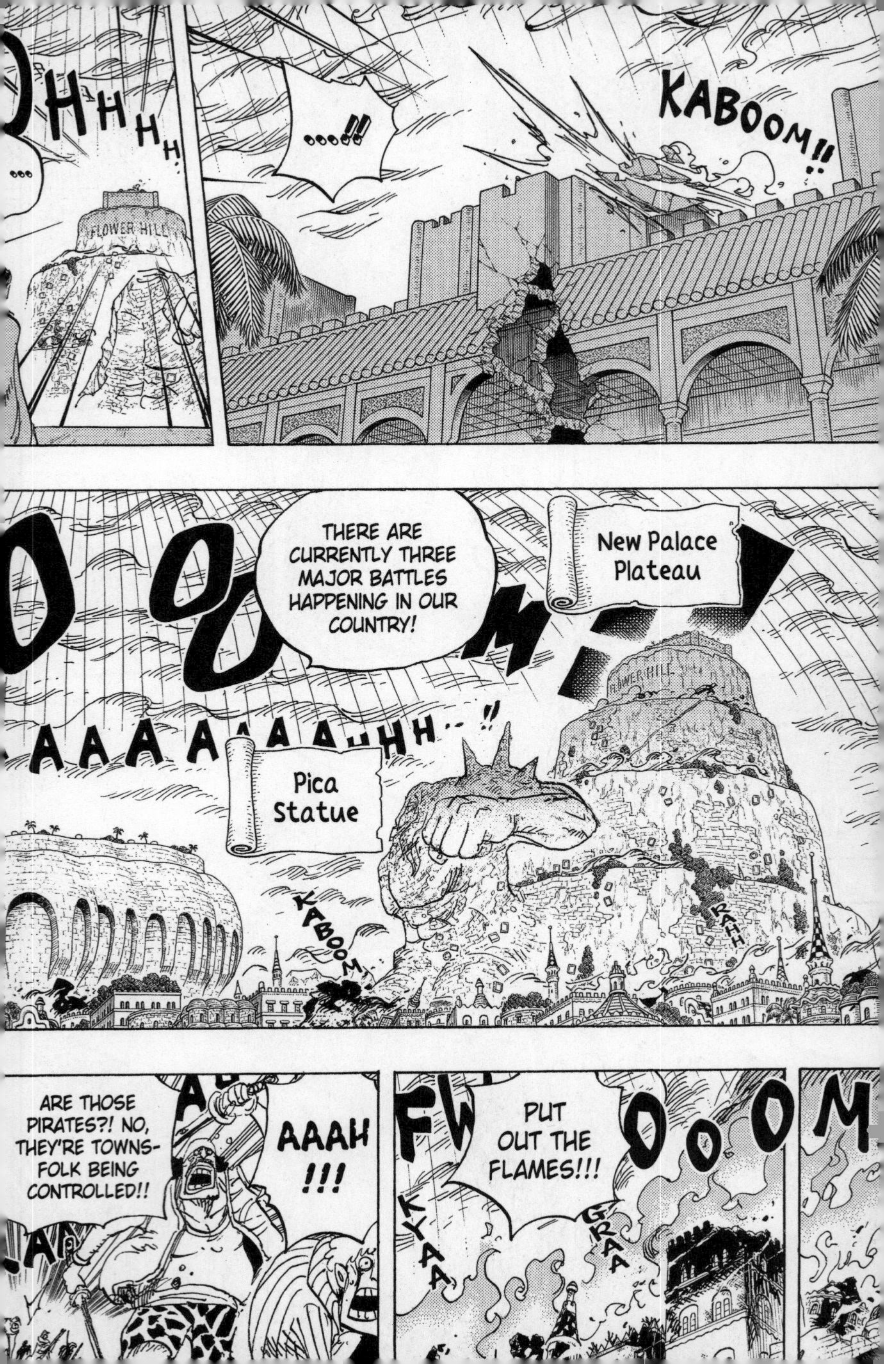
KABOOM!!
....!!
OHHHHH
...
THERE ARE CURRENTLY THREE MAJOR BATTLES HAPPENING IN OUR COUNTRY!
New Palace Plateau
OOOM
AAAAAAAHH...!!
Pica Statue
RAHH
KABOOM
PUT OUT THE FLAMES!!!
FW
OOOM
GRAA
KYAA
ARE THOSE PIRATES?! NO, THEY'RE TOWNSFOLK BEING CONTROLLED!!
AAAH!!!

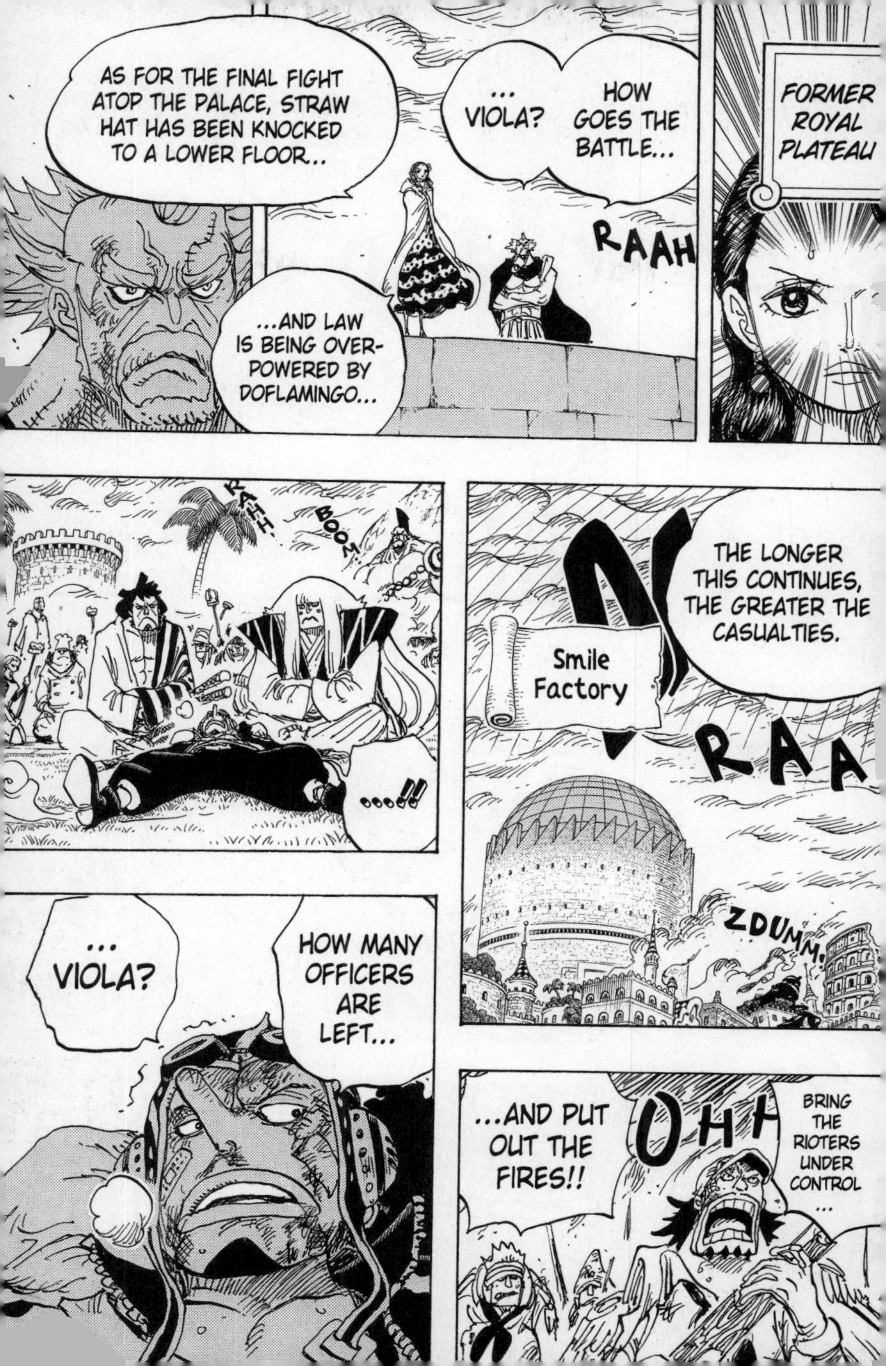
FORMER ROYAL PLATEAU
... VIOLA? HOW GOES THE BATTLE...
RAAH
AS FOR THE FINAL FIGHT ATOP THE PALACE, STRAW HAT HAS BEEN KNOCKED TO A LOWER FLOOR...
...AND LAW IS BEING OVER-POWERED BY DOFLAMINGO...
Smile Factory
THE LONGER THIS CONTINUES, THE GREATER THE CASUALTIES.
RAA
ZDUMM
RAHH
BOOM
...!!
BRING THE RIOTERS UNDER CONTROL ...
OHH
...AND PUT OUT THE FIRES!!
HOW MANY OFFICERS ARE LEFT...
... VIOLA?

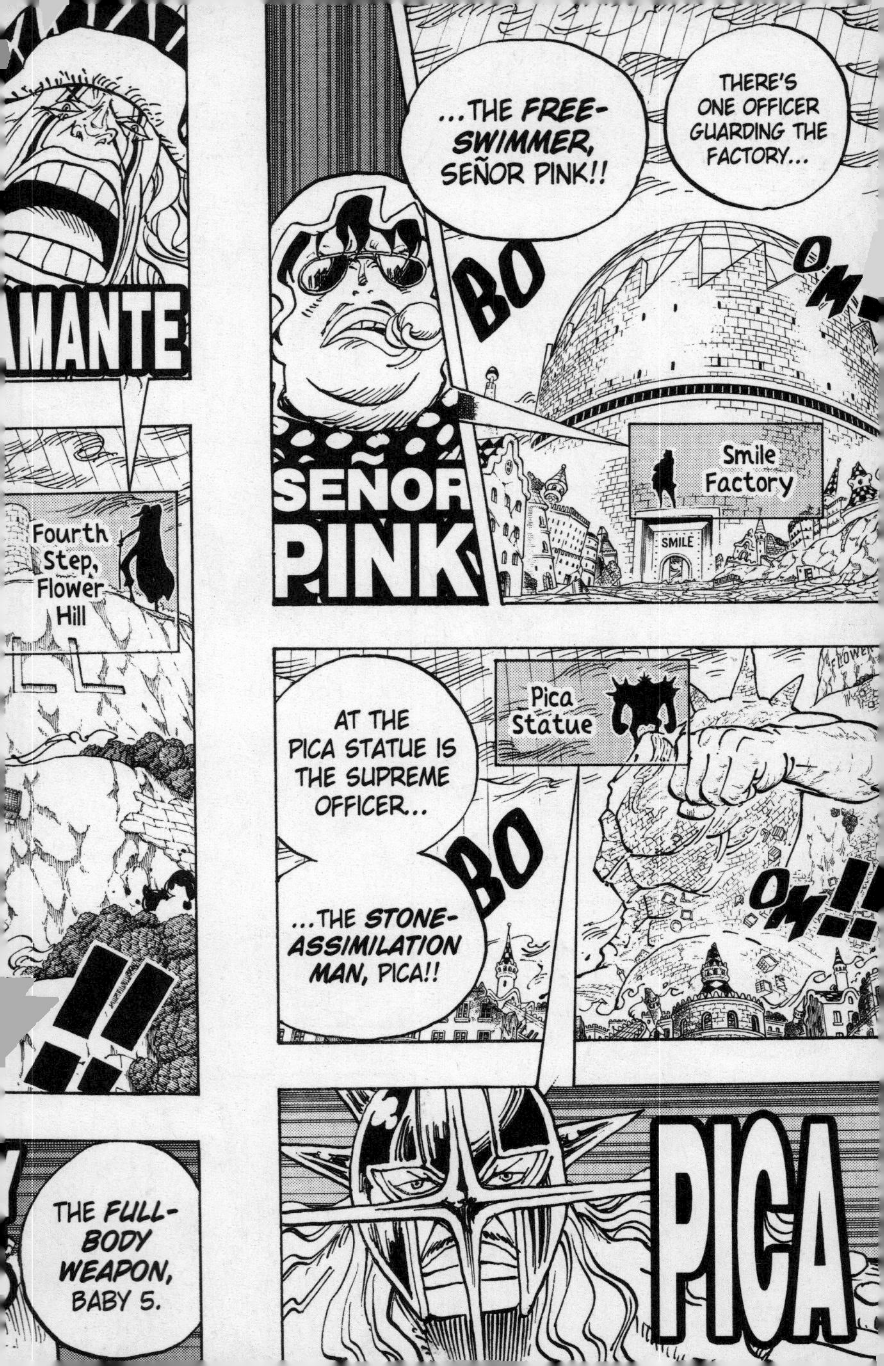
THERE'S ONE OFFICER GUARDING THE FACTORY...
...THE FREE-SWIMMER, SEÑOR PINK!!
BO
OM
Smile Factory
SMILE
SEÑOR PINK
Pica Statue
AT THE PICA STATUE IS THE SUPREME OFFICER...
...THE STONE-ASSIMILATION MAN, PICA!!
BO
OM!!
PICA
AMANTE
Fourth Step, Flower Hill
!!
THE FULL-BODY WEAPON, BABY 5.

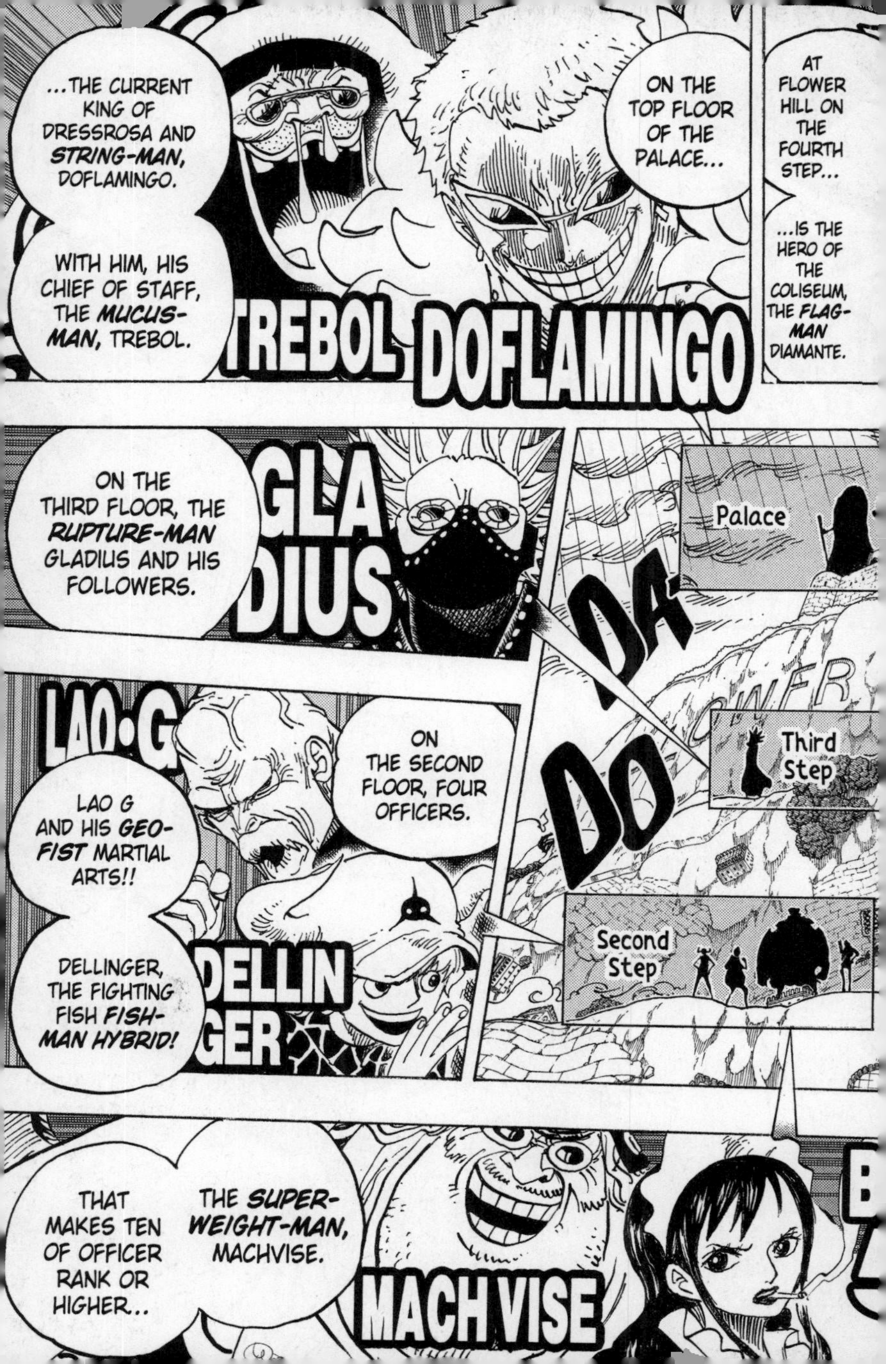
AT FLOWER HILL ON THE FOURTH STEP...
...IS THE HERO OF THE COLISEUM, THE FLAG-MAN DIAMANTE.
ON THE TOP FLOOR OF THE PALACE...
...THE CURRENT KING OF DRESSROSA AND STRING-MAN, DOFLAMINGO.
DOFLAMINGO
WITH HIM, HIS CHIEF OF STAFF, THE MUCUS-MAN, TREBOL.
TREBOL
Palace
DA
DO
Third Step
Second Step
ON THE THIRD FLOOR, THE RUPTURE-MAN GLADIUS AND HIS FOLLOWERS.
GLA DIUS
ON THE SECOND FLOOR, FOUR OFFICERS.
LAO·G
LAO G AND HIS GEO-FIST MARTIAL ARTS!!
DELLINGER, THE FIGHTING FISH FISH-MAN HYBRID!
DELLIN GER
THE SUPER-WEIGHT-MAN, MACHVISE.
MACH VISE
THAT MAKES TEN OF OFFICER RANK OR HIGHER...

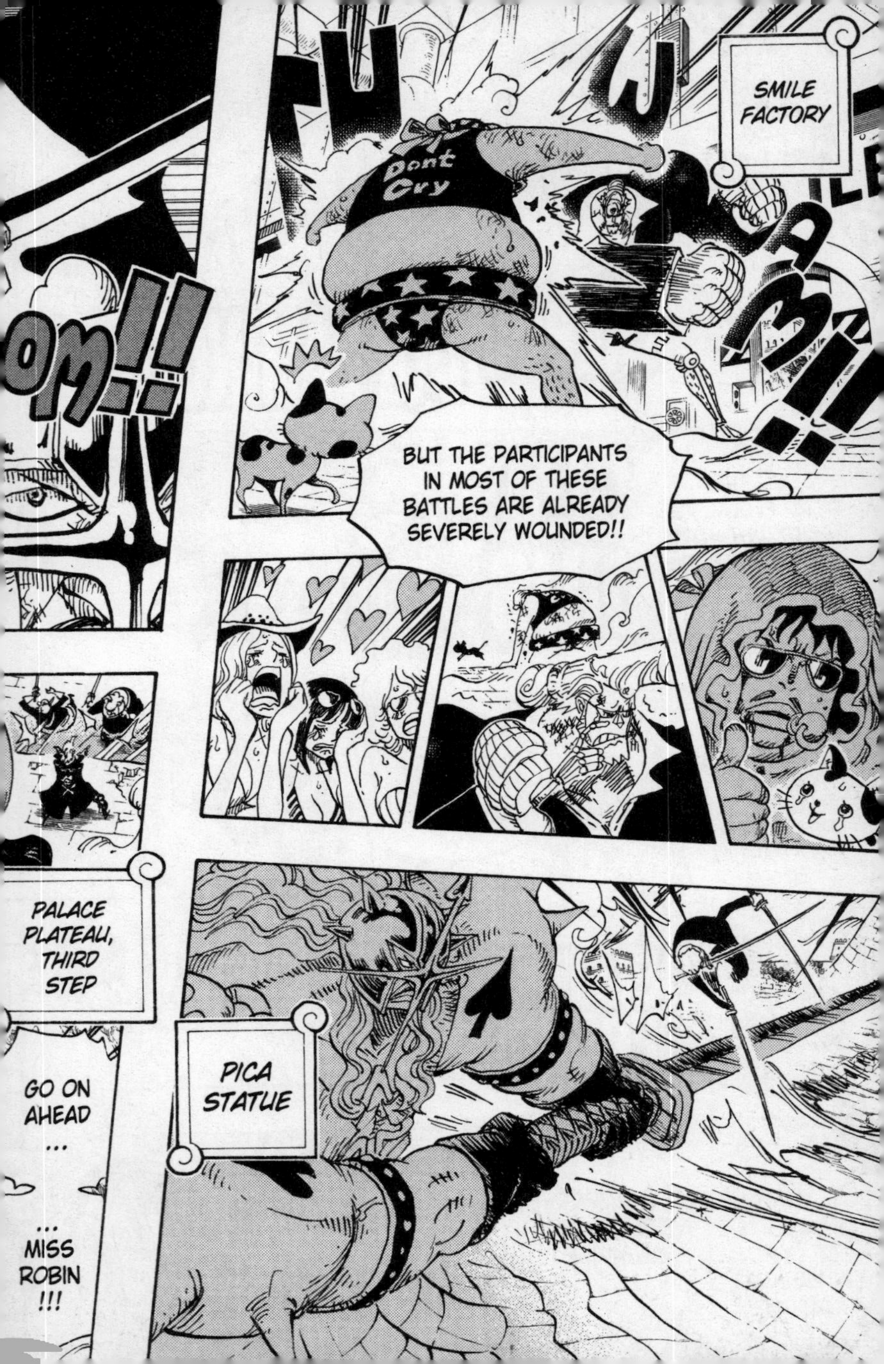
SMILE FACTORY
Dont Cry
BUT THE PARTICIPANTS IN MOST OF THESE BATTLES ARE ALREADY SEVERELY WOUNDED!!
PICA STATUE
PALACE PLATEAU, THIRD STEP
GO ON AHEAD ...
... MISS ROBIN !!!

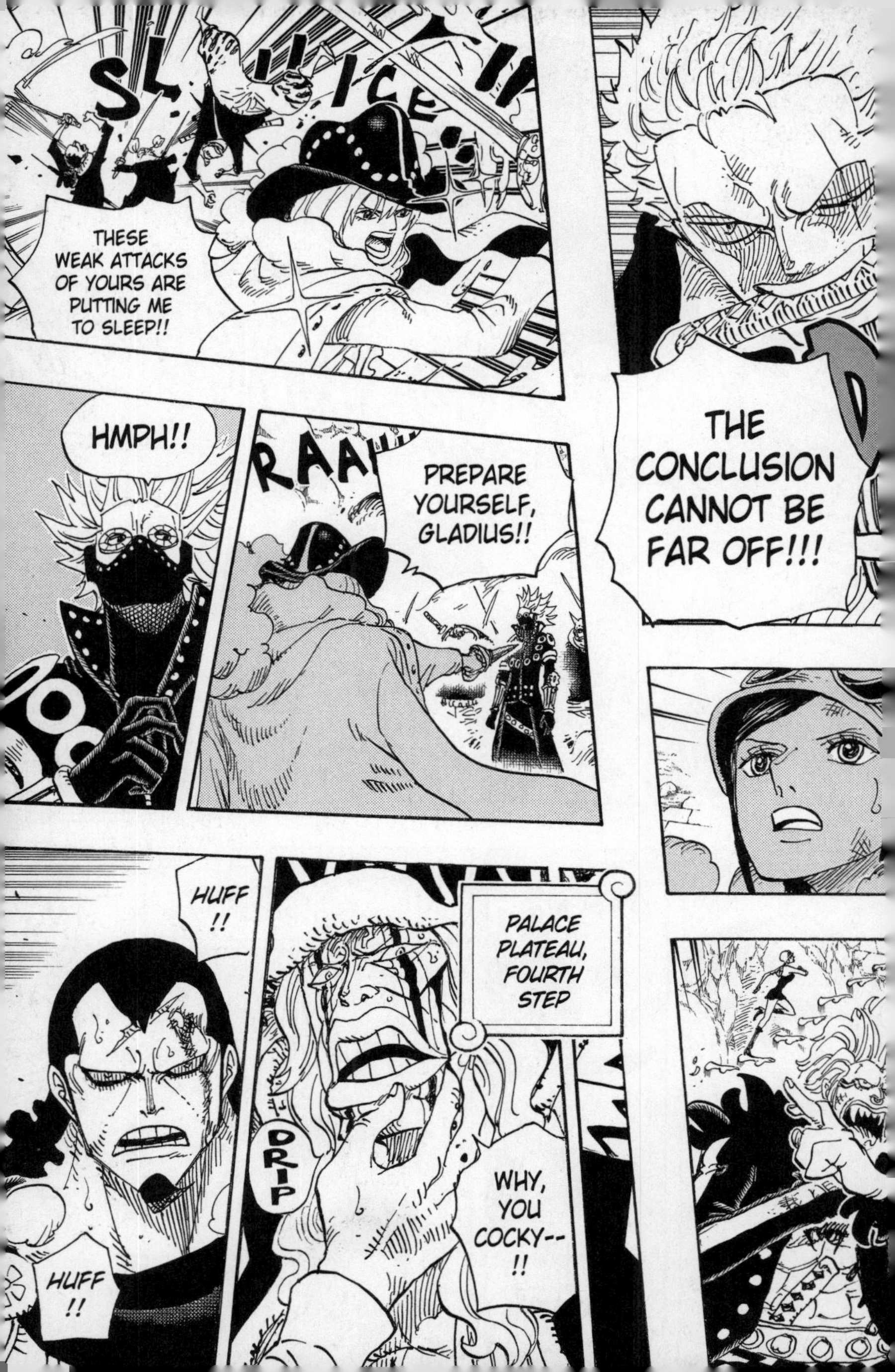
THE CONCLUSION CANNOT BE FAR OFF!!!
SLIIICE!!
THESE WEAK ATTACKS OF YOURS ARE PUTTING ME TO SLEEP!!
PREPARE YOURSELF, GLADIUS!!
RAA
HMPH!!
PALACE PLATEAU, FOURTH STEP
WHY, YOU COCKY-- !!
DRIP
HUFF !!
HUFF !!

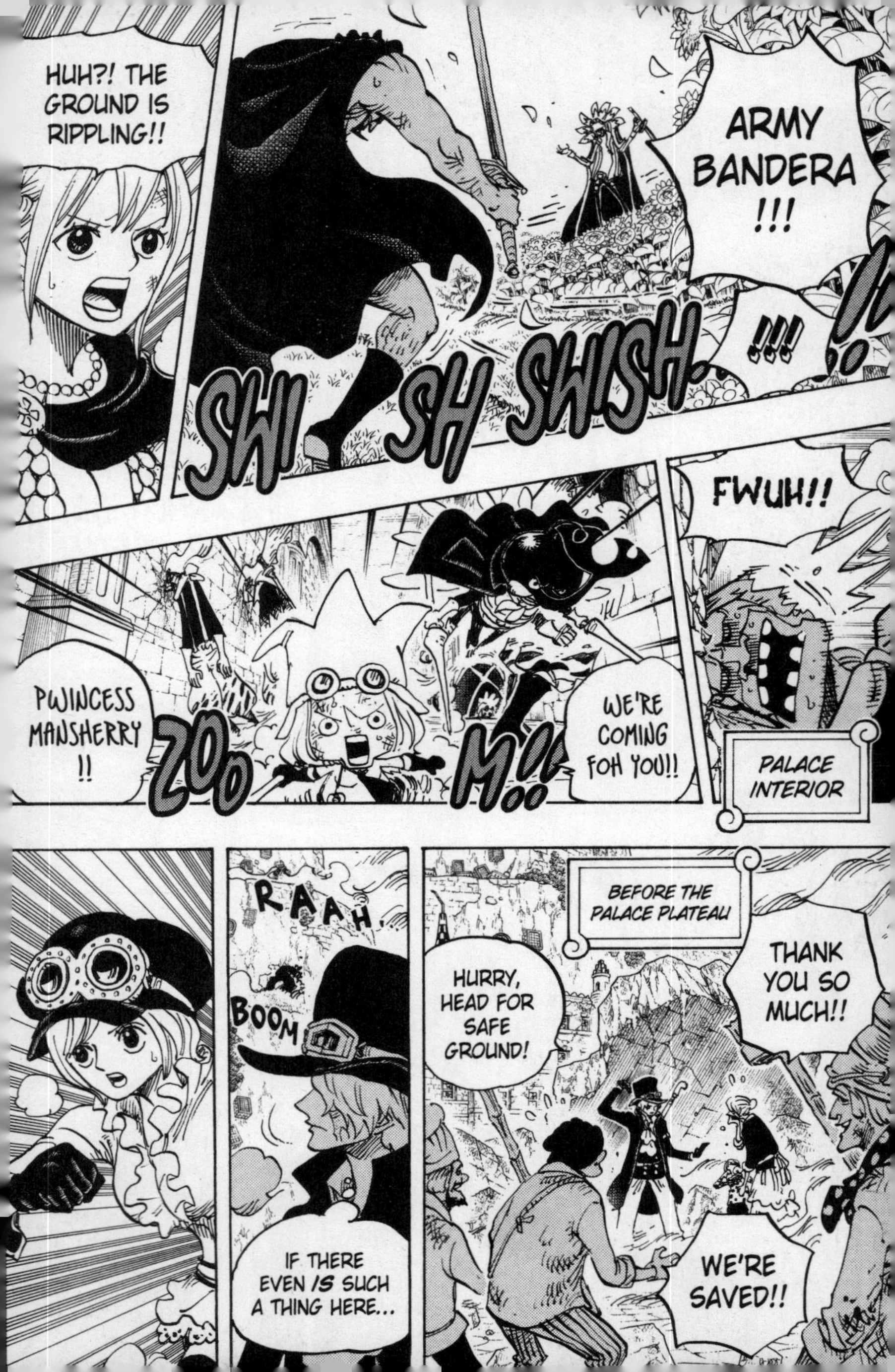
ARMY BANDERA !!!
SHI SH SWISH..!!!
HUH?! THE GROUND IS RIPPLING!!
FWUH!!
PALACE INTERIOR
WE'RE COMING FOH YOU!!
PWINCESS MANSHERRY !!
ZOOM!!
BEFORE THE PALACE PLATEAU
THANK YOU SO MUCH!!
HURRY, HEAD FOR SAFE GROUND!
WE'RE SAVED!!
RAAH..
BOOM
IF THERE EVEN *IS* SUCH A THING HERE...

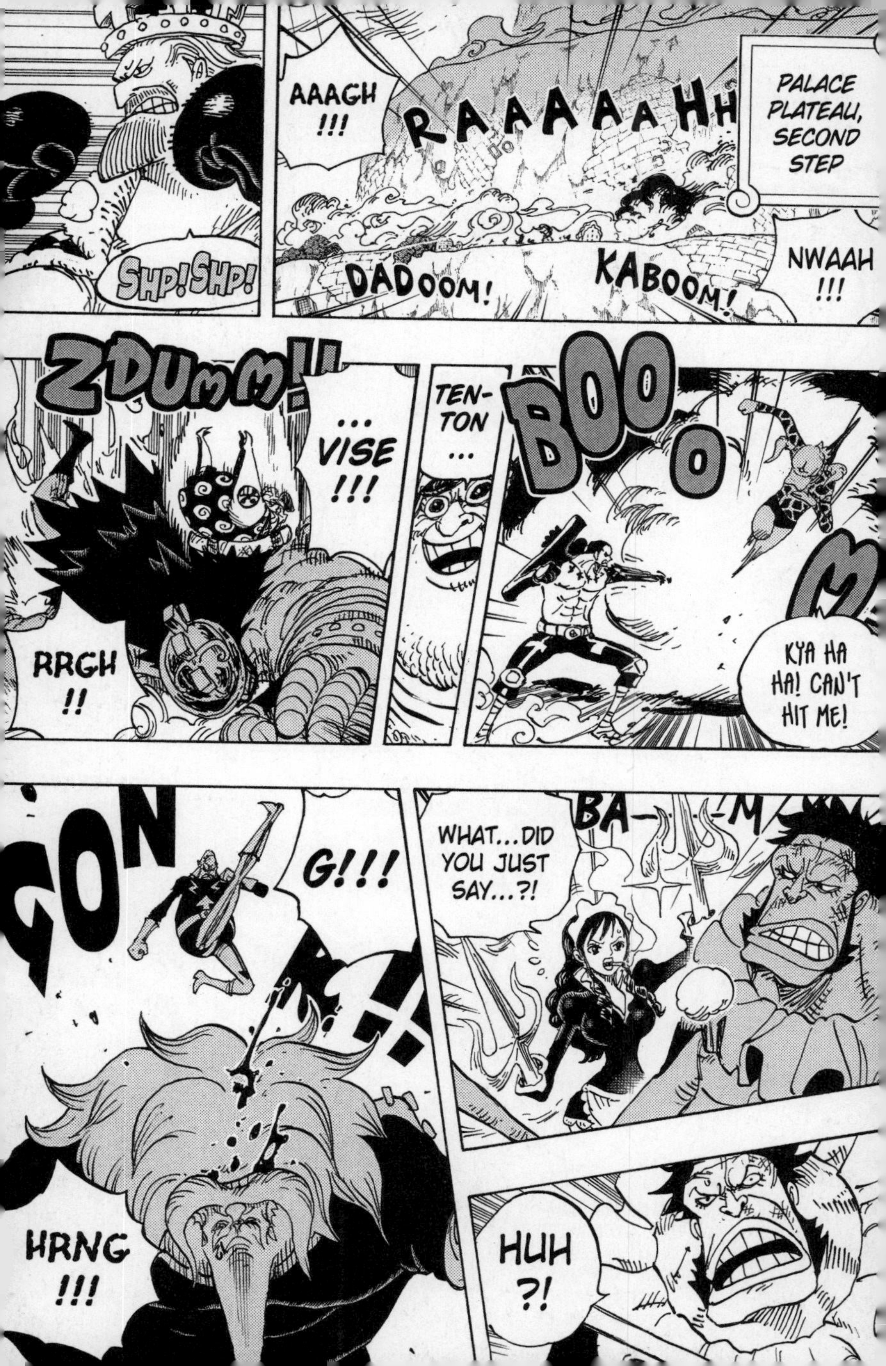

PALACE PLATEAU, SECOND STEP
RAAAAAHH
AAAGH !!!
NWAAH !!!
KABOOM!
DADOOM!
SHP! SHP!
BOOOM
KYA HA HA! CAN'T HIT ME!
TEN-TON ...
... VISE !!!
ZDUMM!!
RRGH !!
BA--M
WHAT...DID YOU JUST SAY...?!
HUH ?!
GON G!!!
HRNG !!!

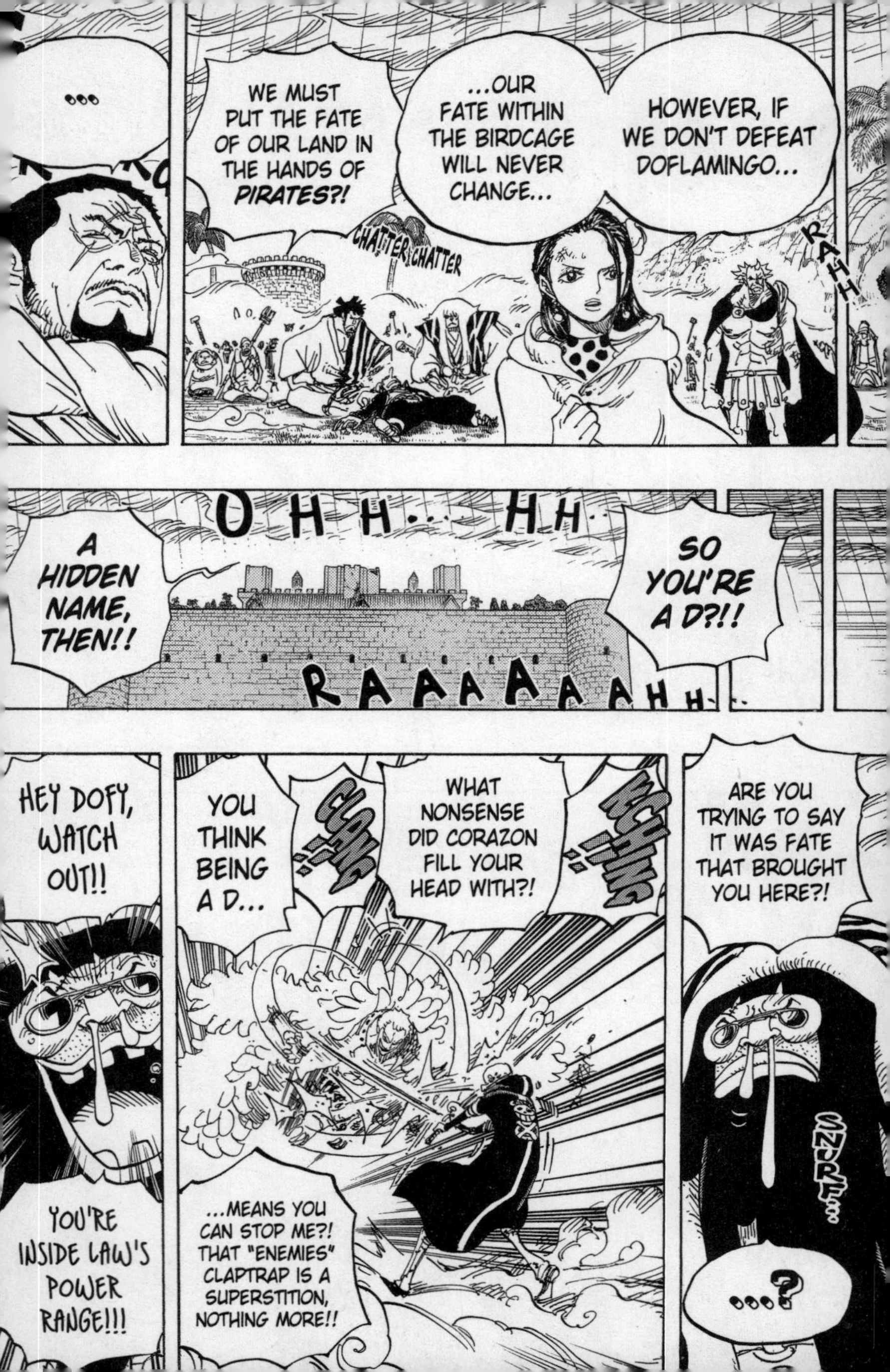
HOWEVER, IF WE DON'T DEFEAT DOFLAMINGO...
...OUR FATE WITHIN THE BIRDCAGE WILL NEVER CHANGE...
RAHH
WE MUST PUT THE FATE OF OUR LAND IN THE HANDS OF PIRATES?!
CHATTER CHATTER
...
SO YOU'RE A D?!!
OHH... HH...
A HIDDEN NAME, THEN!!
RAAAAAAAHHH...
ARE YOU TRYING TO SAY IT WAS FATE THAT BROUGHT YOU HERE?!
SNURF...
...?
WHAT NONSENSE DID CORAZON FILL YOUR HEAD WITH?!
KCHING!!
CLANG!!
YOU THINK BEING A D...
...MEANS YOU CAN STOP ME?! THAT "ENEMIES" CLAPTRAP IS A SUPERSTITION, NOTHING MORE!!
HEY DOFY, WATCH OUT!!
YOU'RE INSIDE LAW'S POWER RANGE!!!

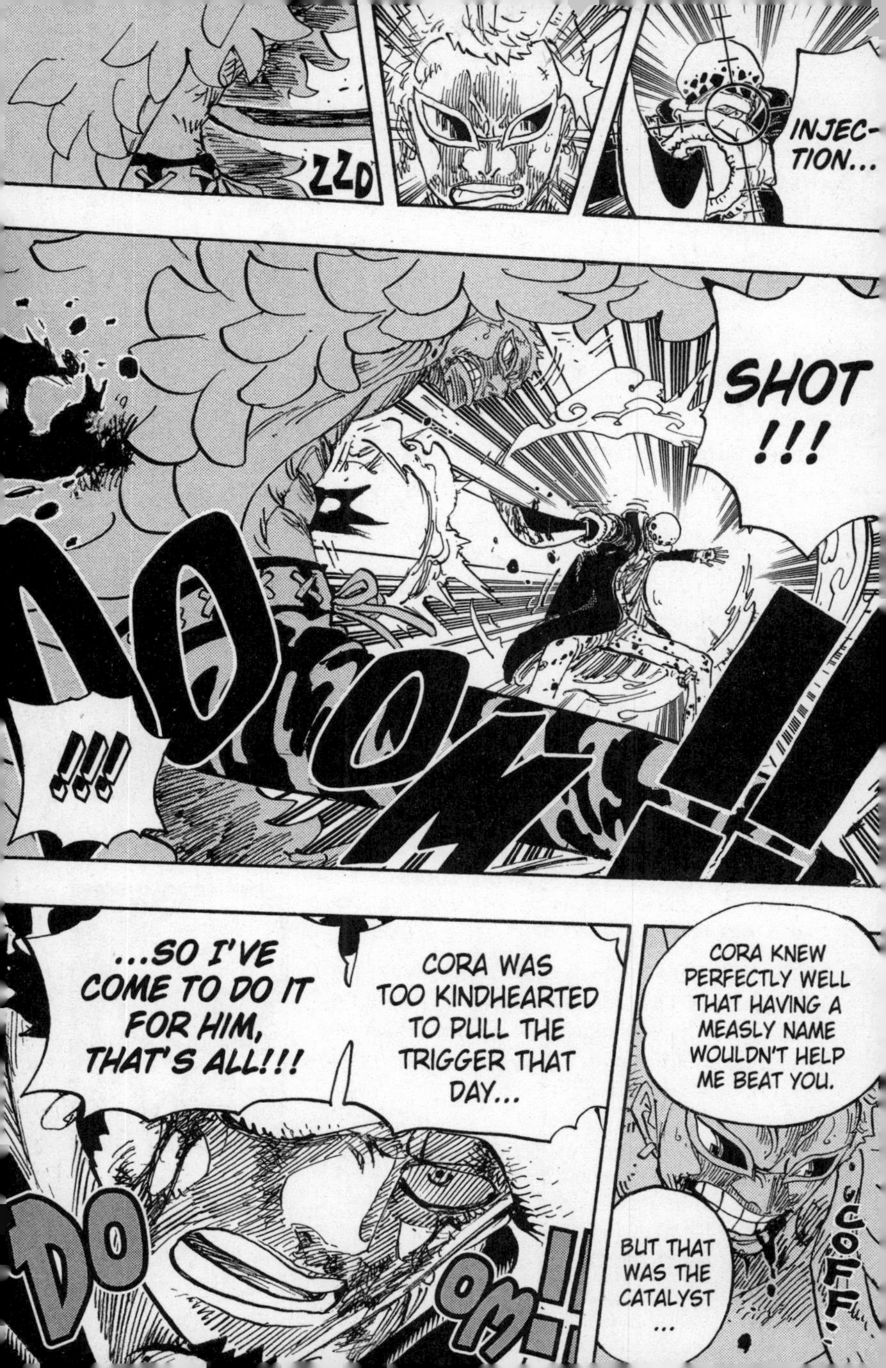
INJEC-TION...
ZZD
SHOT!!!
DOOM!!
!!!
CORA KNEW PERFECTLY WELL THAT HAVING A MEASLY NAME WOULDN'T HELP ME BEAT YOU.
BUT THAT WAS THE CATALYST ...
COFF
CORA WAS TOO KINDHEARTED TO PULL THE TRIGGER THAT DAY...
...SO I'VE COME TO DO IT FOR HIM, THAT'S ALL!!!
DOOM!!

SBS Question Corner

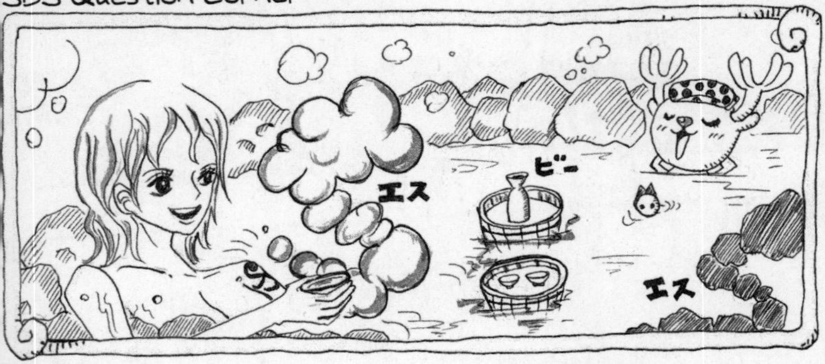
エス
ビー
エス

(Ayumi Yamauchi, Hyogo)

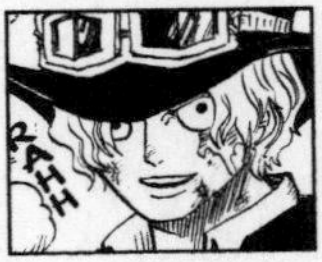
RAHH

Q: Is the scar on Sabo's face...
From when he fought me?!

A: No.

Q: I have a question. The symbol on the back of Law's jacket says "corazon" on it. Is this referring to Law's beloved Cora? Does it mean Law's jacket was custom-made?

--Himeji

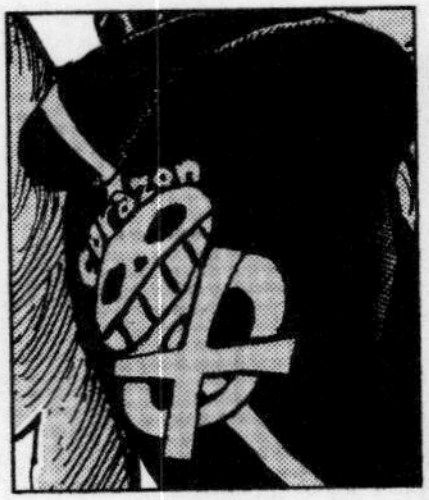
corazon

A: Yes, it says "corazon," which is Spanish for "heart." While this is Cora's code name within the organization, it also makes sense for the captain of the "Heart Pirates" to wear it. And Law's powers make him the "Surgeon of Death" who is able to remove the hearts of others. While this might make the symbol seem frightful to the rest of the world, naturally Law wears it in tribute to Cora. And yes, it's custom-made.

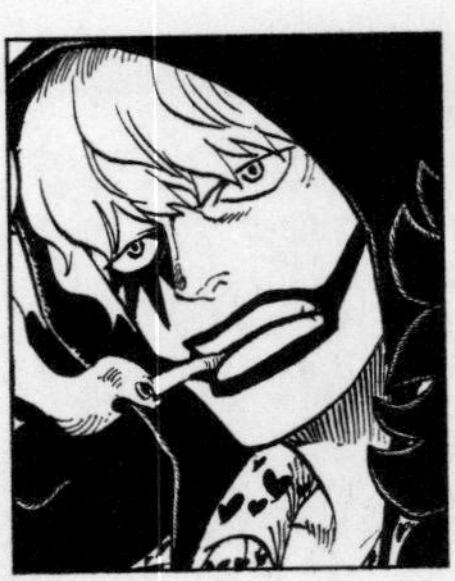

Q: Hello, Oda Sensei. Did the name Rocinante come from the novel by Cervantes? I noticed that in the book, Don Quixote rides a horse named Rocinante, so I thought I'd write in to ask. I'm looking forward to your detailed answer!!

--0196

A: Yes, you're referring to Don Quixote, the satirical novel of the foolish knight of the same name. Here's your detailed explanation!!
I just felt like it.

Chapter 769: BELLAMY THE PIRATE

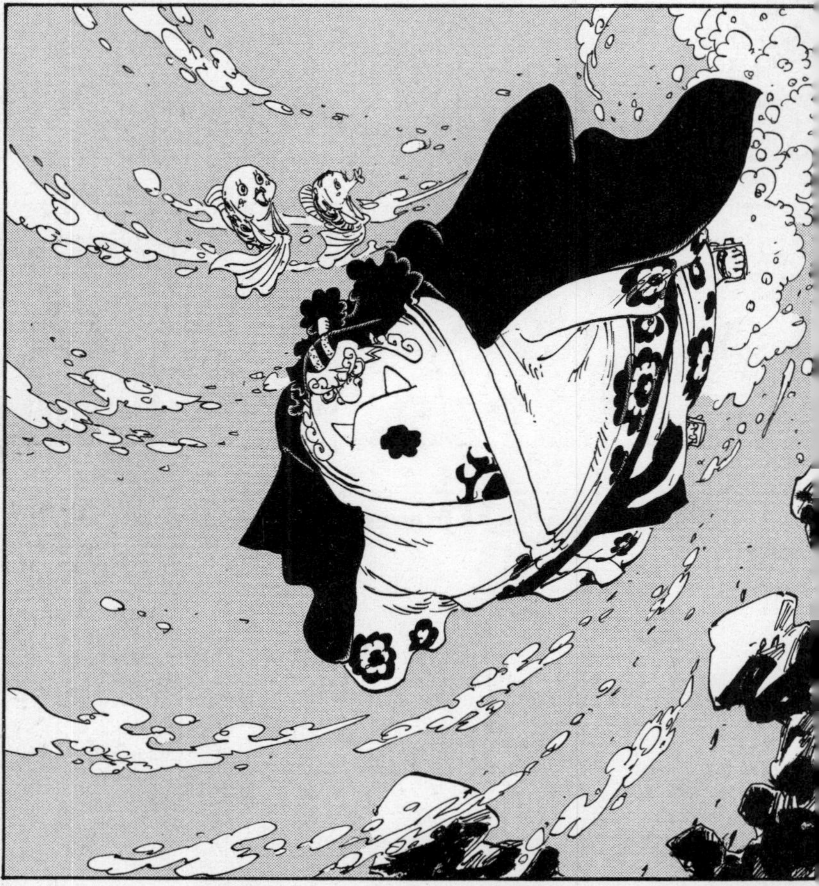

THE SOLITARY JOURNEY OF JIMBEI, FIRST SON OF THE SEA, VOL. 16: "A SHADOW VANISHES INTO THE DEPTHS! THE CULPRIT IS IN THE WATER!!"

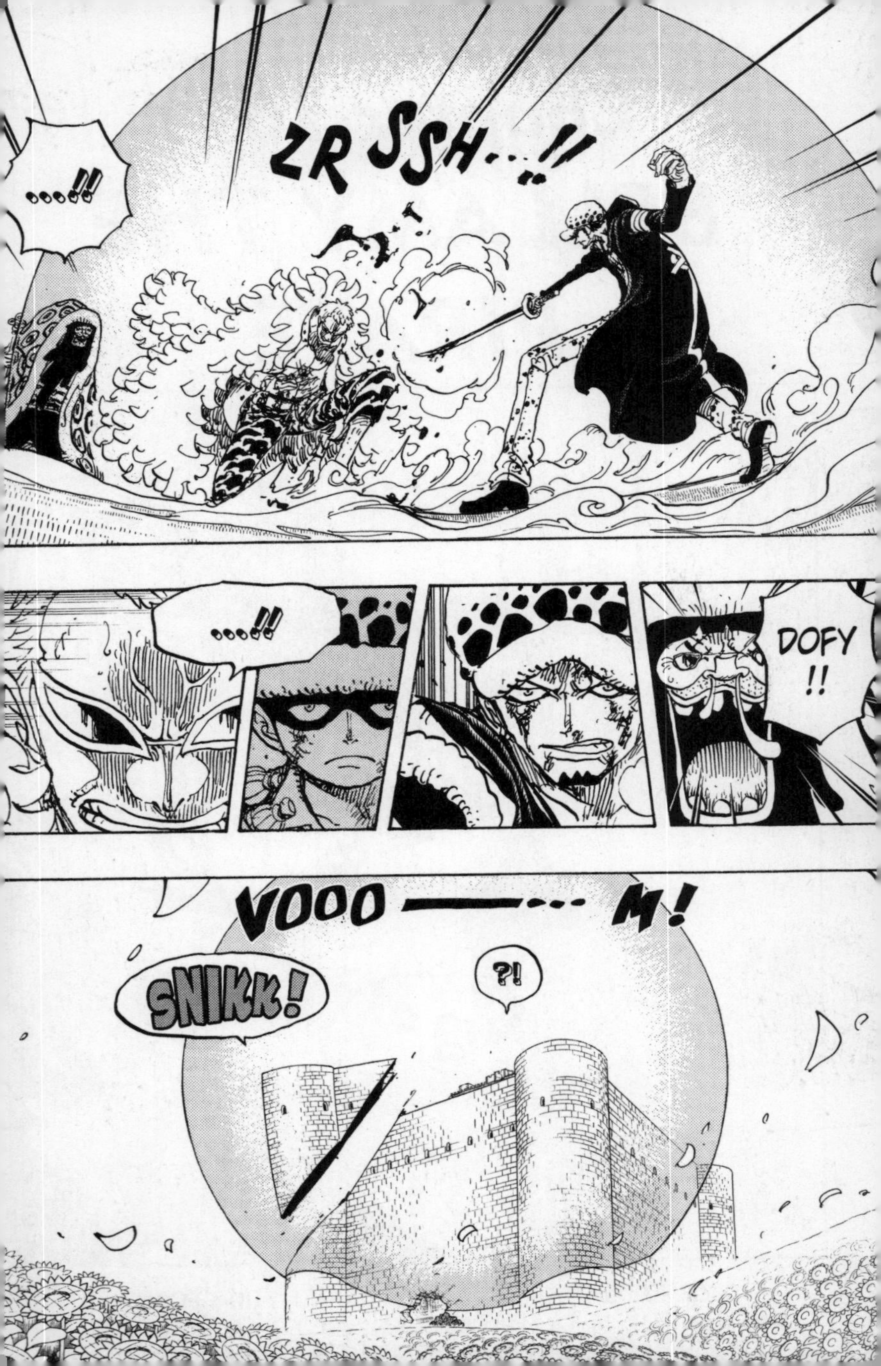
ZR SSH...!!
....!!
DOFY !!
....!!
VOOO———... M!
?!
SNIKK!

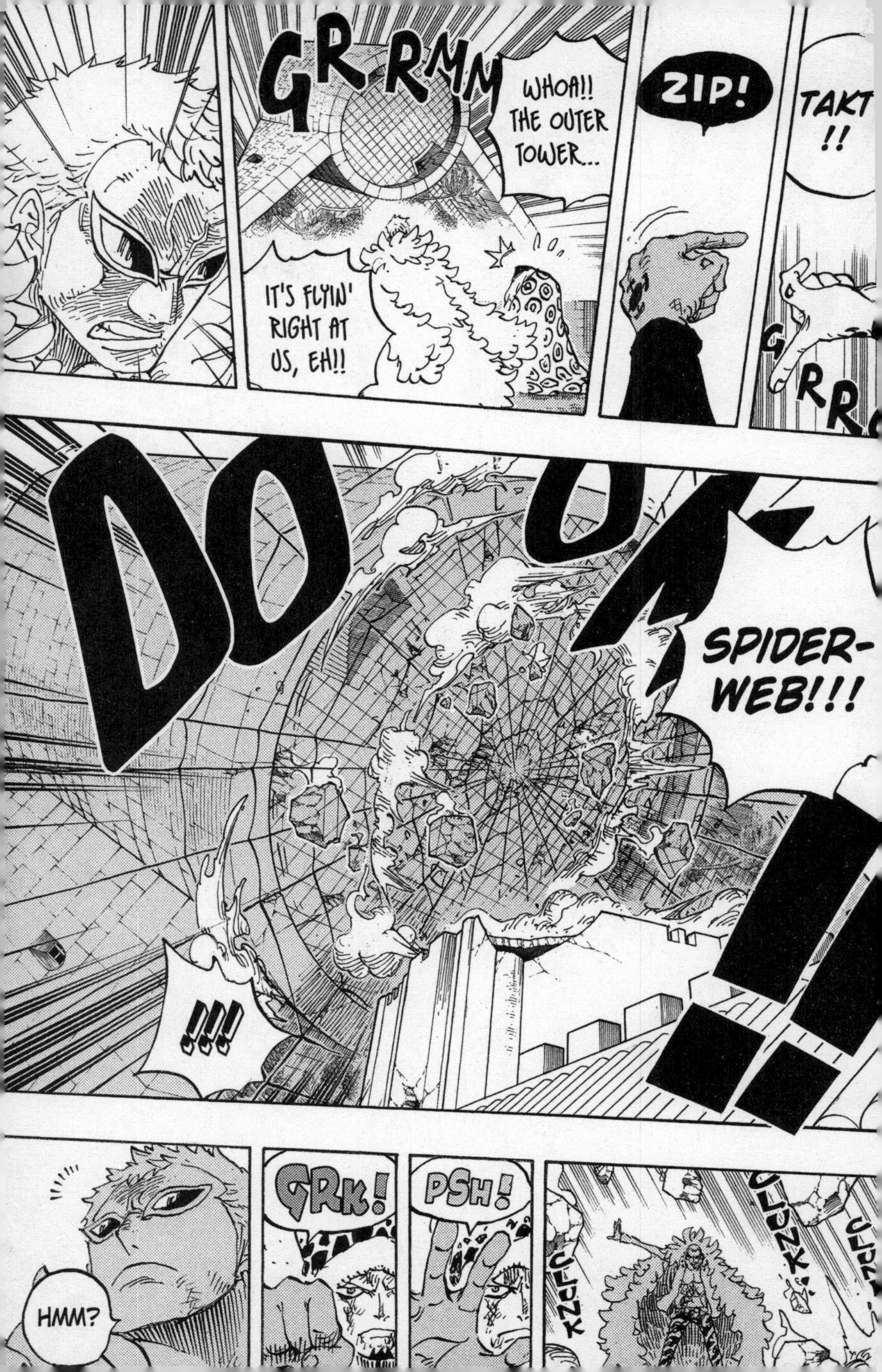
TAKT !!
GRR
ZIP!
GRRMN
WHOA!! THE OUTER TOWER...
IT'S FLYIN' RIGHT AT US, EH!!
SPIDER-WEB!!!
!!!
CLUNK
CLUNK
CLUNK
PSH!
GRK!
HMM?

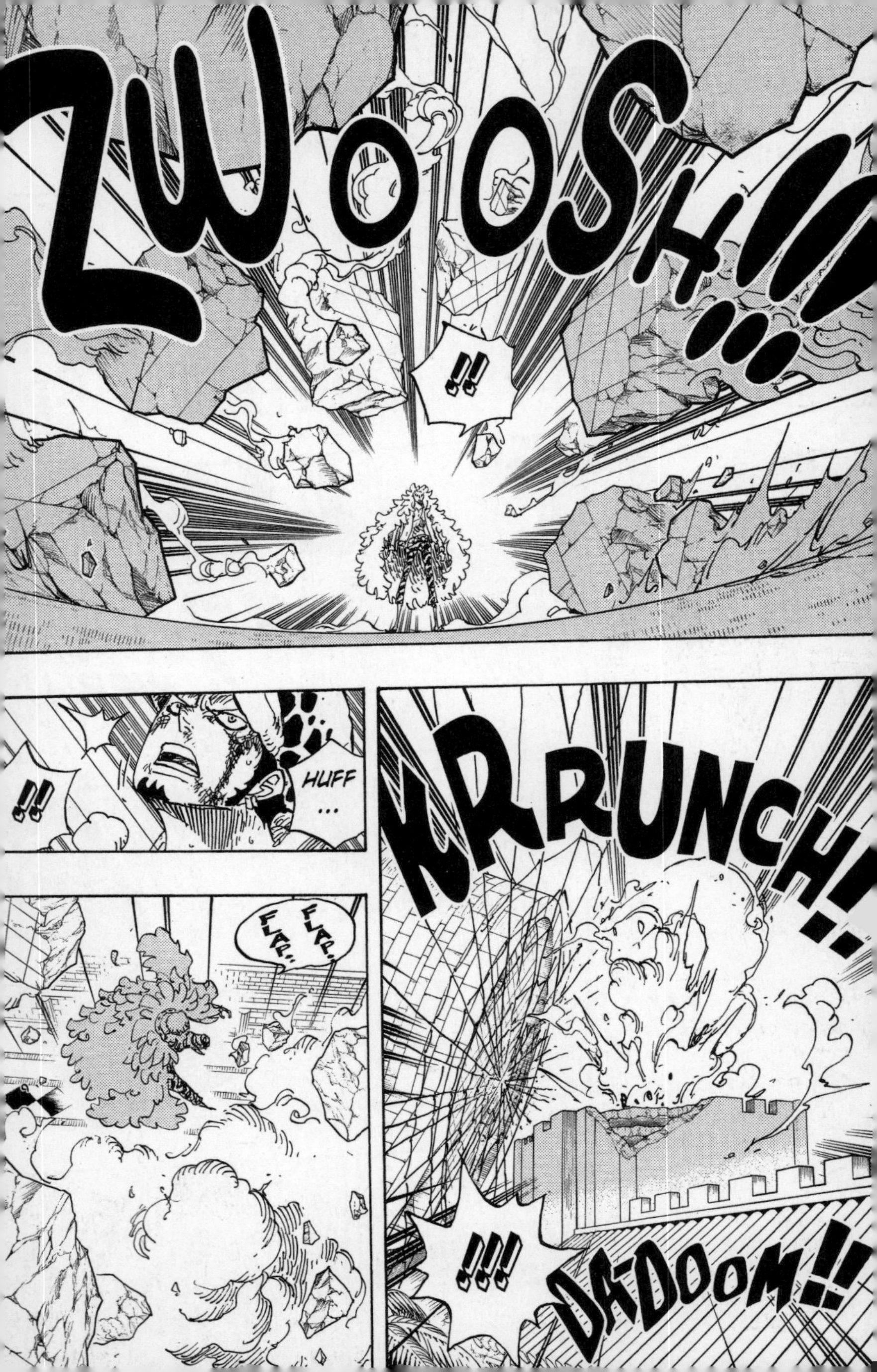
ZWOOSH!!...
!!
KRRUNCH!!
!!!
DADOOM!!
!!
HUFF ...
FLAP. FLAP.

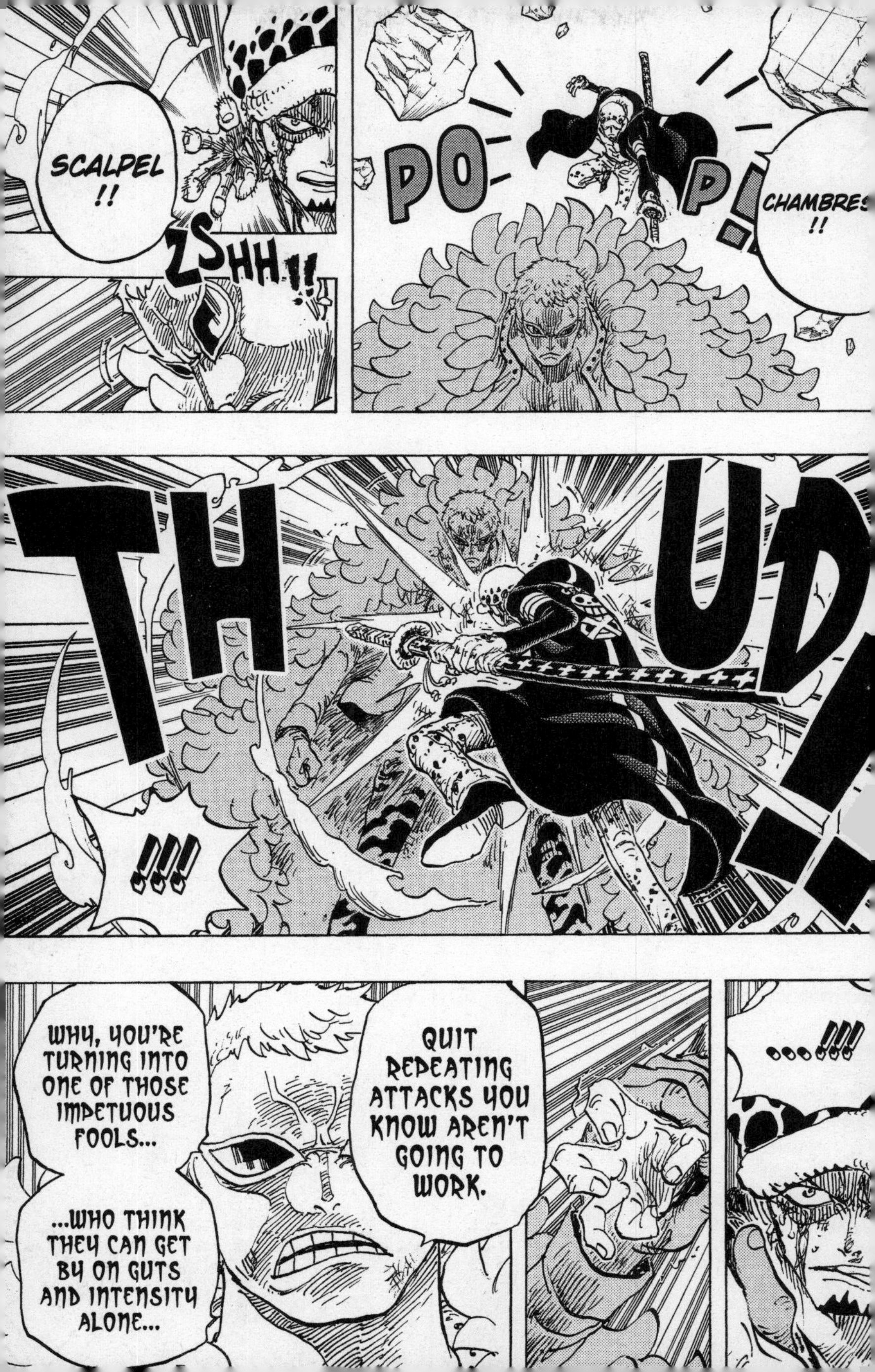

POP!
CHAMBRES !!
SCALPEL !!
ZSHH!!
THUD...!!
!!!
...!!!
QUIT REPEATING ATTACKS YOU KNOW AREN'T GOING TO WORK.
WHY, YOU'RE TURNING INTO ONE OF THOSE IMPETUOUS FOOLS...
...WHO THINK THEY CAN GET BY ON GUTS AND INTENSITY ALONE...

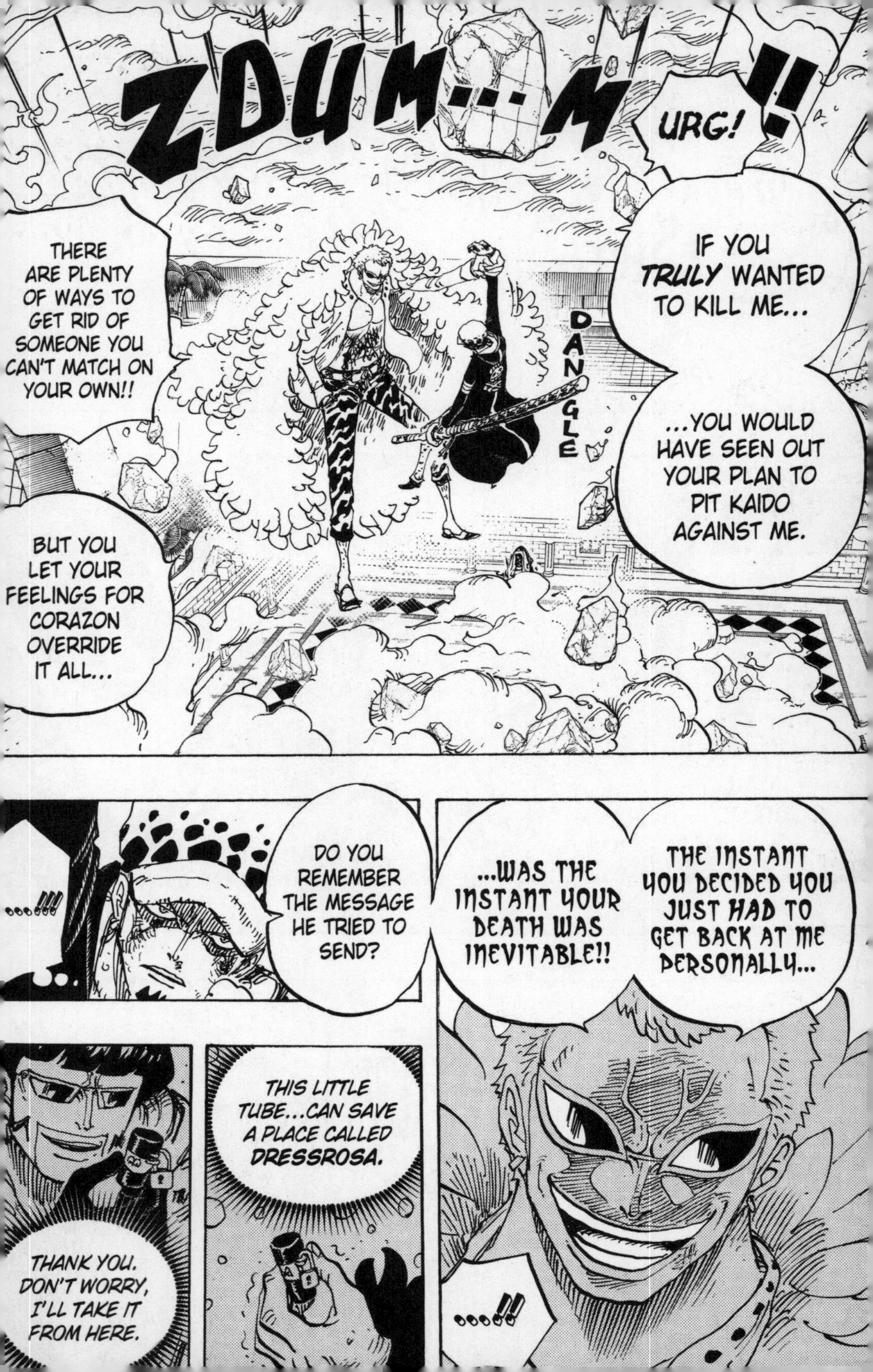
ZDUM...M!!
URG!
DANGLE
IF YOU TRULY WANTED TO KILL ME...
...YOU WOULD HAVE SEEN OUT YOUR PLAN TO PIT KAIDO AGAINST ME.
THERE ARE PLENTY OF WAYS TO GET RID OF SOMEONE YOU CAN'T MATCH ON YOUR OWN!!
BUT YOU LET YOUR FEELINGS FOR CORAZON OVERRIDE IT ALL...
THE INSTANT YOU DECIDED YOU JUST HAD TO GET BACK AT ME PERSONALLY...
...WAS THE INSTANT YOUR DEATH WAS INEVITABLE!!
...!!
DO YOU REMEMBER THE MESSAGE HE TRIED TO SEND?
...!!!
THIS LITTLE TUBE...CAN SAVE A PLACE CALLED DRESSROSA.
THANK YOU. DON'T WORRY, I'LL TAKE IT FROM HERE.

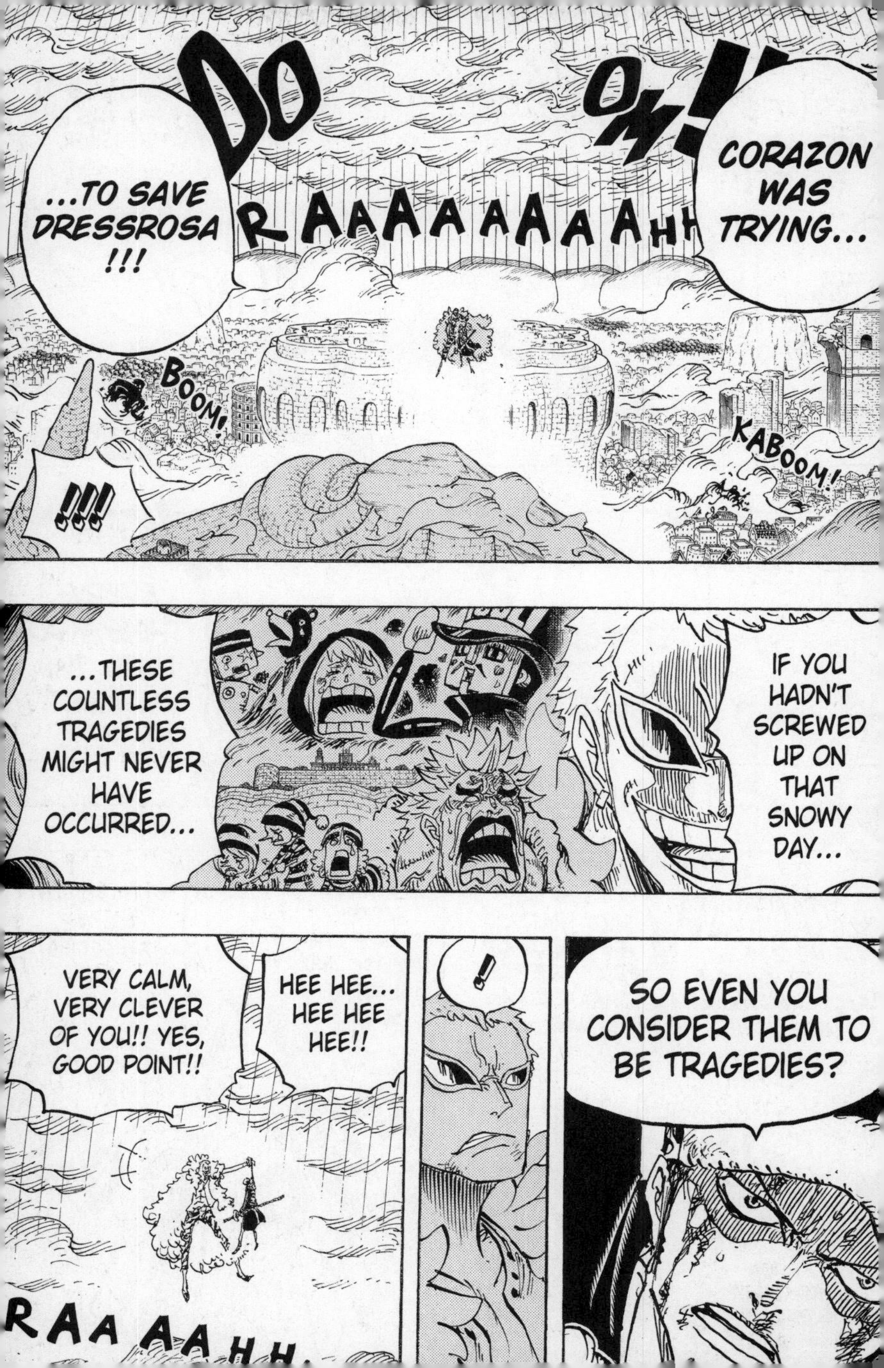
CORAZON WAS TRYING...
DOOM!!
...TO SAVE DRESSROSA!!!
RAAAAAAAAAHH
KABOOM!
BOOM!
!!!
IF YOU HADN'T SCREWED UP ON THAT SNOWY DAY...
...THESE COUNTLESS TRAGEDIES MIGHT NEVER HAVE OCCURRED...
SO EVEN YOU CONSIDER THEM TO BE TRAGEDIES?
!
HEE HEE... HEE HEE HEE!!
VERY CALM, VERY CLEVER OF YOU!! YES, GOOD POINT!!
RAA AAHH.

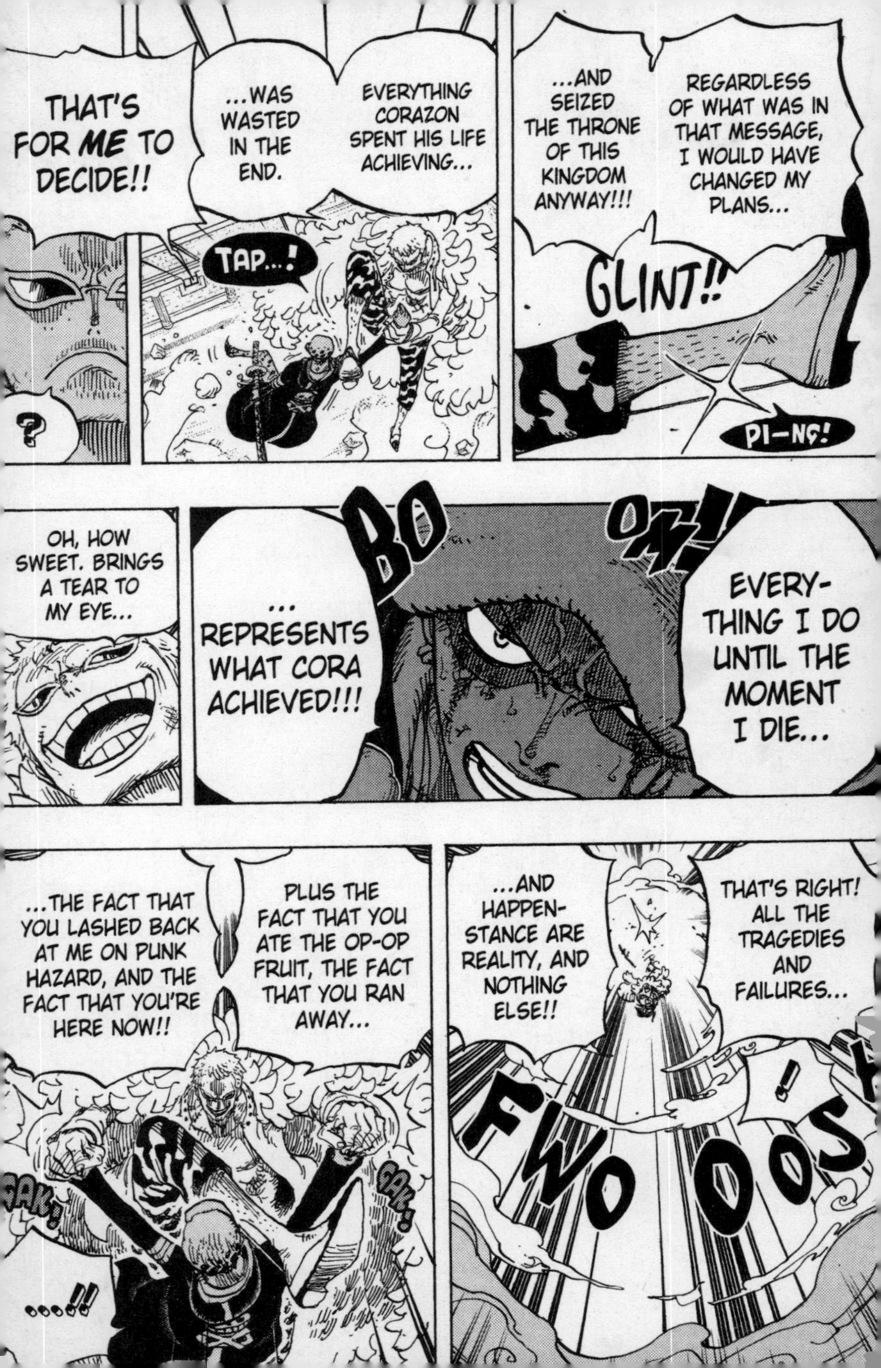
REGARDLESS OF WHAT WAS IN THAT MESSAGE, I WOULD HAVE CHANGED MY PLANS...
...AND SEIZED THE THRONE OF THIS KINGDOM ANYWAY!!!
GLINT!!
PI-NG!
EVERYTHING CORAZON SPENT HIS LIFE ACHIEVING...
...WAS WASTED IN THE END.
TAP...!
THAT'S FOR ME TO DECIDE!!
?
EVERY-THING I DO UNTIL THE MOMENT I DIE...
BOOM!!
... REPRESENTS WHAT CORA ACHIEVED!!!
OH, HOW SWEET. BRINGS A TEAR TO MY EYE...
THAT'S RIGHT! ALL THE TRAGEDIES AND FAILURES...
...AND HAPPEN-STANCE ARE REALITY, AND NOTHING ELSE!!
!
FWOOOS
PLUS THE FACT THAT YOU ATE THE OP-OP FRUIT, THE FACT THAT YOU RAN AWAY...
...THE FACT THAT YOU LASHED BACK AT ME ON PUNK HAZARD, AND THE FACT THAT YOU'RE HERE NOW!!
GAK!
GAK!
....!!

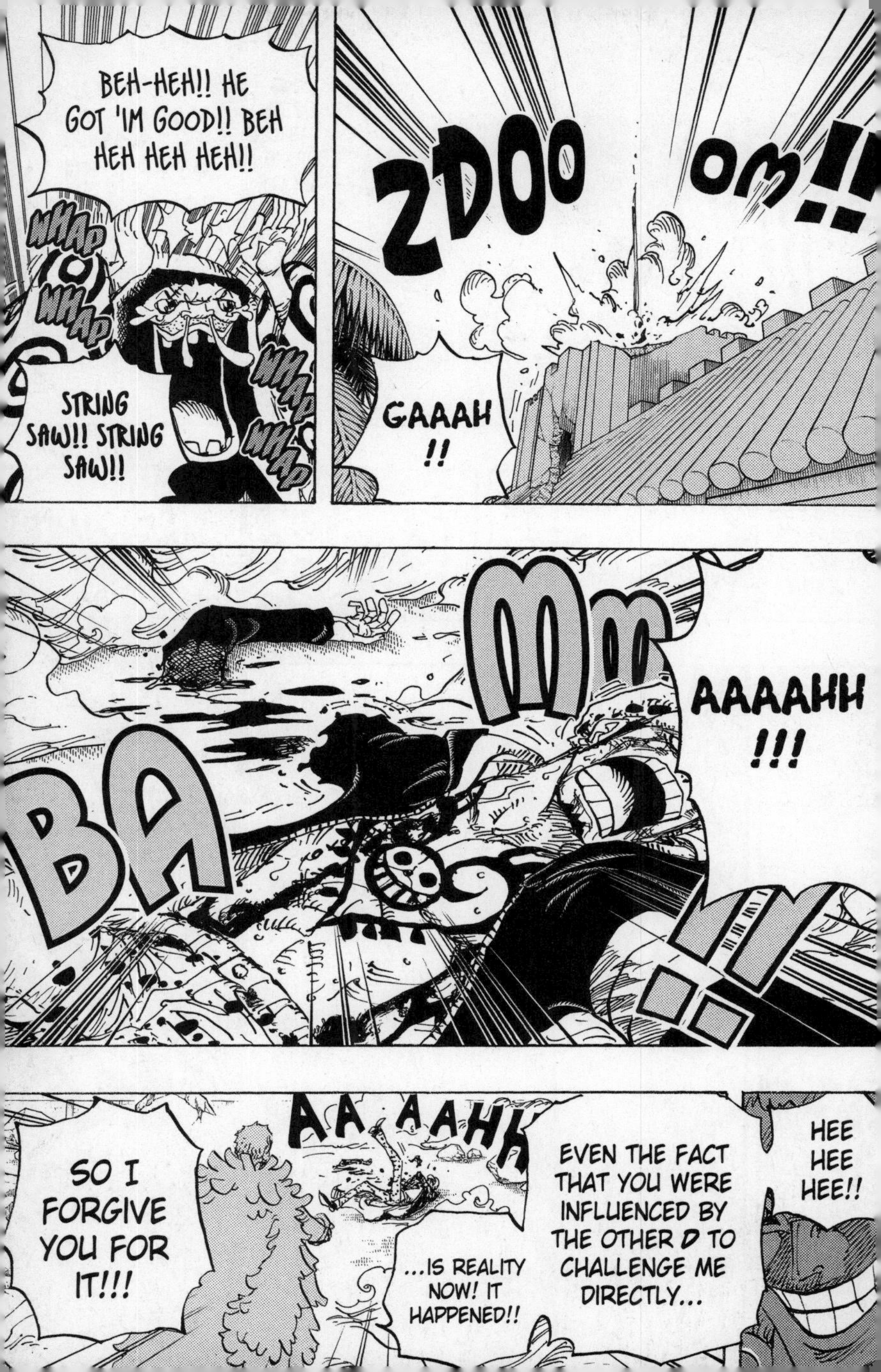
ZDOOOM!!
GAAAH!!
BEH-HEH!! HE GOT 'IM GOOD!! BEH HEH HEH HEH!!
WHAP WHAP
WHAP WHAP
STRING SAW!! STRING SAW!!
AAAAHH!!!
BA MM !!
HEE HEE HEE!!
EVEN THE FACT THAT YOU WERE INFLUENCED BY THE OTHER D TO CHALLENGE ME DIRECTLY...
...IS REALITY NOW! IT HAPPENED!!
AA AAHH
SO I FORGIVE YOU FOR IT!!!

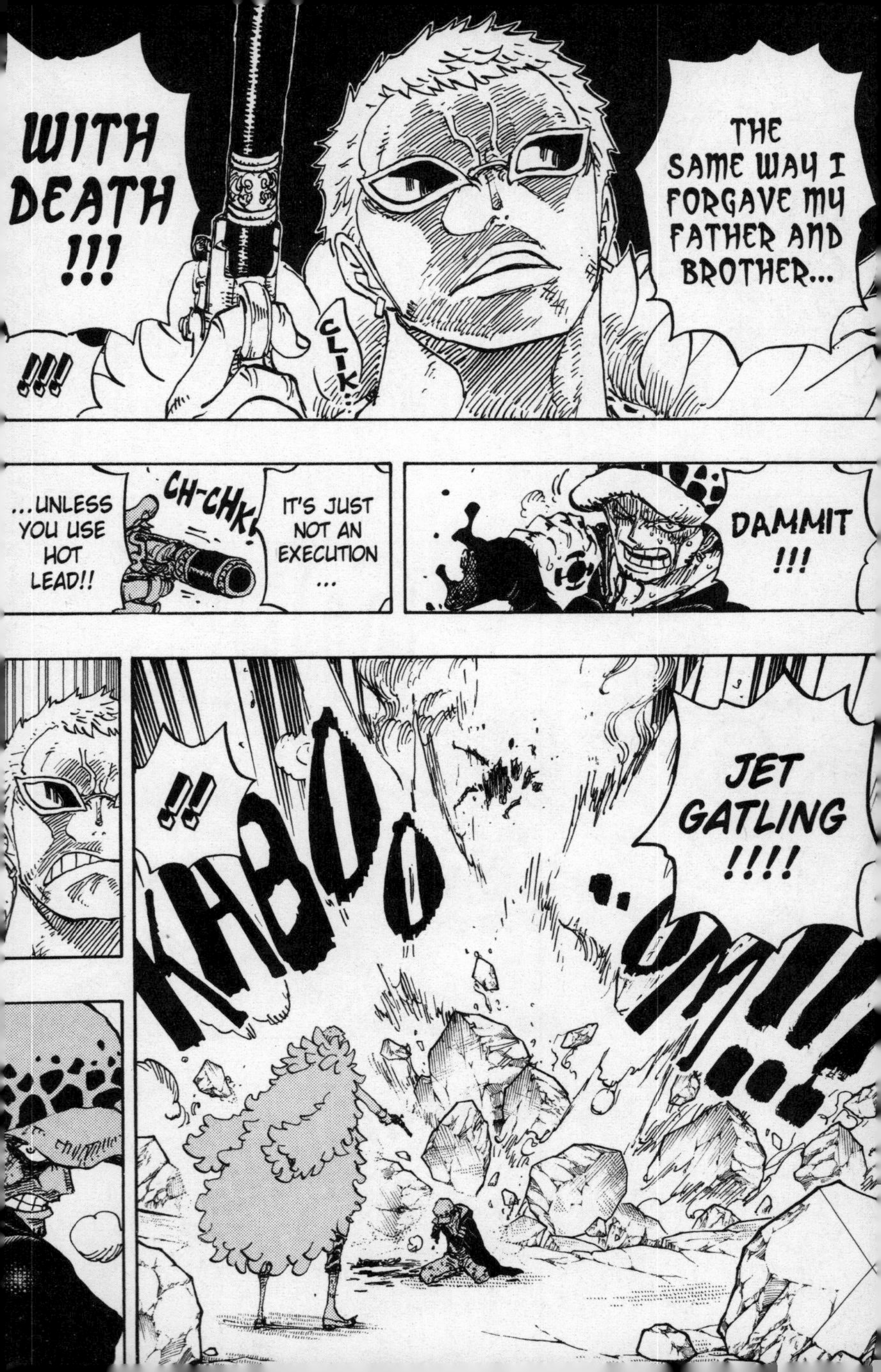
THE SAME WAY I FORGAVE MY FATHER AND BROTHER...
WITH DEATH!!!
CLIK...
!!!
DAMMIT!!!
IT'S JUST NOT AN EXECUTION...
CH-CHK!
...UNLESS YOU USE HOT LEAD!!
JET GATLING!!!!
KHBOOO..OM!!
!!

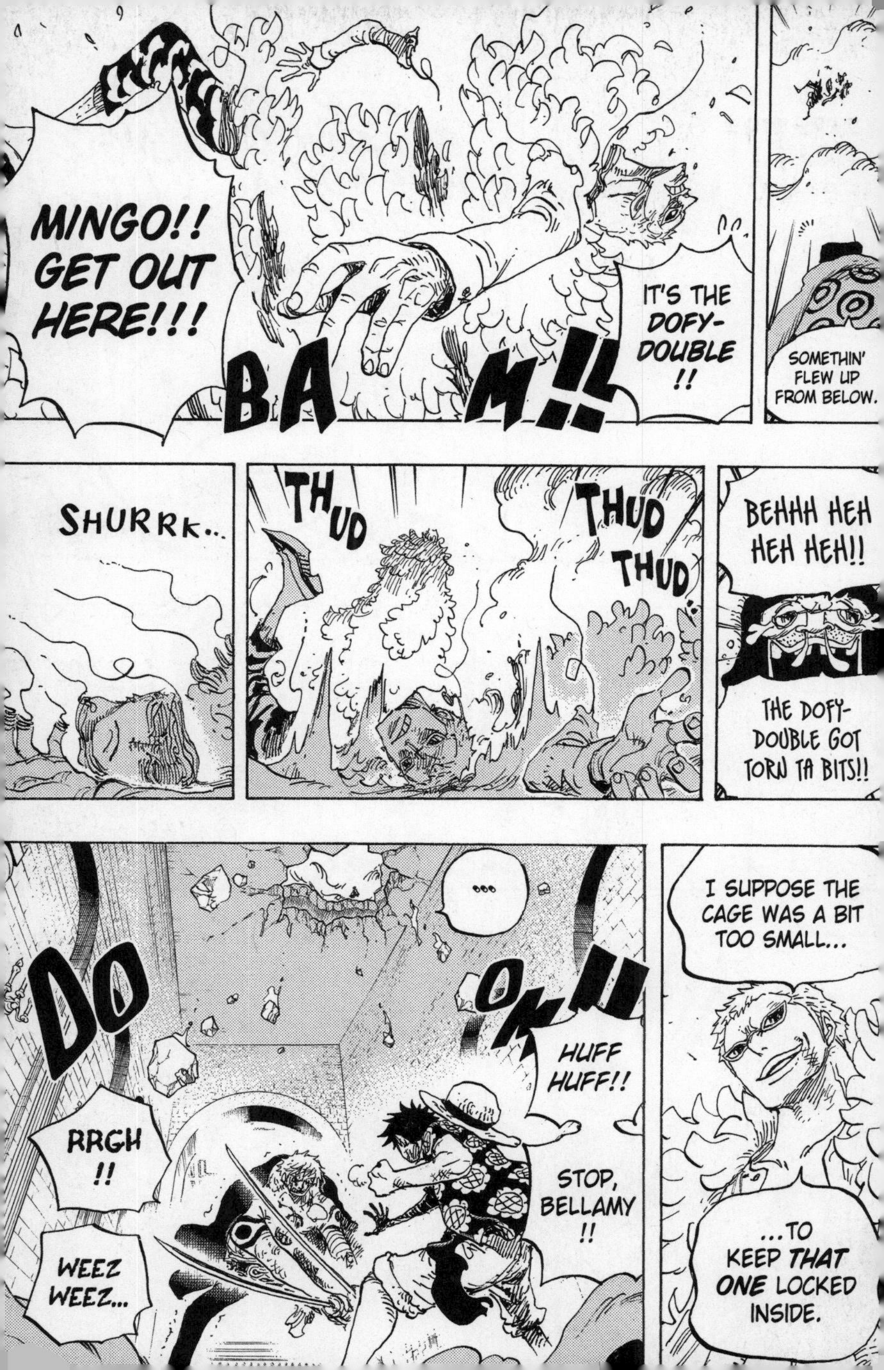
SOMETHIN' FLEW UP FROM BELOW.
IT'S THE DOFY-DOUBLE !!
BAM!!
MINGO!! GET OUT HERE!!!
BEHHH HEH HEH HEH!!
THE DOFY-DOUBLE GOT TORN TA BITS!!
THUD THUD
THUD
SHURRK...
I SUPPOSE THE CAGE WAS A BIT TOO SMALL...
...TO KEEP THAT ONE LOCKED INSIDE.
...
OM!!
HUFF HUFF!!
DO
STOP, BELLAMY !!
RRGH !!
WEEZ WEEZ...

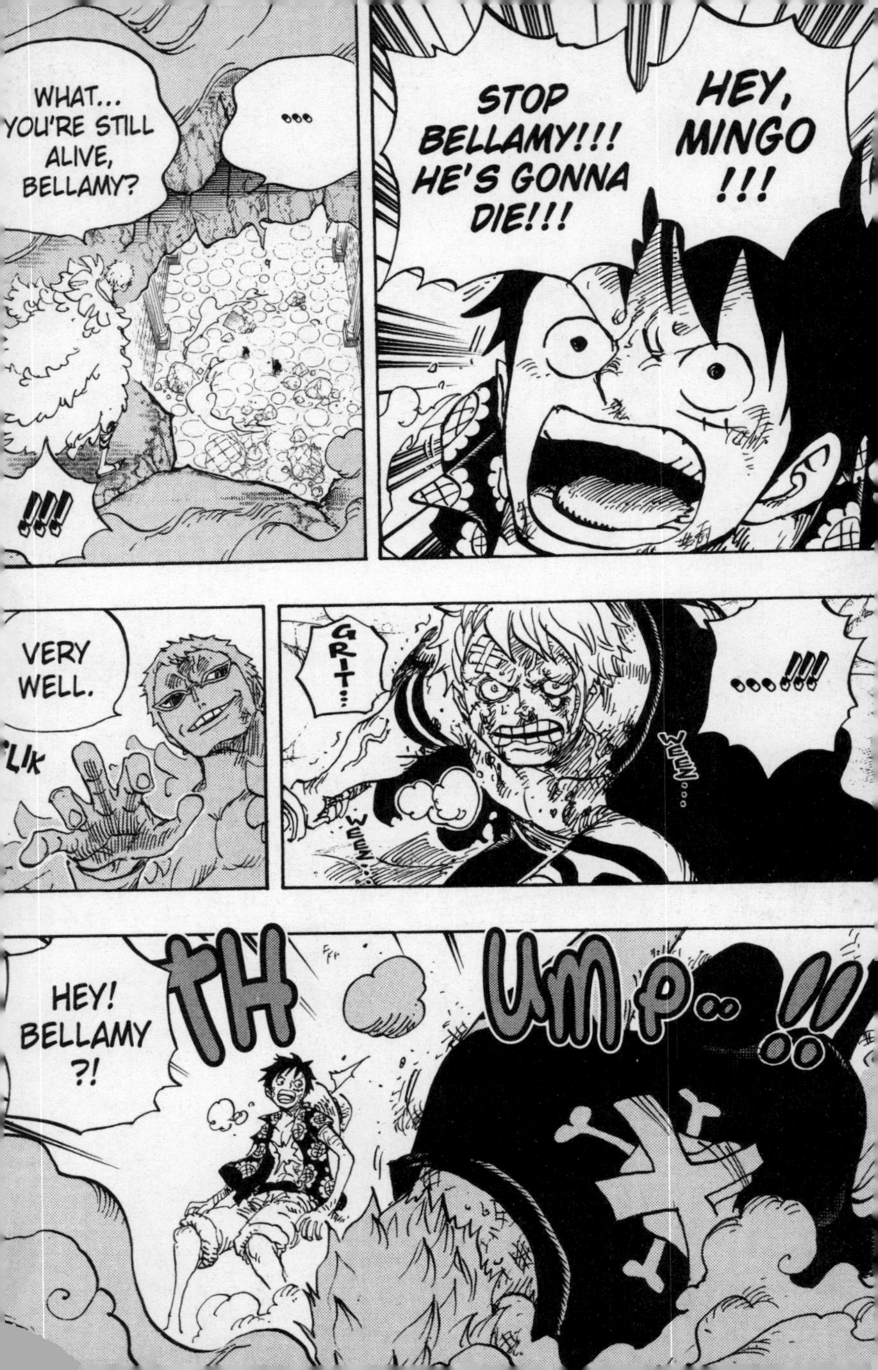
HEY, MINGO!!!
STOP BELLAMY!!! HE'S GONNA DIE!!!
...
WHAT... YOU'RE STILL ALIVE, BELLAMY?
!!!
...!!!
GRIT..
WEEN...
WEEZ...
VERY WELL.
LIK
THUMP..!!
HEY! BELLAMY?!

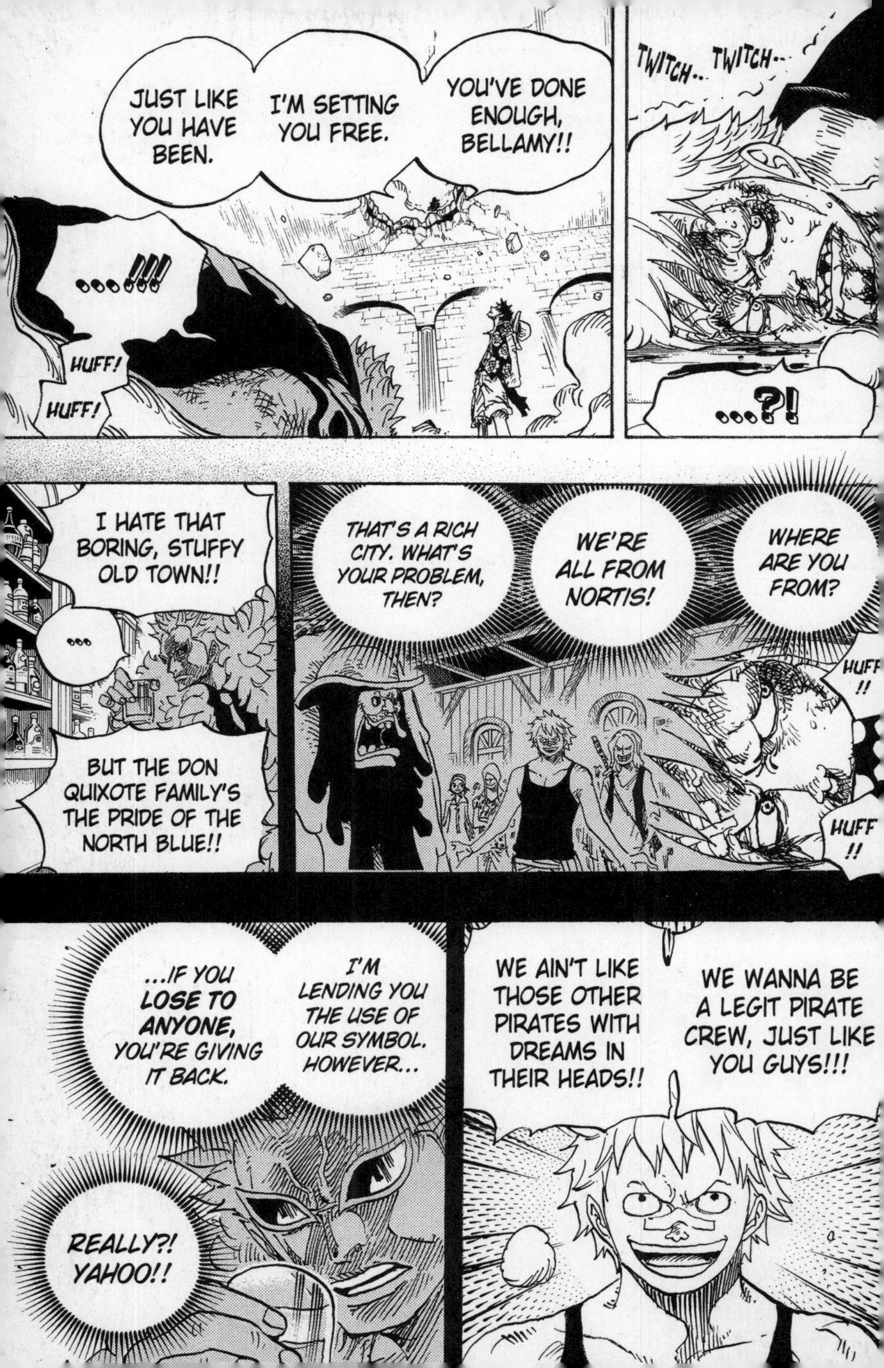
TWITCH... TWITCH...
...?!
YOU'VE DONE ENOUGH, BELLAMY!!
I'M SETTING YOU FREE.
JUST LIKE YOU HAVE BEEN.
...!!!
HUFF!
HUFF!
WHERE ARE YOU FROM?
WE'RE ALL FROM NORTIS!
THAT'S A RICH CITY. WHAT'S YOUR PROBLEM, THEN?
HUFF!!
HUFF!!
I HATE THAT BORING, STUFFY OLD TOWN!!
...
BUT THE DON QUIXOTE FAMILY'S THE PRIDE OF THE NORTH BLUE!!
WE WANNA BE A LEGIT PIRATE CREW, JUST LIKE YOU GUYS!!!
WE AIN'T LIKE THOSE OTHER PIRATES WITH DREAMS IN THEIR HEADS!!
I'M LENDING YOU THE USE OF OUR SYMBOL. HOWEVER...
...IF YOU LOSE TO ANYONE, YOU'RE GIVING IT BACK.
REALLY?! YAHOO!!

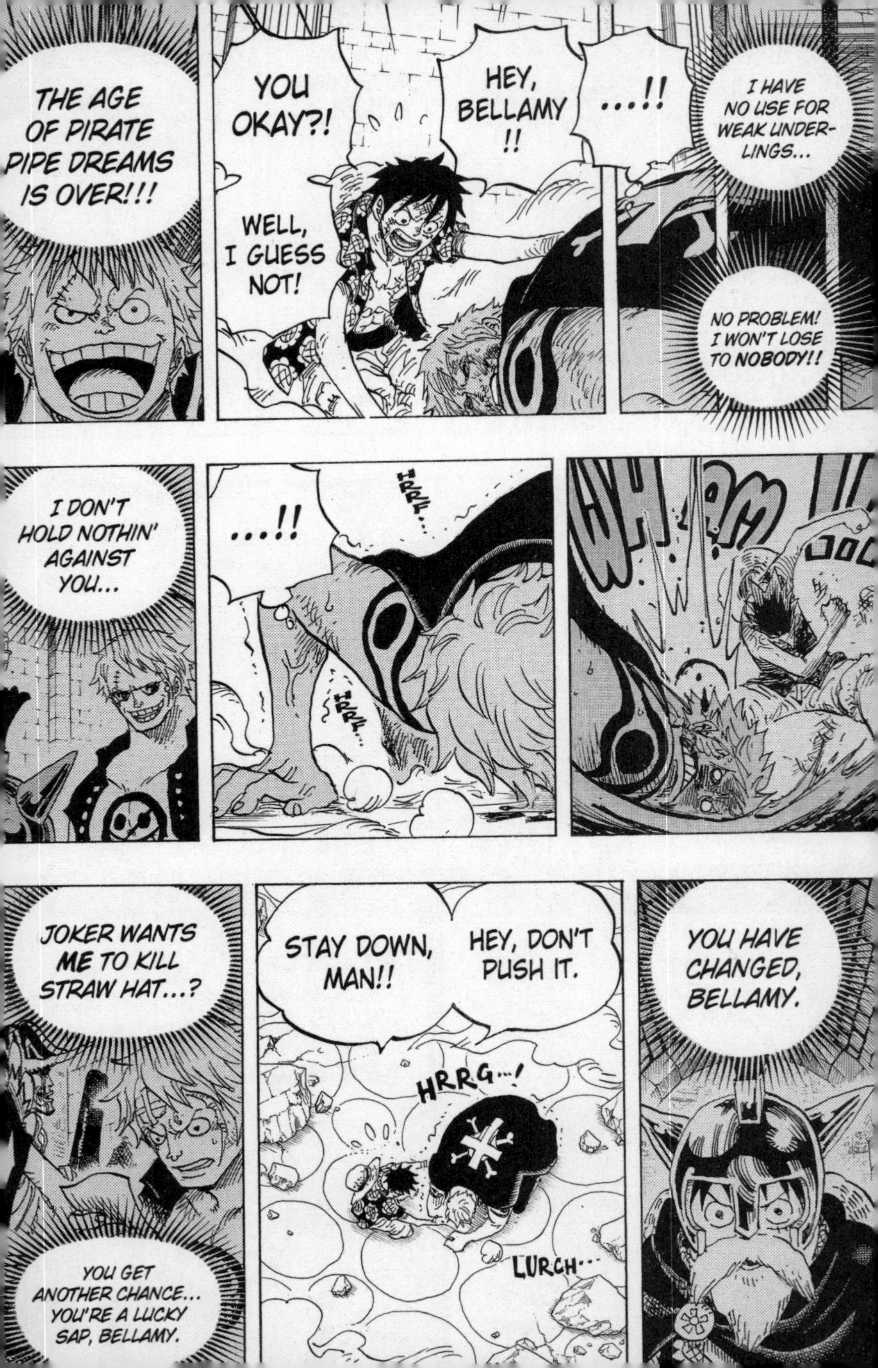
I HAVE NO USE FOR WEAK UNDER-LINGS...
NO PROBLEM! I WON'T LOSE TO NOBODY!!
...!!
HEY, BELLAMY !!
YOU OKAY?!
WELL, I GUESS NOT!
THE AGE OF PIRATE PIPE DREAMS IS OVER!!!
...!!
HRRF...
HRRF...
I DON'T HOLD NOTHIN' AGAINST YOU...
YOU HAVE CHANGED, BELLAMY.
HEY, DON'T PUSH IT.
STAY DOWN, MAN!!
HRRG...!
LURCH...
JOKER WANTS ME TO KILL STRAW HAT...?
YOU GET ANOTHER CHANCE... YOU'RE A LUCKY SAP, BELLAMY.

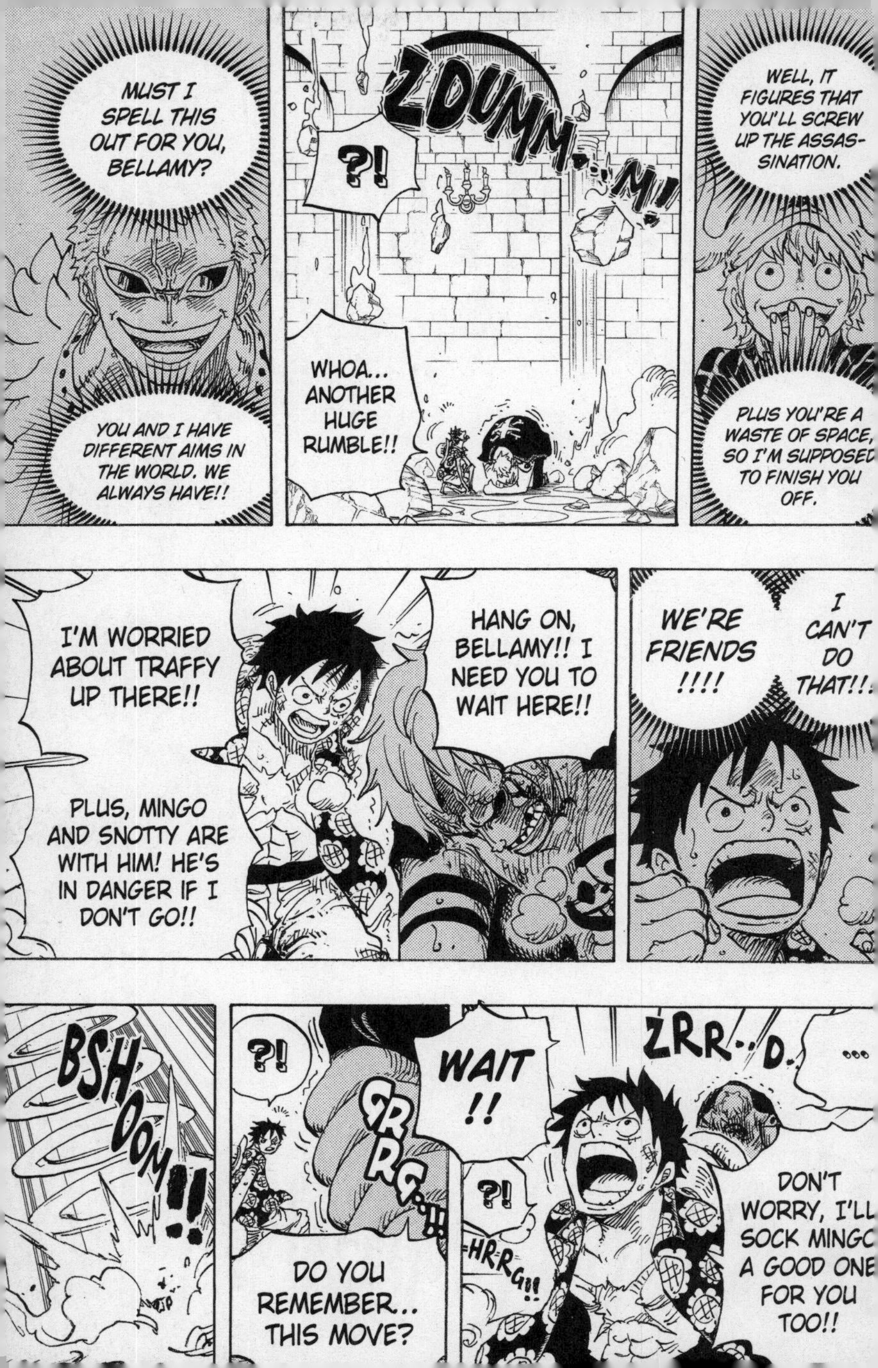
WELL, IT FIGURES THAT YOU'LL SCREW UP THE ASSAS-SINATION.
PLUS YOU'RE A WASTE OF SPACE, SO I'M SUPPOSED TO FINISH YOU OFF.
ZDUMM...M!
?!
WHOA... ANOTHER HUGE RUMBLE!!
MUST I SPELL THIS OUT FOR YOU, BELLAMY?
YOU AND I HAVE DIFFERENT AIMS IN THE WORLD. WE ALWAYS HAVE!!
I CAN'T DO THAT!!
WE'RE FRIENDS!!!!
HANG ON, BELLAMY!! I NEED YOU TO WAIT HERE!!
I'M WORRIED ABOUT TRAFFY UP THERE!!
PLUS, MINGO AND SNOTTY ARE WITH HIM! HE'S IN DANGER IF I DON'T GO!!
ZRR..D..
...
WAIT!!
DON'T WORRY, I'LL SOCK MINGO A GOOD ONE FOR YOU TOO!!
?!
HR-RG!!
?!
GRRG..!!
DO YOU REMEMBER... THIS MOVE?
BSHOOOM!!

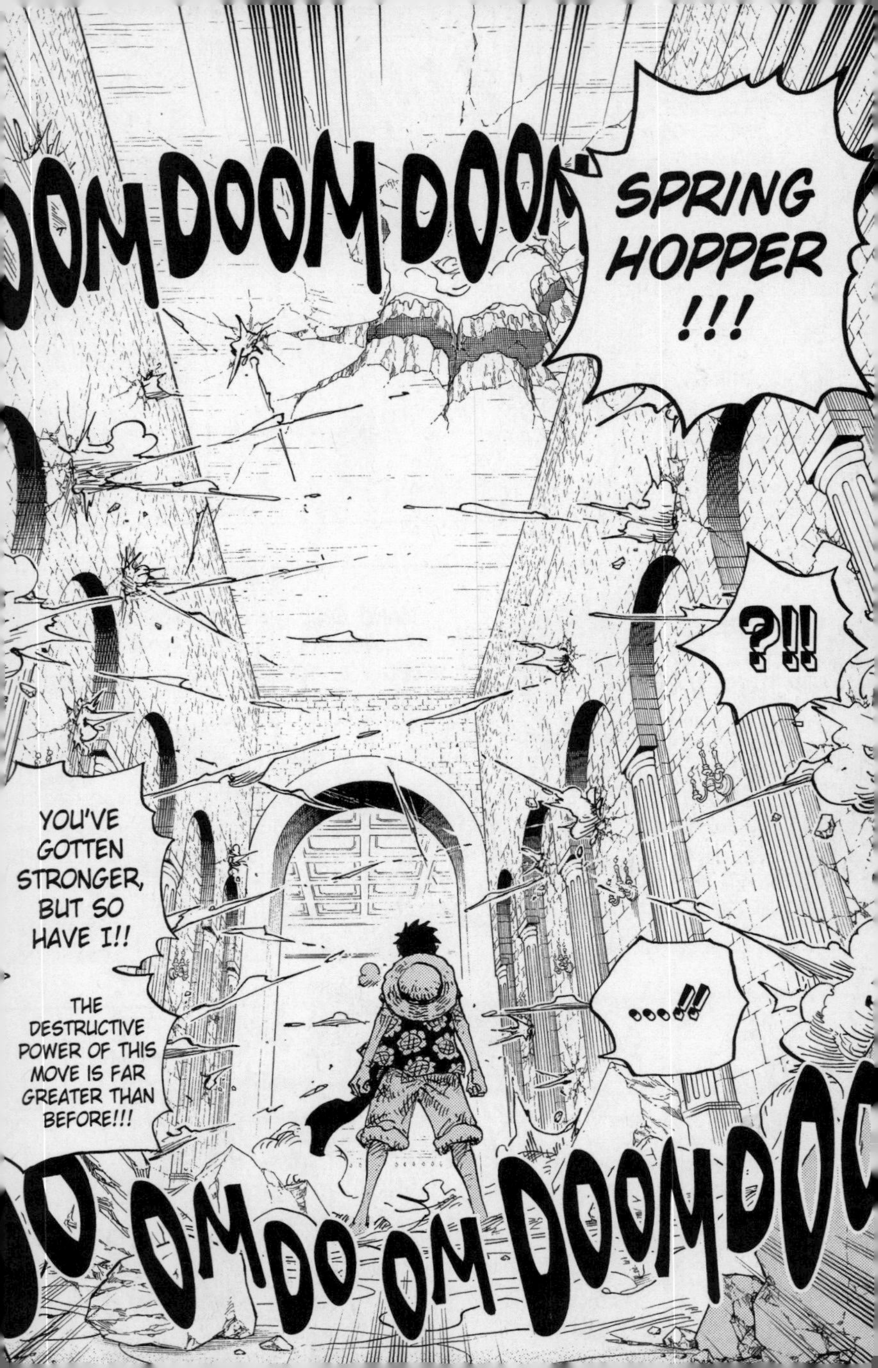
SPRING HOPPER!!!
DOOM DOOM
?!!
...!!
YOU'VE GOTTEN STRONGER, BUT SO HAVE I!!
THE DESTRUCTIVE POWER OF THIS MOVE IS FAR GREATER THAN BEFORE!!!
DOOM DOOM

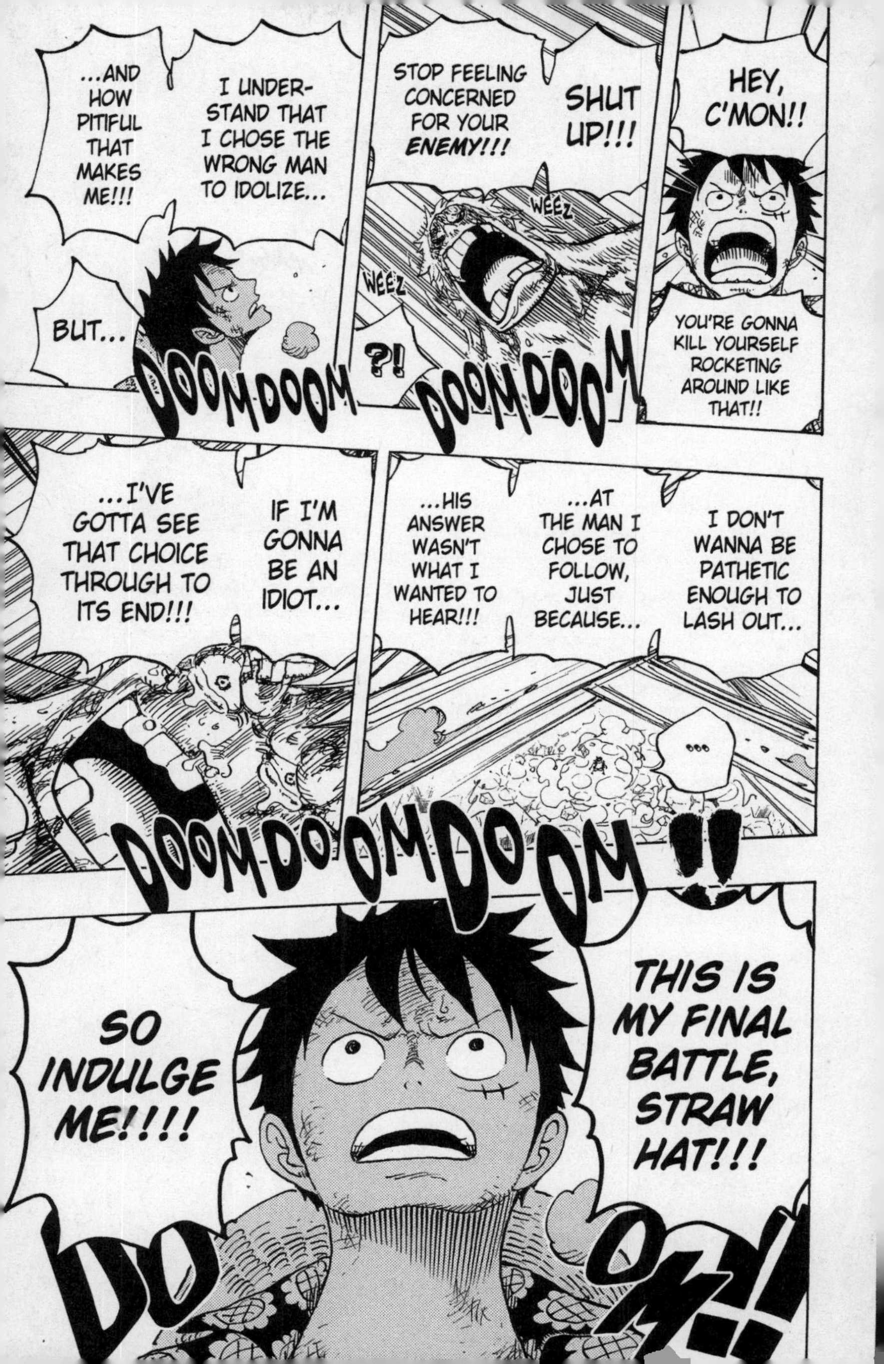
HEY, C'MON!!
YOU'RE GONNA KILL YOURSELF ROCKETING AROUND LIKE THAT!!
SHUT UP!!!
STOP FEELING CONCERNED FOR YOUR *ENEMY!!!*
WEEZ
WEEZ
?!
DOOMDOOM
I UNDER-STAND THAT I CHOSE THE WRONG MAN TO IDOLIZE...
...AND HOW PITIFUL THAT MAKES ME!!!
BUT...
DOOMDOOM
I DON'T WANNA BE PATHETIC ENOUGH TO LASH OUT...
...AT THE MAN I CHOSE TO FOLLOW, JUST BECAUSE...
...HIS ANSWER WASN'T WHAT I WANTED TO HEAR!!!
...
IF I'M GONNA BE AN IDIOT...
...I'VE GOTTA SEE THAT CHOICE THROUGH TO ITS END!!!
DOOMDOOMDOOM!!
THIS IS MY FINAL BATTLE, STRAW HAT!!!
SO INDULGE ME!!!!
DOOM!!

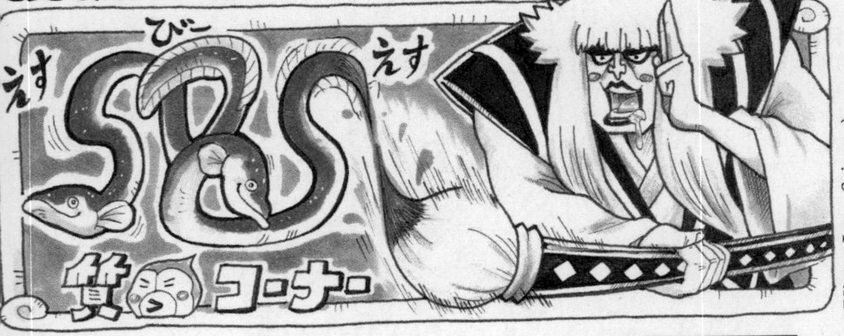
えす
びー
えす
SBS
質
コーナー

(Hippo Iron, Saitama)

Q: Is Gladius's penis capable of bursting too?

--Muranko

A: It is. That's scary!!!

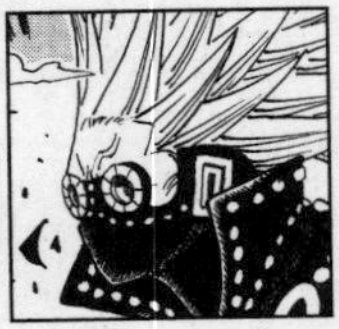

Q: How old is Corazon? Why isn't Sugar present in the flashback scenes of the Dofy Family?

--Roronoa Romugen

A: Corazon is two years younger than Doflamingo. He was 26 when he died. Sugar and Monet joined the family after that incident. The two were rescued from terribly misfortunate circumstances by Doflamingo. They were sisters age 9 and 17 at the time, and they now dedicate their lives in service to the family. They got their Devil Fruit powers after joining. Doflamingo really seems to place a heavy focus on the environments in which people were raised.

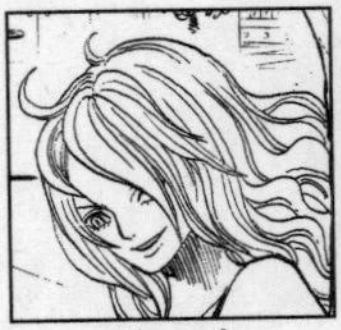

Monet

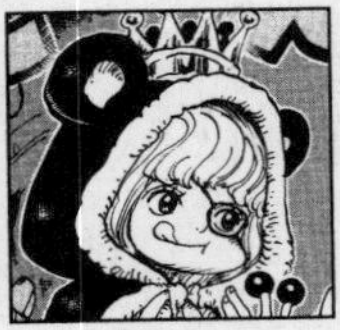

Sugar

Q: Hello, Odacchi! I've decided to do my own palm reading for Luffy! Oh my goodness!! He clearly has the legendary masukake line all the way across the palm!!!
From what I've researched, this is quite an extraordinary line that indicates great and mighty deeds, and it fits Luffy's profile perfectly! No wonder he can use the Haki of the Supreme King! Incredible work, Odacchi!! I can't believe you even design the palms of your characters this way… I'm simply speechless!!!

--Tauteni

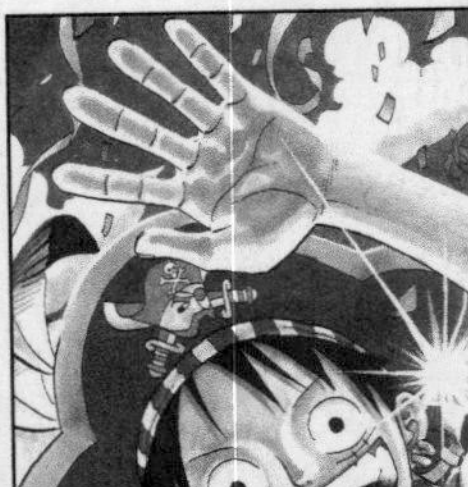

A: ....W...Why, of course.
That's right. I even take the characters', um...p-p-palm readings into account when designing them. Isn't that to be expected? I just knew that this would describe Luffy to a T! Good job noticing that mosu...er, masukake line? Is that right?

Chapter 770:
THE SPEAR OF ELBAPH

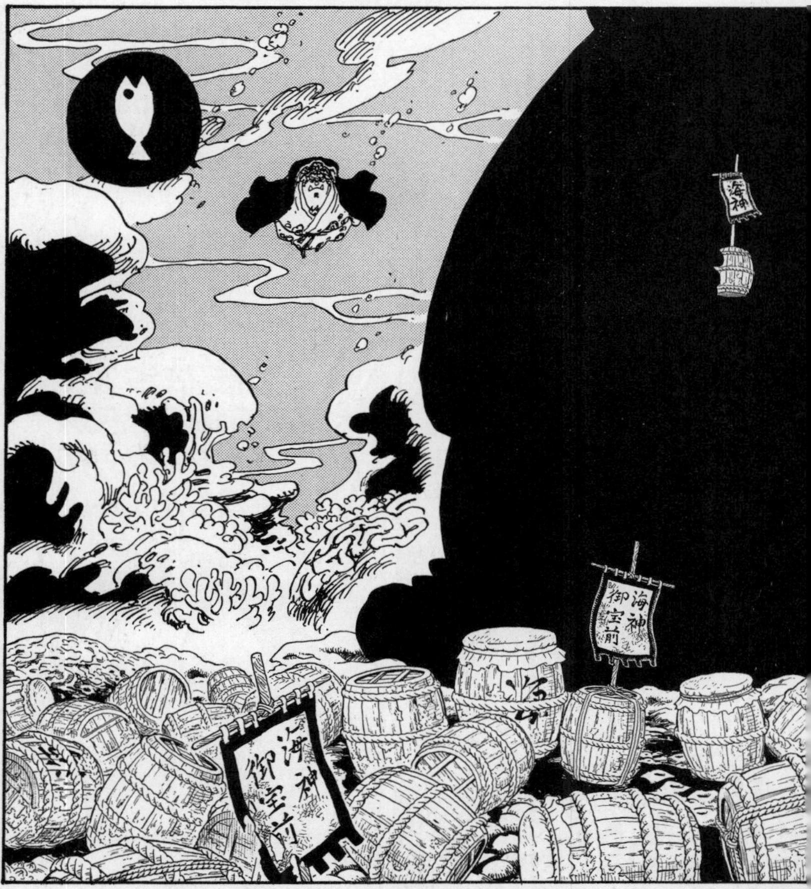
海神
海神
御宝前
海神
御宝前

*TREASURE FOR THE SEA GOD

THE SOLITARY JOURNEY OF JIMBEI, FIRST SON OF THE SEA
VOL. 17: "DISCOVERED! A HUGE MOUND OF OFFERINGS"

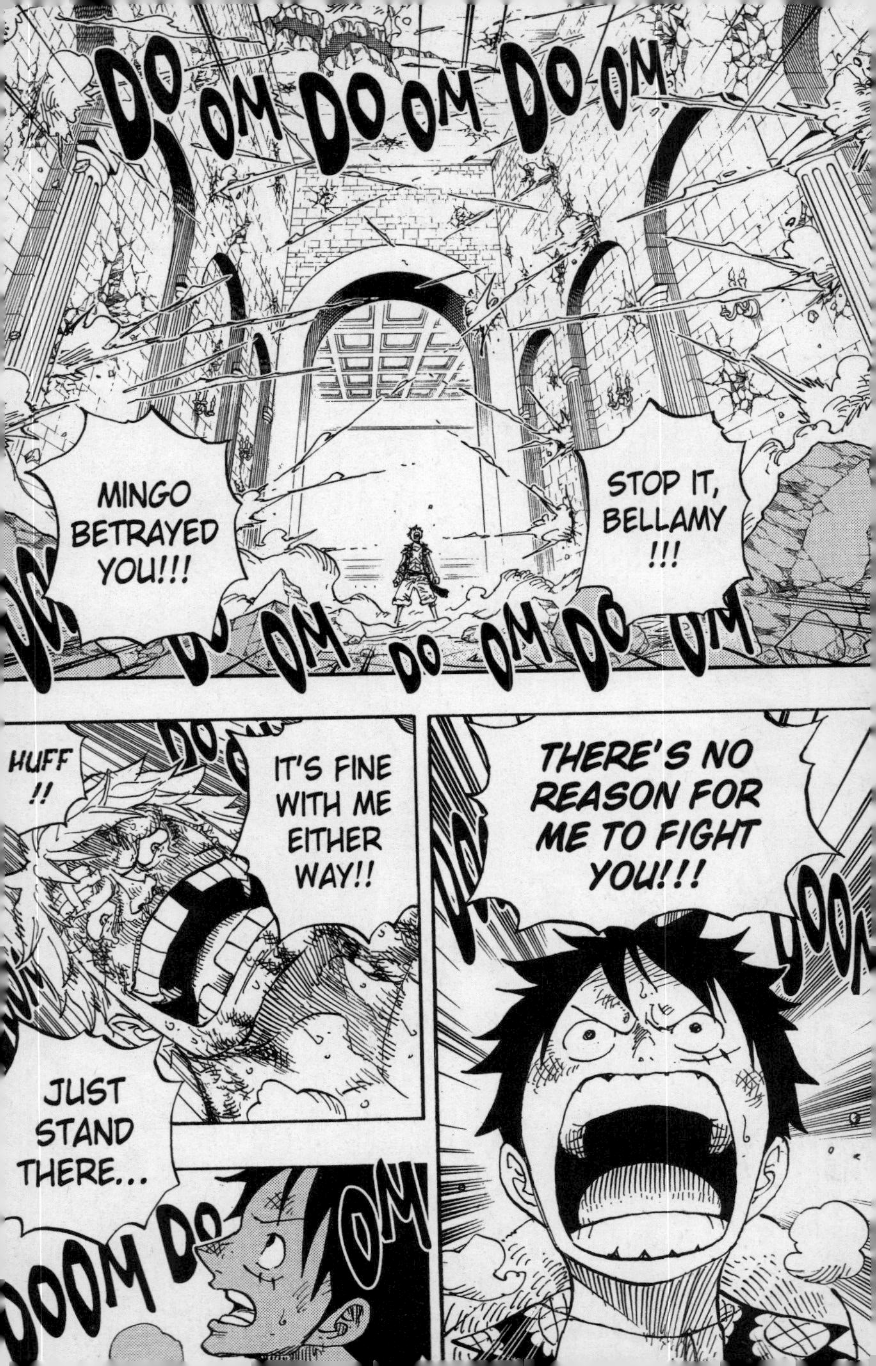
DO-OM DO-OM DO-OM
STOP IT, BELLAMY!!!
MINGO BETRAYED YOU!!!
DO-OM DO-OM DO-OM
THERE'S NO REASON FOR ME TO FIGHT YOU!!!
IT'S FINE WITH ME EITHER WAY!!
HUFF!!
JUST STAND THERE...
DOOM DOOM

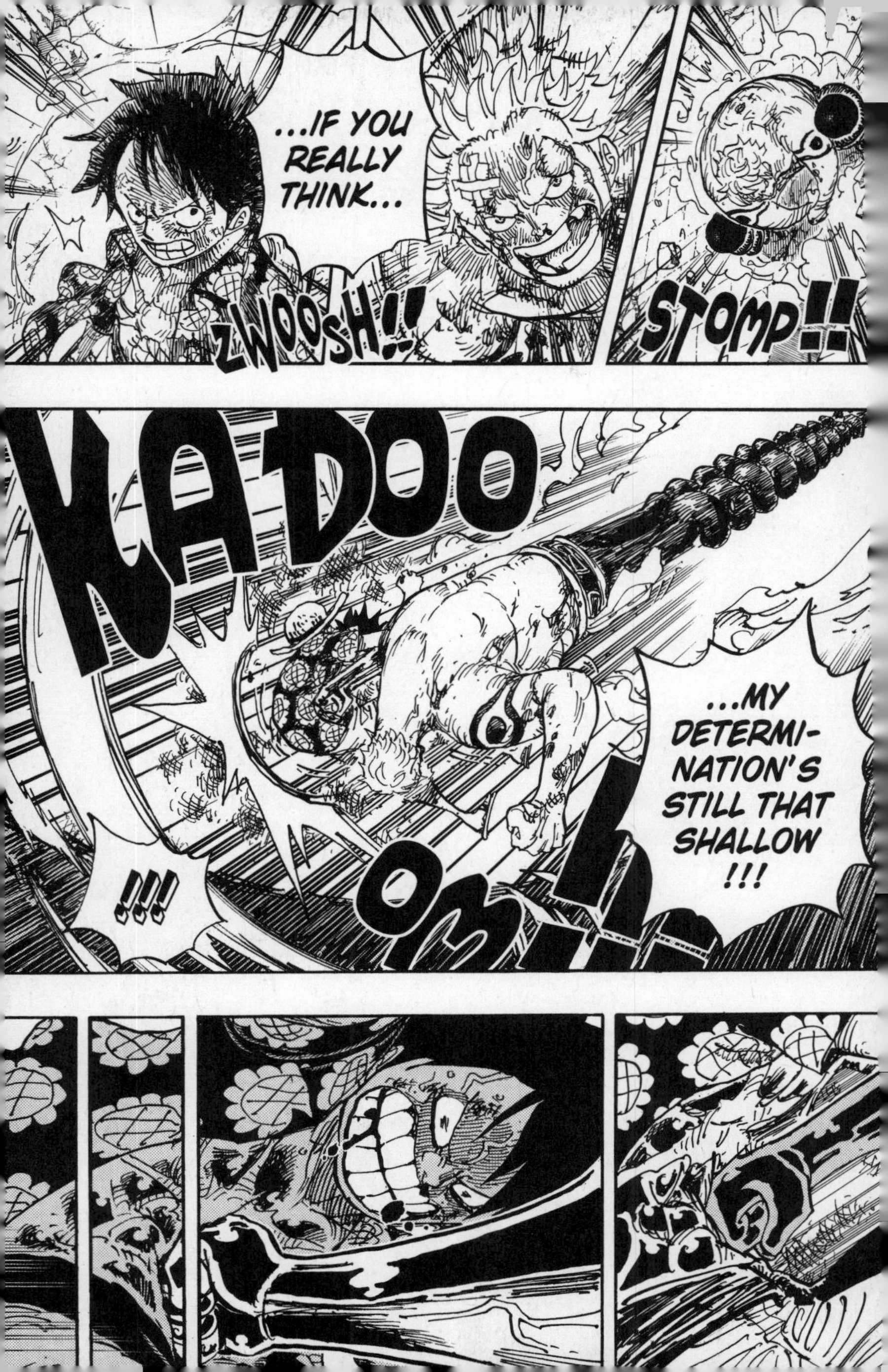
STOMP!!
...IF YOU REALLY THINK...
ZWOOSH!!
...MY DETERMINATION'S STILL THAT SHALLOW!!!
KA-DOOM!!
!!!

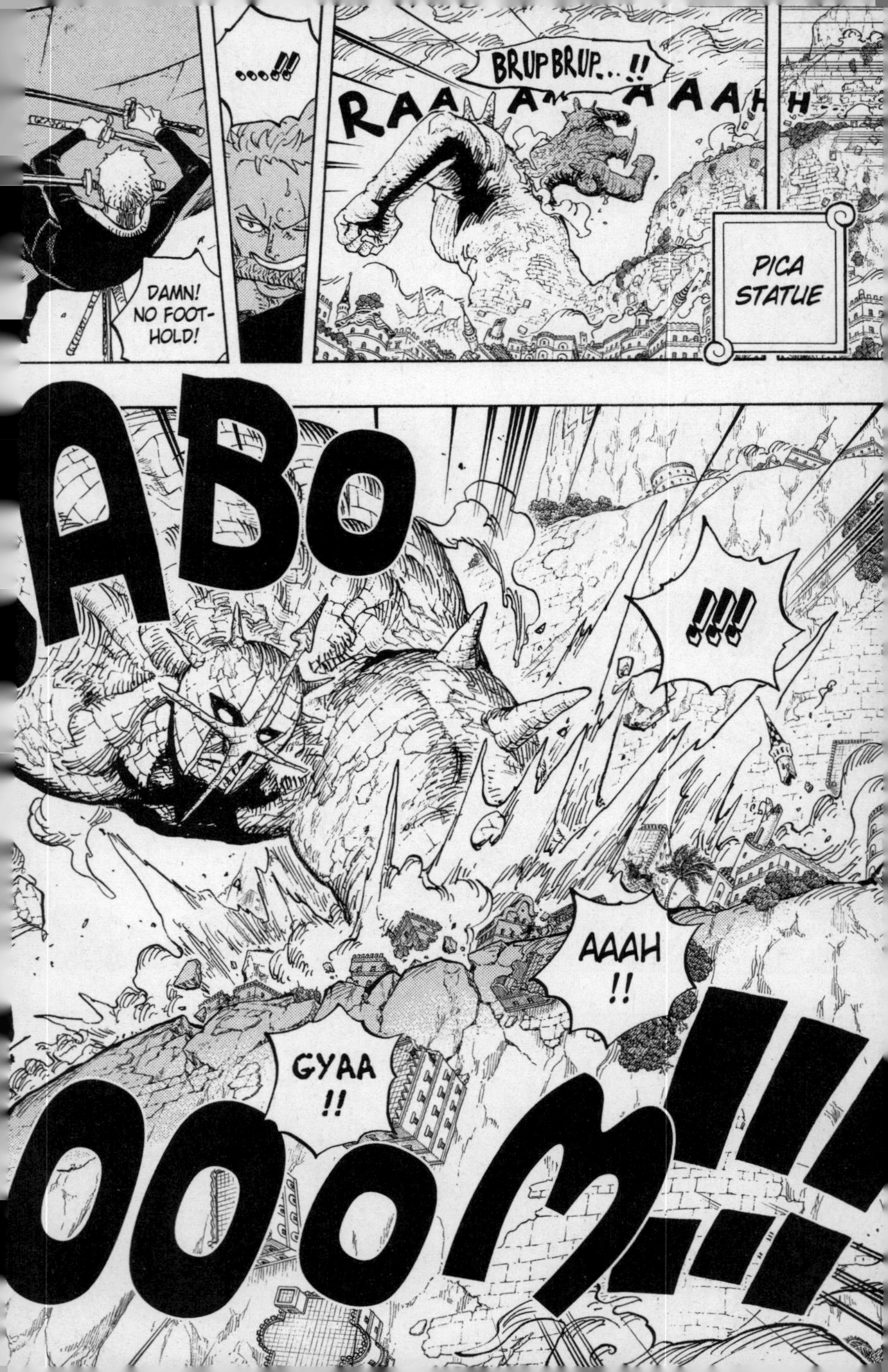
PICA STATUE
BRUP BRUP...!!
RAAAAAAAH
....!!
DAMN! NO FOOT-HOLD!
ABO
OOOM!!!
!!!
AAAH !!
GYAA !!

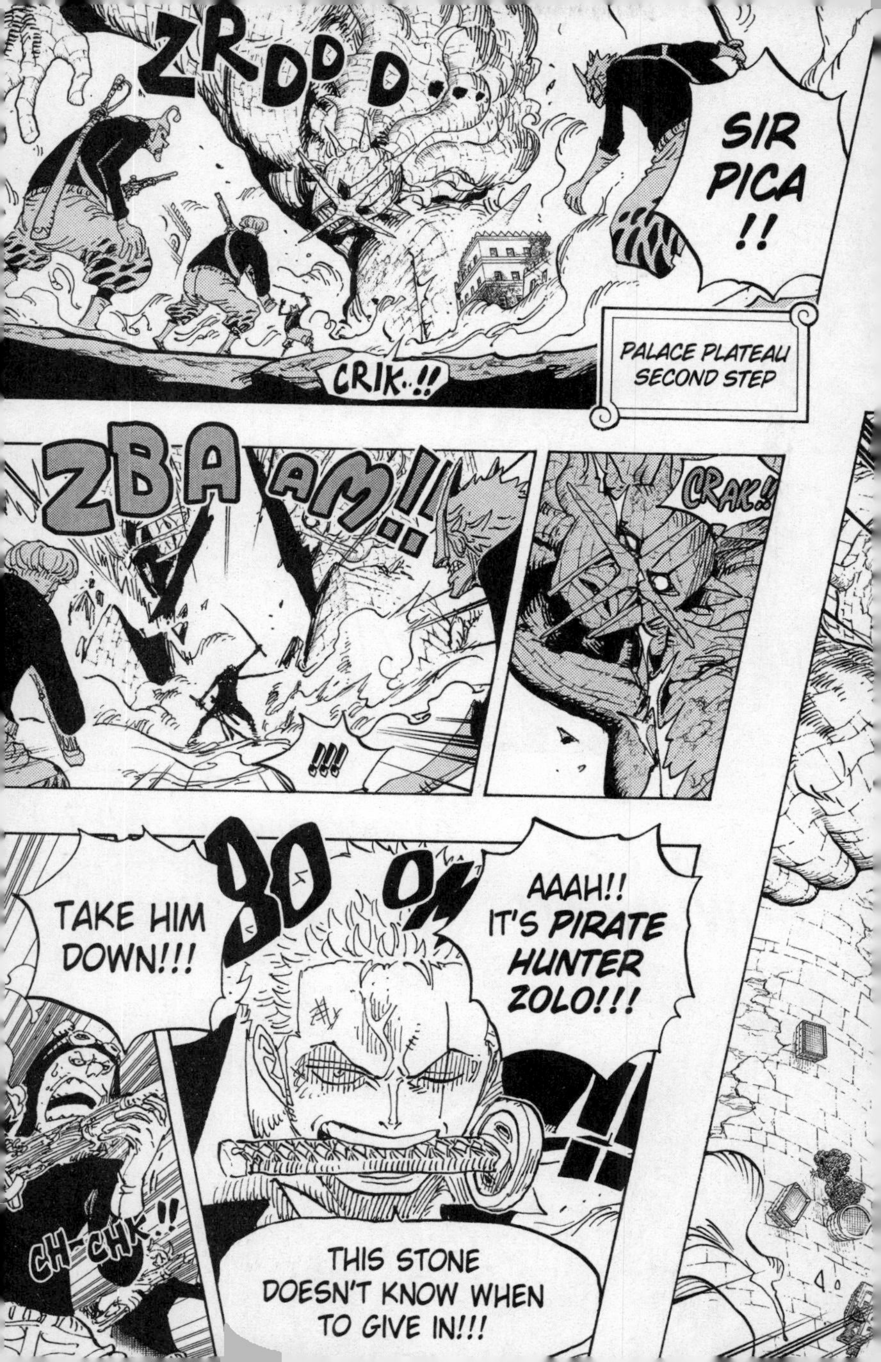
PALACE PLATEAU SECOND STEP
SIR PICA!!
ZRDDD...
CRIK..!!
CRAK..!
ZBAAM!!
!!!
AAAH!! IT'S PIRATE HUNTER ZOLO!!!
BOOM
THIS STONE DOESN'T KNOW WHEN TO GIVE IN!!!
TAKE HIM DOWN!!!
CH-CHK!!

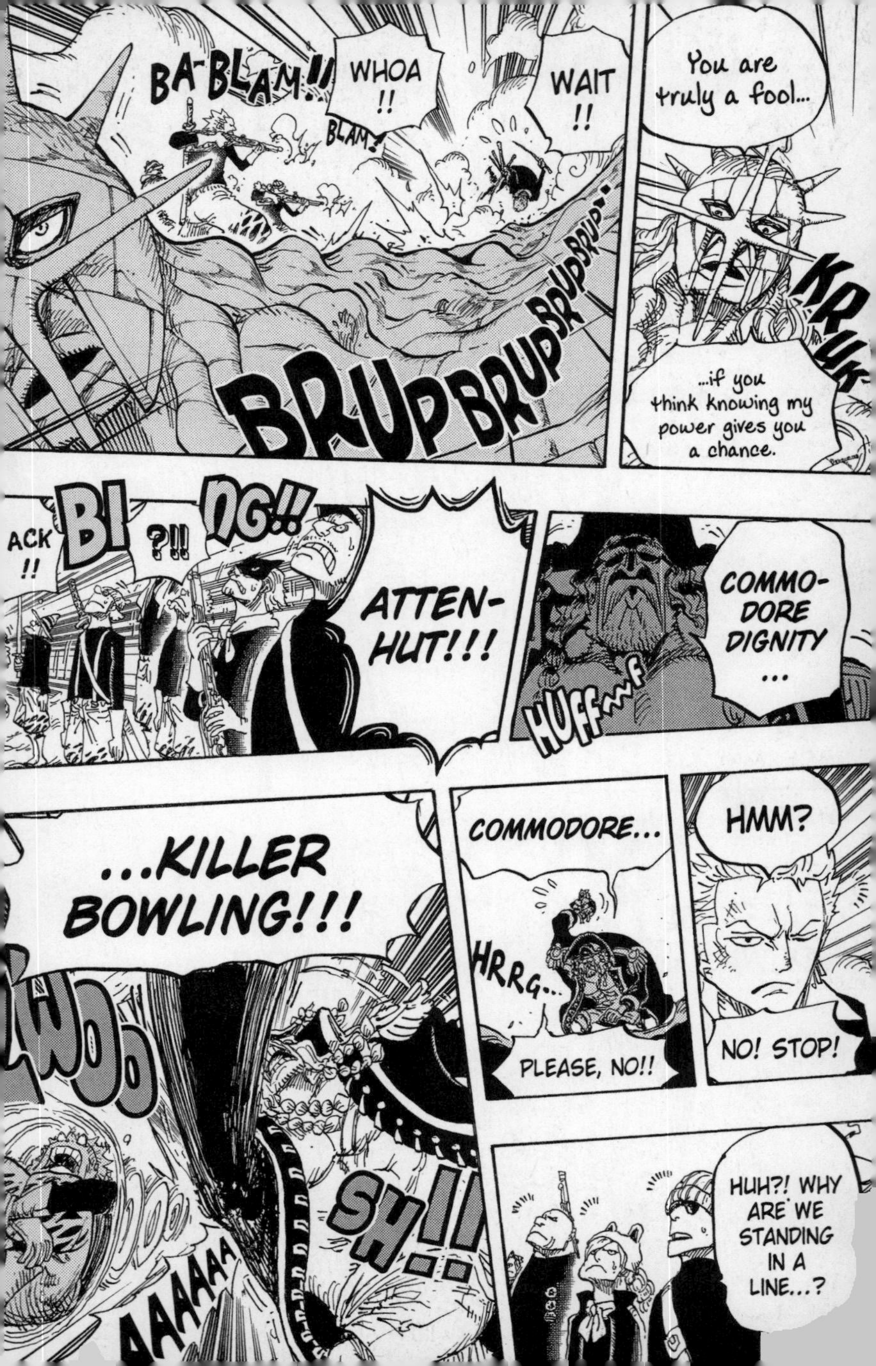
You are truly a fool...
KRUK
...if you think knowing my power gives you a chance.
WAIT !!
WHOA !!
BA-BLAM!!
BLAM!
BRUP BRUP BRUP BRUP BRUP...
COMMODORE DIGNITY ...
HUFF~F
ATTEN-HUT!!!
BI NG!!
?!!
ACK !!
HMM?
NO! STOP!
COMMODORE...
HRRG...
PLEASE, NO!!
HUH?! WHY ARE WE STANDING IN A LINE...?
...KILLER BOWLING!!!
SH!!
AAAAAA

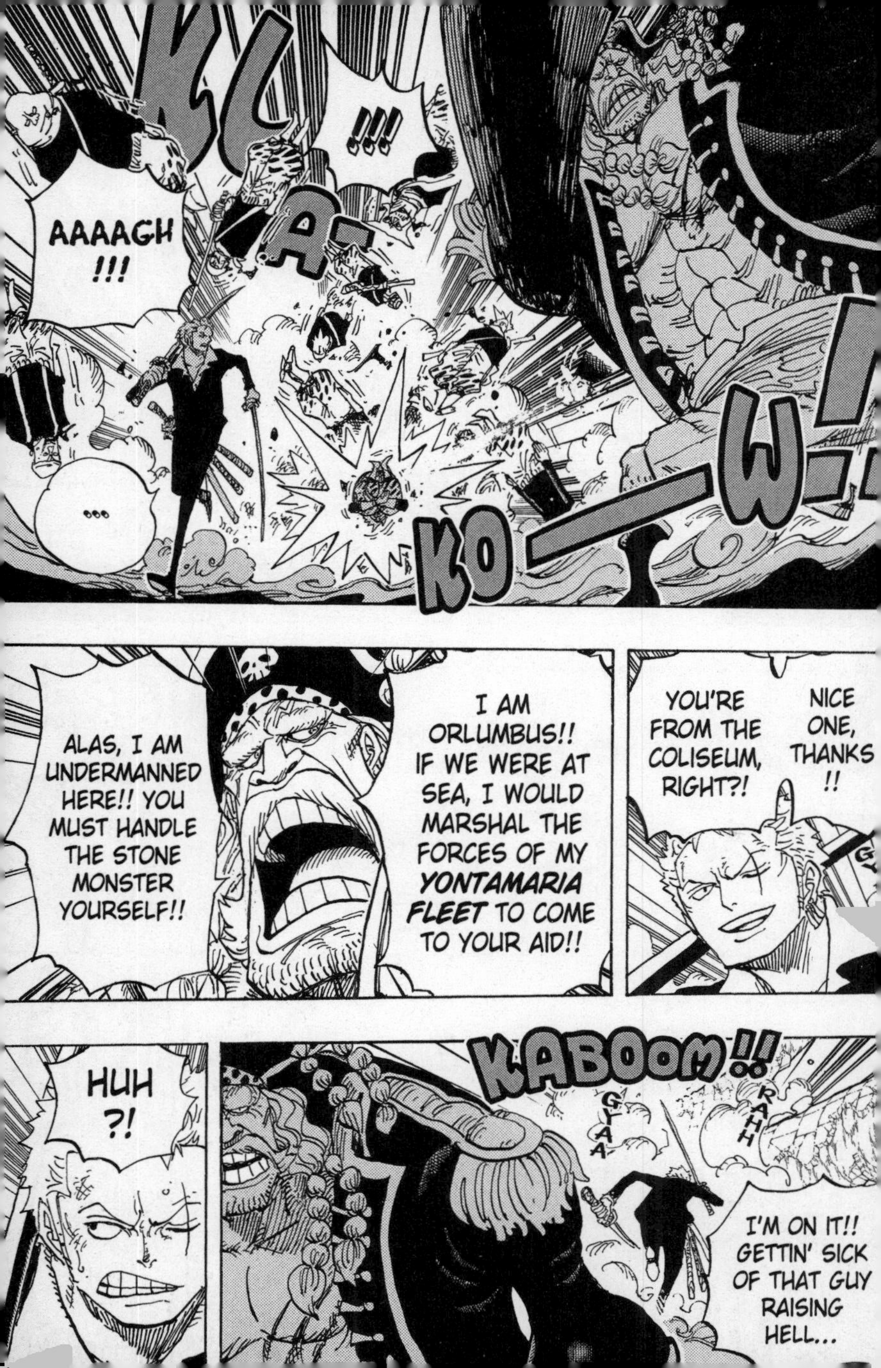
KO—W-!!
KL
A-
!!!
AAAAGH !!!
•••
NICE ONE, THANKS !!
YOU'RE FROM THE COLISEUM, RIGHT?!
I AM ORLUMBUS!! IF WE WERE AT SEA, I WOULD MARSHAL THE FORCES OF MY *YONTAMARIA FLEET* TO COME TO YOUR AID!!
ALAS, I AM UNDERMANNED HERE!! YOU MUST HANDLE THE STONE MONSTER YOURSELF!!
KABOOM!!
RAHH
GYAA
I'M ON IT!! GETTIN' SICK OF THAT GUY RAISING HELL...
HUH ?!

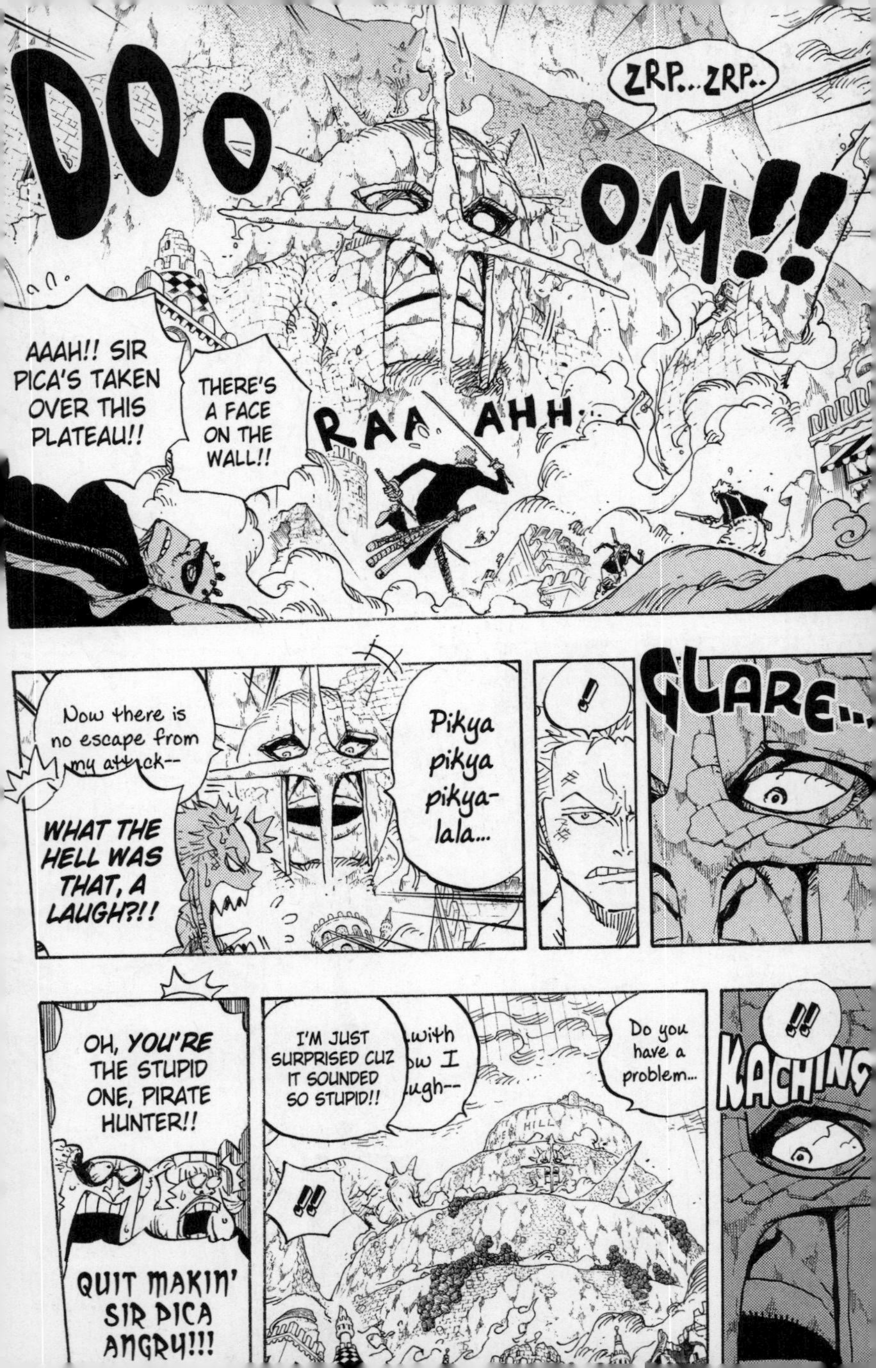
ZRP...ZRP..
DOO
OM!!
RAAAHH
THERE'S A FACE ON THE WALL!!
AAAH!! SIR PICA'S TAKEN OVER THIS PLATEAU!!
GLARE...
!
Pikya pikya pikya-lala...
Now there is no escape from my attack--
WHAT THE HELL WAS THAT, A LAUGH?!!
!!
KACHING
Do you have a problem...
with ow I ugh--
I'M JUST SURPRISED CUZ IT SOUNDED SO STUPID!!
!!
OH, YOU'RE THE STUPID ONE, PIRATE HUNTER!!
QUIT MAKIN' SIR PICA ANGRY!!!

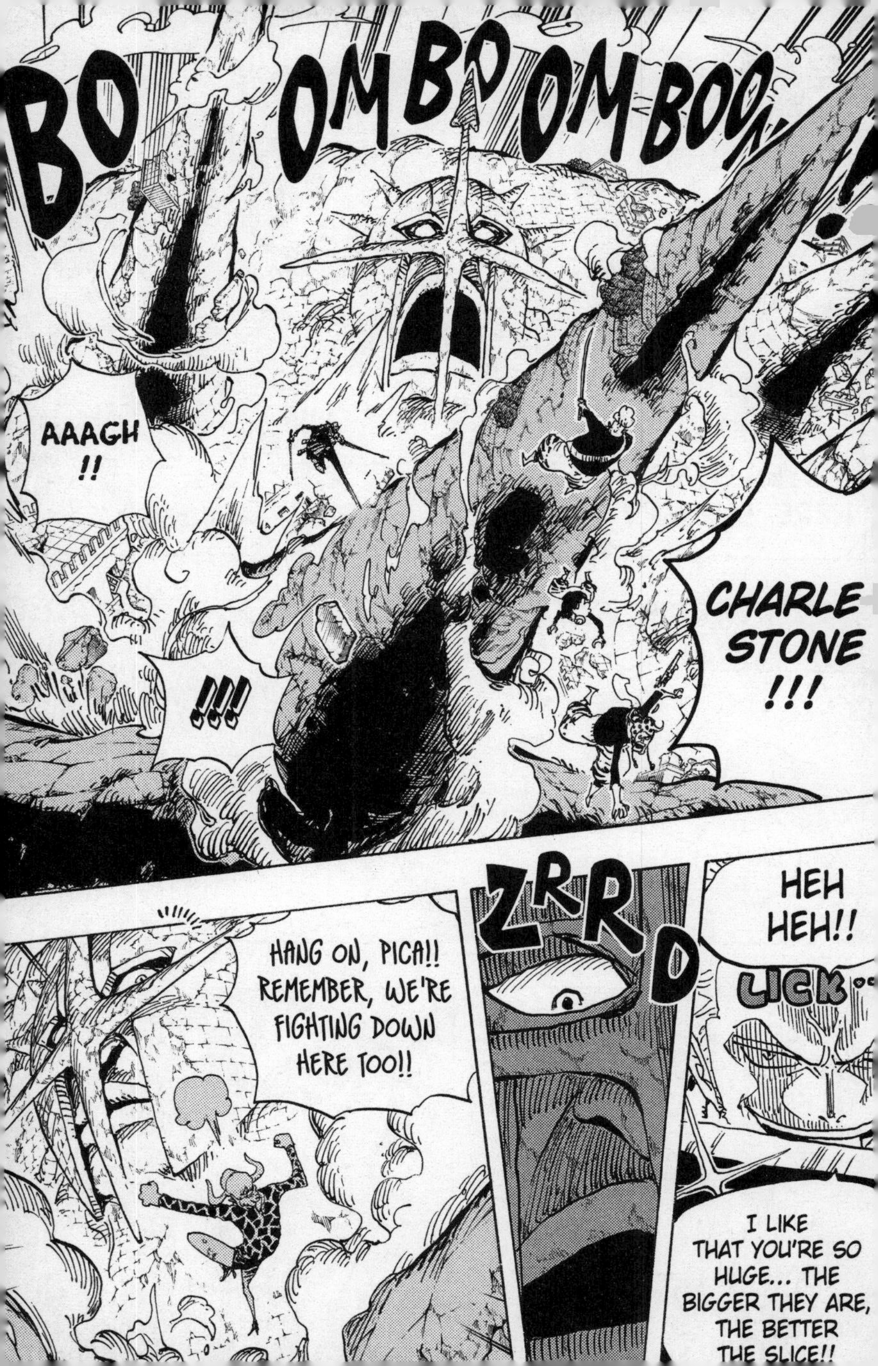
BOOMBOOMBOOOM
CHARLE STONE!!!
AAAGH!!
!!!
HEH HEH!!
LICK
I LIKE THAT YOU'RE SO HUGE... THE BIGGER THEY ARE, THE BETTER THE SLICE!!
ZRRRD
HANG ON, PICA!! REMEMBER, WE'RE FIGHTING DOWN HERE TOO!!

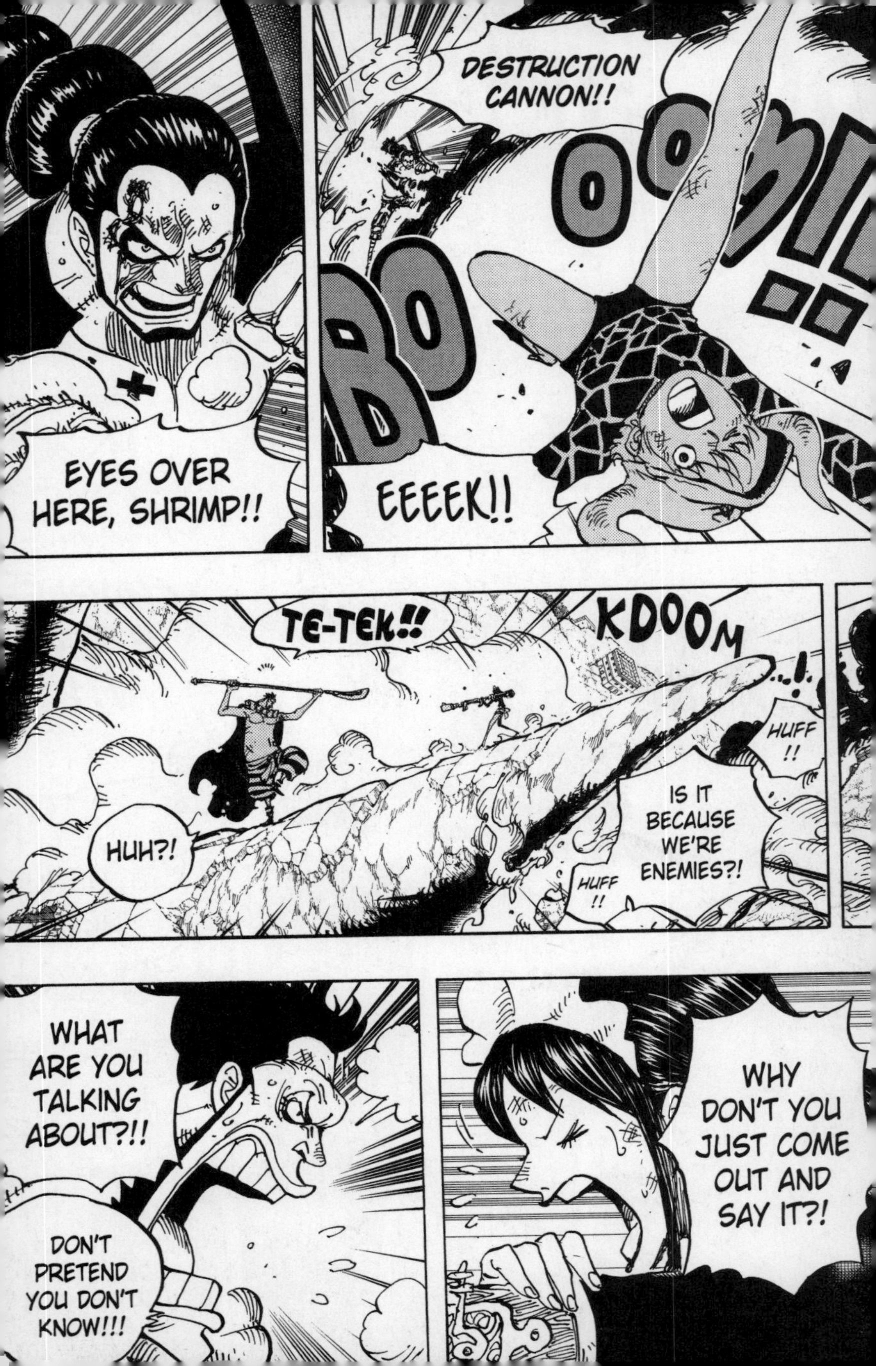
DESTRUCTION CANNON!!
BOOOM!!
EEEEK!!
EYES OVER HERE, SHRIMP!!
KDOOM
TE-TEK!!
...!
HUFF!!
IS IT BECAUSE WE'RE ENEMIES?!
HUFF!!
HUH?!
WHY DON'T YOU JUST COME OUT AND SAY IT?!
WHAT ARE YOU TALKING ABOUT?!!
DON'T PRETEND YOU DON'T KNOW!!!

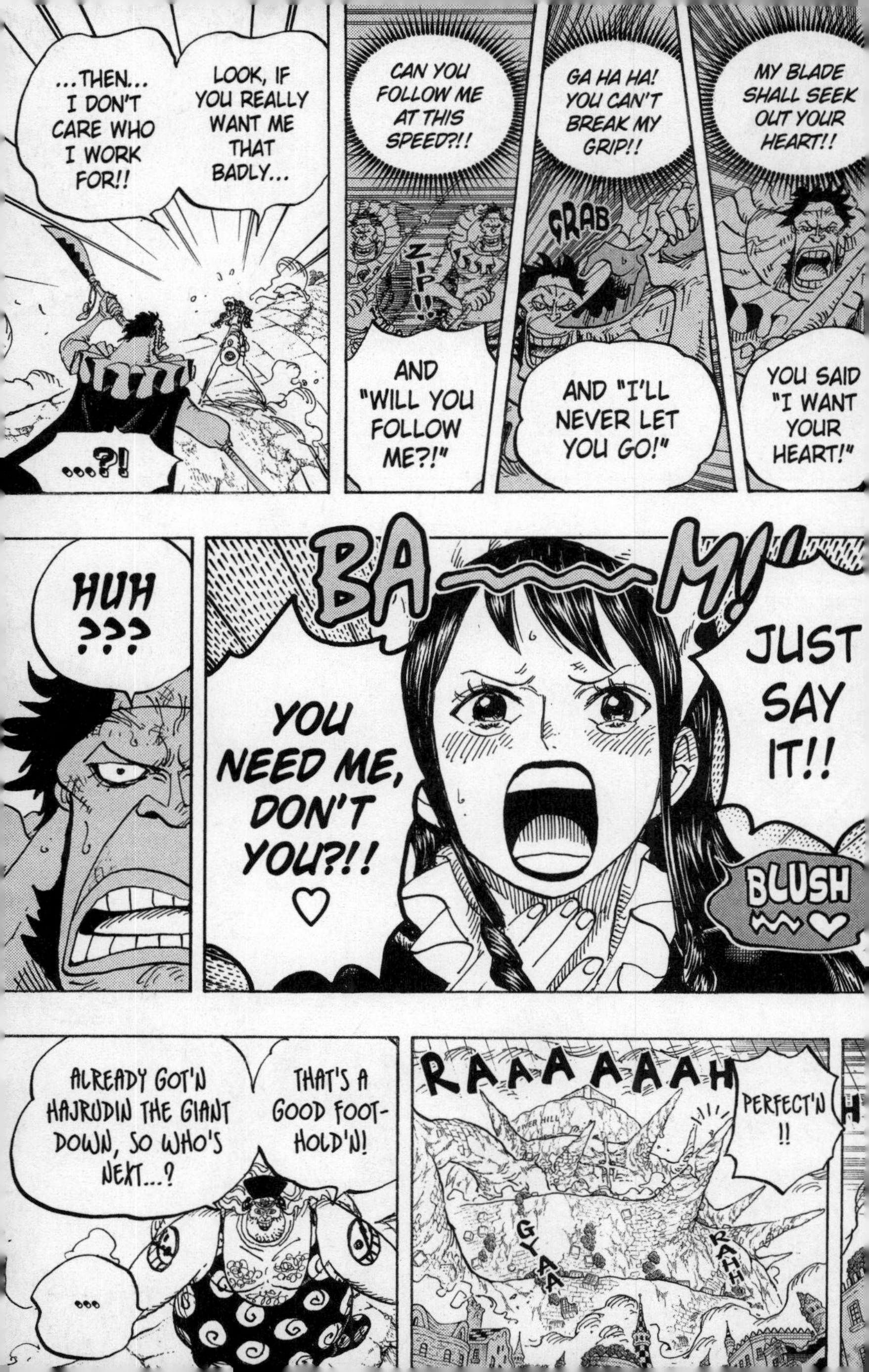
MY BLADE SHALL SEEK OUT YOUR HEART!!
YOU SAID "I WANT YOUR HEART!"
GA HA HA! YOU CAN'T BREAK MY GRIP!!
GRAB
AND "I'LL NEVER LET YOU GO!"
CAN YOU FOLLOW ME AT THIS SPEED?!!
ZIP!!
AND "WILL YOU FOLLOW ME?!"
LOOK, IF YOU REALLY WANT ME THAT BADLY...
...THEN... I DON'T CARE WHO I WORK FOR!!
...?!
BA~~M!
JUST SAY IT!!
YOU NEED ME, DON'T YOU?!! ♡
BLUSH ~♡
HUH ???
RAAAAAAH
PERFECT'N !!
RAHH
GYAA
THAT'S A GOOD FOOT-HOLD'N!
ALREADY GOT'N HAJRUDIN THE GIANT DOWN, SO WHO'S NEXT...?
...

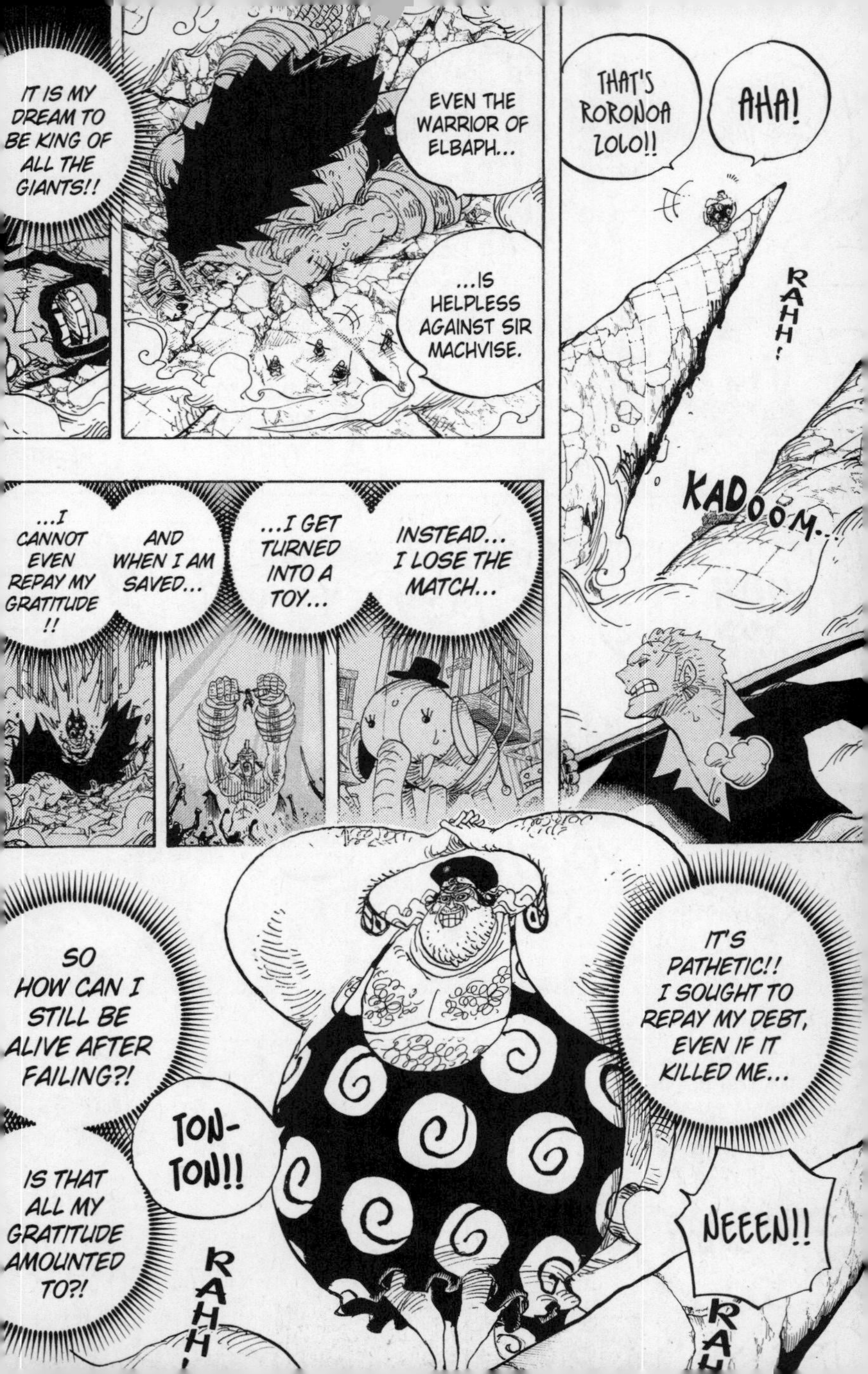
AHA!
THAT'S RORONOA ZOLO!!
RAHH!
KADOOM...
EVEN THE WARRIOR OF ELBAPH...
...IS HELPLESS AGAINST SIR MACHVISE.
IT IS MY DREAM TO BE KING OF ALL THE GIANTS!!
INSTEAD... I LOSE THE MATCH...
...I GET TURNED INTO A TOY...
AND WHEN I AM SAVED...
...I CANNOT EVEN REPAY MY GRATITUDE!!
IT'S PATHETIC!! I SOUGHT TO REPAY MY DEBT, EVEN IF IT KILLED ME...
NEEEN!!
RAH
TON-TON!!
SO HOW CAN I STILL BE ALIVE AFTER FAILING?!
IS THAT ALL MY GRATITUDE AMOUNTED TO?!
RAHH!

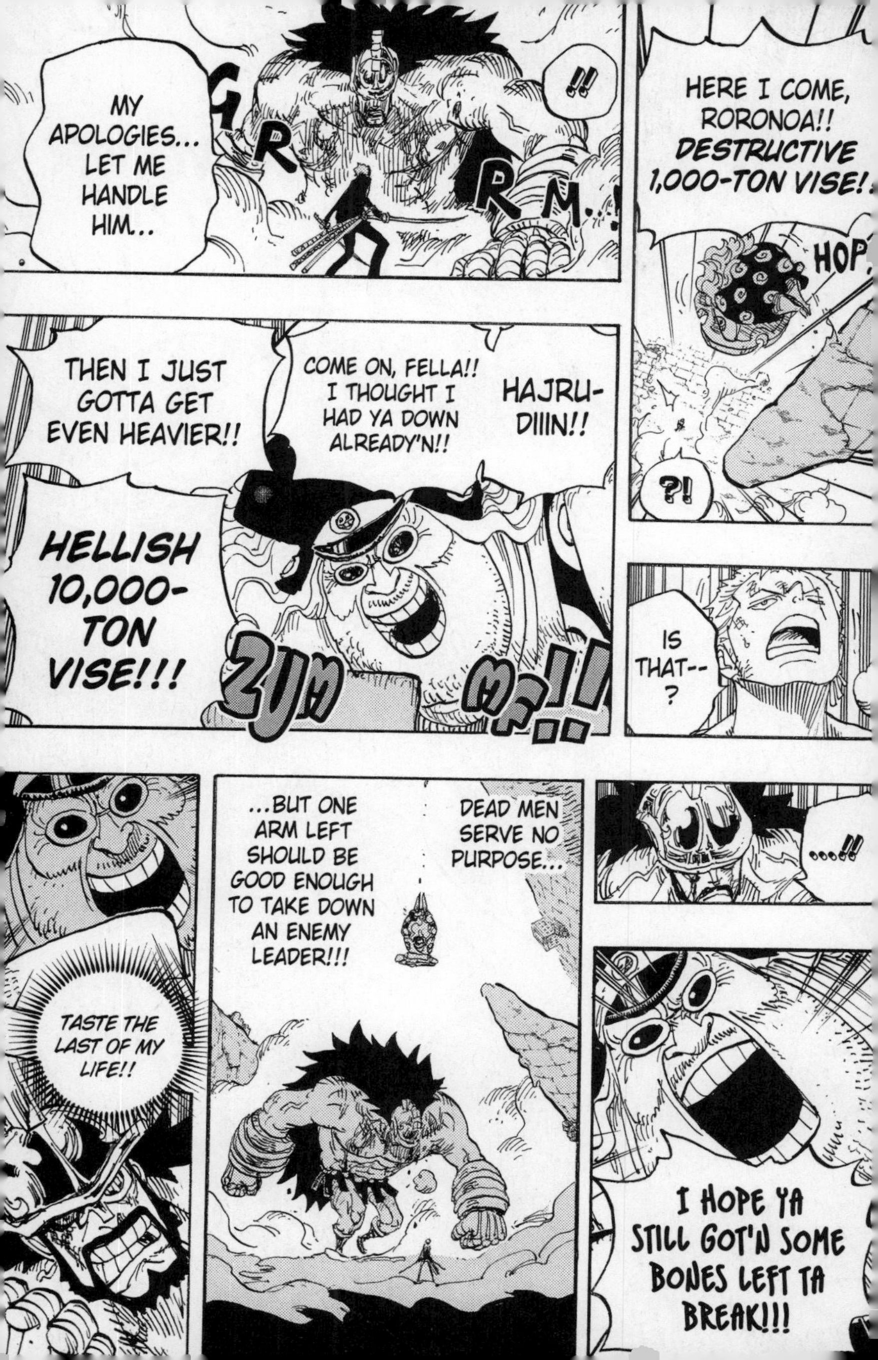
HERE I COME, RORONOA!! DESTRUCTIVE 1,000-TON VISE!!
HOP
?!
MY APOLOGIES... LET ME HANDLE HIM...
!!
GRRM...
IS THAT--?
THEN I JUST GOTTA GET EVEN HEAVIER!!
COME ON, FELLA!! I THOUGHT I HAD YA DOWN ALREADY'N!!
HAJRU-DIIIN!!
HELLISH 10,000-TON VISE!!!
ZUMMF!!
....!!
I HOPE YA STILL GOT'N SOME BONES LEFT TA BREAK!!!
DEAD MEN SERVE NO PURPOSE...
...BUT ONE ARM LEFT SHOULD BE GOOD ENOUGH TO TAKE DOWN AN ENEMY LEADER!!!
TASTE THE LAST OF MY LIFE!!

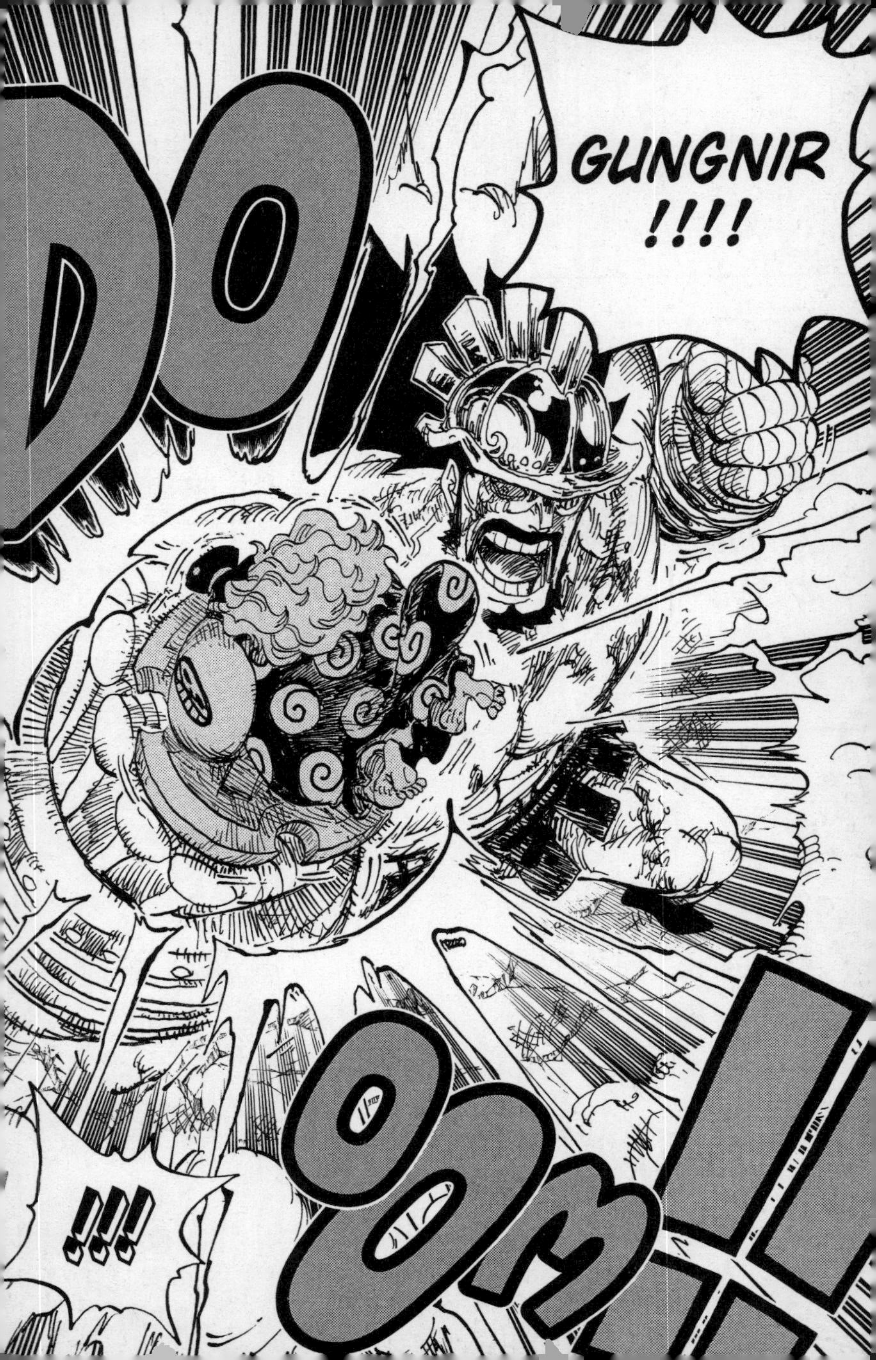
GUNGNIR !!!!
DO
!!!

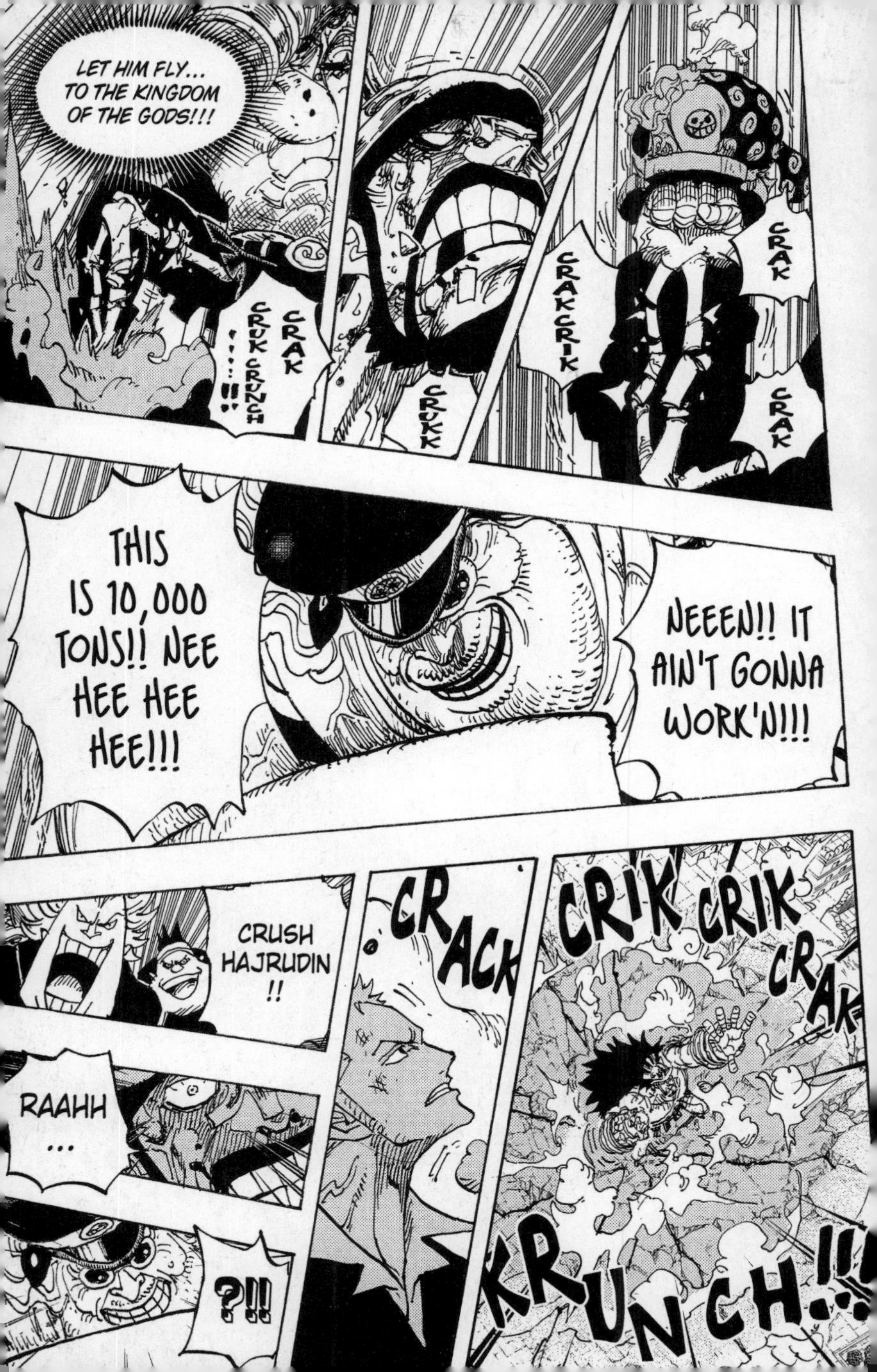
CRAK
CRAKCRIK
CRAK
CRUKK
LET HIM FLY... TO THE KINGDOM OF THE GODS!!!
CRAK
CRUK CRUNCH
……!!
NEEEN!! IT AIN'T GONNA WORK'N!!!
THIS IS 10,000 TONS!! NEE HEE HEE HEE!!!
CRIK CRIK CRAK
KRUNCH!!!
CRACK
CRUSH HAJRUDIN !!
RAAHH ...
?!!

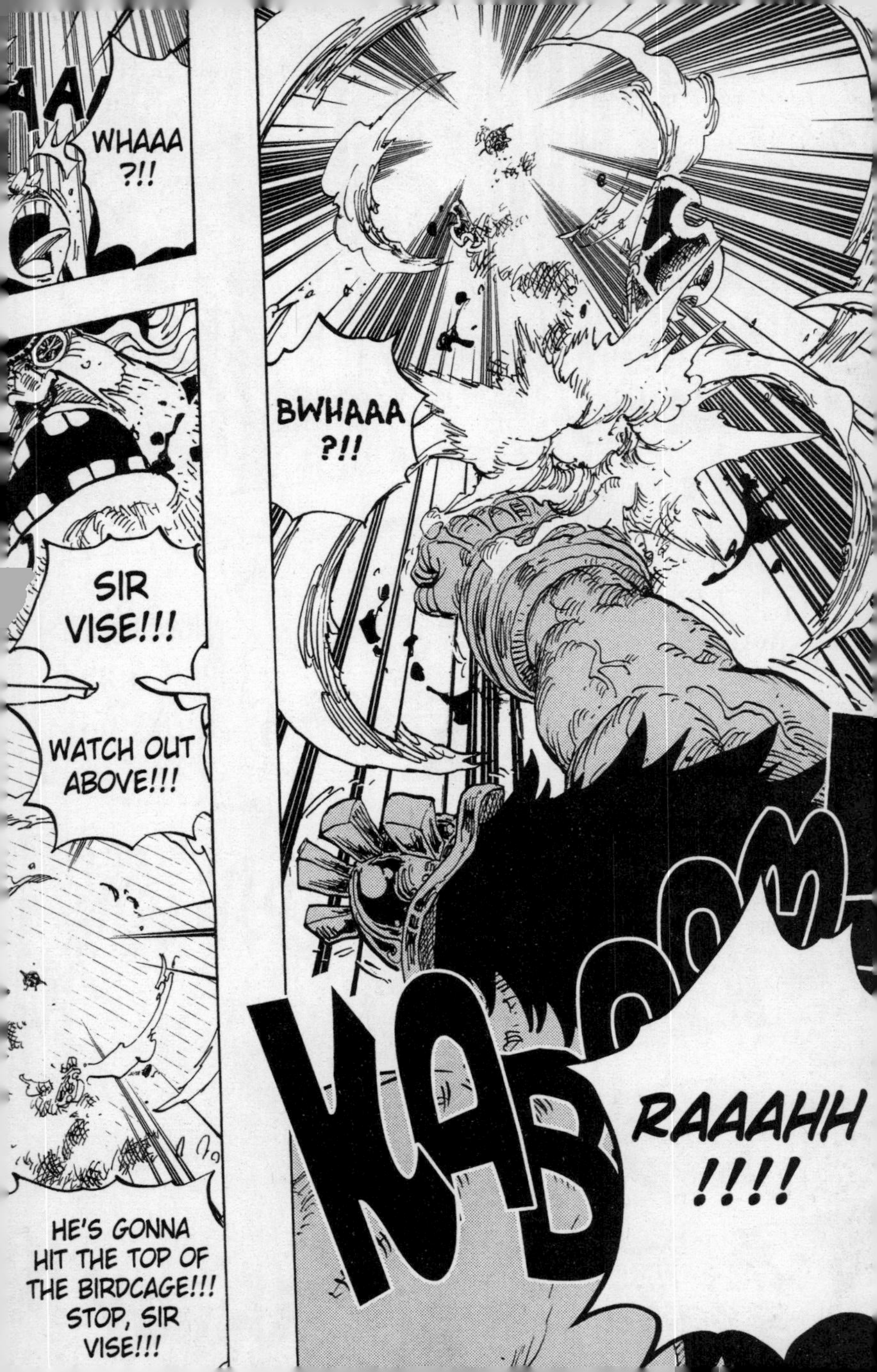
BWHAAA ?!!
KABOOM
RAAAHH !!!!
WHAAA ?!!
SIR VISE!!!
WATCH OUT ABOVE!!!
HE'S GONNA HIT THE TOP OF THE BIRDCAGE!!! STOP, SIR VISE!!!

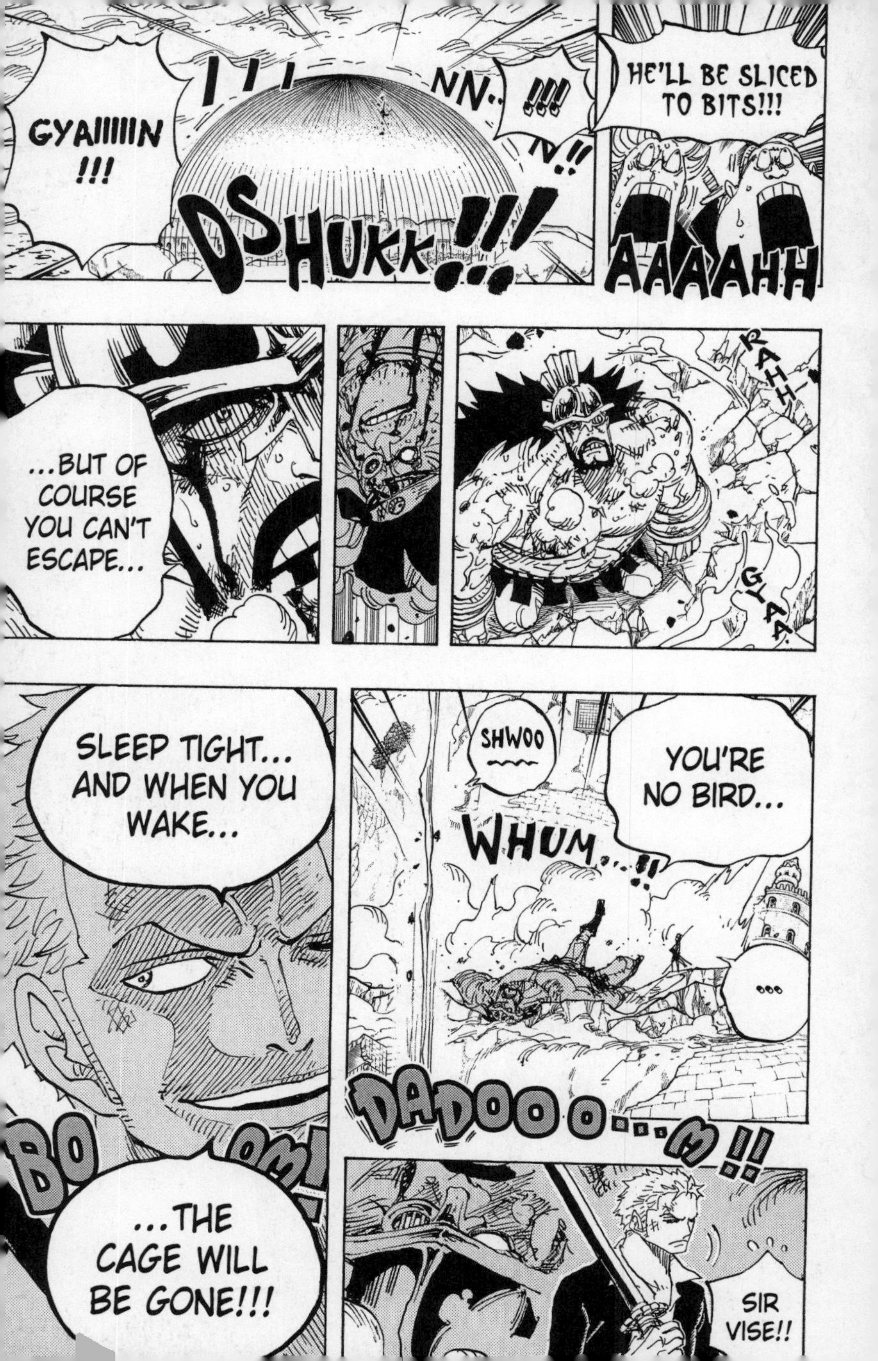
HE'LL BE SLICED TO BITS!!!
AAAAHH
NN...!!!
N!!
GYAIIIIIN !!!
DSHUKK!!!
RAHH
GYAA
...BUT OF COURSE YOU CAN'T ESCAPE...
YOU'RE NO BIRD...
SHWOO
WHUM...!!
...
DADOOO...M!!
SIR VISE!!
SLEEP TIGHT... AND WHEN YOU WAKE...
BOOM!
...THE CAGE WILL BE GONE!!!

AI, DON OF THE HAPPOSUI ARMY

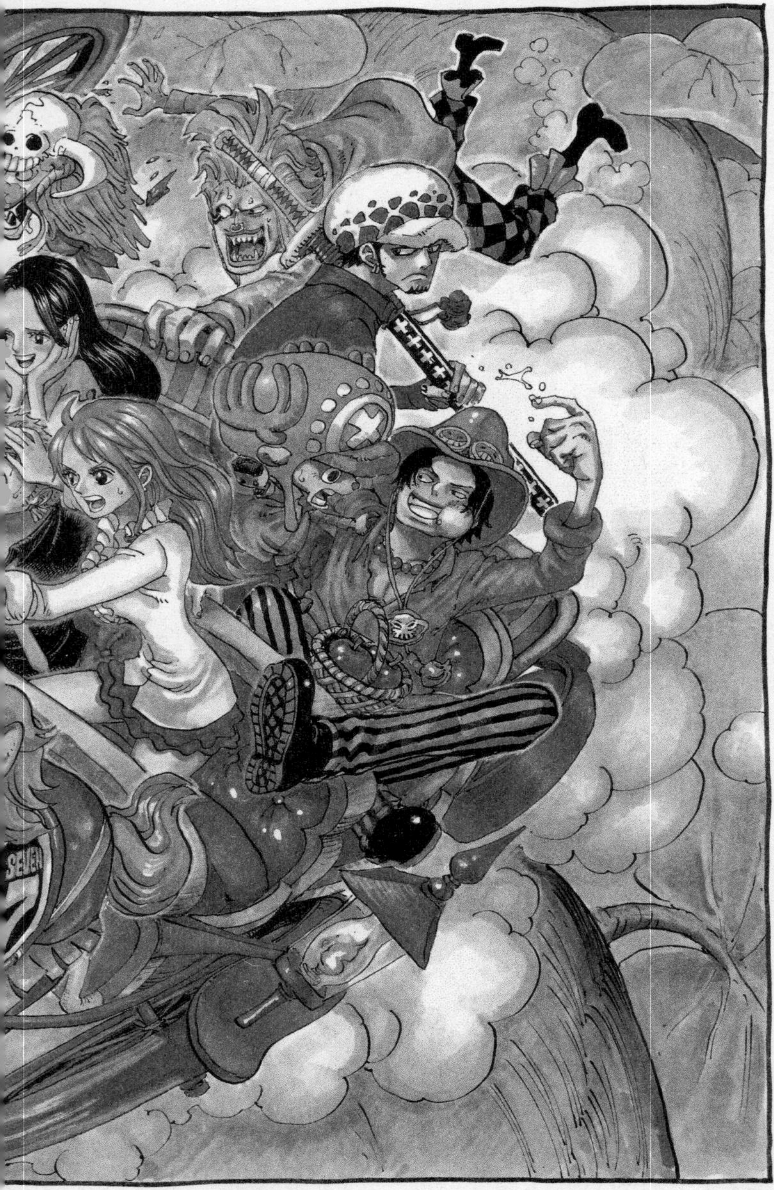

Chapter 771

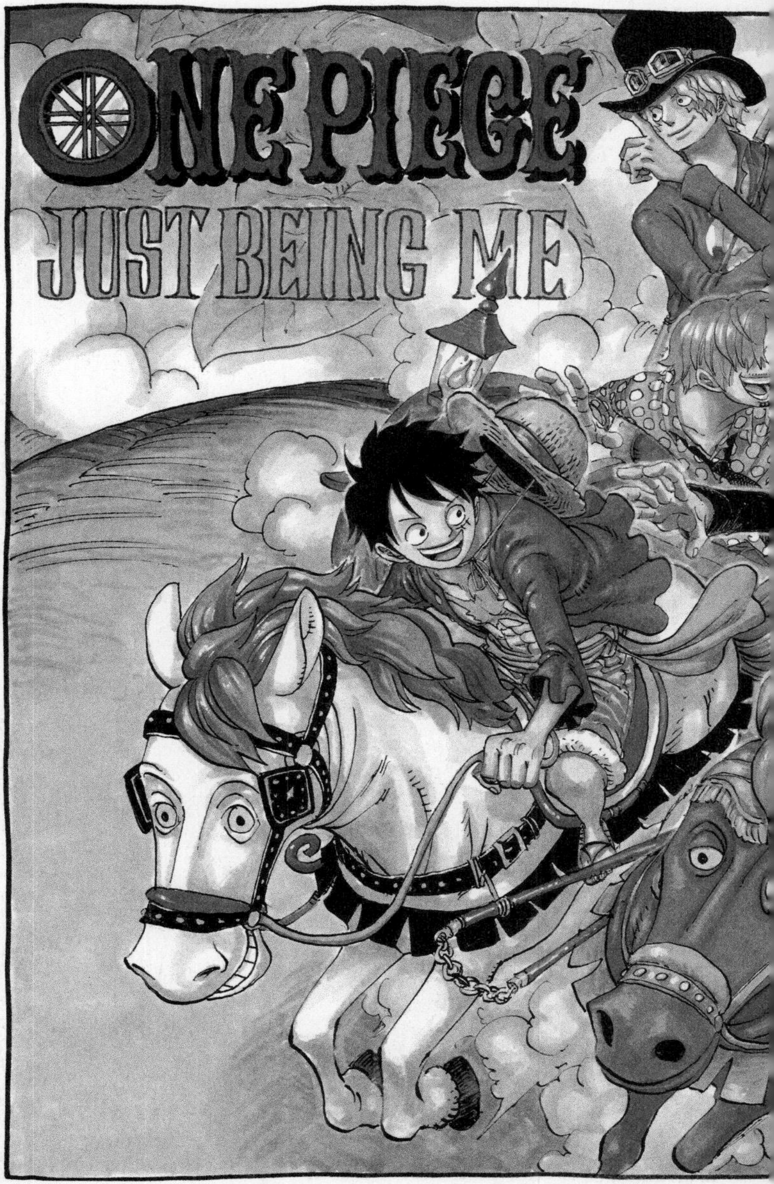
ONE PIECE
JUST BEING ME

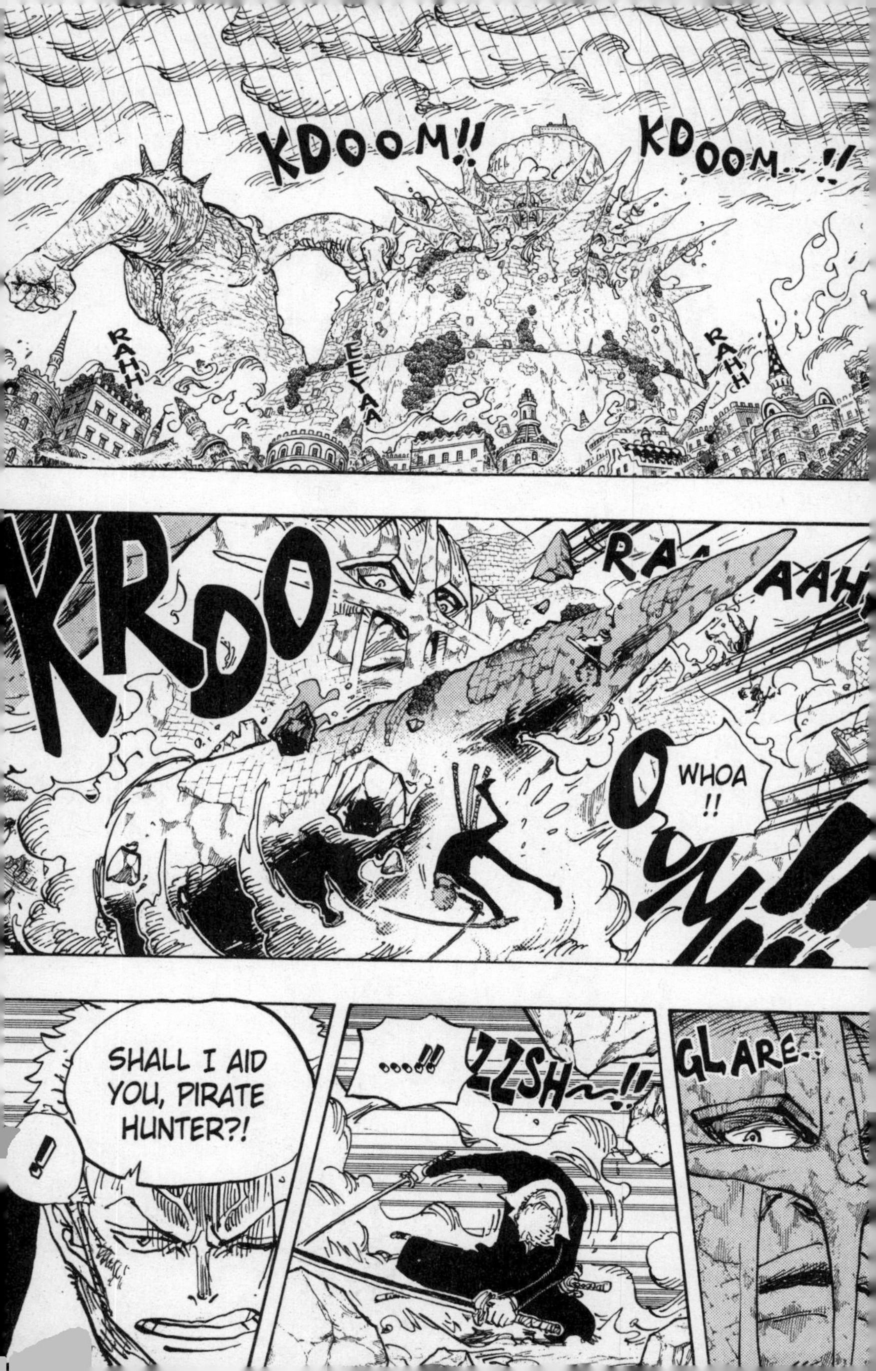
KDOOM...!!
KDOOM!!
RAHH
EEYAA
RAHH
RAAAAHH
WHOA !!
KRDOOOM!!
GLARE..
ZZSH~!!
...!!
SHALL I AID YOU, PIRATE HUNTER?!
!

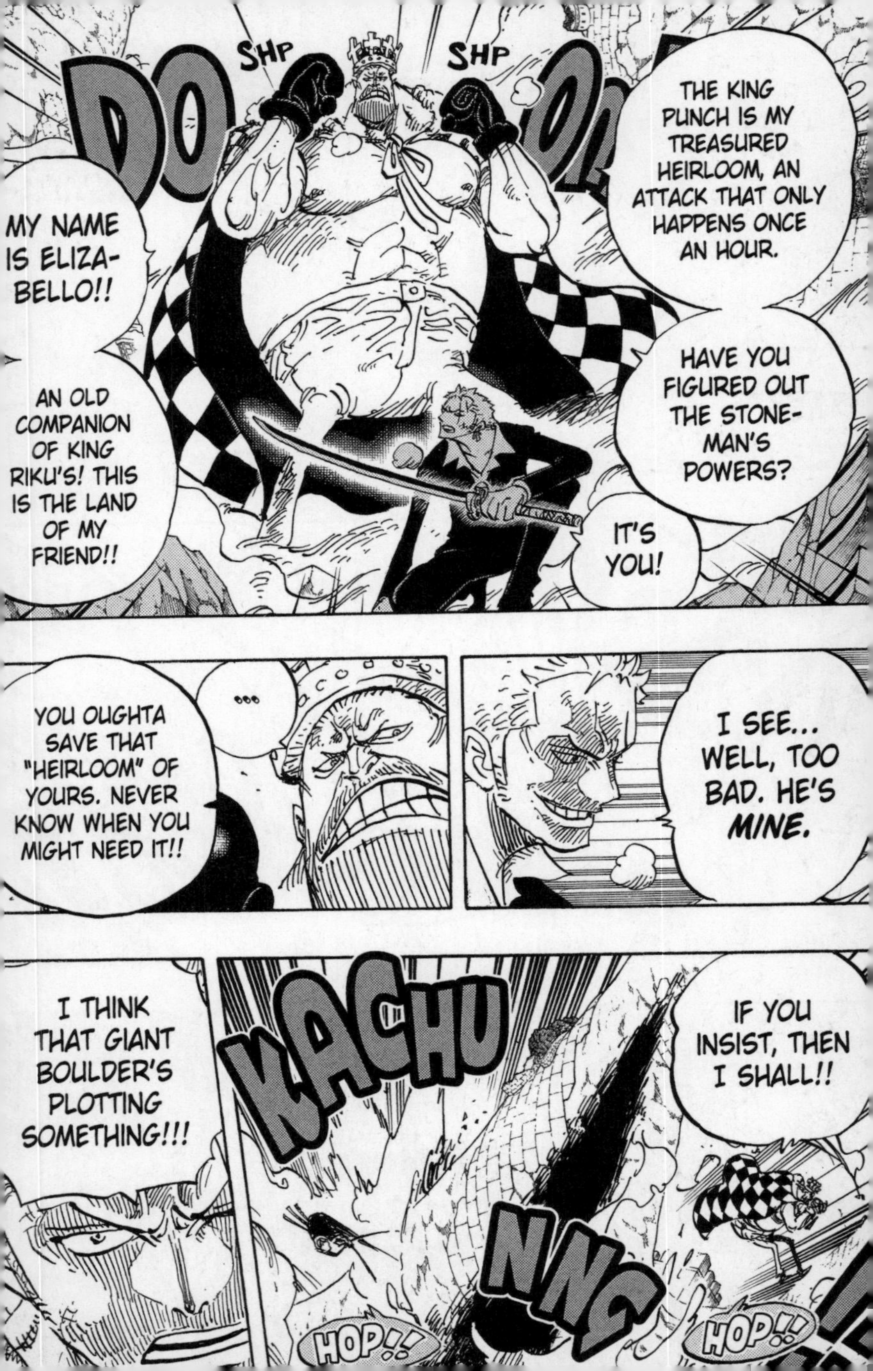
SHP
SHP
DO
THE KING PUNCH IS MY TREASURED HEIRLOOM, AN ATTACK THAT ONLY HAPPENS ONCE AN HOUR.
MY NAME IS ELIZA-BELLO!!
HAVE YOU FIGURED OUT THE STONE-MAN'S POWERS?
AN OLD COMPANION OF KING RIKU'S! THIS IS THE LAND OF MY FRIEND!!
IT'S YOU!
I SEE... WELL, TOO BAD. HE'S MINE.
...
YOU OUGHTA SAVE THAT "HEIRLOOM" OF YOURS. NEVER KNOW WHEN YOU MIGHT NEED IT!!
IF YOU INSIST, THEN I SHALL!!
HOP!!
KACHU
NNNG
HOP!!
I THINK THAT GIANT BOULDER'S PLOTTING SOMETHING!!!

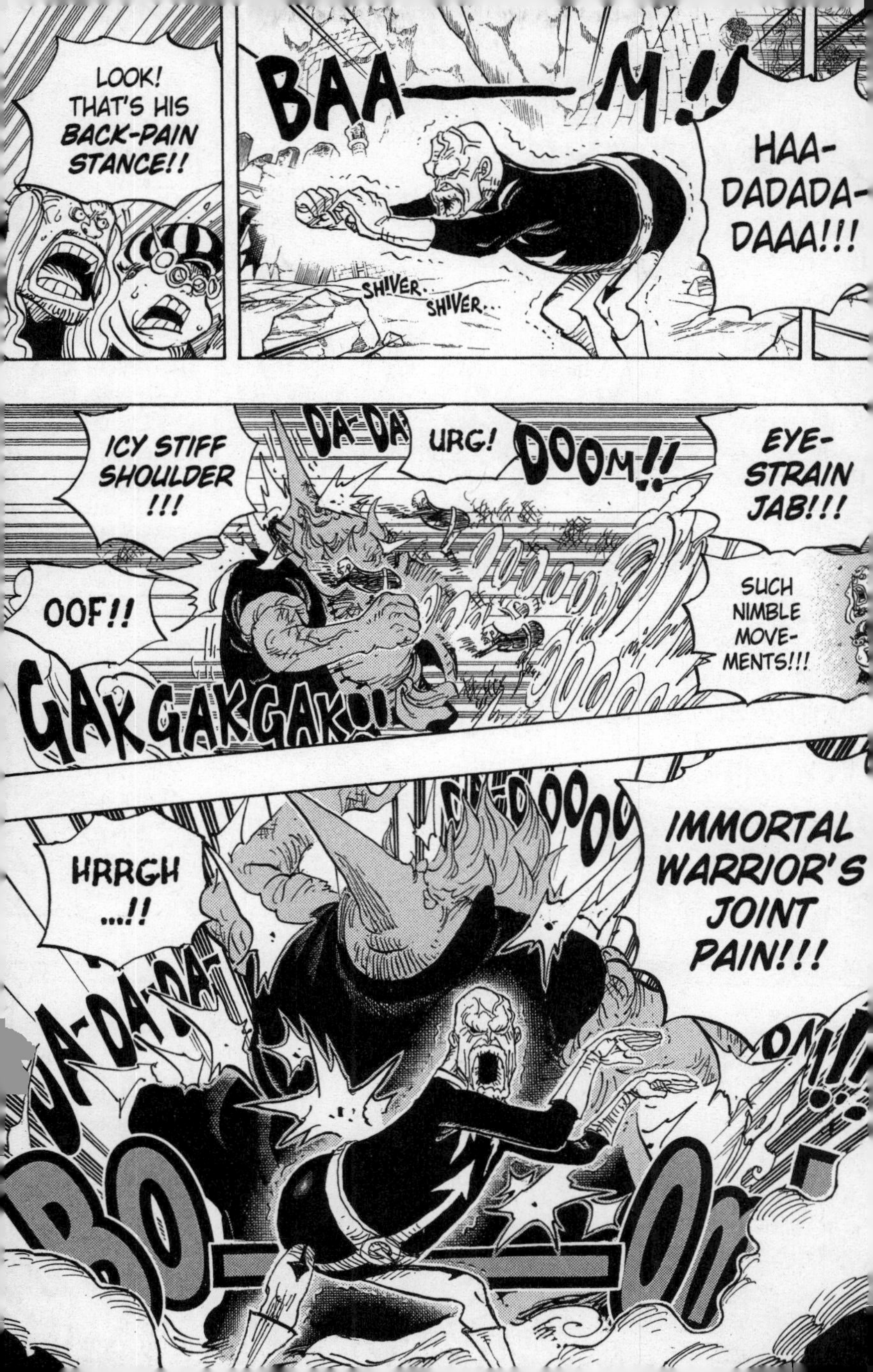
BAA—M!!
HAA-DADADA-DAAA!!!
SHIVER...
SHIVER...
LOOK! THAT'S HIS BACK-PAIN STANCE!!
EYE-STRAIN JAB!!!
DOOM!!
URG!
DA-DA
ICY STIFF SHOULDER!!!
SUCH NIMBLE MOVEMENTS!!!
OOF!!
GAKGAKGAK!!
IMMORTAL WARRIOR'S JOINT PAIN!!!
HRRGH...!!

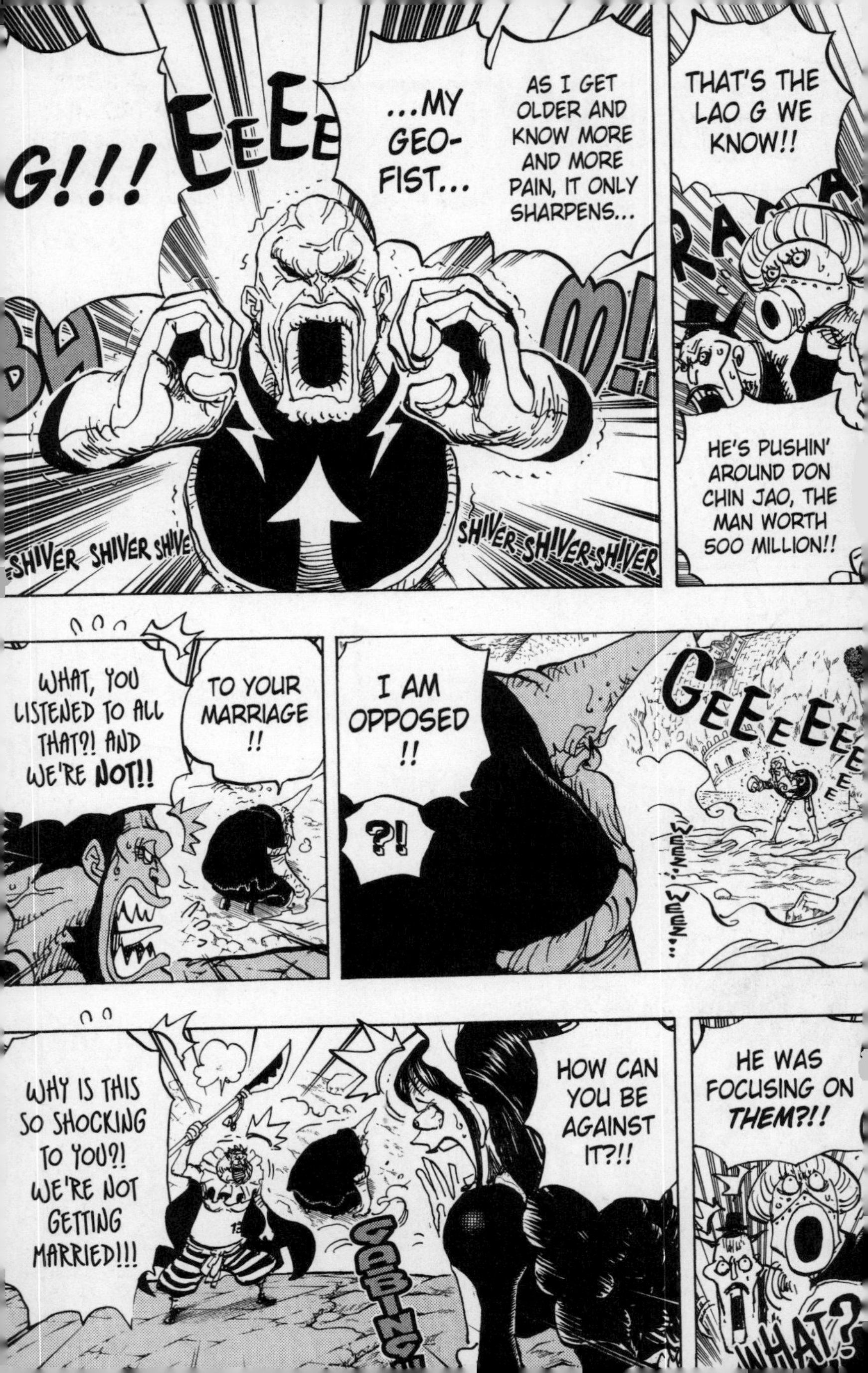
THAT'S THE LAO G WE KNOW!!
HE'S PUSHIN' AROUND DON CHIN JAO, THE MAN WORTH 500 MILLION!!
AS I GET OLDER AND KNOW MORE AND MORE PAIN, IT ONLY SHARPENS...
...MY GEO-FIST...
EEEE
G!!!
SHIVER SHIVER SHIVER
SHIVER SHIVER SHIVE
GEEEEEEE
WEEN... WEEN...
I AM OPPOSED !!
?!
TO YOUR MARRIAGE !!
WHAT, YOU LISTENED TO ALL THAT?! AND WE'RE NOT!!
HE WAS FOCUSING ON THEM?!!
WHAT?
HOW CAN YOU BE AGAINST IT?!!
WHY IS THIS SO SHOCKING TO YOU?! WE'RE NOT GETTING MARRIED!!!

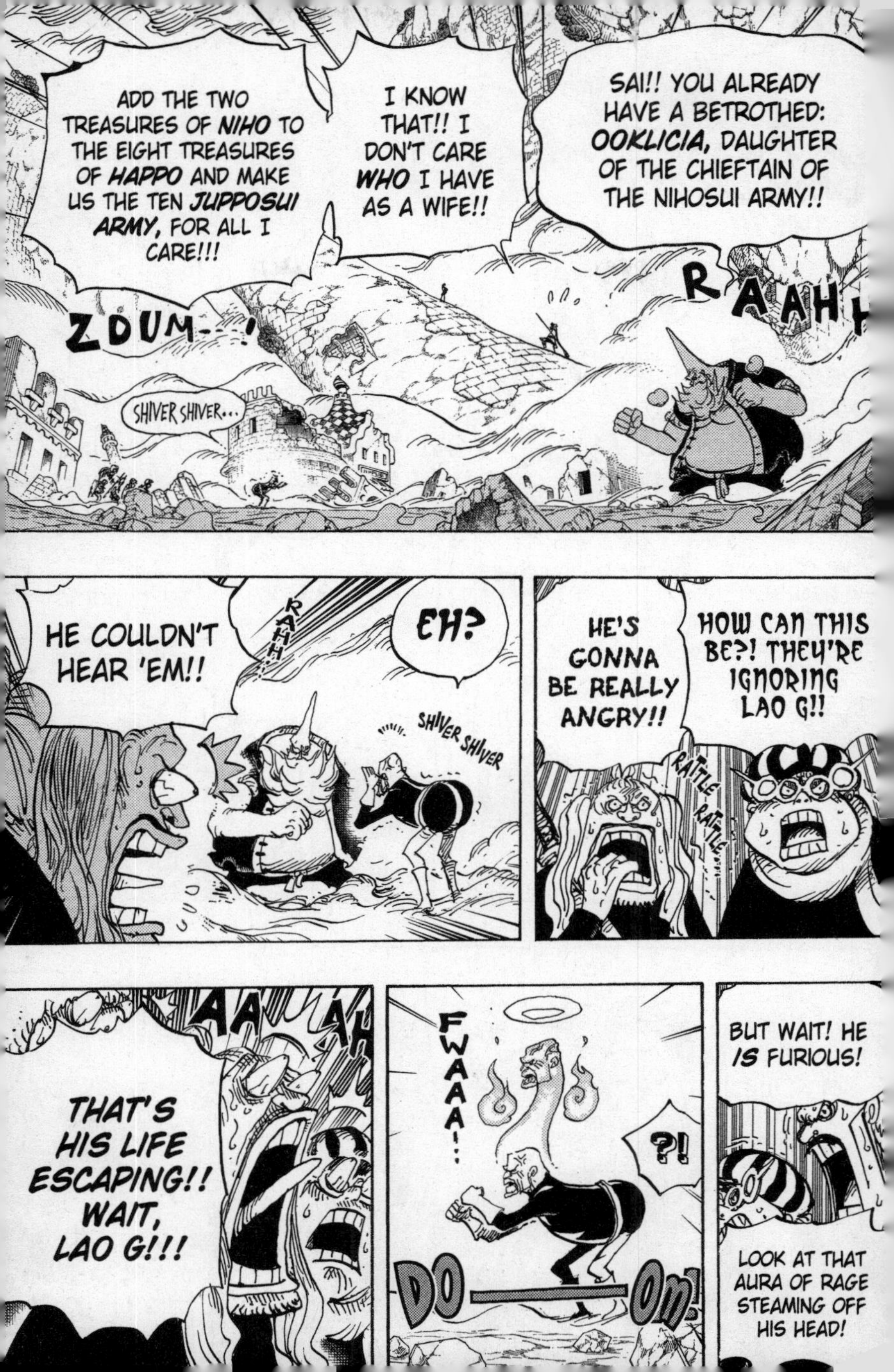
SAI!! YOU ALREADY HAVE A BETROTHED: OOKLICIA, DAUGHTER OF THE CHIEFTAIN OF THE NIHOSUI ARMY!!
I KNOW THAT!! I DON'T CARE WHO I HAVE AS A WIFE!!
ADD THE TWO TREASURES OF NIHO TO THE EIGHT TREASURES OF HAPPO AND MAKE US THE TEN JUPPOSUI ARMY, FOR ALL I CARE!!!
RAAHH
ZDUM
SHIVER SHIVER...
HOW CAN THIS BE?! THEY'RE IGNORING LAO G!!
HE'S GONNA BE REALLY ANGRY!!
RATTLE RATTLE
EH?
RAHH
HE COULDN'T HEAR 'EM!!
SHIVER SHIVER
BUT WAIT! HE IS FURIOUS!
LOOK AT THAT AURA OF RAGE STEAMING OFF HIS HEAD!
FWAAAA!
?!
DO—OM
AAAAH
THAT'S HIS LIFE ESCAPING!! WAIT, LAO G!!!

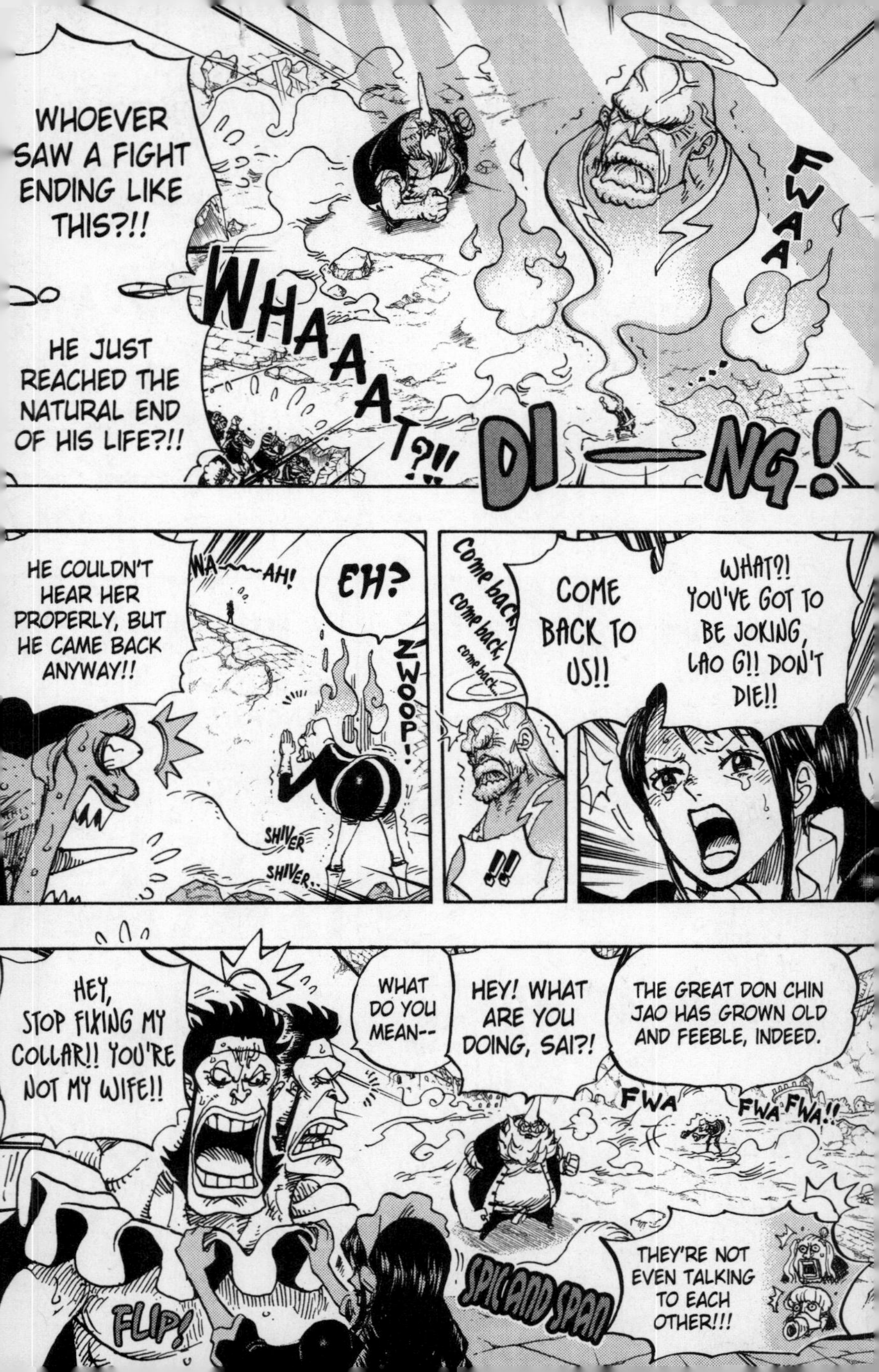
FWAA
DI—NG!
WHAAAAT?!!
WHOEVER SAW A FIGHT ENDING LIKE THIS?!!
HE JUST REACHED THE NATURAL END OF HIS LIFE?!!
WHAT?! YOU'VE GOT TO BE JOKING, LAO G!! DON'T DIE!!
come back, come back, come back...
COME BACK TO US!!
!!
EH?
ZWOOP!
WA---AH!
HE COULDN'T HEAR HER PROPERLY, BUT HE CAME BACK ANYWAY!!
SHIVER SHIVER...
THE GREAT DON CHIN JAO HAS GROWN OLD AND FEEBLE, INDEED.
HEY! WHAT ARE YOU DOING, SAI?!
WHAT DO YOU MEAN--
FWA FWA FWA!!
HEY, STOP FIXING MY COLLAR!! YOU'RE NOT MY WIFE!!
THEY'RE NOT EVEN TALKING TO EACH OTHER!!!
SPIC AND SPAN
FLIP!

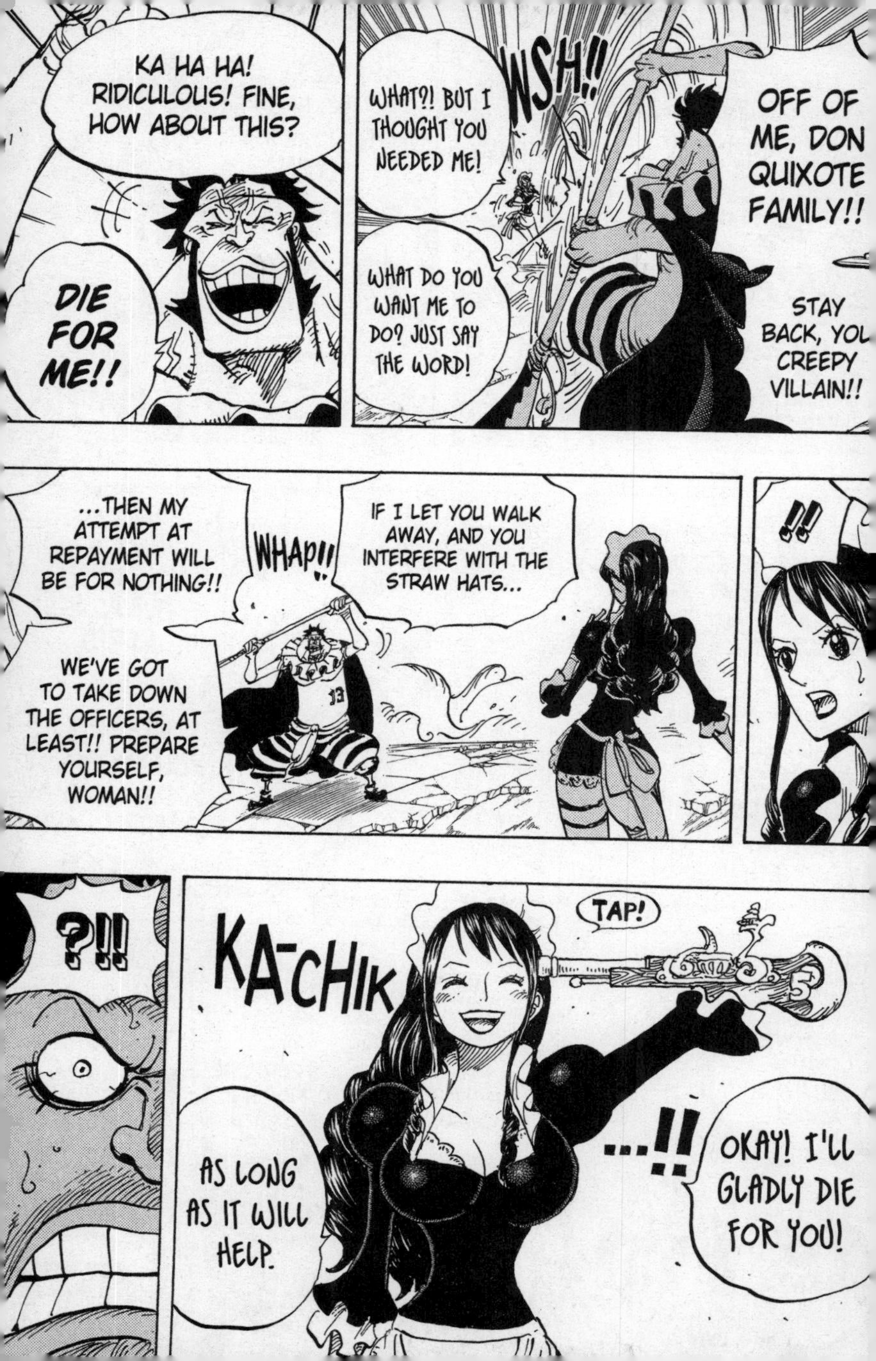
OFF OF ME, DON QUIXOTE FAMILY!!
STAY BACK, YOU CREEPY VILLAIN!!
WSH!!
WHAT?! BUT I THOUGHT YOU NEEDED ME!
WHAT DO YOU WANT ME TO DO? JUST SAY THE WORD!
KA HA HA! RIDICULOUS! FINE, HOW ABOUT THIS?
DIE FOR ME!!
!!
IF I LET YOU WALK AWAY, AND YOU INTERFERE WITH THE STRAW HATS...
WHAP!!
...THEN MY ATTEMPT AT REPAYMENT WILL BE FOR NOTHING!!
WE'VE GOT TO TAKE DOWN THE OFFICERS, AT LEAST!! PREPARE YOURSELF, WOMAN!!
TAP!
KA-CHIK
OKAY! I'LL GLADLY DIE FOR YOU!
...!!
AS LONG AS IT WILL HELP.
?!!

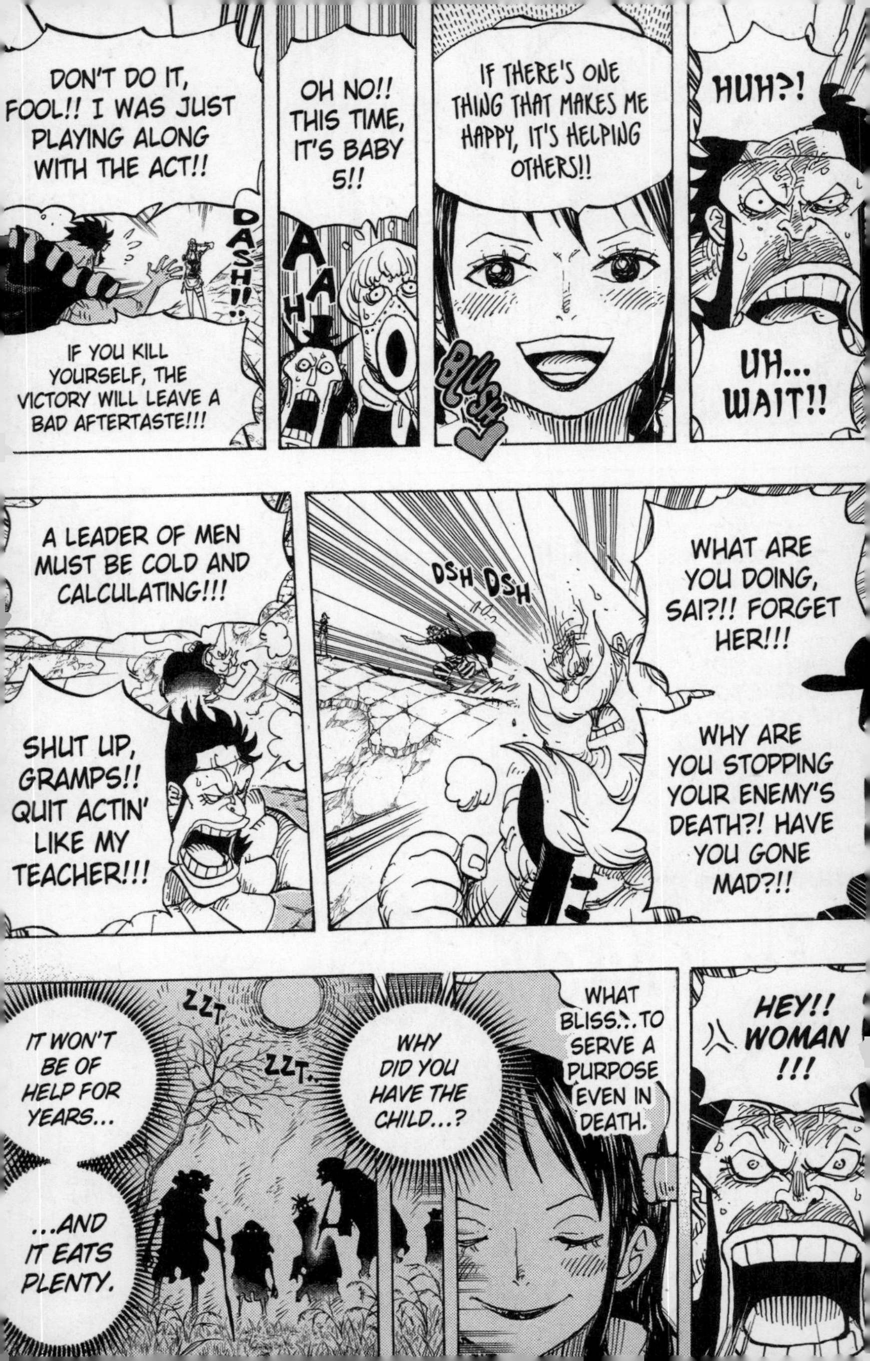
HUH?!
UH... WAIT!!
IF THERE'S ONE THING THAT MAKES ME HAPPY, IT'S HELPING OTHERS!!
BLUSH
OH NO!! THIS TIME, IT'S BABY 5!!
AAH
DON'T DO IT, FOOL!! I WAS JUST PLAYING ALONG WITH THE ACT!!
DASH!!
IF YOU KILL YOURSELF, THE VICTORY WILL LEAVE A BAD AFTERTASTE!!!
WHAT ARE YOU DOING, SAI?!! FORGET HER!!!
DSH DSH
WHY ARE YOU STOPPING YOUR ENEMY'S DEATH?! HAVE YOU GONE MAD?!!
A LEADER OF MEN MUST BE COLD AND CALCULATING!!!
SHUT UP, GRAMPS!! QUIT ACTIN' LIKE MY TEACHER!!!
HEY!! WOMAN!!!
WHAT BLISS...TO SERVE A PURPOSE EVEN IN DEATH.
ZZT
ZZT...
WHY DID YOU HAVE THE CHILD...?
IT WON'T BE OF HELP FOR YEARS...
...AND IT EATS PLENTY.

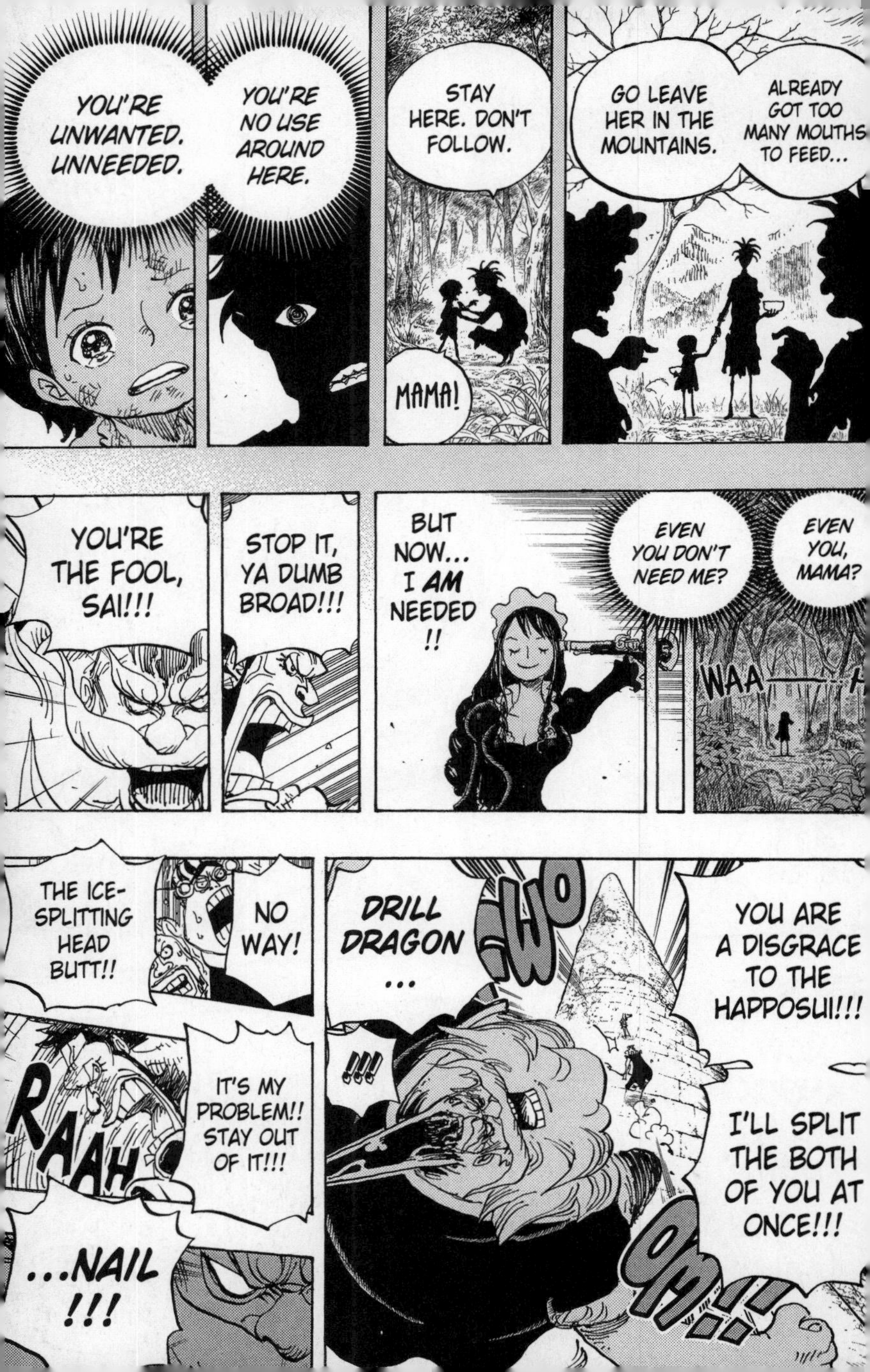
ALREADY GOT TOO MANY MOUTHS TO FEED...
GO LEAVE HER IN THE MOUNTAINS.
STAY HERE. DON'T FOLLOW.
MAMA!
YOU'RE NO USE AROUND HERE.
YOU'RE UNWANTED. UNNEEDED.
EVEN YOU, MAMA?
EVEN YOU DON'T NEED ME?
WAA——H
BUT NOW... I AM NEEDED!!
STOP IT, YA DUMB BROAD!!!
YOU'RE THE FOOL, SAI!!!
YOU ARE A DISGRACE TO THE HAPPOSUI!!!
DRILL DRAGON...
!!!
I'LL SPLIT THE BOTH OF YOU AT ONCE!!!
NO WAY!
THE ICE-SPLITTING HEAD BUTT!!
IT'S MY PROBLEM!! STAY OUT OF IT!!!
RAAH
...NAIL!!!

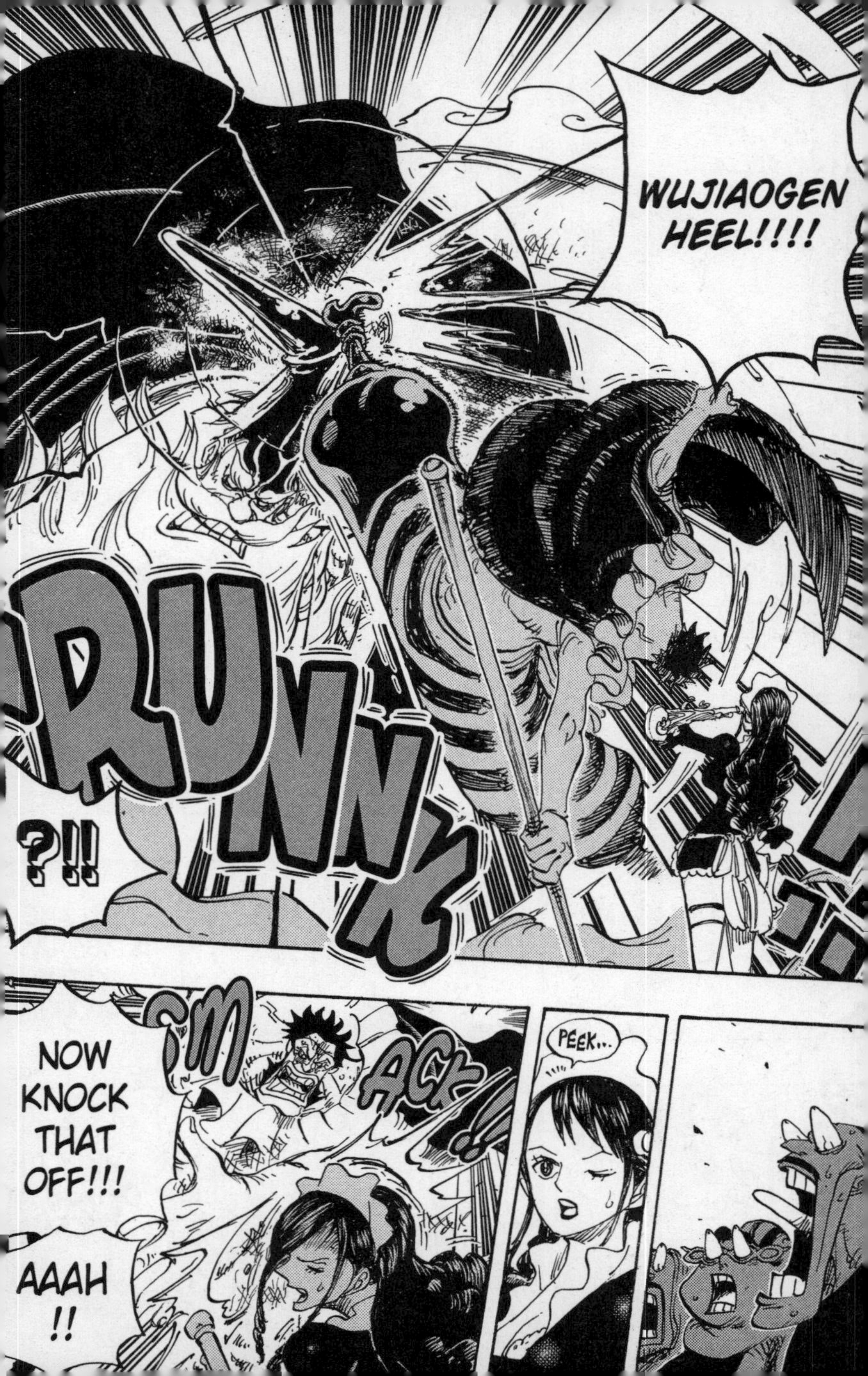
WUJIAOGEN HEEL!!!!
?!!
PEEK...
NOW KNOCK THAT OFF!!!
AAAH !!

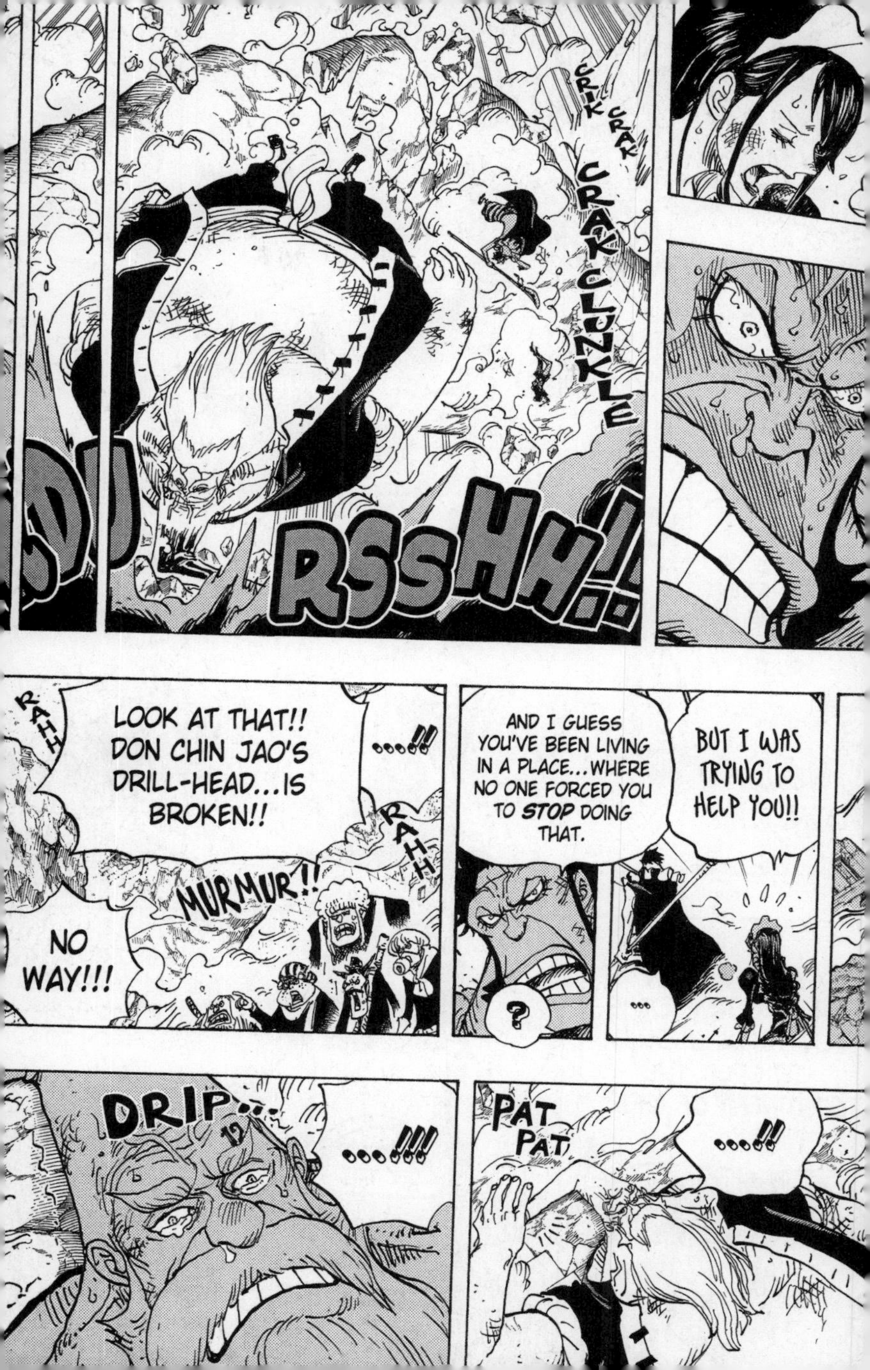
CRIK CRAK
CRAK CLUNKLE
RSSHH!!
BUT I WAS TRYING TO HELP YOU!!
...
AND I GUESS YOU'VE BEEN LIVING IN A PLACE...WHERE NO ONE FORCED YOU TO STOP DOING THAT.
?
...!!
RAHH
LOOK AT THAT!! DON CHIN JAO'S DRILL-HEAD...IS BROKEN!!
RAHH
MURMUR!!
NO WAY!!!
PAT PAT
...!!
DRIP...
...!!!

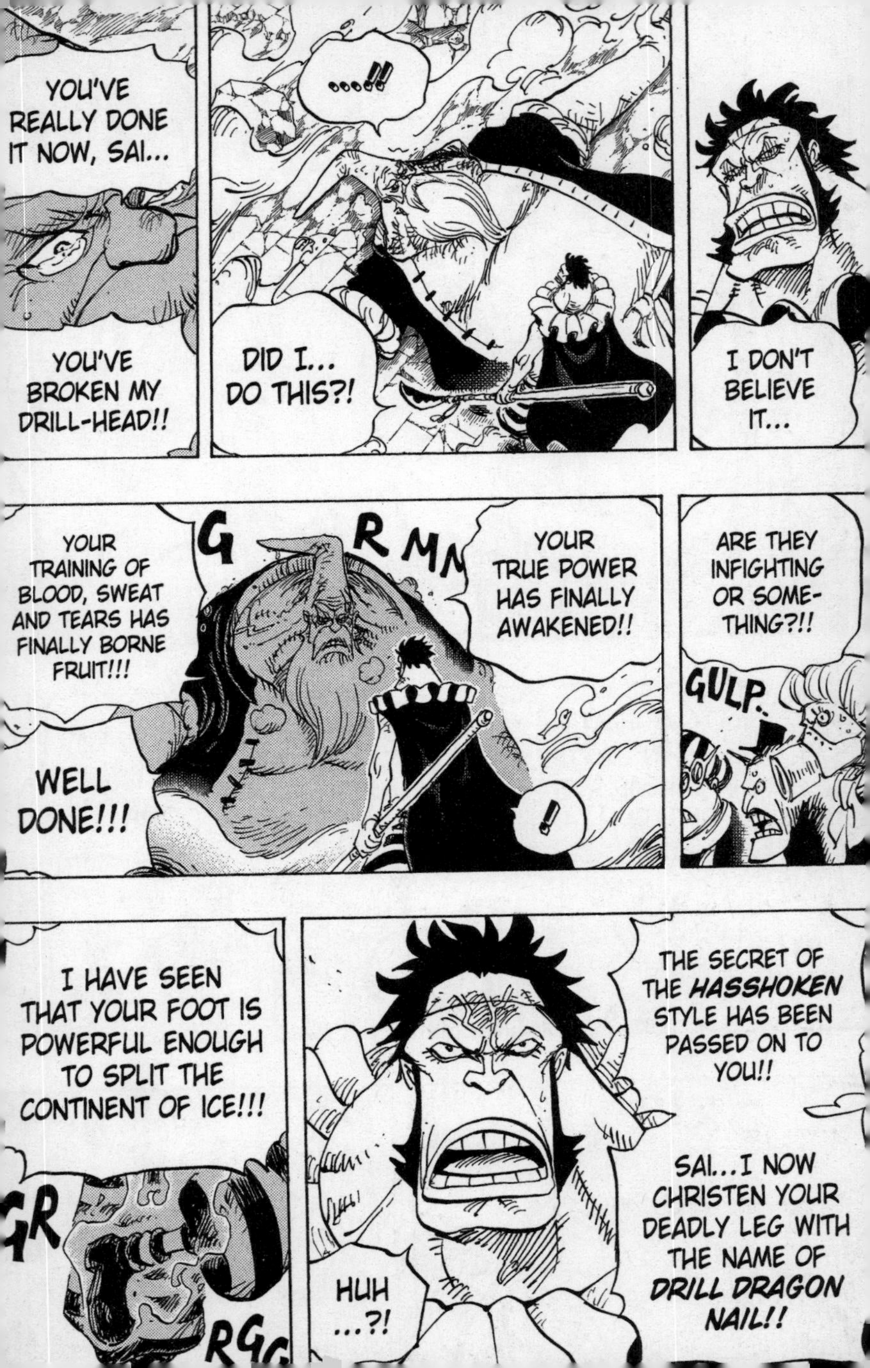
I DON'T BELIEVE IT...
....!!
DID I... DO THIS?!
YOU'VE REALLY DONE IT NOW, SAI...
YOU'VE BROKEN MY DRILL-HEAD!!
ARE THEY INFIGHTING OR SOMETHING?!!
GULP..
YOUR TRUE POWER HAS FINALLY AWAKENED!!
GRMM
YOUR TRAINING OF BLOOD, SWEAT AND TEARS HAS FINALLY BORNE FRUIT!!!
!
WELL DONE!!!
THE SECRET OF THE *HASSHOKEN* STYLE HAS BEEN PASSED ON TO YOU!!
SAI...I NOW CHRISTEN YOUR DEADLY LEG WITH THE NAME OF *DRILL DRAGON NAIL!!*
HUH ...?!
I HAVE SEEN THAT YOUR FOOT IS POWERFUL ENOUGH TO SPLIT THE CONTINENT OF ICE!!!
GR
RGG

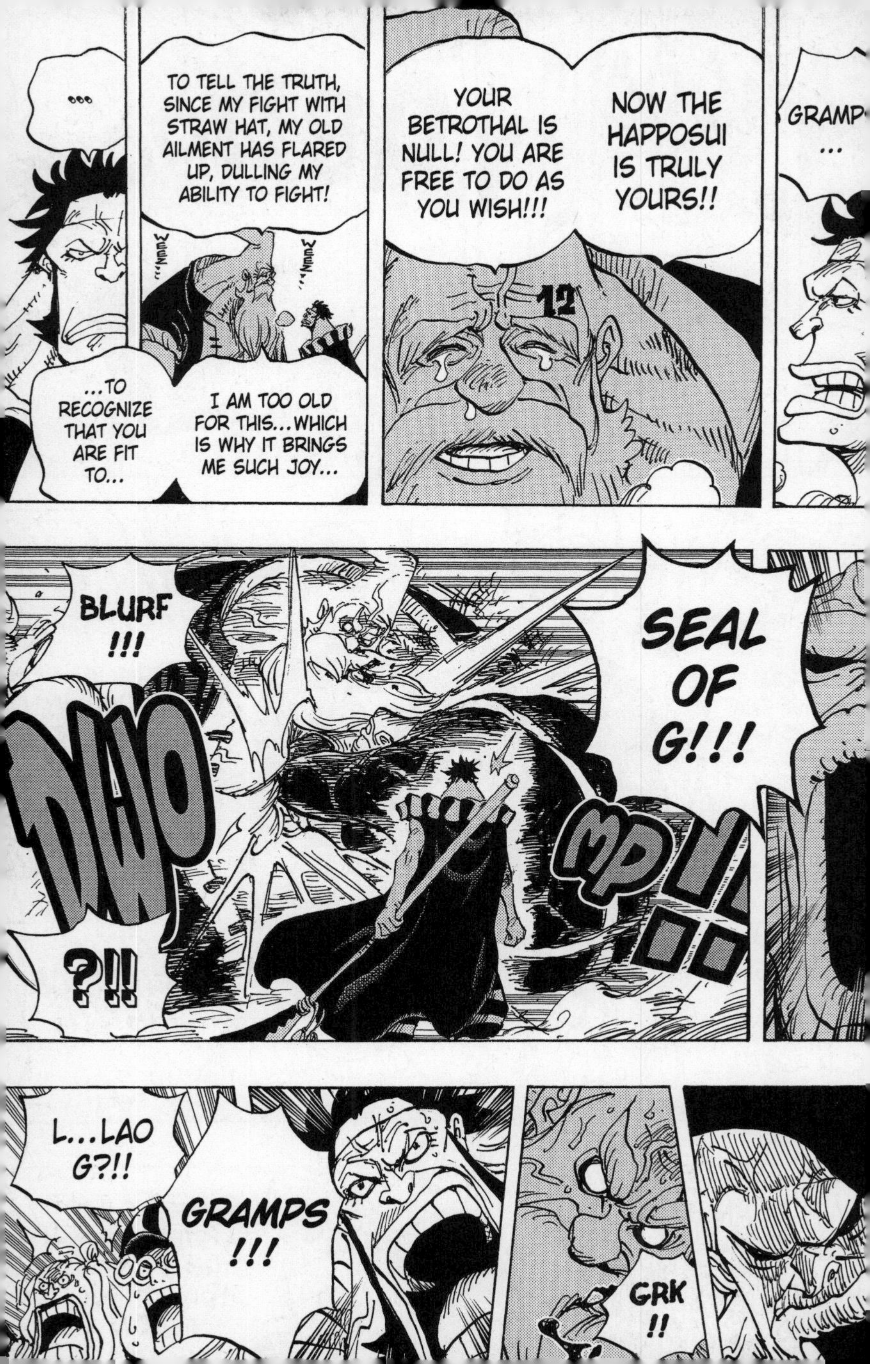
GRAMPS...
NOW THE HAPPOSUI IS TRULY YOURS!!
YOUR BETROTHAL IS NULL! YOU ARE FREE TO DO AS YOU WISH!!!
12
TO TELL THE TRUTH, SINCE MY FIGHT WITH STRAW HAT, MY OLD AILMENT HAS FLARED UP, DULLING MY ABILITY TO FIGHT!
WEEN...
WEEN...
I AM TOO OLD FOR THIS...WHICH IS WHY IT BRINGS ME SUCH JOY...
...TO RECOGNIZE THAT YOU ARE FIT TO...
...
SEAL OF G!!!
BLURF !!!
?!!
GRK !!
GRAMPS !!!
L...LAO G?!!

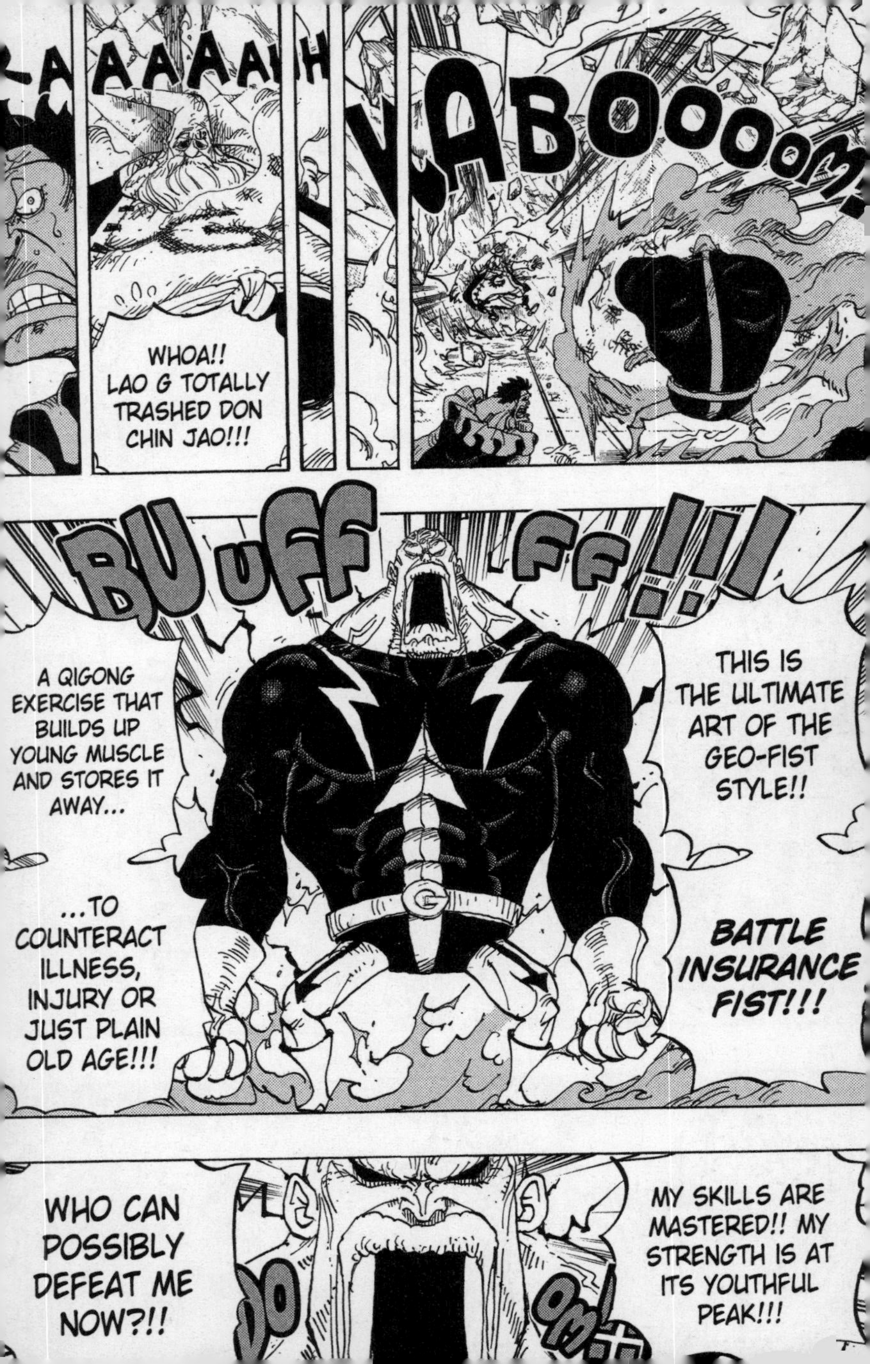
VABOOOOM!
AAAAAHH
WHOA!! LAO G TOTALLY TRASHED DON CHIN JAO!!!
BUFFFF!!!
THIS IS THE ULTIMATE ART OF THE GEO-FIST STYLE!!
A QIGONG EXERCISE THAT BUILDS UP YOUNG MUSCLE AND STORES IT AWAY...
...TO COUNTERACT ILLNESS, INJURY OR JUST PLAIN OLD AGE!!!
BATTLE INSURANCE FIST!!!
MY SKILLS ARE MASTERED!! MY STRENGTH IS AT ITS YOUTHFUL PEAK!!!
WHO CAN POSSIBLY DEFEAT ME NOW?!!

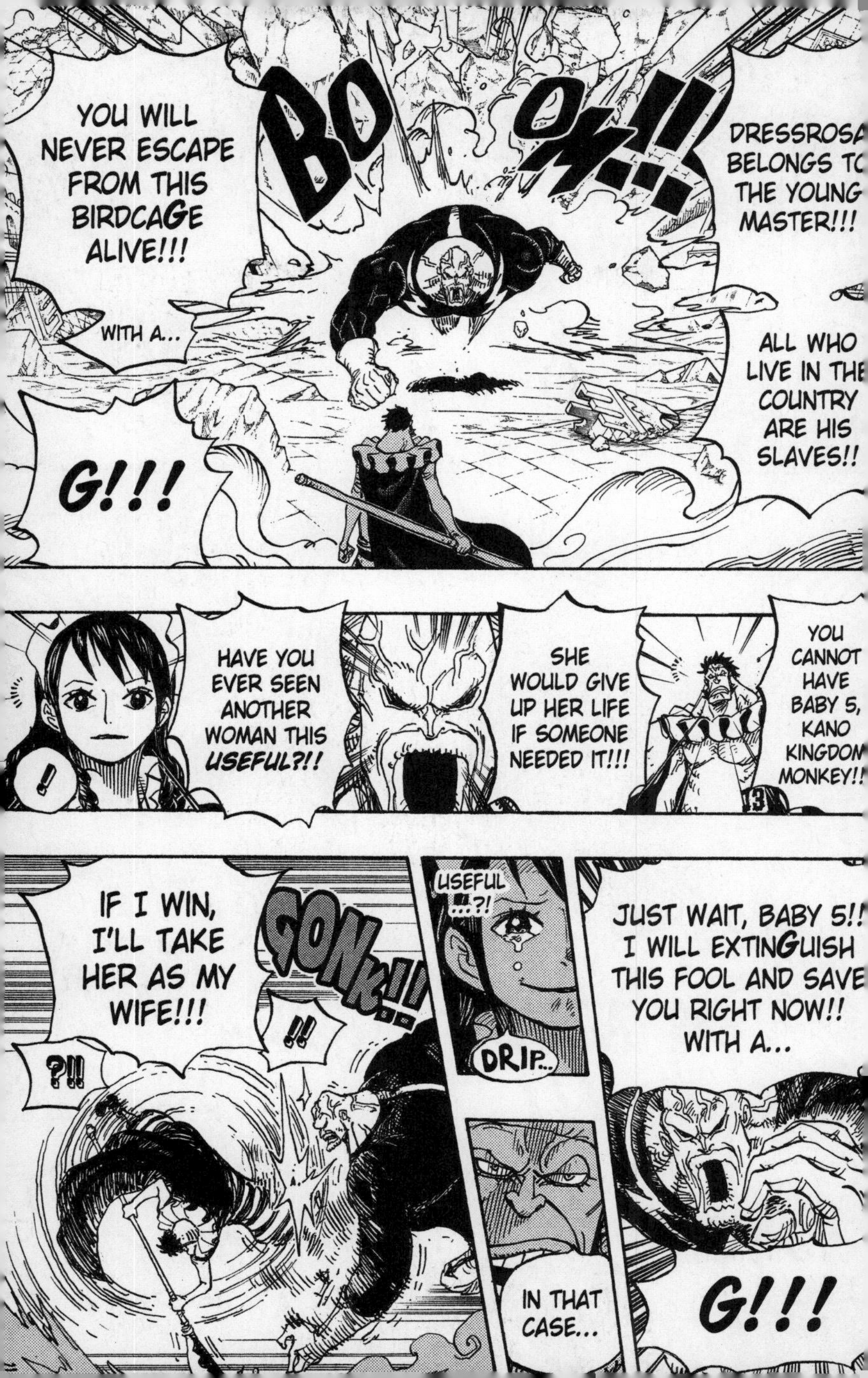
DRESSROSA BELONGS TO THE YOUNG MASTER!!!
ALL WHO LIVE IN THE COUNTRY ARE HIS SLAVES!!
BO OM!!
YOU WILL NEVER ESCAPE FROM THIS BIRDCAGE ALIVE!!!
WITH A...
G!!!
YOU CANNOT HAVE BABY 5, KANO KINGDOM MONKEY!!
SHE WOULD GIVE UP HER LIFE IF SOMEONE NEEDED IT!!!
HAVE YOU EVER SEEN ANOTHER WOMAN THIS USEFUL?!!
!
JUST WAIT, BABY 5!! I WILL EXTINGUISH THIS FOOL AND SAVE YOU RIGHT NOW!! WITH A...
G!!!
USEFUL ...?!
DRIP...
IN THAT CASE...
IF I WIN, I'LL TAKE HER AS MY WIFE!!!
GONK!!!
!!
?!!

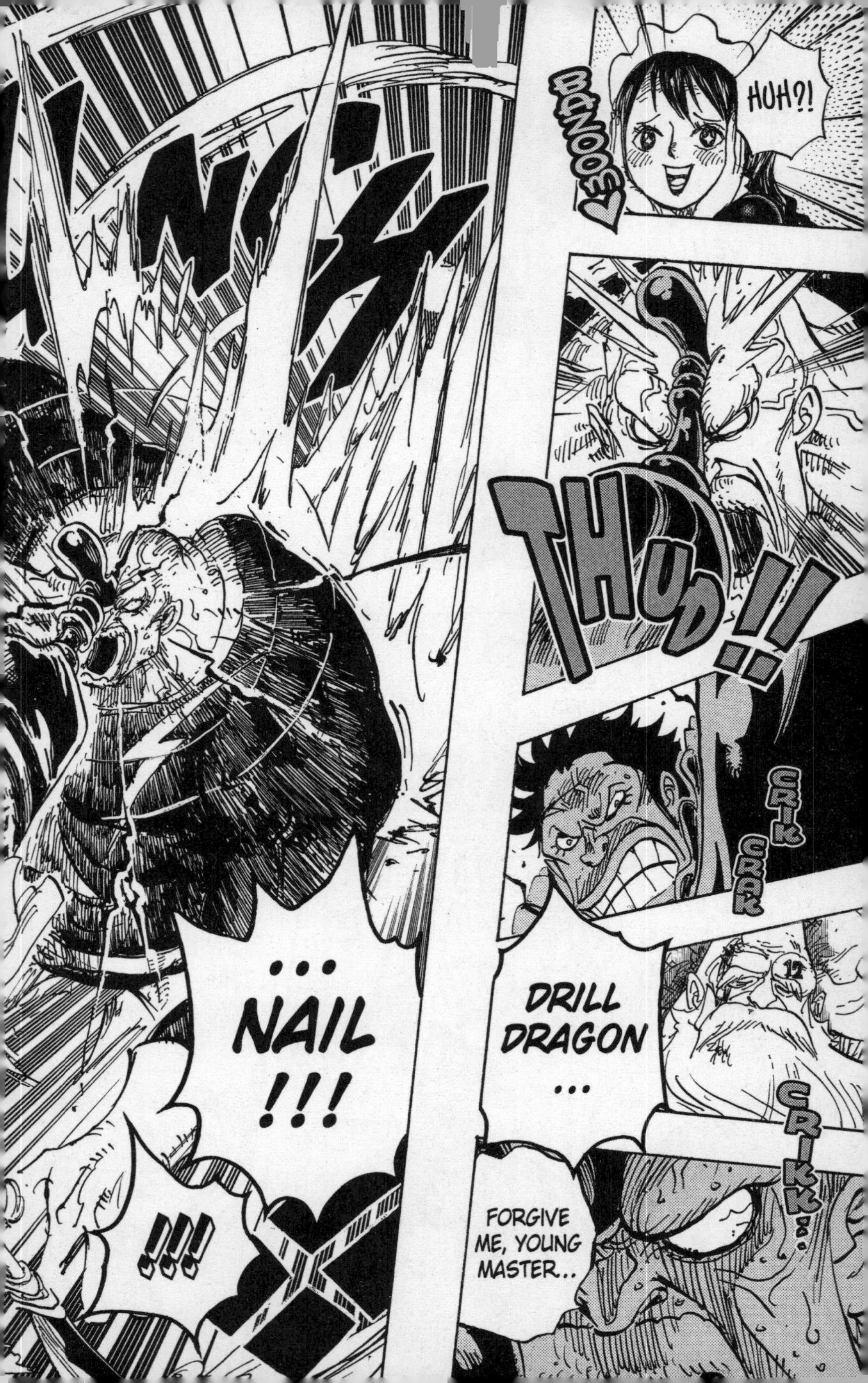
HUH?!
THUD!!
CRIK
CRAK
DRILL DRAGON ...
CRIKKK
FORGIVE ME, YOUNG MASTER...
... NAIL !!!
!!!

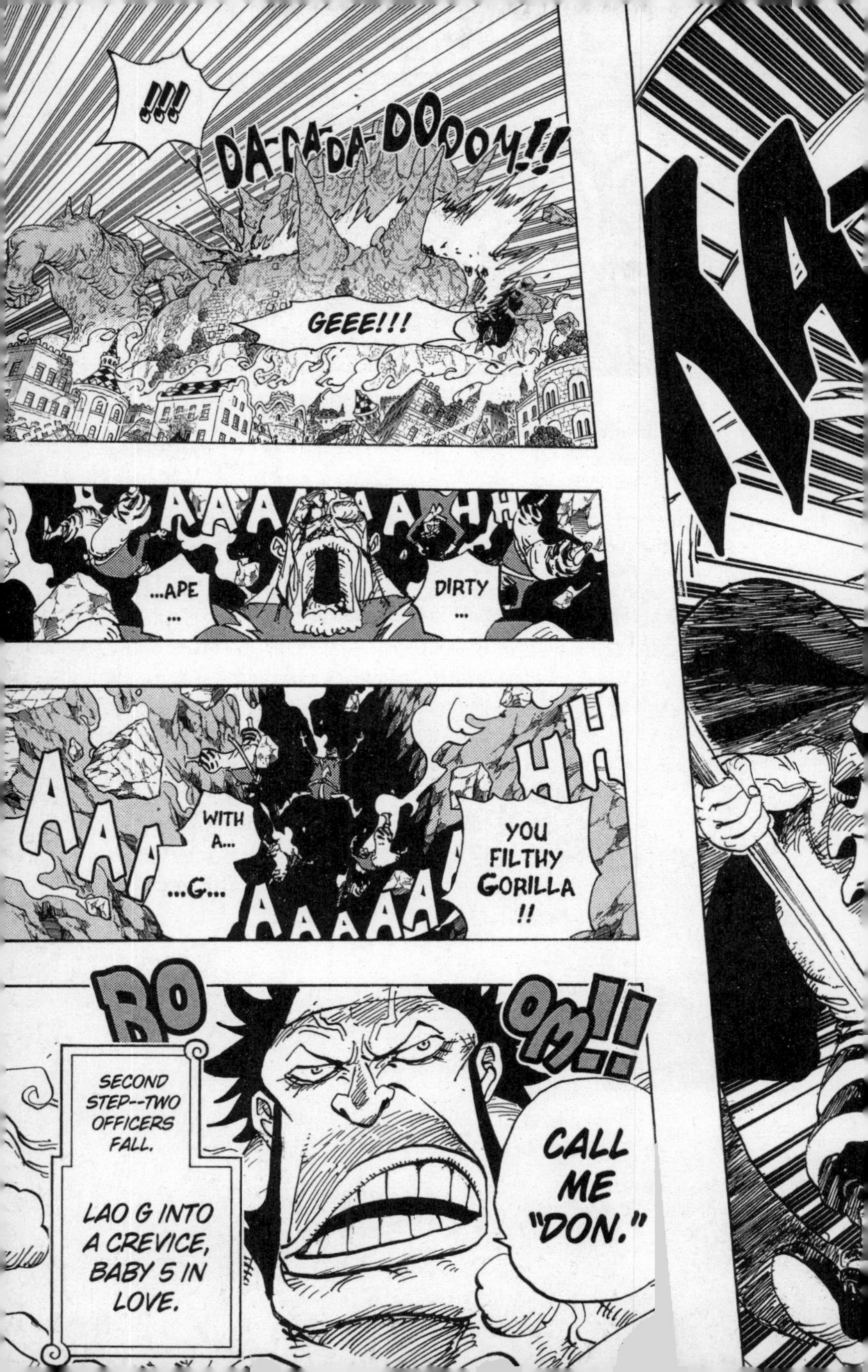

!!!
DA-DA-DA-DOOOM!!
GEEE!!!
AAAAAAAHH
DIRTY ...
...APE ...
HH
YOU FILTHY GORILLA !!
WITH A...
...G...
AAAAAAAA
BOOM!!
CALL ME "DON."
SECOND STEP--TWO OFFICERS FALL.
LAO G INTO A CREVICE, BABY 5 IN LOVE.

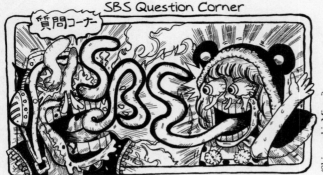

SBS Question Corner

質問コーナー
SBS

(Shimayuki, Miyagi)

Q: A question for Ei-chan. If you ate a single bite of a Devil Fruit, and someone else ate the leftovers, would they get the powers too? Thanks for the answer!!

-- ☆ Monkey ☆

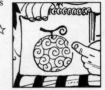

A: Uh, they won't. The instant someone takes a bite, the power belongs to that person, and the rest is just a really gross fruit. Nobody seems to realize this, because they always eat the entire fruit afterward.

Q: Tell us the height and age for the revolutionaries Sabo, Koala and Hack, and what kind of fish-man species Hack is! Also, can Hack's birthday be August 9, since ha*(chi)* is 8, and ku is 9?

--Katana★Romance

A: Yep. That's the only choice for his birthday.

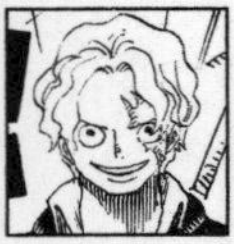

6'1"
22 years old

Sabo

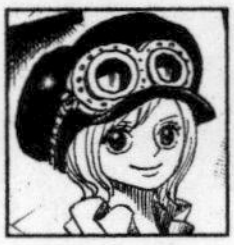

5'3"
23 years old

Koala

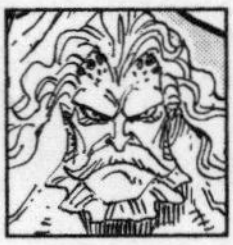

9'2"
38 years old
(Soldierfish fish-man)

Hack

Q: Congrats on your marriage, Baby 5 and Sai!! I couldn't help but wonder what kind of woman Ooklicia, Sai's betrothed, is though! Her name sounds a bit gorilla-ish… I get the impression that she's a quite hardy individual…

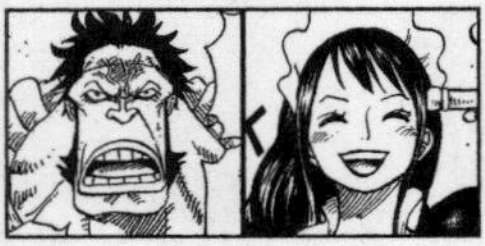

--Heidi Senpai

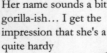

A: I've heard she's a woman with beautiful hair and a cool gaze. ➡

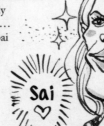

Sai
♡

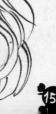

Chapter 772: CABBAGE & LOMEO

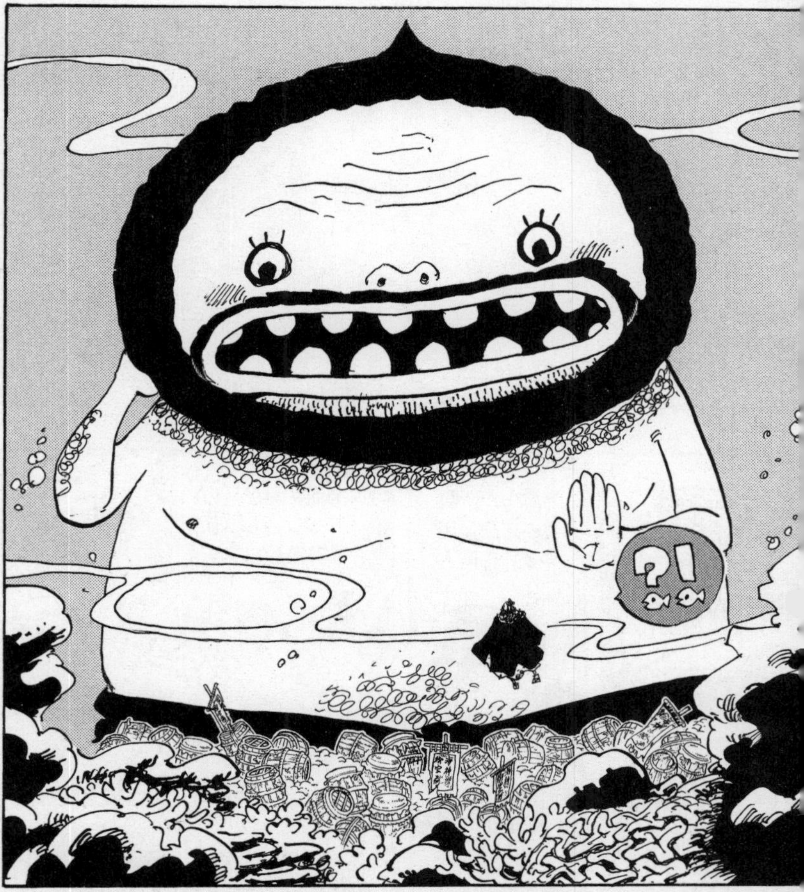
?!

THE SOLITARY JOURNEY OF JIMBEI, FIRST SON OF THE SEA, VOL. 18: "THE GIANT MONK, SEA GOD WADATSUMI APPEARS, 'NO NEED TO THANK ME'!"

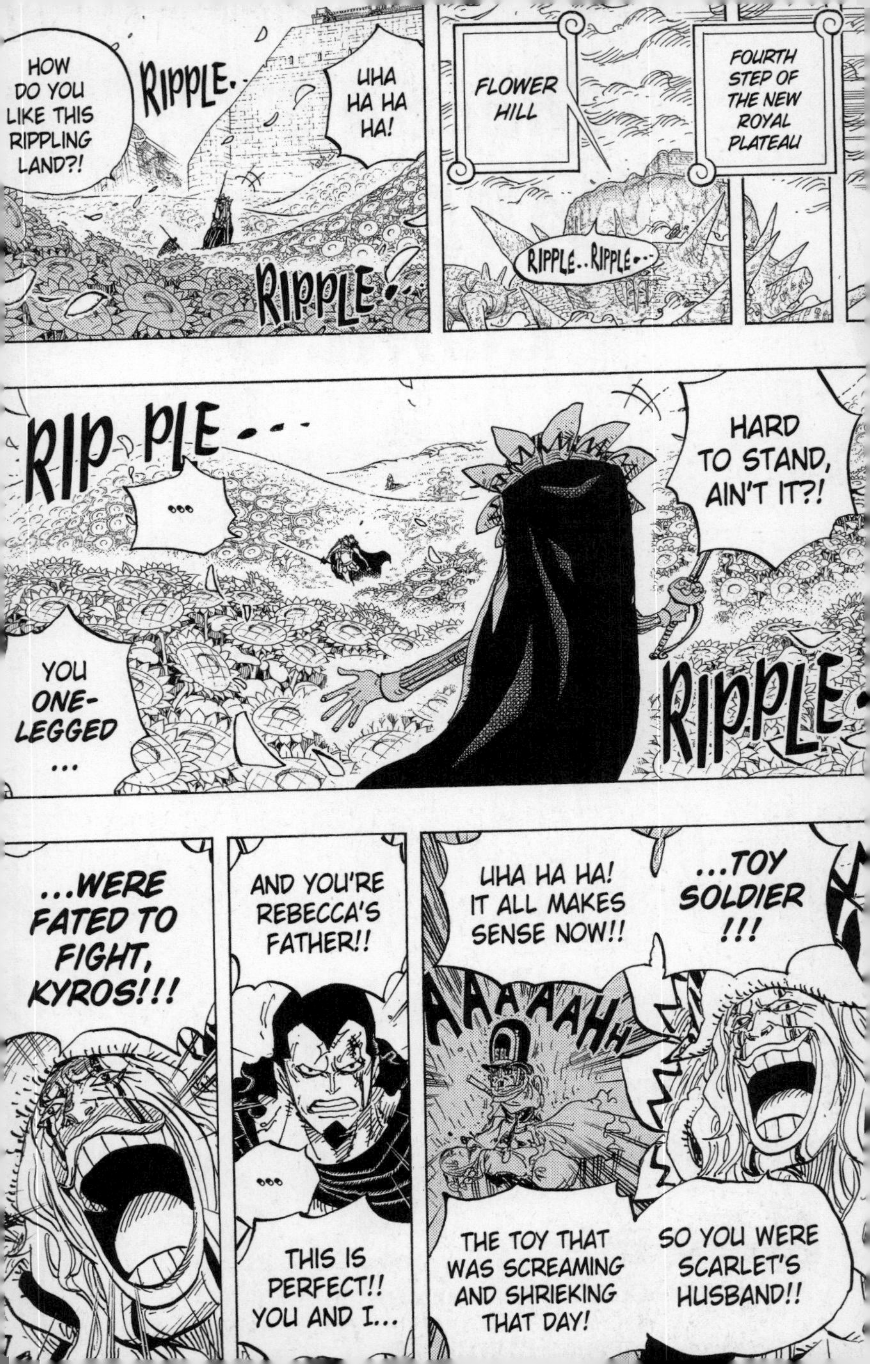
FOURTH STEP OF THE NEW ROYAL PLATEAU
FLOWER HILL
RIPPLE.. RIPPLE...
UHA HA HA HA!
RIPPLE.
HOW DO YOU LIKE THIS RIPPLING LAND?!
RIPPLE!
HARD TO STAND, AIN'T IT?!
RIPPLE
RIP PLE...
...
YOU ONE-LEGGED ...
...TOY SOLDIER!!!
UHA HA HA! IT ALL MAKES SENSE NOW!!
AAAAAHH
SO YOU WERE SCARLET'S HUSBAND!!
THE TOY THAT WAS SCREAMING AND SHRIEKING THAT DAY!
AND YOU'RE REBECCA'S FATHER!!
...
THIS IS PERFECT!! YOU AND I...
...WERE FATED TO FIGHT, KYROS!!!

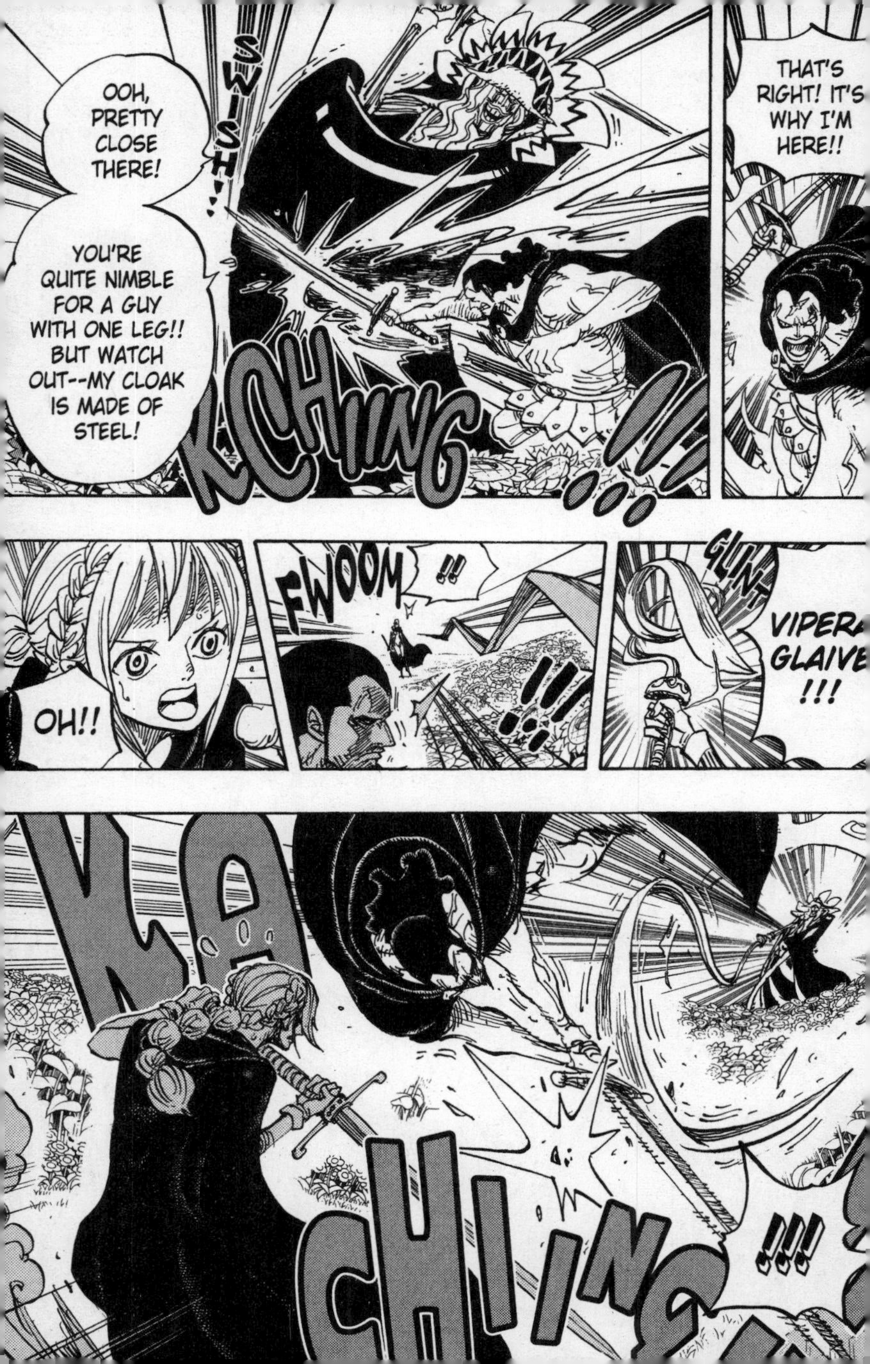
THAT'S RIGHT! IT'S WHY I'M HERE!!
SWISH
OOH, PRETTY CLOSE THERE!
YOU'RE QUITE NIMBLE FOR A GUY WITH ONE LEG!! BUT WATCH OUT--MY CLOAK IS MADE OF STEEL!
KCHIING
GLINT
VIPER GLAIVE!!!
FWOOM!!
!!!
OH!!
CHIING!!!

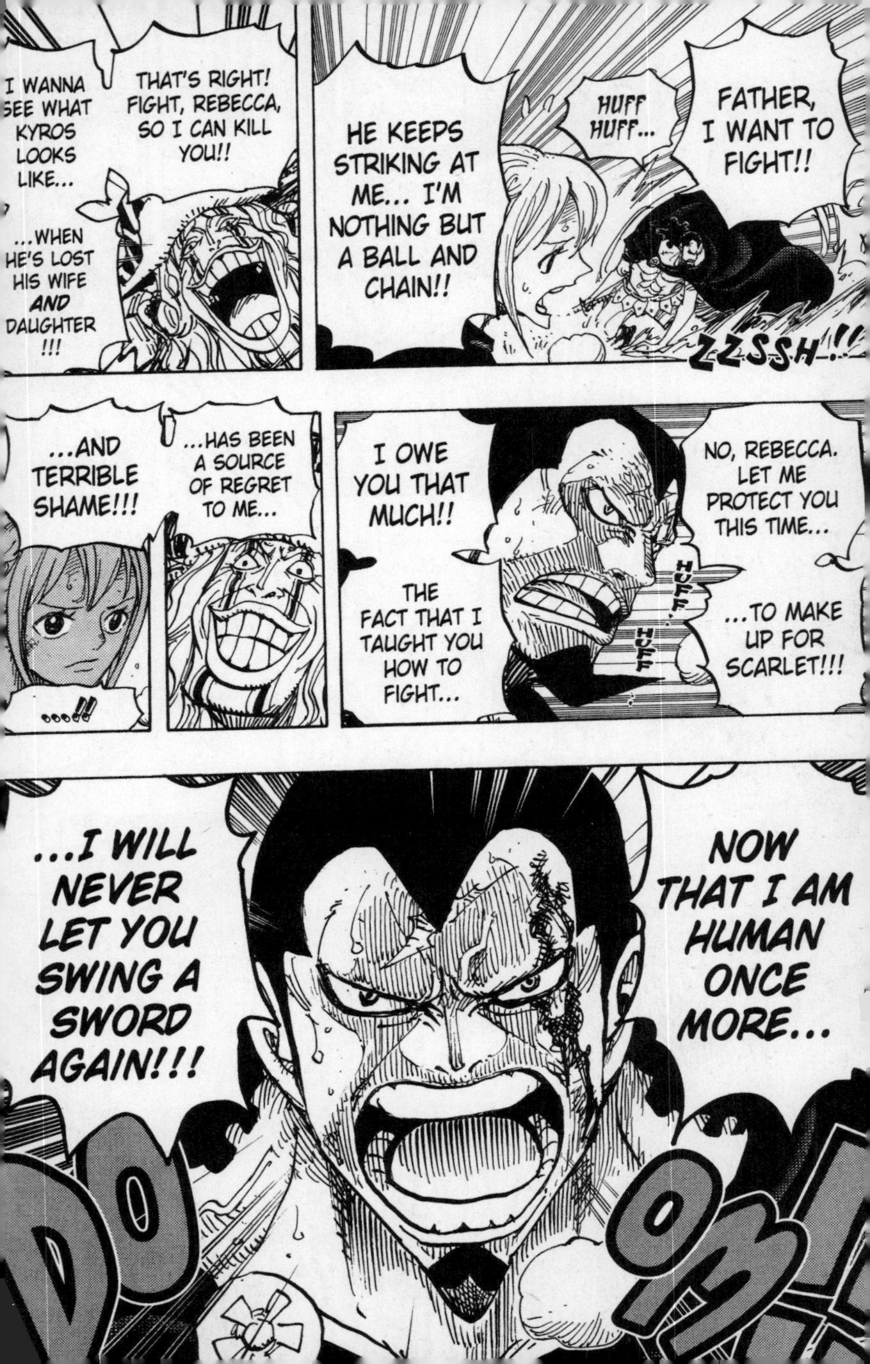
HUFF HUFF...
FATHER, I WANT TO FIGHT!!
HE KEEPS STRIKING AT ME... I'M NOTHING BUT A BALL AND CHAIN!!
ZZSSH!!
THAT'S RIGHT! FIGHT, REBECCA, SO I CAN KILL YOU!!
I WANNA SEE WHAT KYROS LOOKS LIKE...
...WHEN HE'S LOST HIS WIFE AND DAUGHTER!!!
NO, REBECCA. LET ME PROTECT YOU THIS TIME...
...TO MAKE UP FOR SCARLET!!!
HUFF HUFF
I OWE YOU THAT MUCH!!
THE FACT THAT I TAUGHT YOU HOW TO FIGHT...
...HAS BEEN A SOURCE OF REGRET TO ME...
...AND TERRIBLE SHAME!!!
...!!
NOW THAT I AM HUMAN ONCE MORE...
...I WILL NEVER LET YOU SWING A SWORD AGAIN!!!

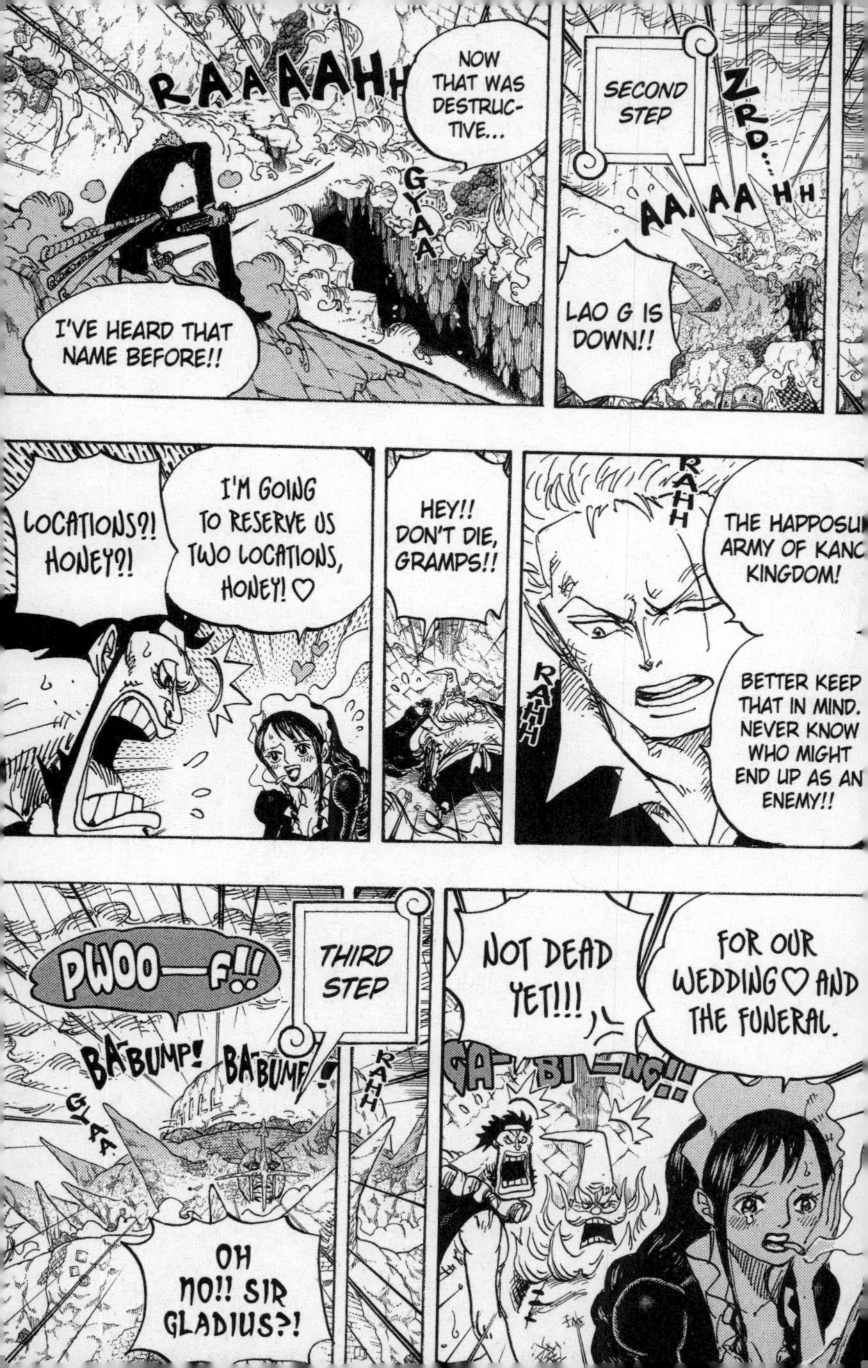
SECOND STEP
ZRD...
AAAAAHH
LAO G IS DOWN!!
NOW THAT WAS DESTRUCTIVE...
RAAAAHH
GYAA
I'VE HEARD THAT NAME BEFORE!!
RAHH
THE HAPPOSUI ARMY OF KANO KINGDOM!
RAHH
BETTER KEEP THAT IN MIND. NEVER KNOW WHO MIGHT END UP AS AN ENEMY!!
HEY!! DON'T DIE, GRAMPS!!
I'M GOING TO RESERVE US TWO LOCATIONS, HONEY! ♡
LOCATIONS?! HONEY?!
FOR OUR WEDDING ♡ AND THE FUNERAL.
NOT DEAD YET!!!
GA-BI—NG!!
THIRD STEP
RAHH
PWOO—F!!
BA-BUMP! BA-BUMP!
GYAA
OH NO!! SIR GLADIUS?!

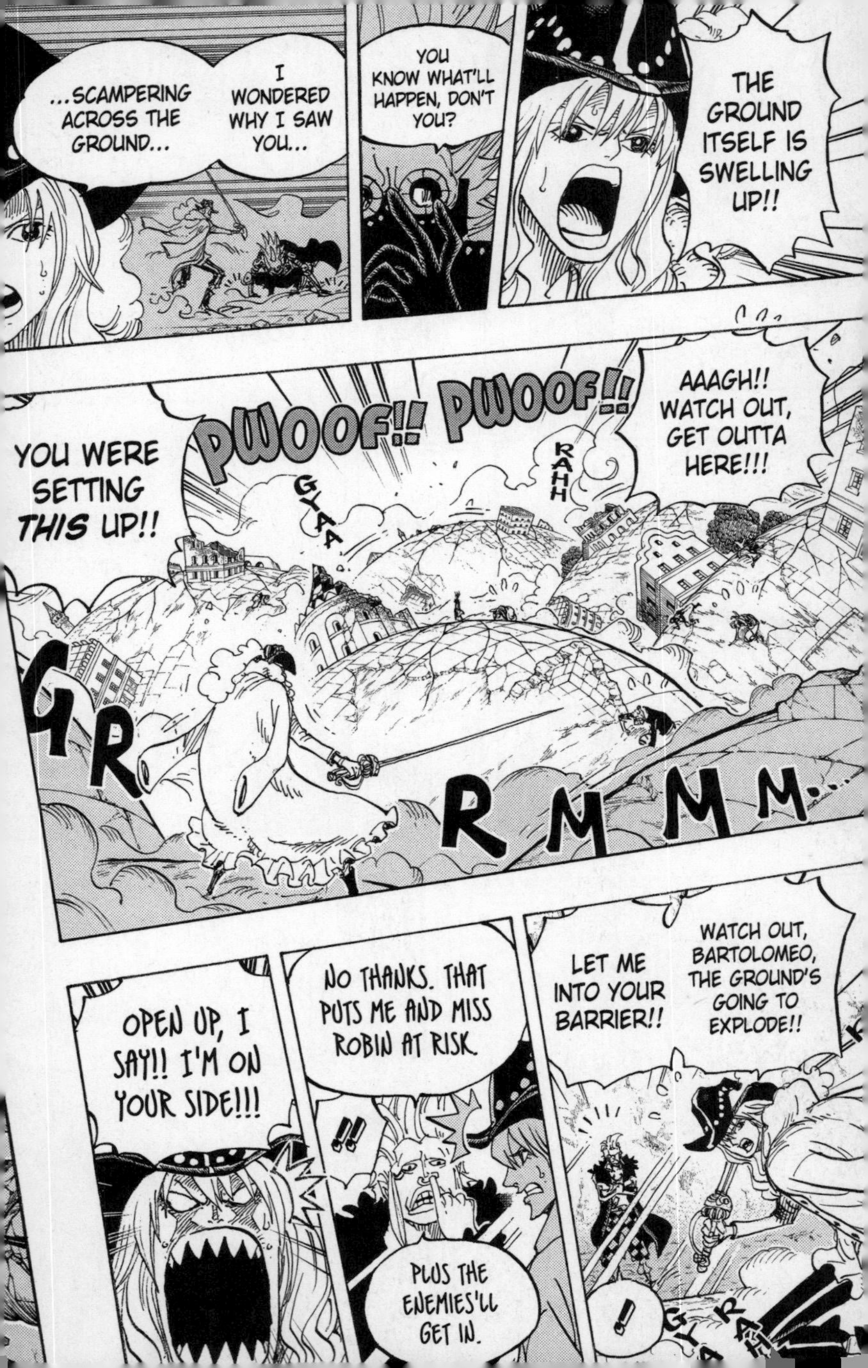
THE GROUND ITSELF IS SWELLING UP!!
YOU KNOW WHAT'LL HAPPEN, DON'T YOU?
I WONDERED WHY I SAW YOU...
...SCAMPERING ACROSS THE GROUND...
AAAGH!! WATCH OUT, GET OUTTA HERE!!!
PWOOF!! PWOOF!!
RAHH
GYAA
YOU WERE SETTING THIS UP!!
RMMM...
WATCH OUT, BARTOLOMEO, THE GROUND'S GOING TO EXPLODE!!
LET ME INTO YOUR BARRIER!!
!
NO THANKS. THAT PUTS ME AND MISS ROBIN AT RISK.
!!
PLUS THE ENEMIES'LL GET IN.
OPEN UP, I SAY!! I'M ON YOUR SIDE!!!

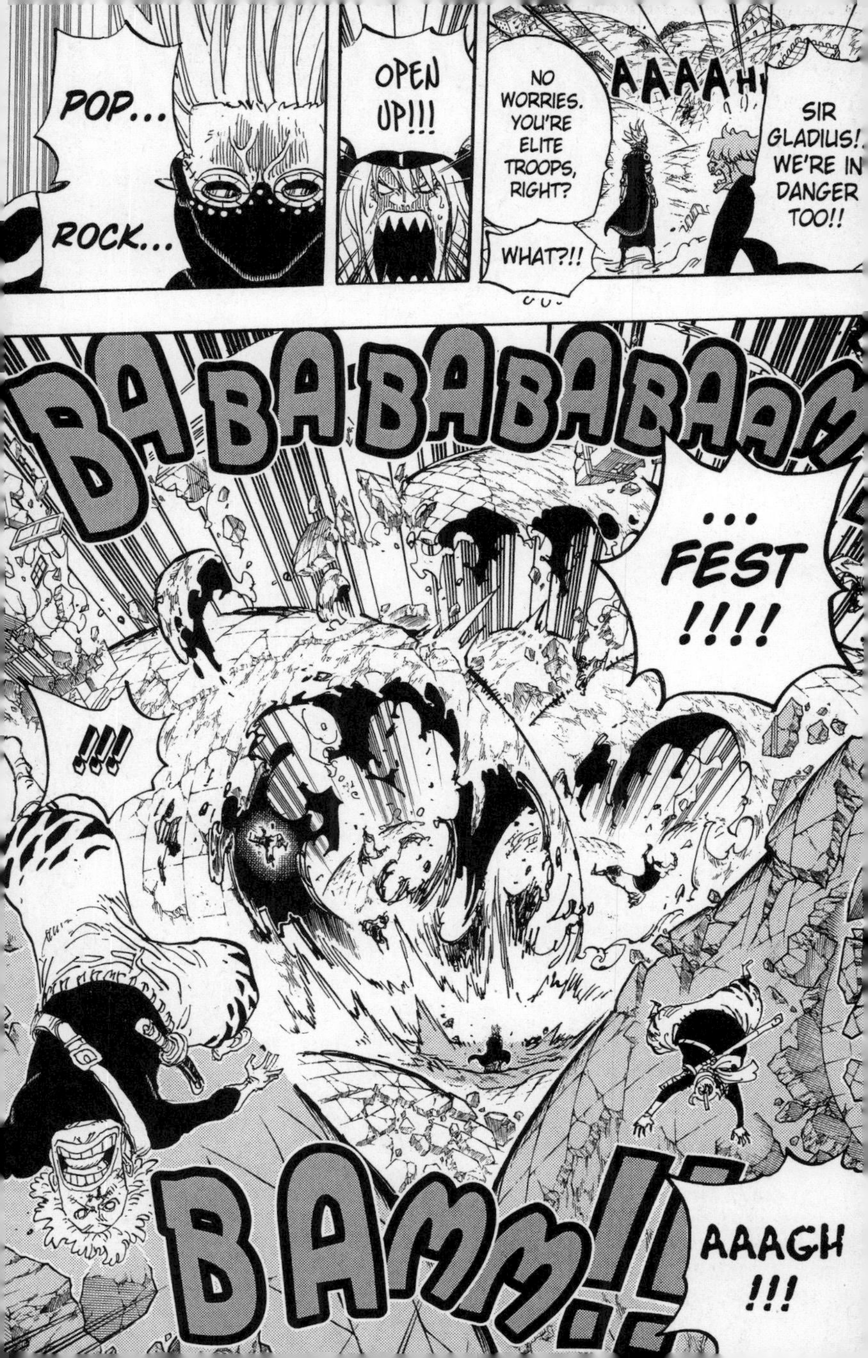
SIR GLADIUS!! WE'RE IN DANGER TOO!!
AAAAH
NO WORRIES. YOU'RE ELITE TROOPS, RIGHT?
WHAT?!!
OPEN UP!!!
POP...
ROCK...
BABABABABAAAM
... FEST !!!!
!!!
BAMM!!
AAAGH !!!

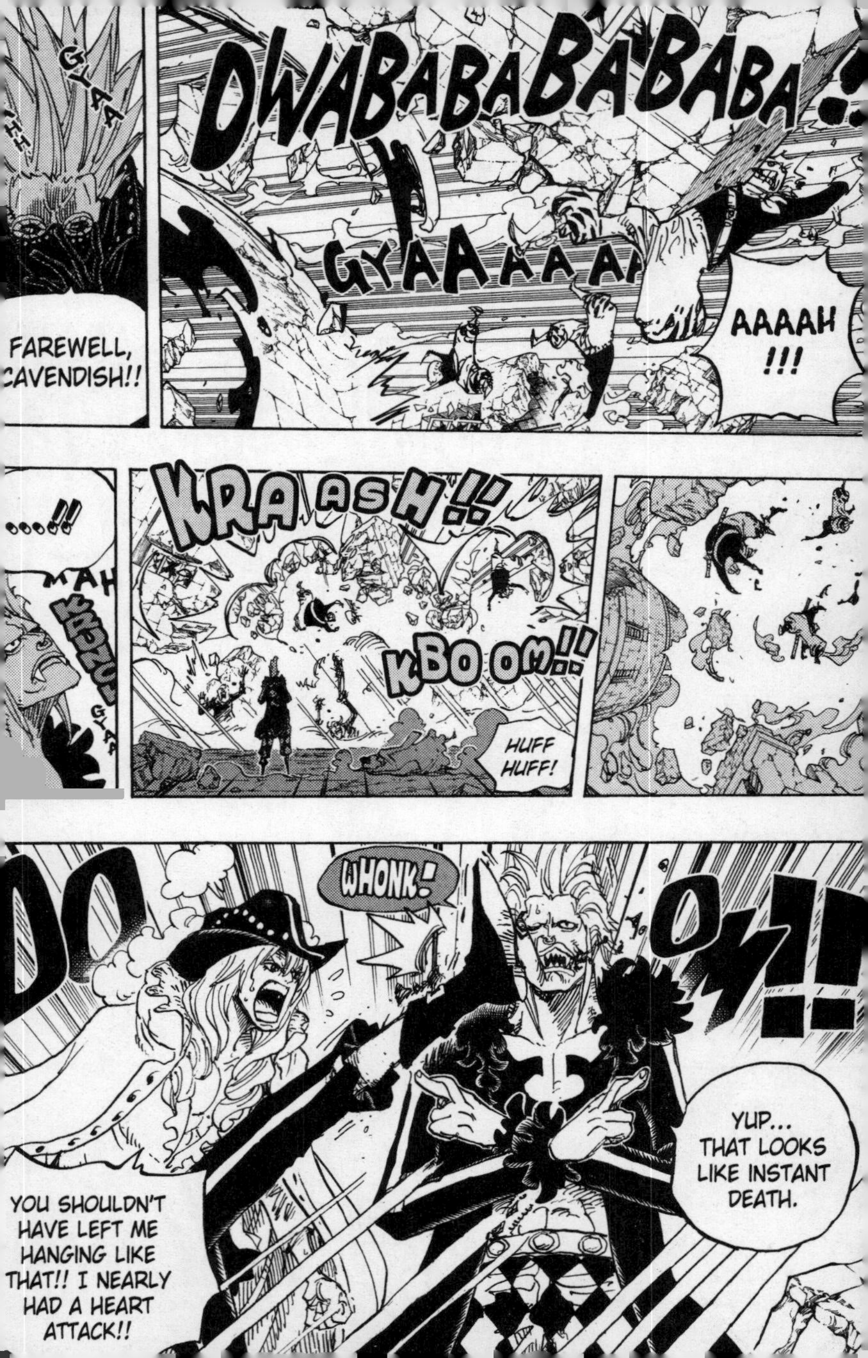
DWABABABABABA!!
AAAAH!!!
GYAAAAAAH
GYAA
FAREWELL, CAVENDISH!!
KRAASH!!
KBOOM!!
HUFF HUFF!
....!!
MAH
GYAA
YUP... THAT LOOKS LIKE INSTANT DEATH.
DO
O!!
WHONK!
YOU SHOULDN'T HAVE LEFT ME HANGING LIKE THAT!! I NEARLY HAD A HEART ATTACK!!

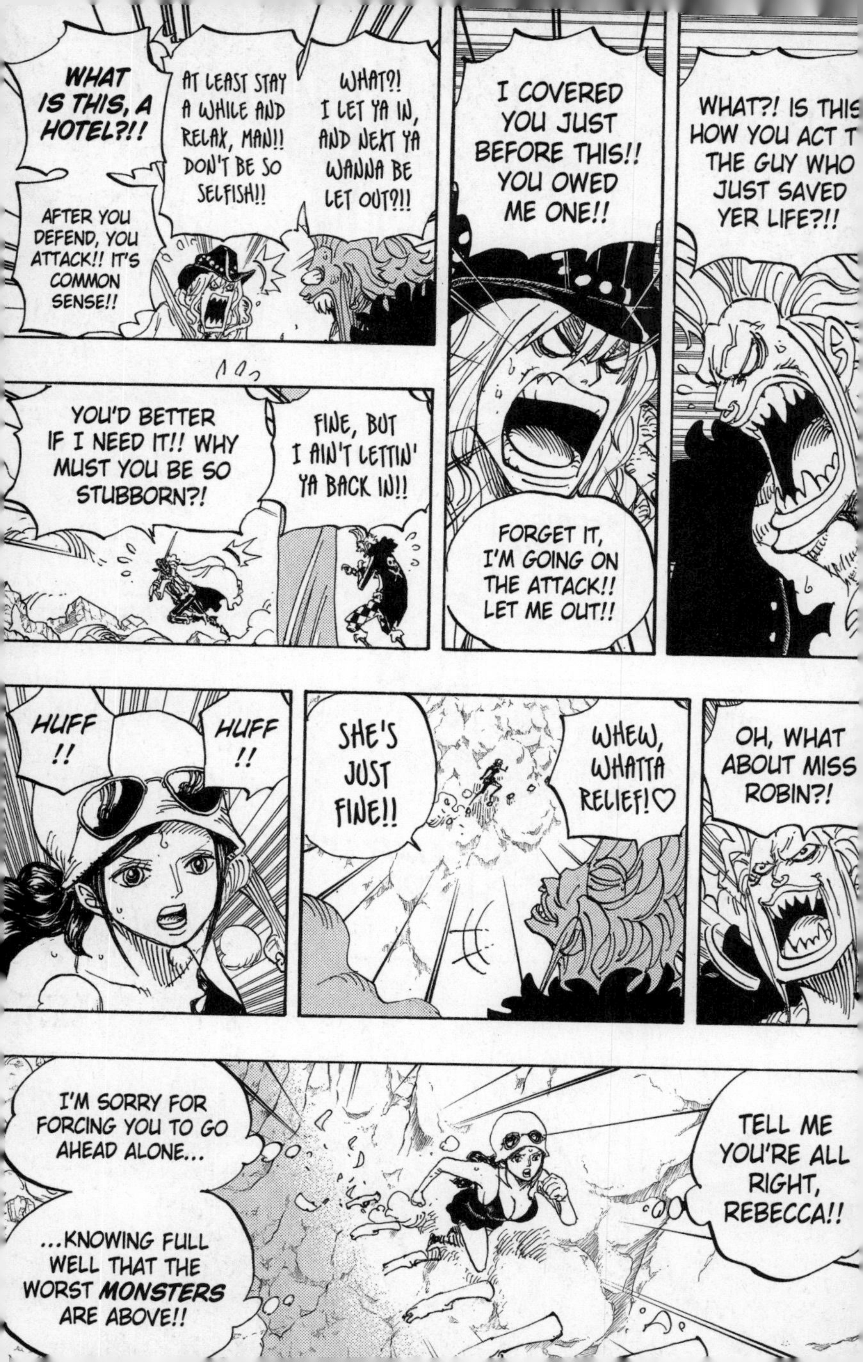
WHAT?! IS THIS HOW YOU ACT T THE GUY WHO JUST SAVED YER LIFE?!!
I COVERED YOU JUST BEFORE THIS!! YOU OWED ME ONE!!
FORGET IT, I'M GOING ON THE ATTACK!! LET ME OUT!!
WHAT?! I LET YA IN, AND NEXT YA WANNA BE LET OUT?!!
AT LEAST STAY A WHILE AND RELAX, MAN!! DON'T BE SO SELFISH!!
WHAT IS THIS, A HOTEL?!!
AFTER YOU DEFEND, YOU ATTACK!! IT'S COMMON SENSE!!
FINE, BUT I AIN'T LETTIN' YA BACK IN!!
YOU'D BETTER IF I NEED IT!! WHY MUST YOU BE SO STUBBORN?!
OH, WHAT ABOUT MISS ROBIN?!
WHEW, WHATTA RELIEF!♡
SHE'S JUST FINE!!
HUFF!!
HUFF!!
TELL ME YOU'RE ALL RIGHT, REBECCA!!
I'M SORRY FOR FORCING YOU TO GO AHEAD ALONE...
...KNOWING FULL WELL THAT THE WORST MONSTERS ARE ABOVE!!

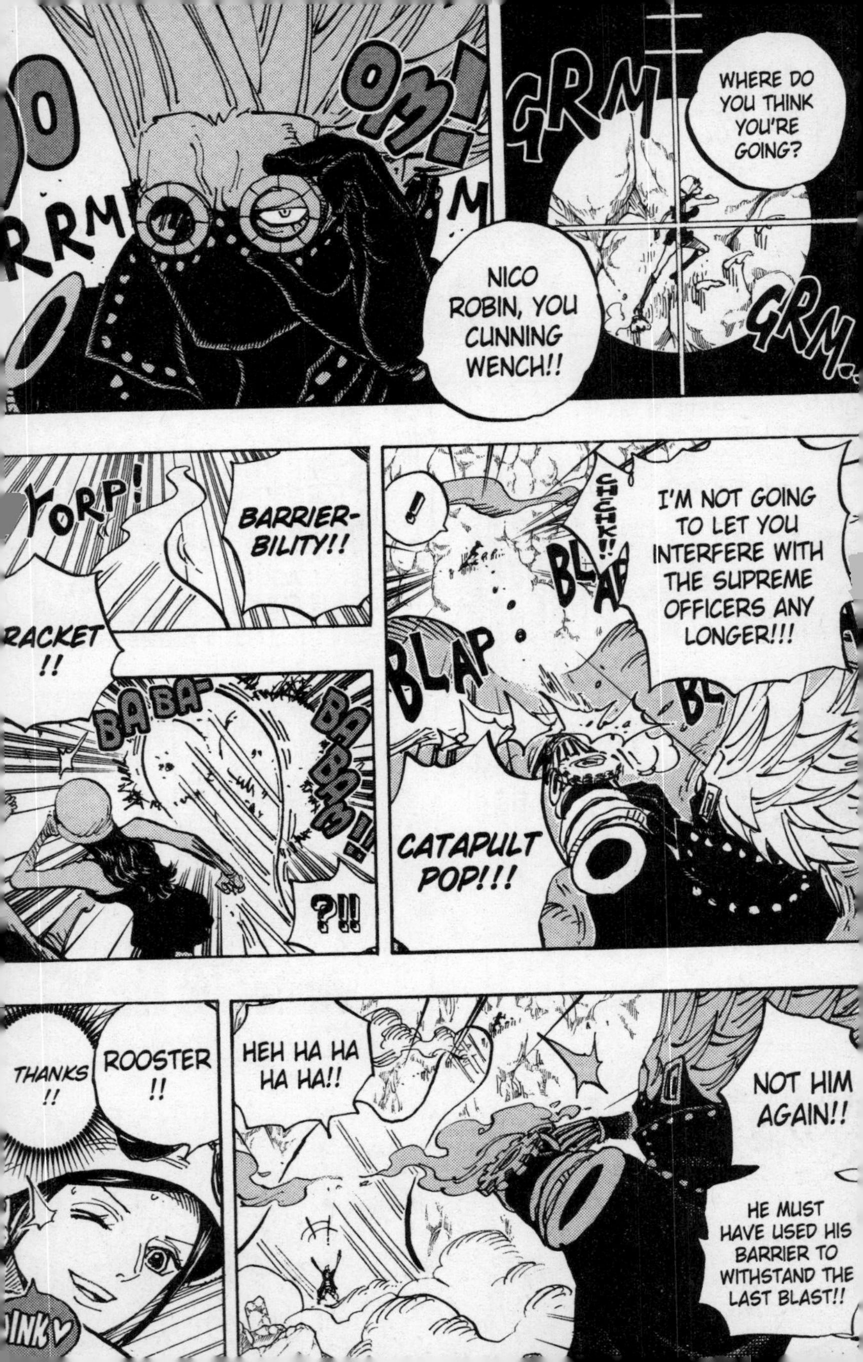
GRM
WHERE DO YOU THINK YOU'RE GOING?
GRM..
OO
RRRM
OM!
RM
NICO ROBIN, YOU CUNNING WENCH!!
!
CHCHK!!
BLAP
BLAP
BL
I'M NOT GOING TO LET YOU INTERFERE WITH THE SUPREME OFFICERS ANY LONGER!!!
CATAPULT POP!!!
YORP!
BARRIER-BILITY!!
RACKET !!
BA BA-
BA BAM!!!
?!!
NOT HIM AGAIN!!
HE MUST HAVE USED HIS BARRIER TO WITHSTAND THE LAST BLAST!!
HEH HA HA HA HA!!
ROOSTER !!
THANKS !!
INK♥

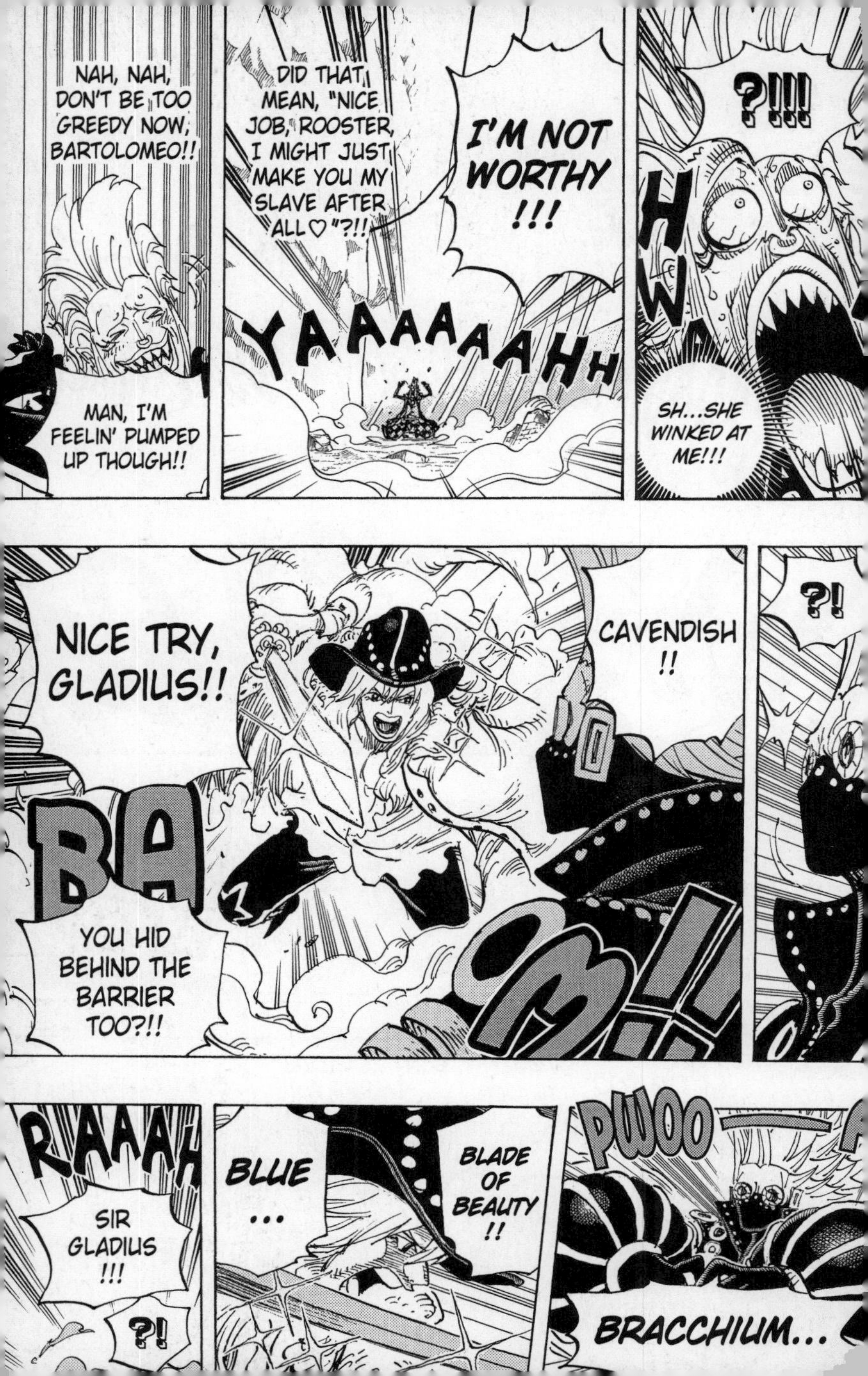
?!!!
HWA
SH...SHE WINKED AT ME!!!
DID THAT MEAN, "NICE JOB, ROOSTER, I MIGHT JUST MAKE YOU MY SLAVE AFTER ALL♡"?!!
I'M NOT WORTHY!!!
YAAAAAAHH
NAH, NAH, DON'T BE TOO GREEDY NOW, BARTOLOMEO!!
MAN, I'M FEELIN' PUMPED UP THOUGH!!
?!
CAVENDISH!!
NICE TRY, GLADIUS!!
BA
M!!
YOU HID BEHIND THE BARRIER TOO?!!
PWOO
BRACCHIUM...
BLADE OF BEAUTY!!
BLUE...
RAAAH
SIR GLADIUS!!!
?!

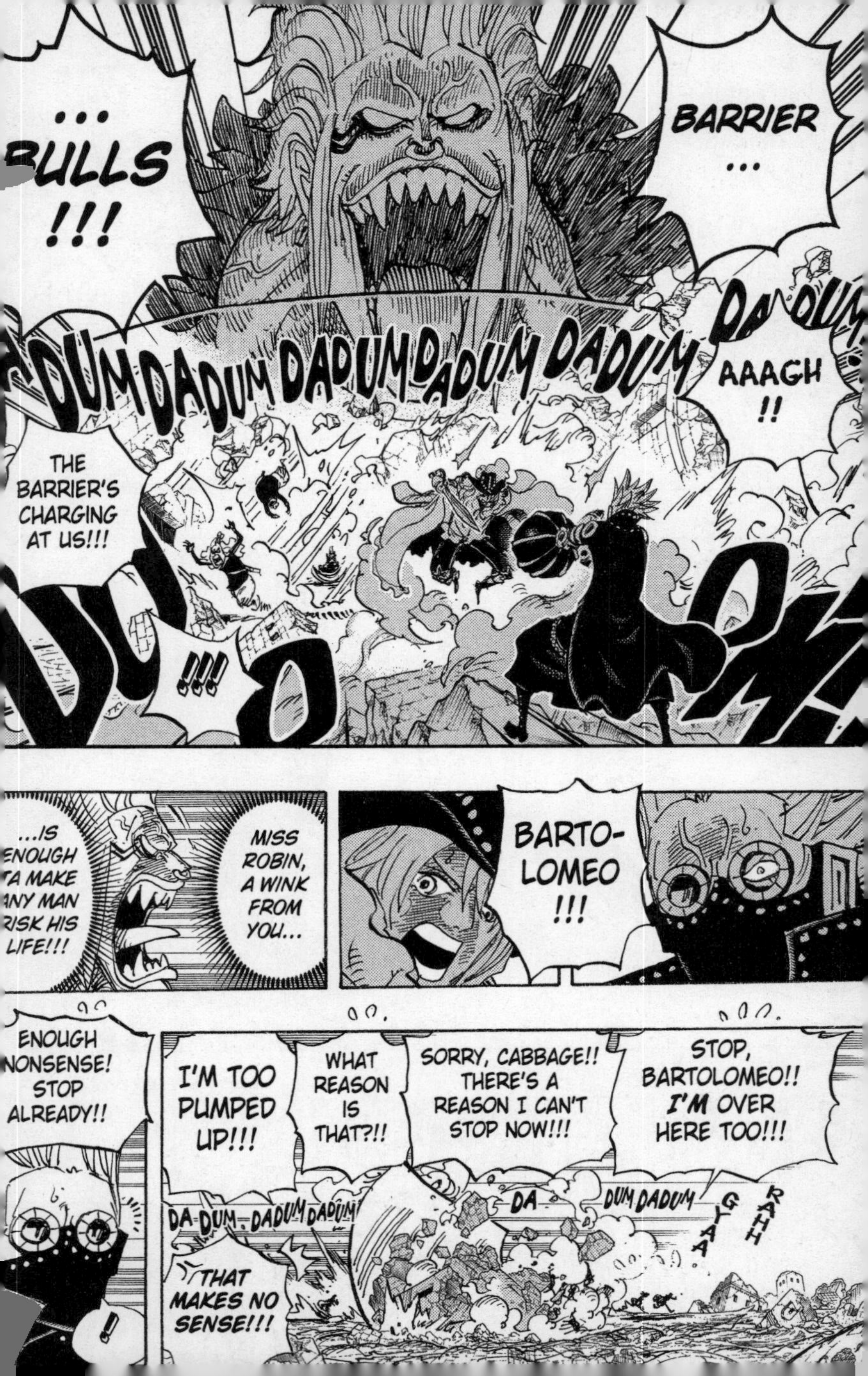
BARRIER ...
... BULLS !!!
DA DUM
DUMDADUM DADUM DADUM DADUM DADUM
AAAGH !!
THE BARRIER'S CHARGING AT US!!!
!!!
BARTO-LOMEO !!!
MISS ROBIN, A WINK FROM YOU...
...IS ENOUGH TA MAKE ANY MAN RISK HIS LIFE!!!
STOP, BARTOLOMEO!! *I'M* OVER HERE TOO!!!
SORRY, CABBAGE!! THERE'S A REASON I CAN'T STOP NOW!!!
WHAT REASON IS THAT?!!
I'M TOO PUMPED UP!!!
RAHH
GYAA
DA DUM DADUM
DA-DUM DADUM DADUM
THAT MAKES NO SENSE!!!
ENOUGH NONSENSE! STOP ALREADY!!
!

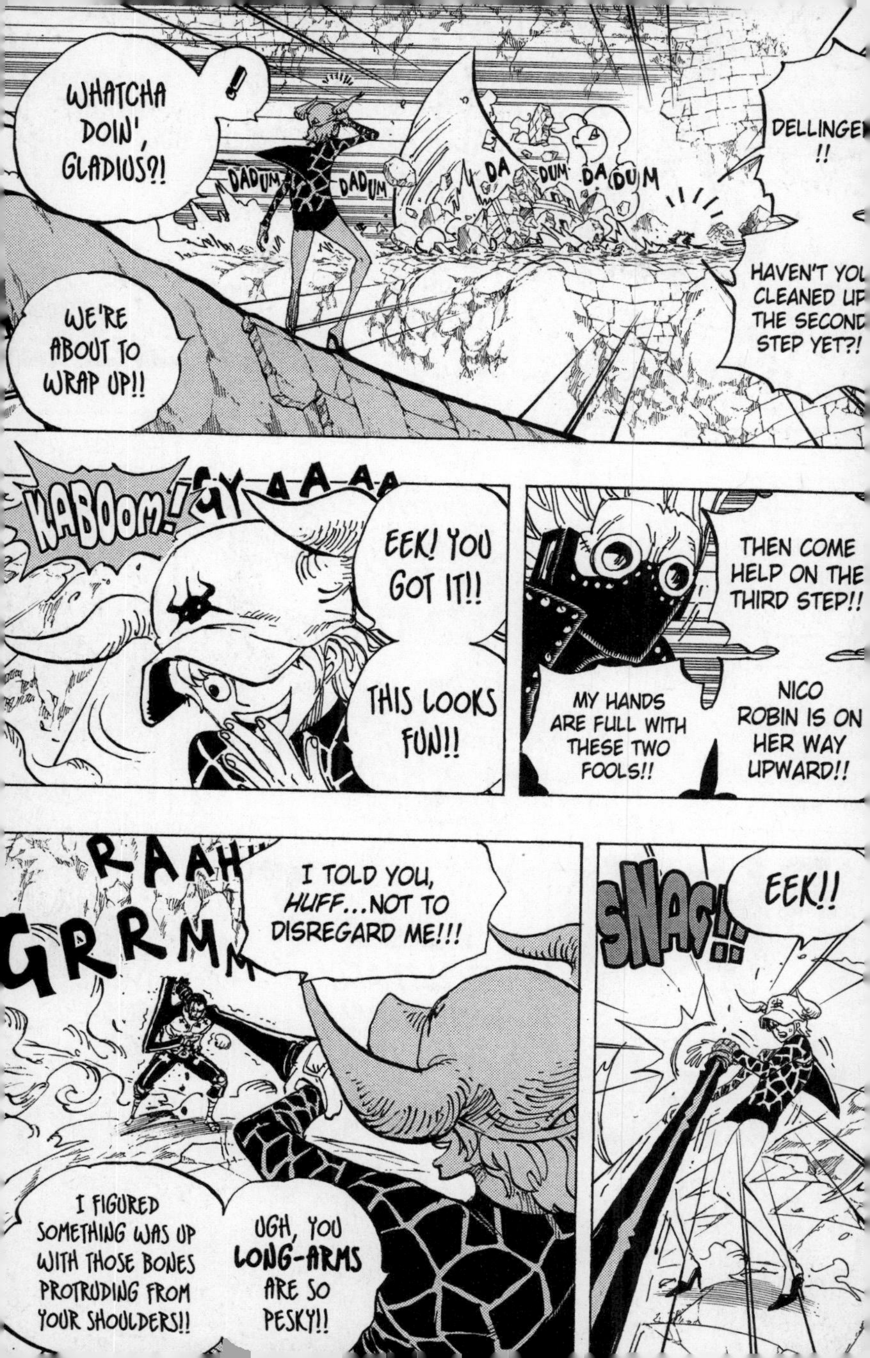
DELLINGE !!
HAVEN'T YO CLEANED UP THE SECOND STEP YET?!
DA DUM DA DUM
DADUM DADUM
!
WHATCHA DOIN', GLADIUS?!
WE'RE ABOUT TO WRAP UP!!
THEN COME HELP ON THE THIRD STEP!!
NICO ROBIN IS ON HER WAY UPWARD!!
MY HANDS ARE FULL WITH THESE TWO FOOLS!!
KABOOM!
GYAAAA
EEK! YOU GOT IT!!
THIS LOOKS FUN!!
SNAG!!
EEK!!
RAAH
GRRMM
I TOLD YOU, HUFF...NOT TO DISREGARD ME!!!
UGH, YOU LONG-ARMS ARE SO PESKY!!
I FIGURED SOMETHING WAS UP WITH THOSE BONES PROTRUDING FROM YOUR SHOULDERS!!

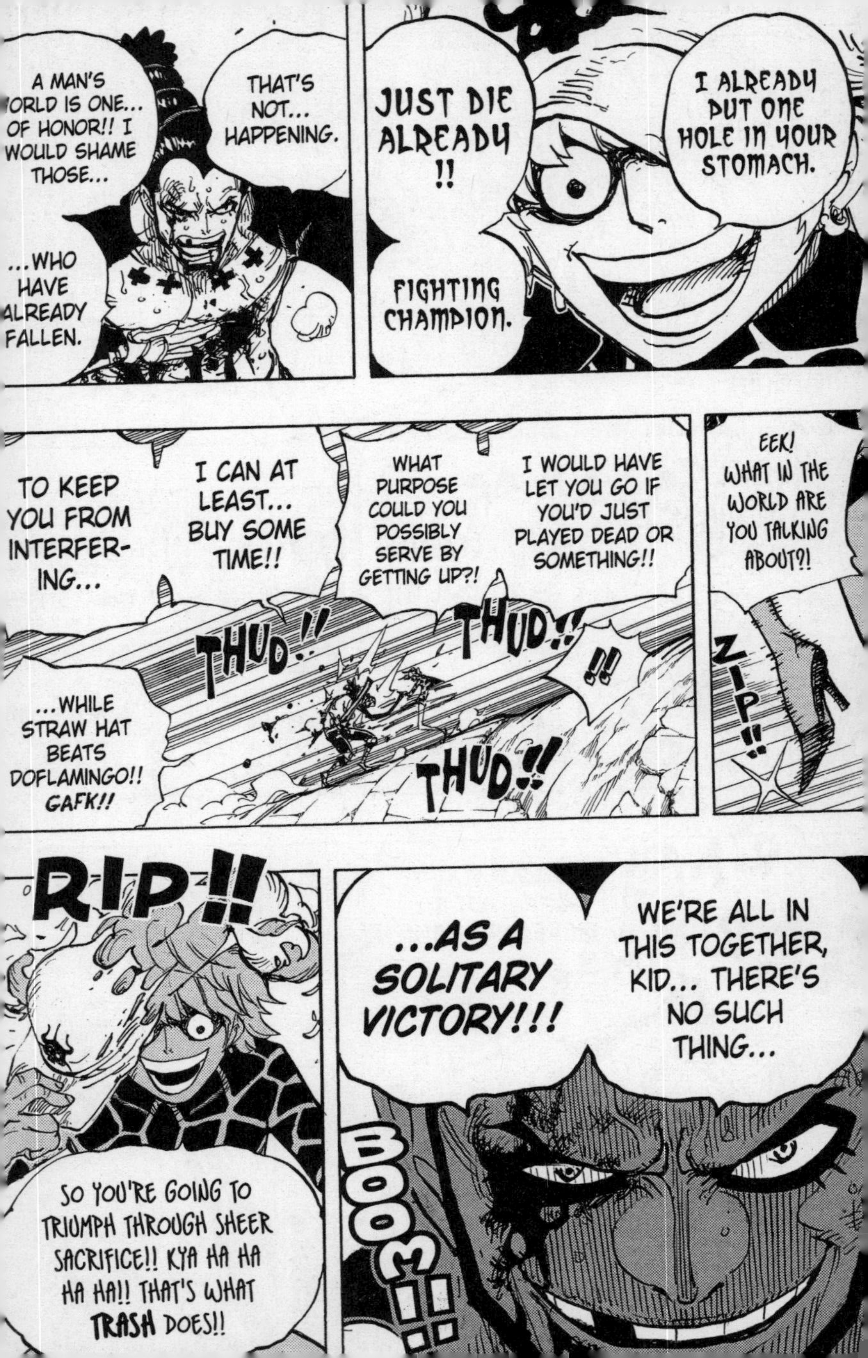

I ALREADY PUT ONE HOLE IN YOUR STOMACH.
JUST DIE ALREADY !!
FIGHTING CHAMPION.
THAT'S NOT... HAPPENING.
A MAN'S WORLD IS ONE... OF HONOR!! I WOULD SHAME THOSE...
...WHO HAVE ALREADY FALLEN.
EEK! WHAT IN THE WORLD ARE YOU TALKING ABOUT?!
ZIP!!
I WOULD HAVE LET YOU GO IF YOU'D JUST PLAYED DEAD OR SOMETHING!!
WHAT PURPOSE COULD YOU POSSIBLY SERVE BY GETTING UP?!
I CAN AT LEAST... BUY SOME TIME!!
TO KEEP YOU FROM INTERFER-ING...
THUD!!
!!
THUD!!
THUD!!
...WHILE STRAW HAT BEATS DOFLAMINGO!! GAFK!!
WE'RE ALL IN THIS TOGETHER, KID... THERE'S NO SUCH THING...
...AS A SOLITARY VICTORY!!!
BOOM!!
RIP!!
SO YOU'RE GOING TO TRIUMPH THROUGH SHEER SACRIFICE!! KYA HA HA HA HA!! THAT'S WHAT TRASH DOES!!

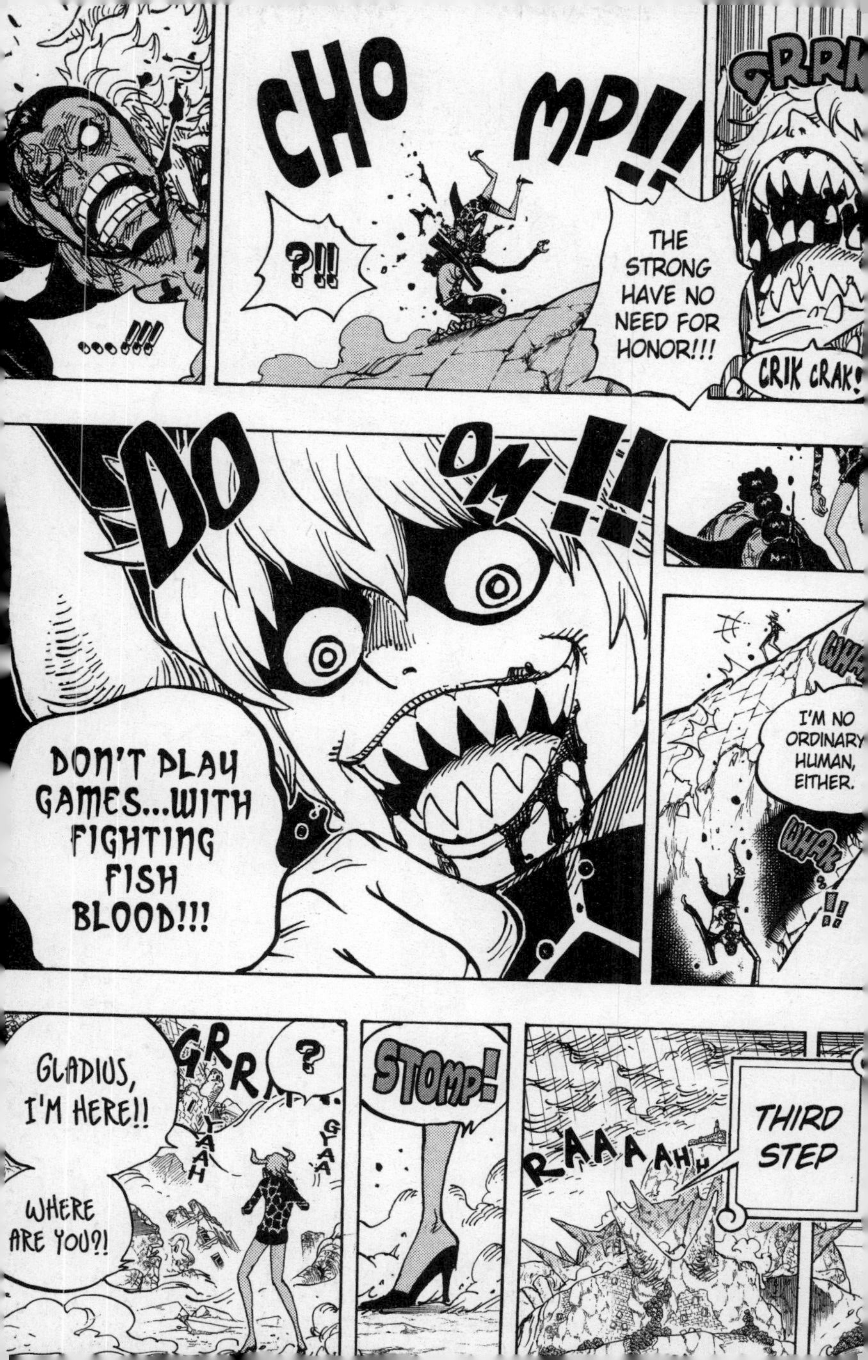
GRRK
THE STRONG HAVE NO NEED FOR HONOR!!!
CRIK CRAK!
CHOMP!!
?!!
...!!!
WHAK
I'M NO ORDINARY HUMAN, EITHER.
WHAK
!!
DOOM!!
DON'T PLAY GAMES...WITH FIGHTING FISH BLOOD!!!
THIRD STEP
RAAAAHH
STOMP!
?
GRRR
GLADIUS, I'M HERE!!
WHERE ARE YOU?!
GYAAH
GYAA

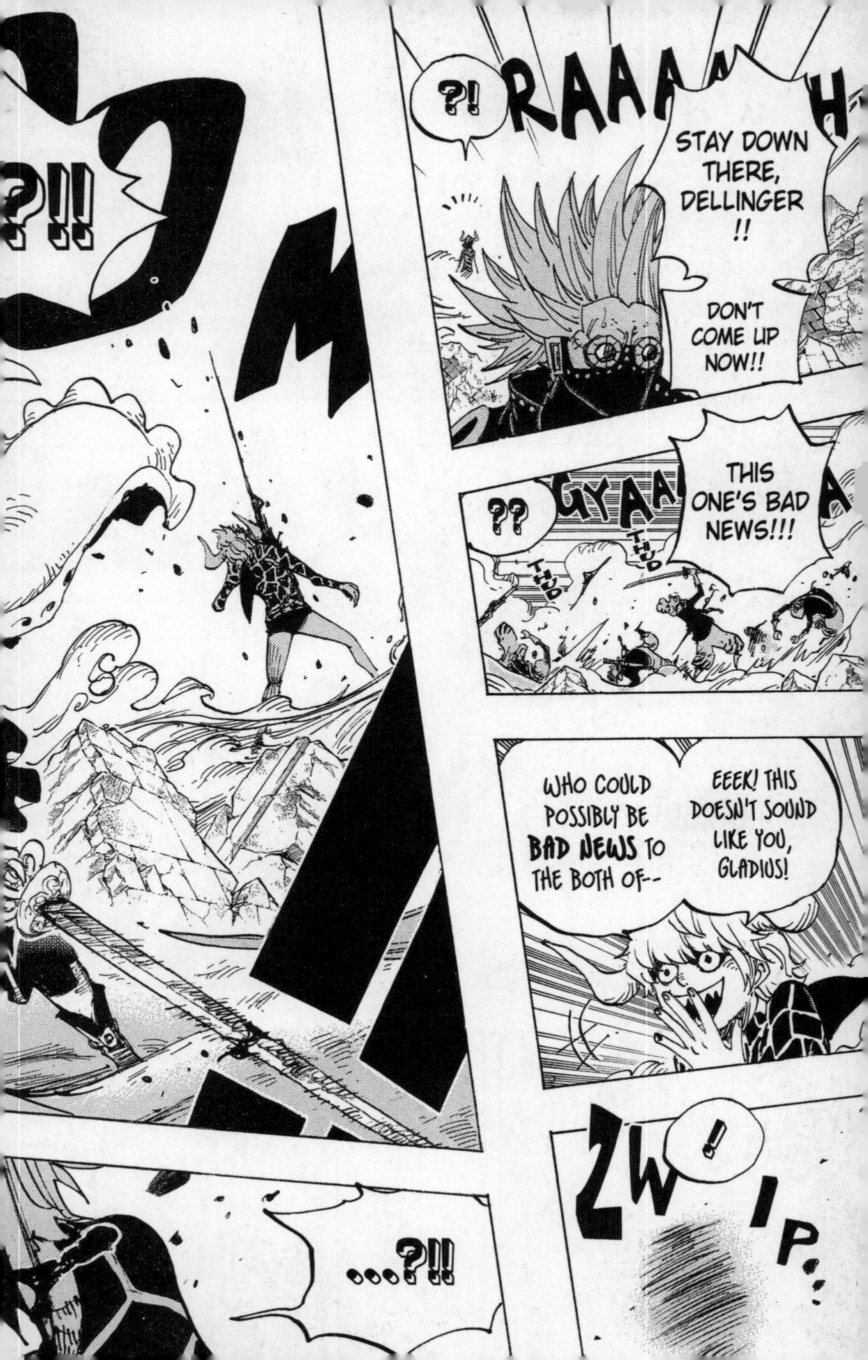
?!
RAAAAAH
STAY DOWN THERE, DELLINGER!!
DON'T COME UP NOW!!
??
GYAAAA
THUD
THUD
THIS ONE'S BAD NEWS!!!
EEEK! THIS DOESN'T SOUND LIKE YOU, GLADIUS!
WHO COULD POSSIBLY BE BAD NEWS TO THE BOTH OF--
?!!
ZWIP
!
...?!!

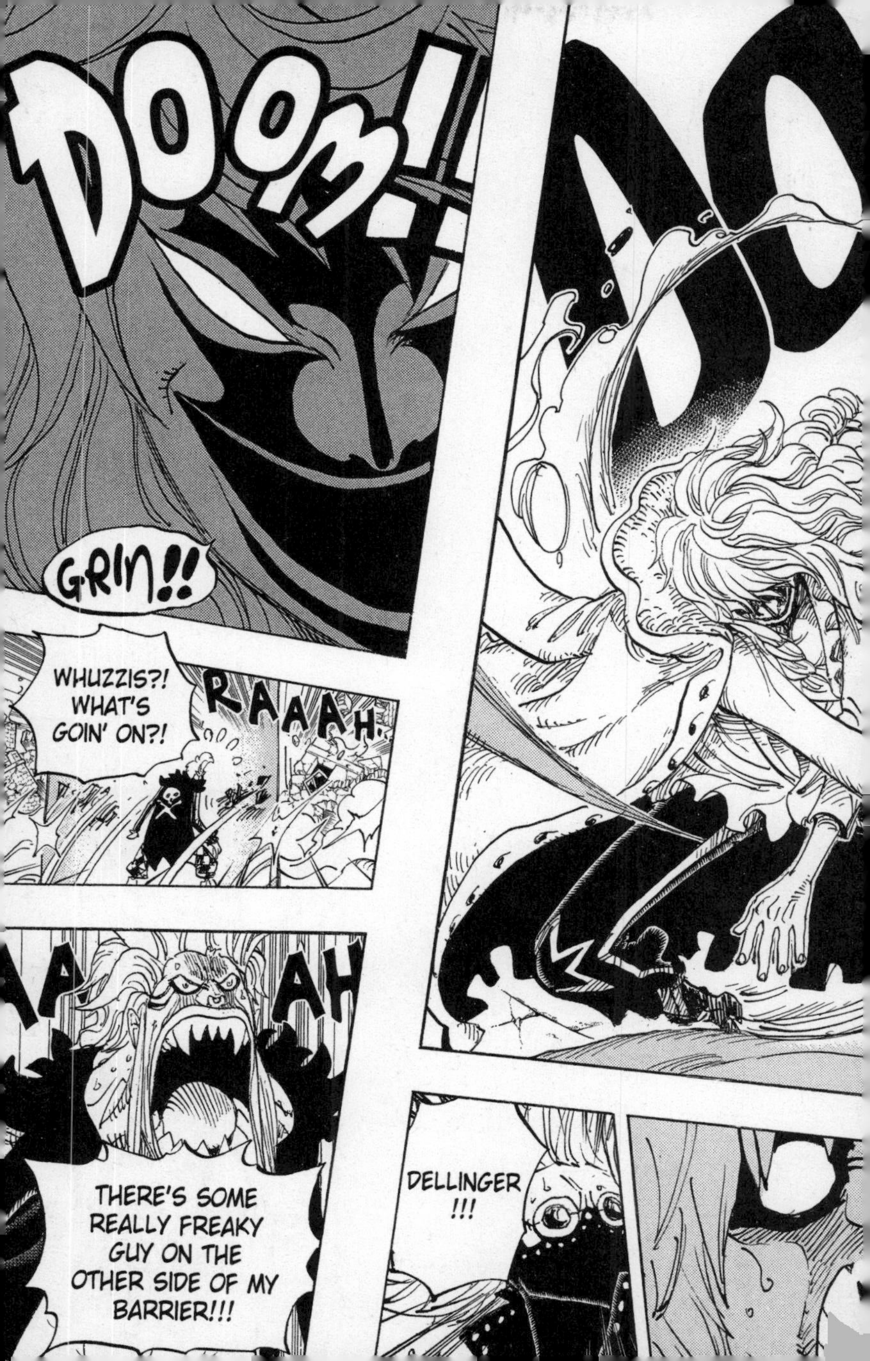
DOOM!!
GRIN!!
RAAAH
WHUZZIS?! WHAT'S GOIN' ON?!
DELLINGER !!!
AH
THERE'S SOME REALLY FREAKY GUY ON THE OTHER SIDE OF MY BARRIER!!!

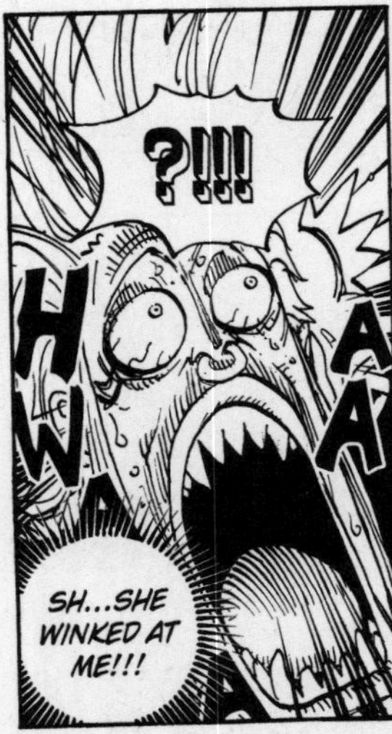
?!!!
HWA
AA
SH...SHE WINKED AT ME!!!

Chapter 773:
HALF 'N HALF

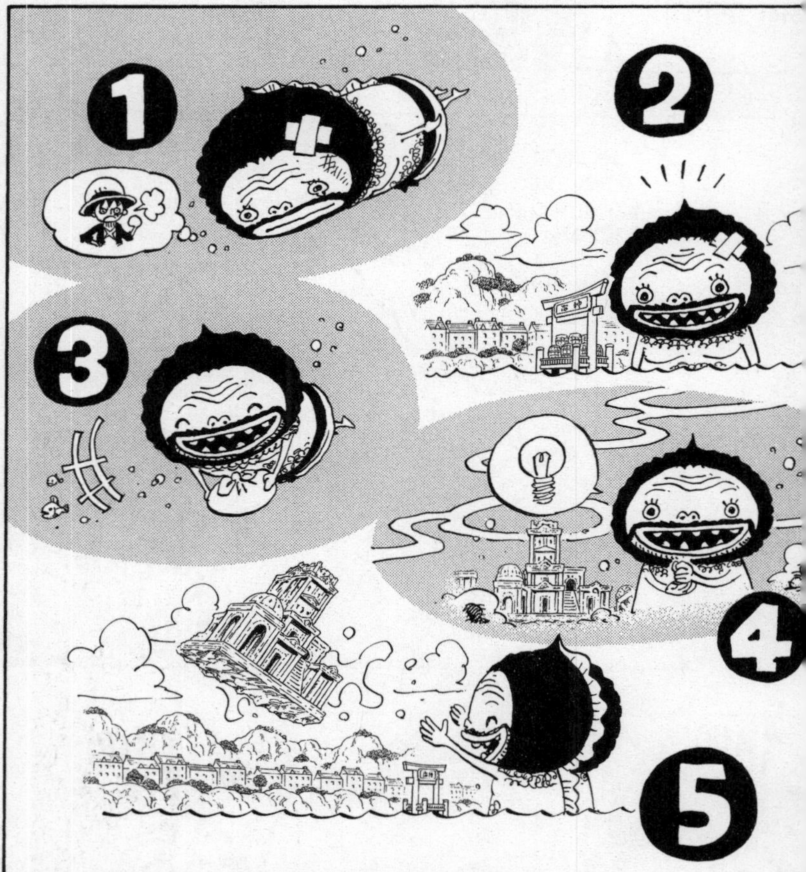
1
2
3
4
5

THE SOLITARY JOURNEY OF JIMBEI, FIRST SON OF THE SEA, VOL. 19: "AS THANKS FOR THE OFFERINGS, I JUST GAVE YOU THE UNDERWATER HUMANS' HOUSE"

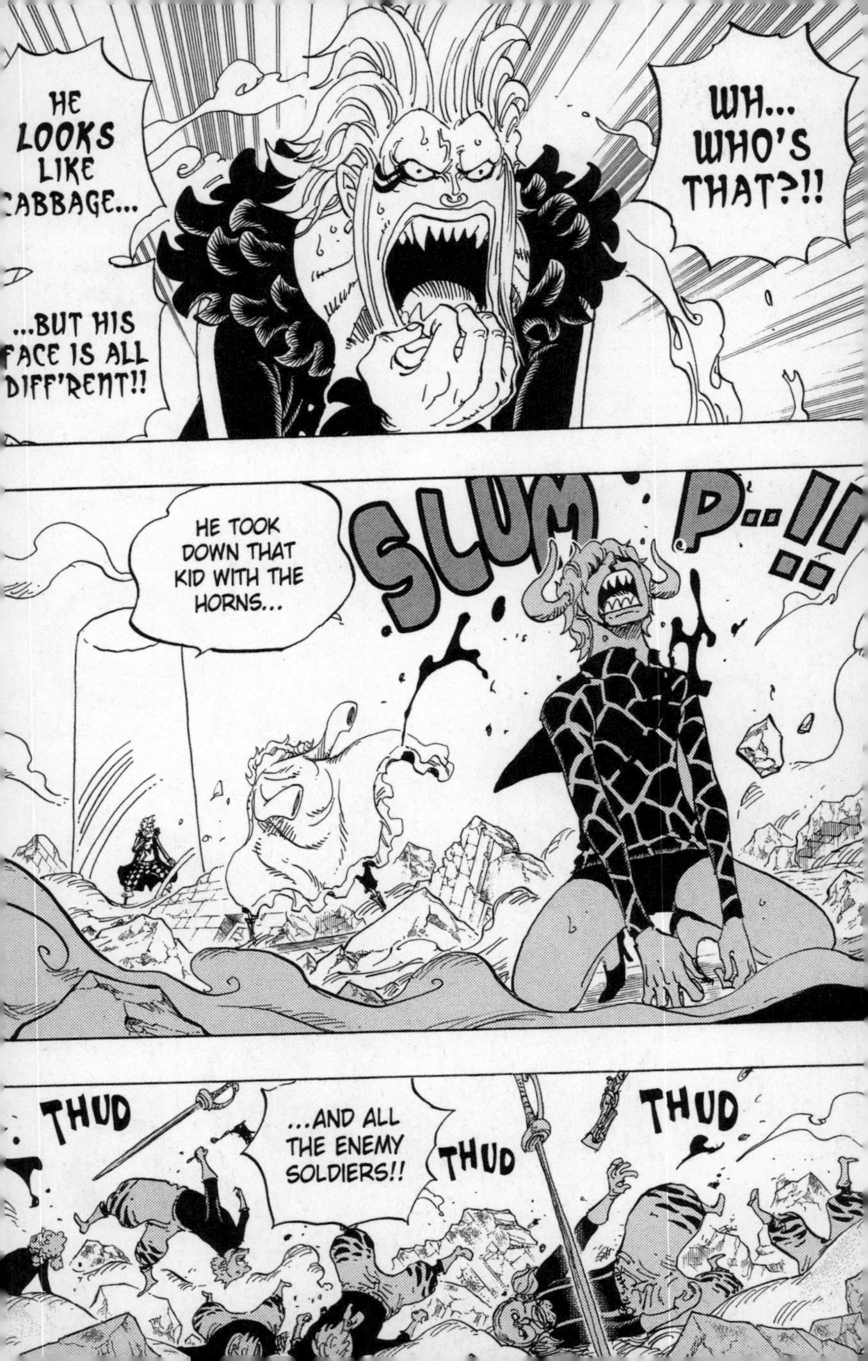
WH... WHO'S THAT?!!
HE LOOKS LIKE CABBAGE...
...BUT HIS FACE IS ALL DIFF'RENT!!
SLUMP..!!
HE TOOK DOWN THAT KID WITH THE HORNS...
THUD
THUD
...AND ALL THE ENEMY SOLDIERS!!
THUD

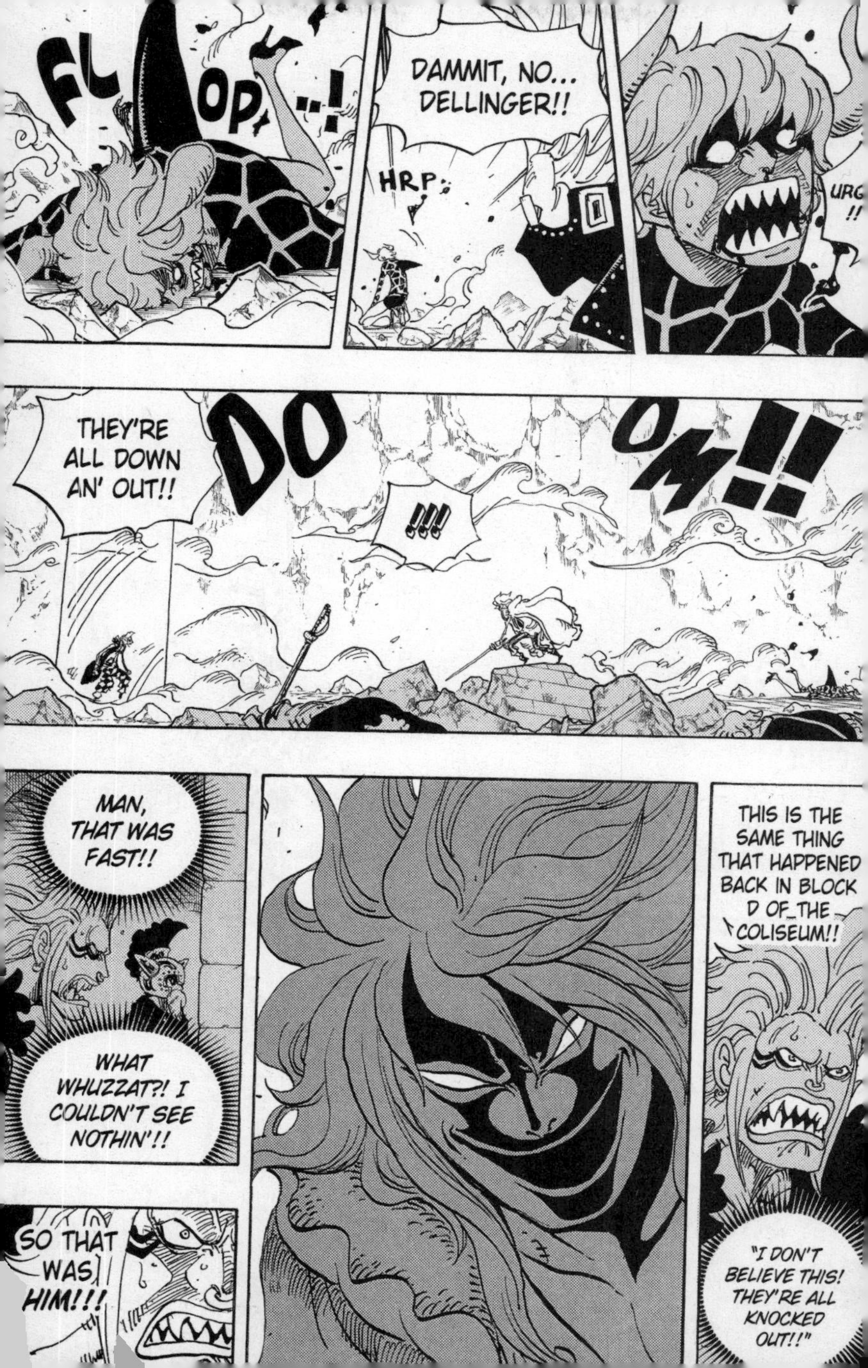
URG!!
DAMMIT, NO... DELLINGER!!
HRP
FLOP...!
DOOM!!
!!!
THEY'RE ALL DOWN AN' OUT!!
THIS IS THE SAME THING THAT HAPPENED BACK IN BLOCK D OF THE COLISEUM!!
"I DON'T BELIEVE THIS! THEY'RE ALL KNOCKED OUT!!"
MAN, THAT WAS FAST!!
WHAT WHUZZAT?! I COULDN'T SEE NOTHIN'!!
SO THAT WAS HIM!!!

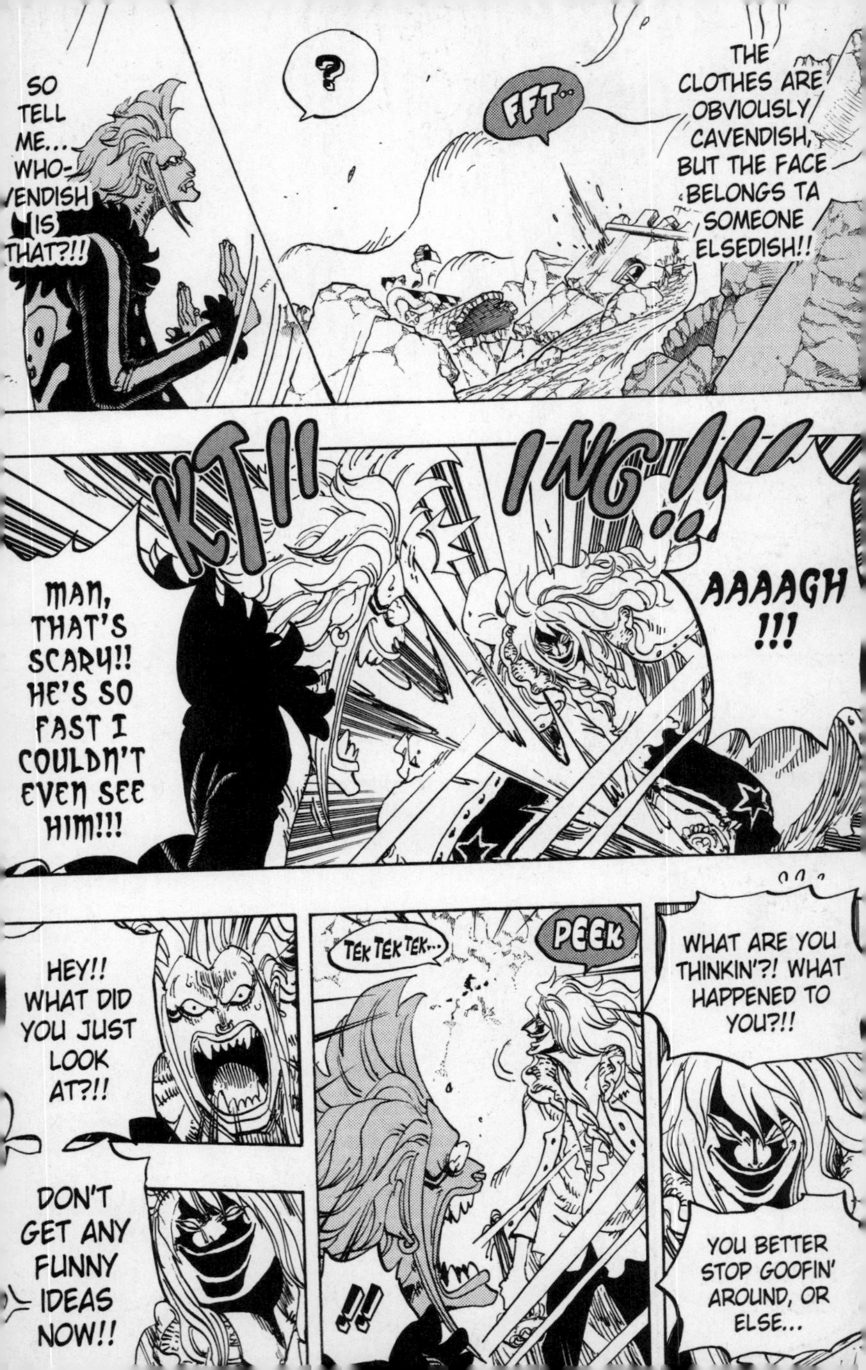
THE CLOTHES ARE OBVIOUSLY CAVENDISH, BUT THE FACE BELONGS TA SOMEONE ELSEDISH!!
FFT..
?
SO TELL ME... WHO-VENDISH IS THAT?!!
KT!! ING!!
AAAAGH!!!
MAN, THAT'S SCARY!! HE'S SO FAST I COULDN'T EVEN SEE HIM!!!
WHAT ARE YOU THINKIN'?! WHAT HAPPENED TO YOU?!!
YOU BETTER STOP GOOFIN' AROUND, OR ELSE...
PEEK
TEK TEK TEK...
!!
HEY!! WHAT DID YOU JUST LOOK AT?!!
DON'T GET ANY FUNNY IDEAS NOW!!

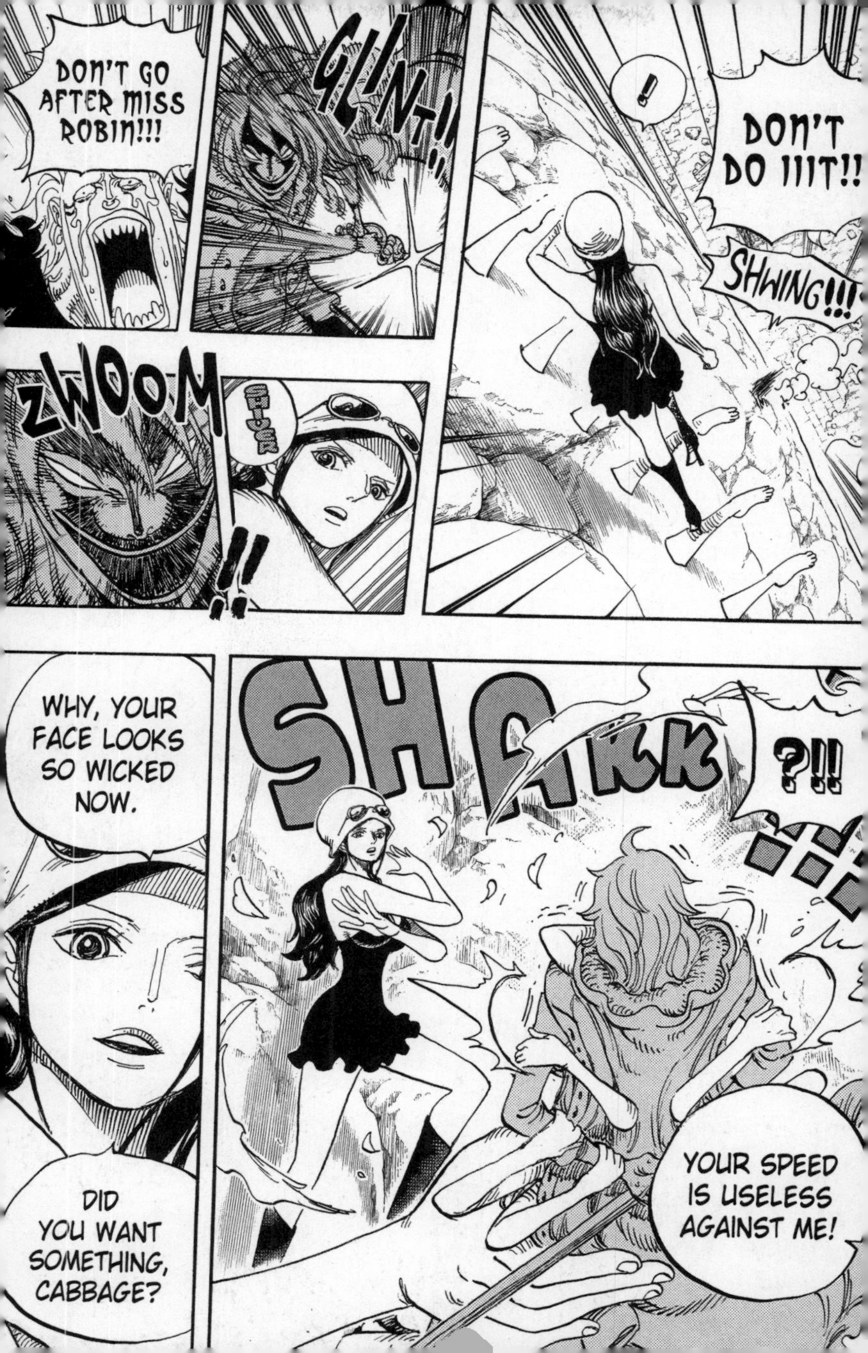
!
DON'T DO IIIT!!
SHWING!!!
GLINT!!
DON'T GO AFTER MISS ROBIN!!!
SHIVER
!!
ZWOOM
SHAKK
?!!
YOUR SPEED IS USELESS AGAINST ME!
WHY, YOUR FACE LOOKS SO WICKED NOW.
DID YOU WANT SOMETHING, CABBAGE?

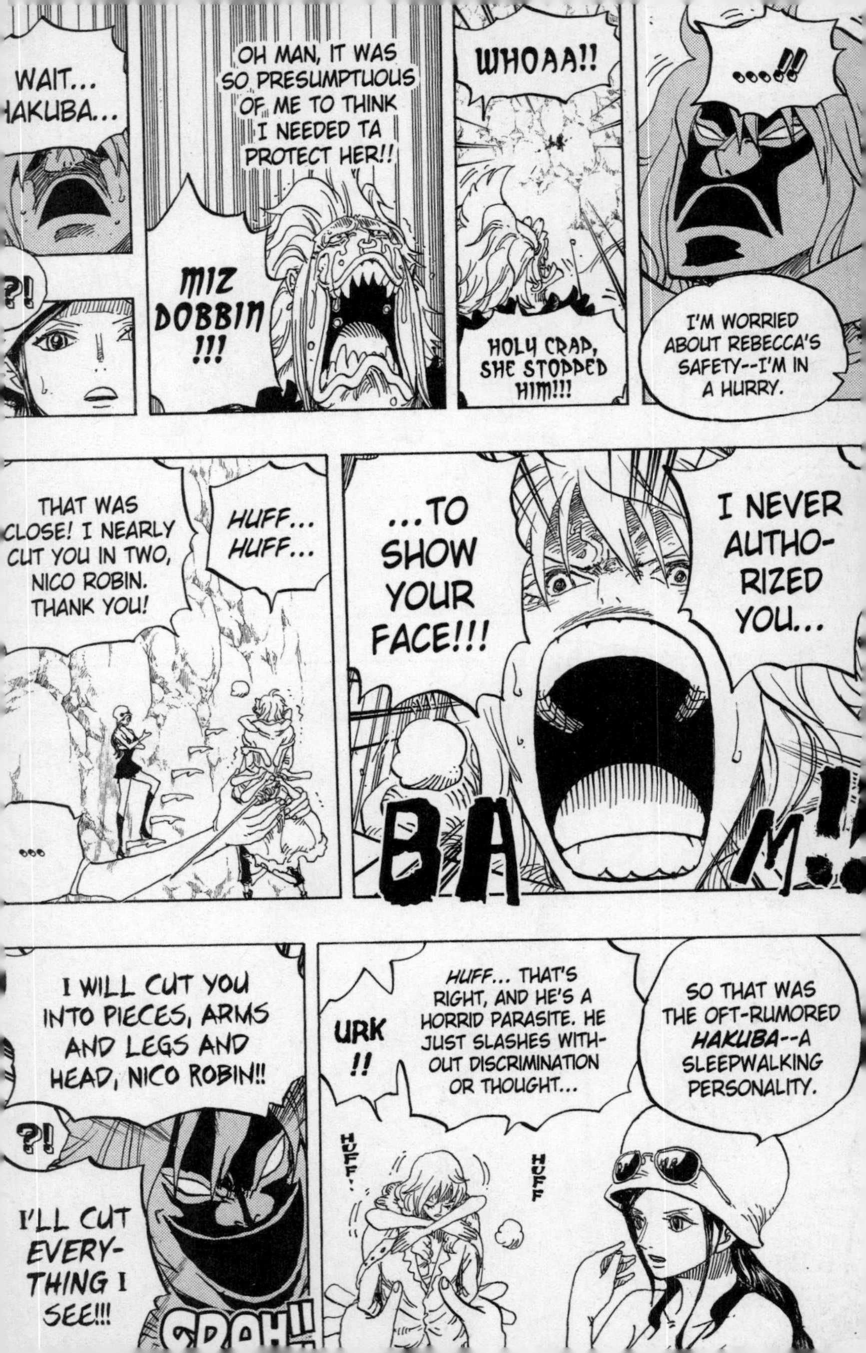
...!!
I'M WORRIED ABOUT REBECCA'S SAFETY--I'M IN A HURRY.
WHOAA!!
HOLY CRAP, SHE STOPPED HIM!!!
OH MAN, IT WAS SO PRESUMPTUOUS OF ME TO THINK I NEEDED TA PROTECT HER!!
MIZ DOBBIN!!!
WAIT... HAKUBA...
?!
I NEVER AUTHORIZED YOU...
...TO SHOW YOUR FACE!!!
BAM!!
HUFF... HUFF...
THAT WAS CLOSE! I NEARLY CUT YOU IN TWO, NICO ROBIN. THANK YOU!
...
SO THAT WAS THE OFT-RUMORED HAKUBA--A SLEEPWALKING PERSONALITY.
HUFF... THAT'S RIGHT, AND HE'S A HORRID PARASITE. HE JUST SLASHES WITHOUT DISCRIMINATION OR THOUGHT...
URK !!
HUFF
HUFF
I WILL CUT YOU INTO PIECES, ARMS AND LEGS AND HEAD, NICO ROBIN!!
?!
I'LL CUT EVERYTHING I SEE!!!

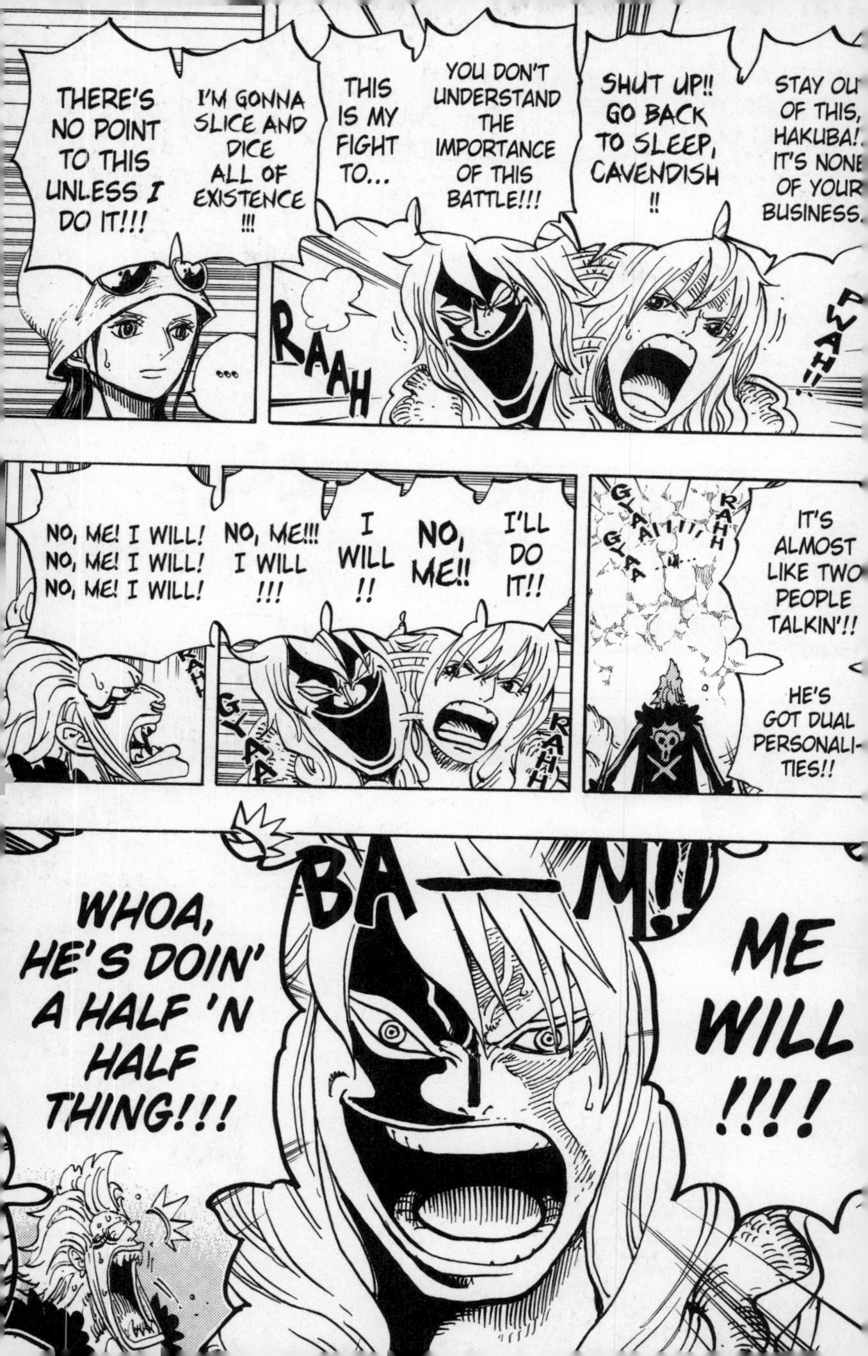
STAY OUT OF THIS, HAKUBA!! IT'S NONE OF YOUR BUSINESS.
SHUT UP!! GO BACK TO SLEEP, CAVENDISH!!
YOU DON'T UNDERSTAND THE IMPORTANCE OF THIS BATTLE!!!
THIS IS MY FIGHT TO...
PWAH!!
RAAH
I'M GONNA SLICE AND DICE ALL OF EXISTENCE!!!
THERE'S NO POINT TO THIS UNLESS I DO IT!!!
...
IT'S ALMOST LIKE TWO PEOPLE TALKIN'!!
HE'S GOT DUAL PERSONALITIES!!
RAHH
GYAA GYAA
I'LL DO IT!!
NO, ME!!
I WILL!!
NO, ME!!! I WILL!!!
NO, ME! I WILL! NO, ME! I WILL! NO, ME! I WILL!
RAHH
GYAA
RAHH
ME WILL!!!!
BA—M!!
WHOA, HE'S DOIN' A HALF 'N HALF THING!!!

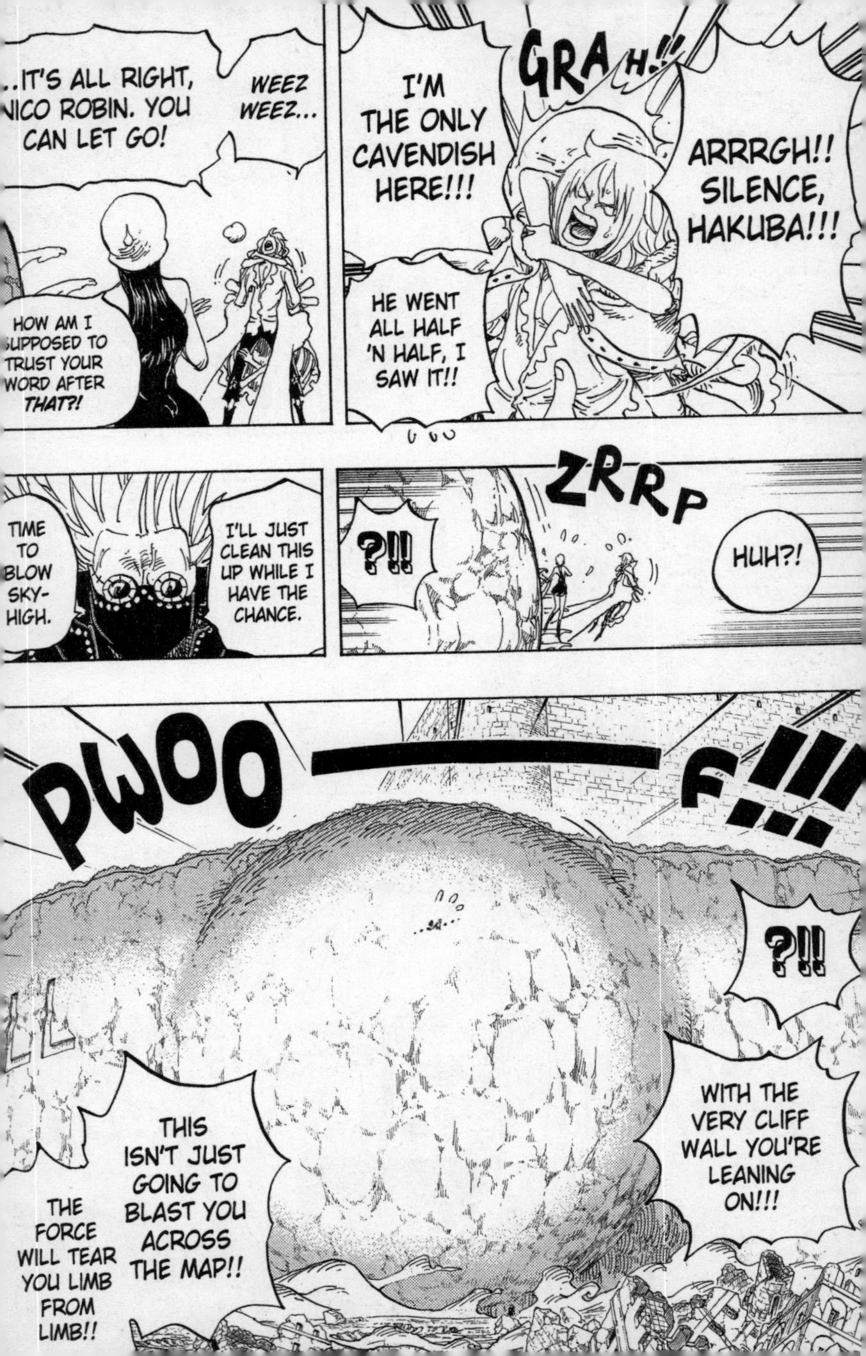
GRAAH!!
ARRRGH!! SILENCE, HAKUBA!!!
I'M THE ONLY CAVENDISH HERE!!!
HE WENT ALL HALF 'N HALF, I SAW IT!!
WEEZ WEEZ...
..IT'S ALL RIGHT, NICO ROBIN. YOU CAN LET GO!
HOW AM I SUPPOSED TO TRUST YOUR WORD AFTER THAT?!
ZRRP
HUH?!
?!!
I'LL JUST CLEAN THIS UP WHILE I HAVE THE CHANCE.
TIME TO BLOW SKY-HIGH.
PWOO—F!!!
?!!
WITH THE VERY CLIFF WALL YOU'RE LEANING ON!!!
THIS ISN'T JUST GOING TO BLAST YOU ACROSS THE MAP!!
THE FORCE WILL TEAR YOU LIMB FROM LIMB!!

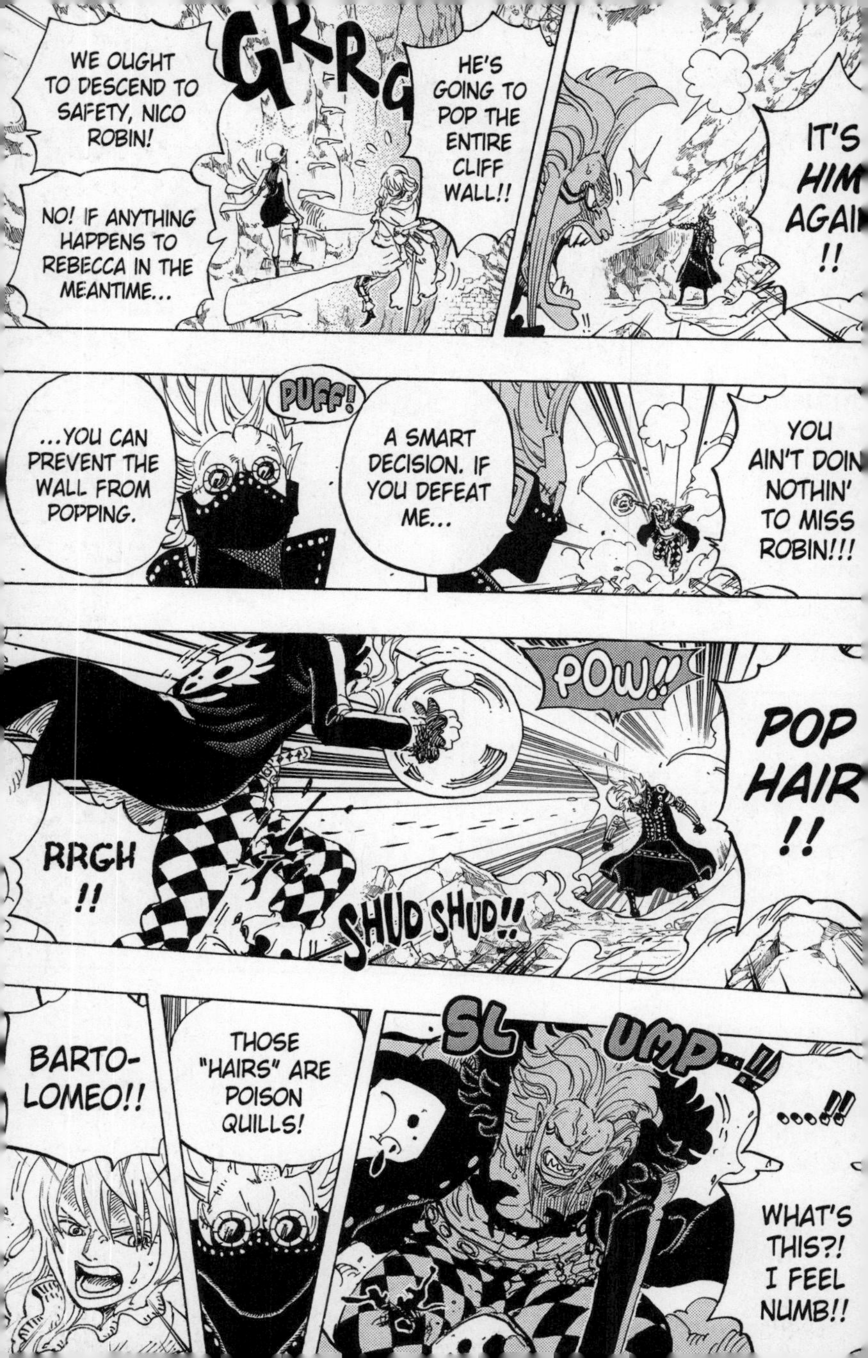

IT'S HIM AGAI !!
GRRG
HE'S GOING TO POP THE ENTIRE CLIFF WALL!!
WE OUGHT TO DESCEND TO SAFETY, NICO ROBIN!
NO! IF ANYTHING HAPPENS TO REBECCA IN THE MEANTIME...
YOU AIN'T DOIN NOTHIN' TO MISS ROBIN!!!
PUFF!
A SMART DECISION. IF YOU DEFEAT ME...
...YOU CAN PREVENT THE WALL FROM POPPING.
POP HAIR !!
POW!!
SHUD SHUD!!
RRGH !!
SLUMP...!!
.....!!
WHAT'S THIS?! I FEEL NUMB!!
THOSE "HAIRS" ARE POISON QUILLS!
BARTO-LOMEO!!

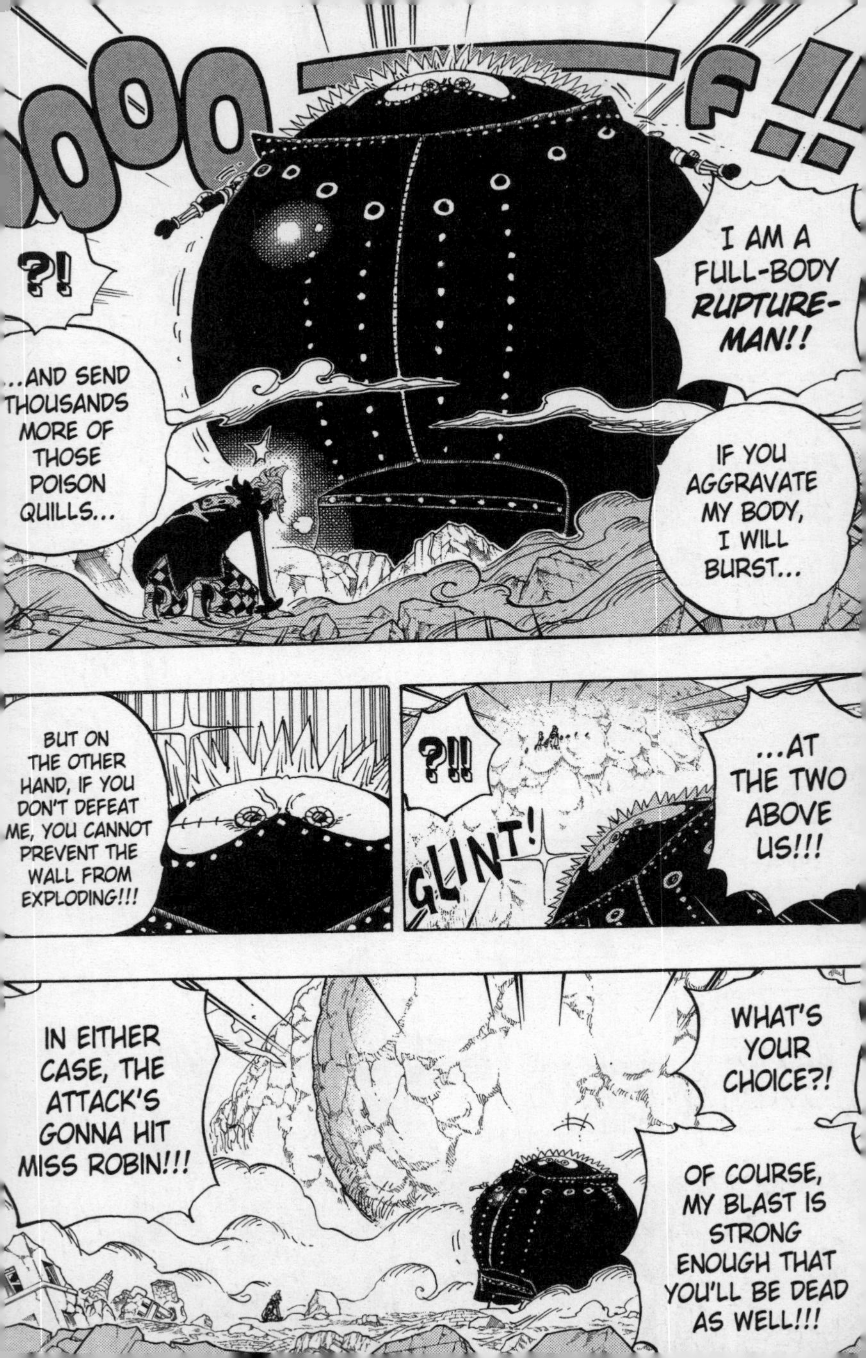
OOOO—F!!
I AM A FULL-BODY RUPTURE-MAN!!
?!
IF YOU AGGRAVATE MY BODY, I WILL BURST...
...AND SEND THOUSANDS MORE OF THOSE POISON QUILLS...
...AT THE TWO ABOVE US!!!
?!!
GLINT!
BUT ON THE OTHER HAND, IF YOU DON'T DEFEAT ME, YOU CANNOT PREVENT THE WALL FROM EXPLODING!!!
WHAT'S YOUR CHOICE?!
OF COURSE, MY BLAST IS STRONG ENOUGH THAT YOU'LL BE DEAD AS WELL!!!
IN EITHER CASE, THE ATTACK'S GONNA HIT MISS ROBIN!!!

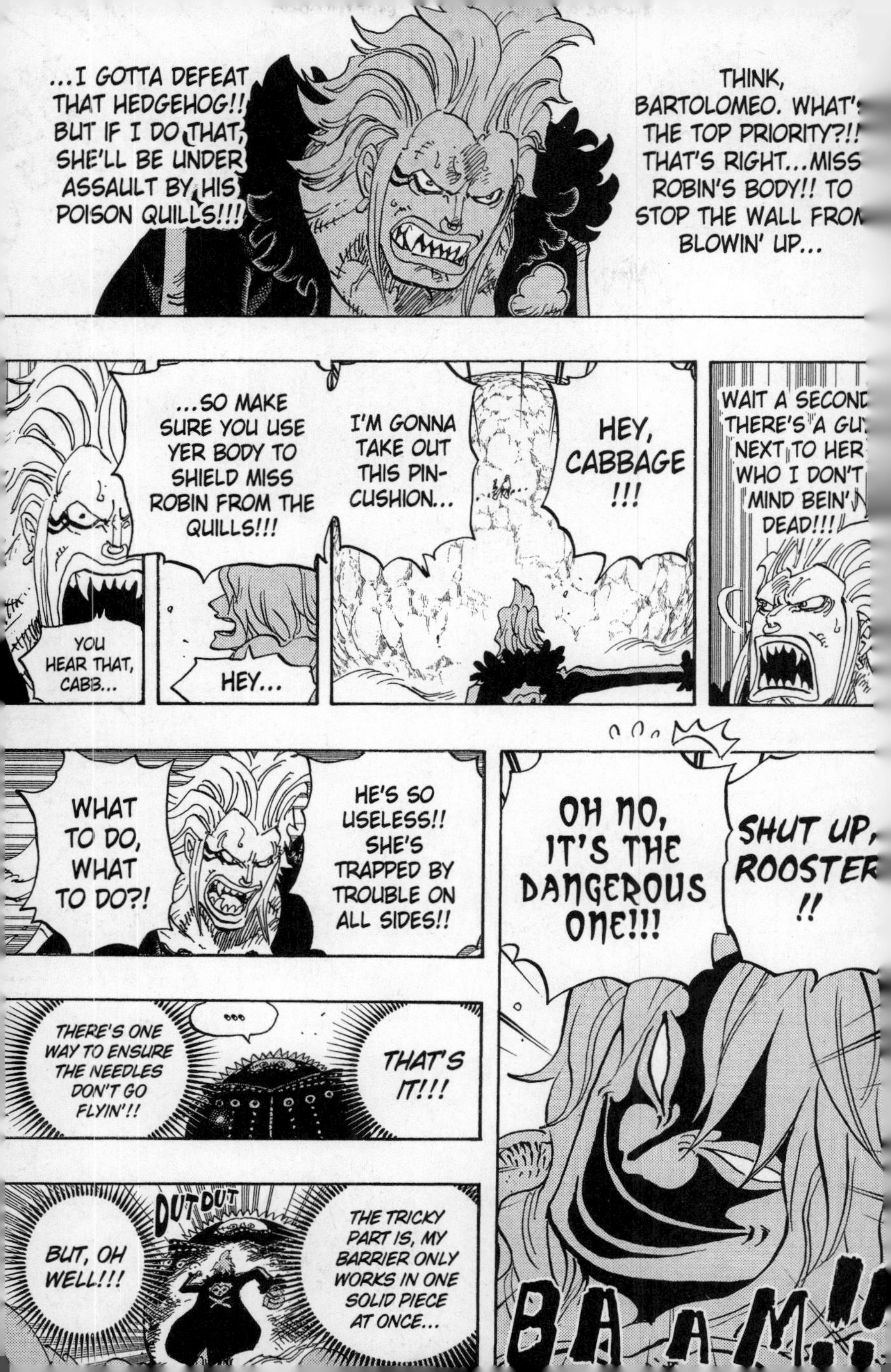
THINK, BARTOLOMEO. WHAT'S THE TOP PRIORITY?!! THAT'S RIGHT...MISS ROBIN'S BODY!! TO STOP THE WALL FROM BLOWIN' UP...
...I GOTTA DEFEAT THAT HEDGEHOG!! BUT IF I DO THAT, SHE'LL BE UNDER ASSAULT BY HIS POISON QUILLS!!!
WAIT A SECOND THERE'S A GUY NEXT TO HER WHO I DON'T MIND BEIN' DEAD!!!
HEY, CABBAGE!!!
I'M GONNA TAKE OUT THIS PIN-CUSHION...
...SO MAKE SURE YOU USE YER BODY TO SHIELD MISS ROBIN FROM THE QUILLS!!!
HEY...
YOU HEAR THAT, CABB...
SHUT UP, ROOSTER!!
OH NO, IT'S THE DANGEROUS ONE!!!
BAAM!!
HE'S SO USELESS!! SHE'S TRAPPED BY TROUBLE ON ALL SIDES!!
WHAT TO DO, WHAT TO DO?!
...
THAT'S IT!!!
THERE'S ONE WAY TO ENSURE THE NEEDLES DON'T GO FLYIN'!!
DUT DUT
THE TRICKY PART IS, MY BARRIER ONLY WORKS IN ONE SOLID PIECE AT ONCE...
BUT, OH WELL!!!

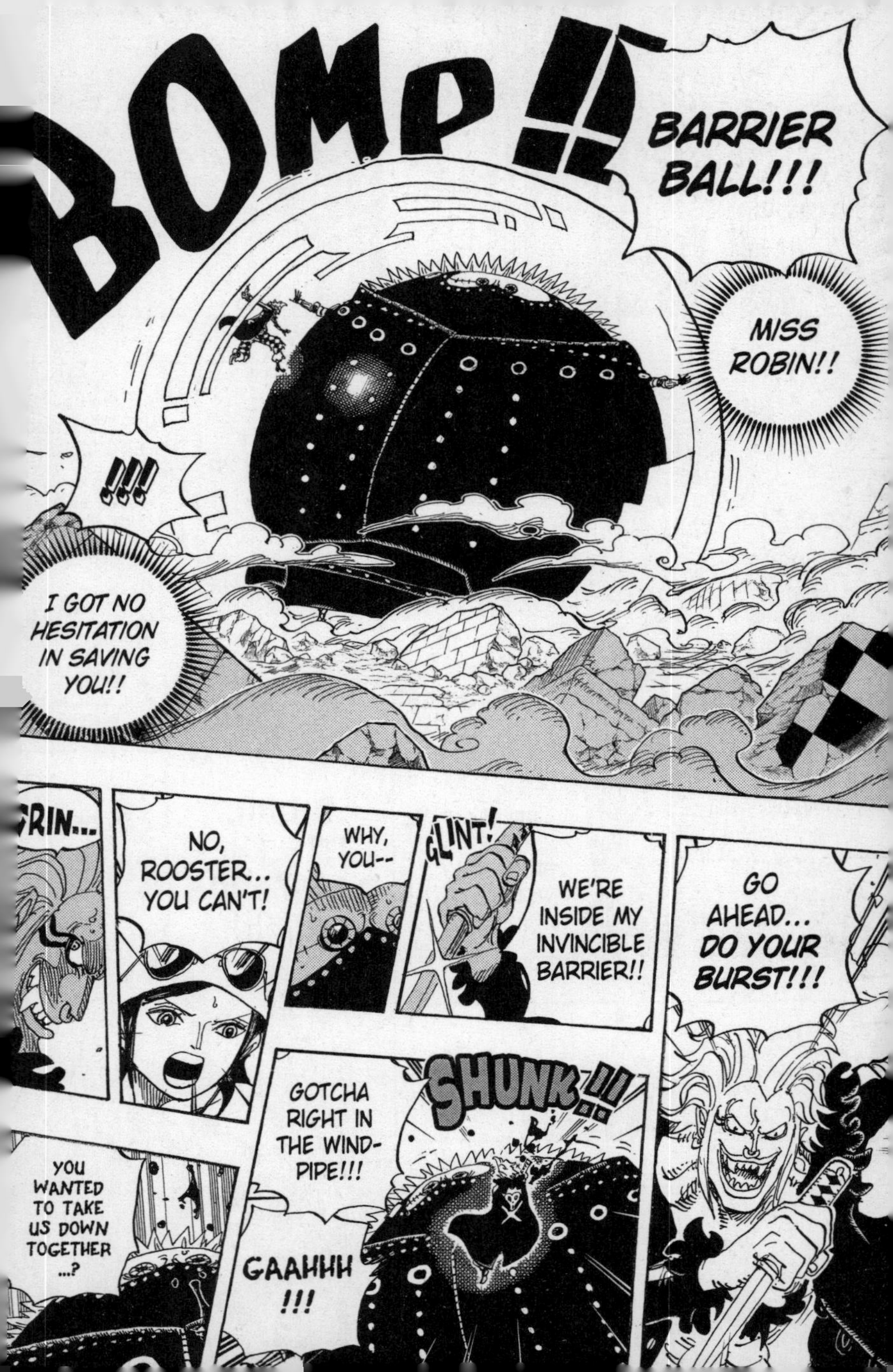

BARRIER BALL!!!
BOMP!!
MISS ROBIN!!
!!!
I GOT NO HESITATION IN SAVING YOU!!
GO AHEAD... DO YOUR BURST!!!
GLINT!
WE'RE INSIDE MY INVINCIBLE BARRIER!!
WHY, YOU--
NO, ROOSTER... YOU CAN'T!
GRIN...
SHUNK!!!
GOTCHA RIGHT IN THE WIND-PIPE!!!
GAAHHH!!!
YOU WANTED TO TAKE US DOWN TOGETHER...?

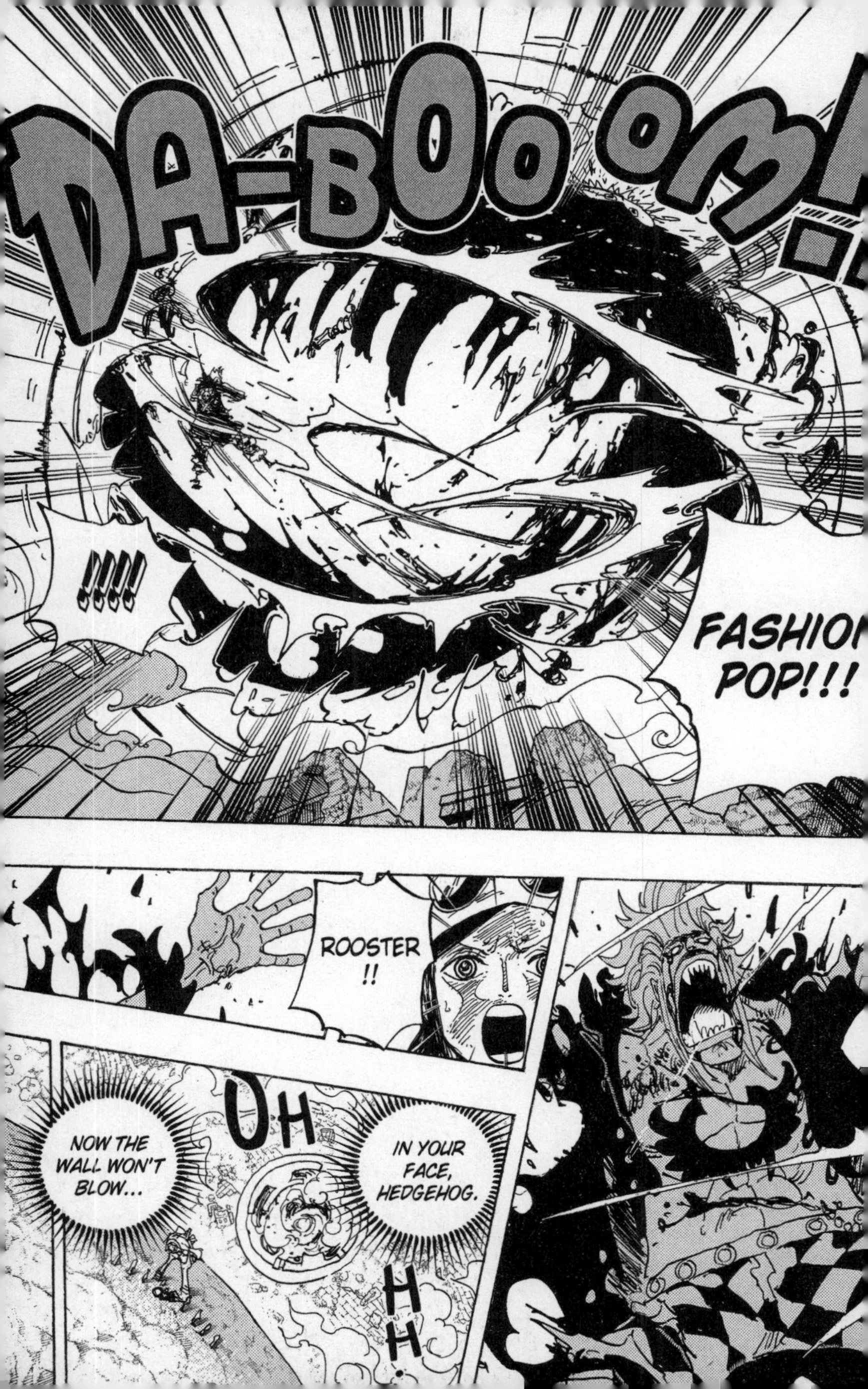
DA-BOOOOM!!
FASHION POP!!!
!!!!
ROOSTER !!
UH
IN YOUR FACE, HEDGEHOG.
NOW THE WALL WON'T BLOW...
HH

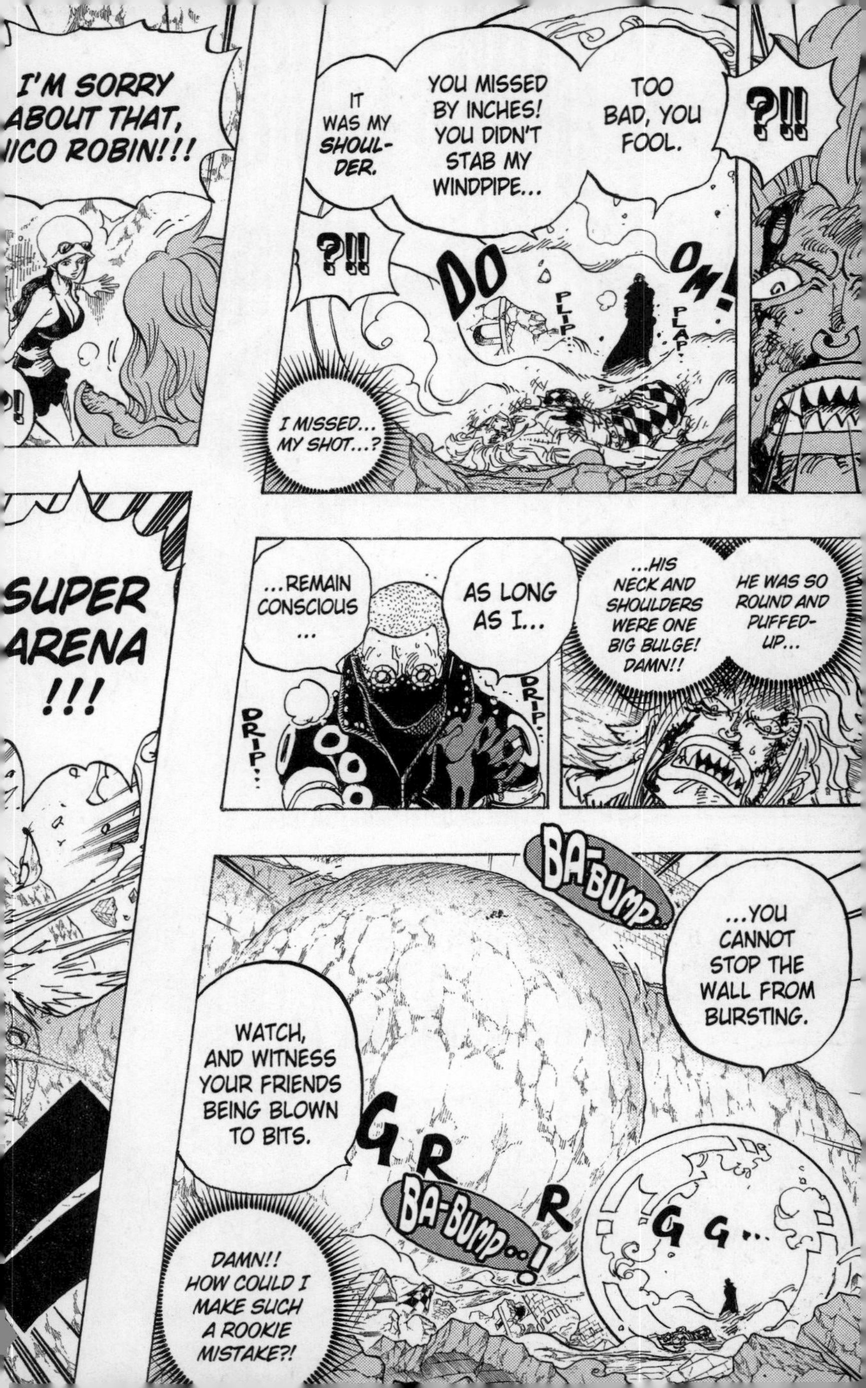
?!!
TOO BAD, YOU FOOL.
YOU MISSED BY INCHES! YOU DIDN'T STAB MY WINDPIPE...
IT WAS MY SHOUL-DER.
?!!
DOOM!
FLIP
FLAP
I MISSED... MY SHOT...?
HE WAS SO ROUND AND PUFFED-UP...
...HIS NECK AND SHOULDERS WERE ONE BIG BULGE! DAMN!!
AS LONG AS I...
...REMAIN CONSCIOUS ...
DRIP
DRIP
BA-BUMP
...YOU CANNOT STOP THE WALL FROM BURSTING.
WATCH, AND WITNESS YOUR FRIENDS BEING BLOWN TO BITS.
GRRRGG...
BA-BUMP..!
DAMN!! HOW COULD I MAKE SUCH A ROOKIE MISTAKE?!
I'M SORRY ABOUT THAT, ICO ROBIN!!!
SUPER ARENA !!!

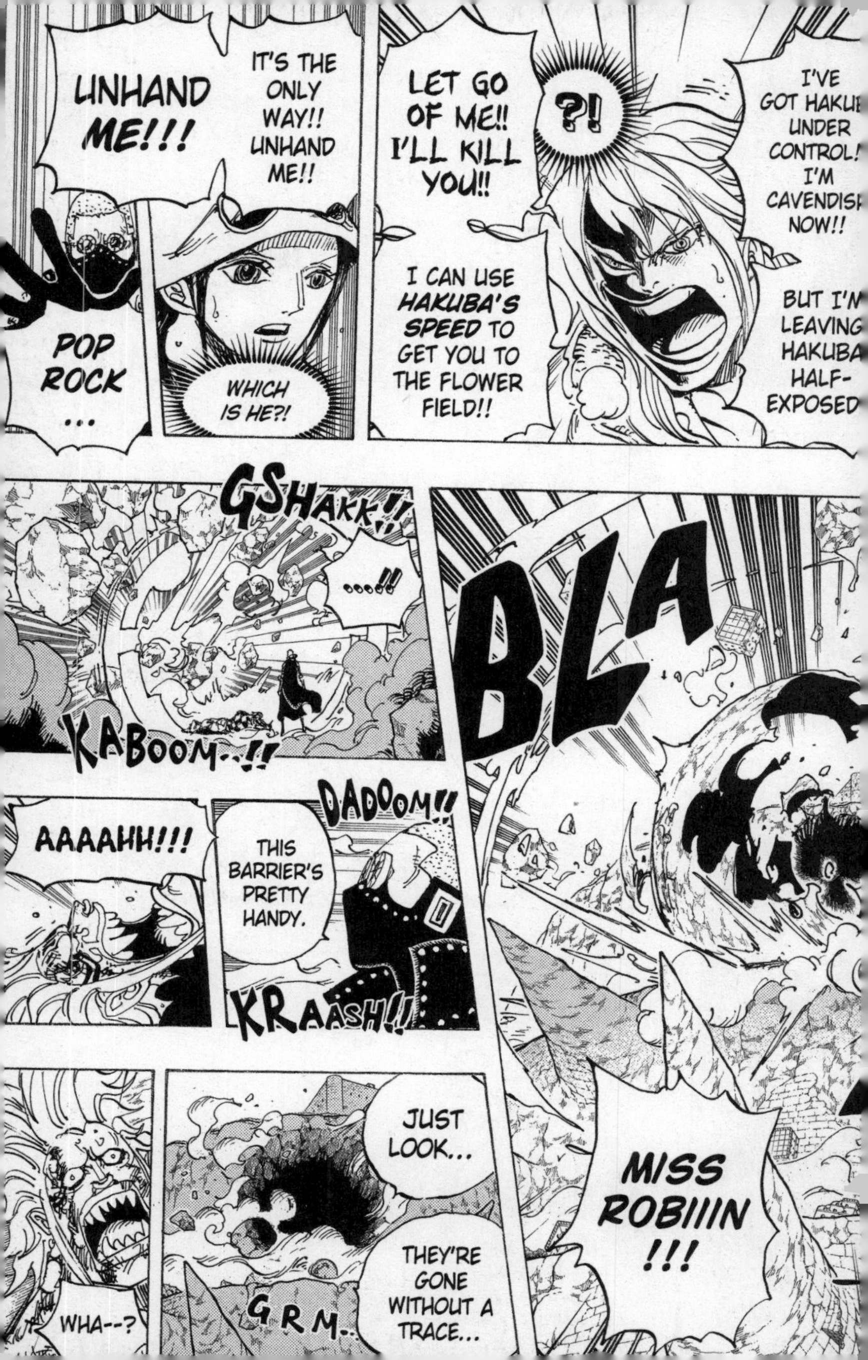

I'VE GOT HAKUB UNDER CONTROL! I'M CAVENDISH NOW!!
BUT I'M LEAVING HAKUBA HALF-EXPOSED
?!
LET GO OF ME!! I'LL KILL YOU!!
I CAN USE HAKUBA'S SPEED TO GET YOU TO THE FLOWER FIELD!!
IT'S THE ONLY WAY!! UNHAND ME!!
WHICH IS HE?!
UNHAND ME!!!
POP ROCK ...
BLA
MISS ROBIIIN !!!
GSHAKK!!
....!!
KABOOM..!!
DADOOM!!
THIS BARRIER'S PRETTY HANDY.
KRAASH!!
AAAAHH!!!
JUST LOOK...
THEY'RE GONE WITHOUT A TRACE...
GRM..
WHA--?

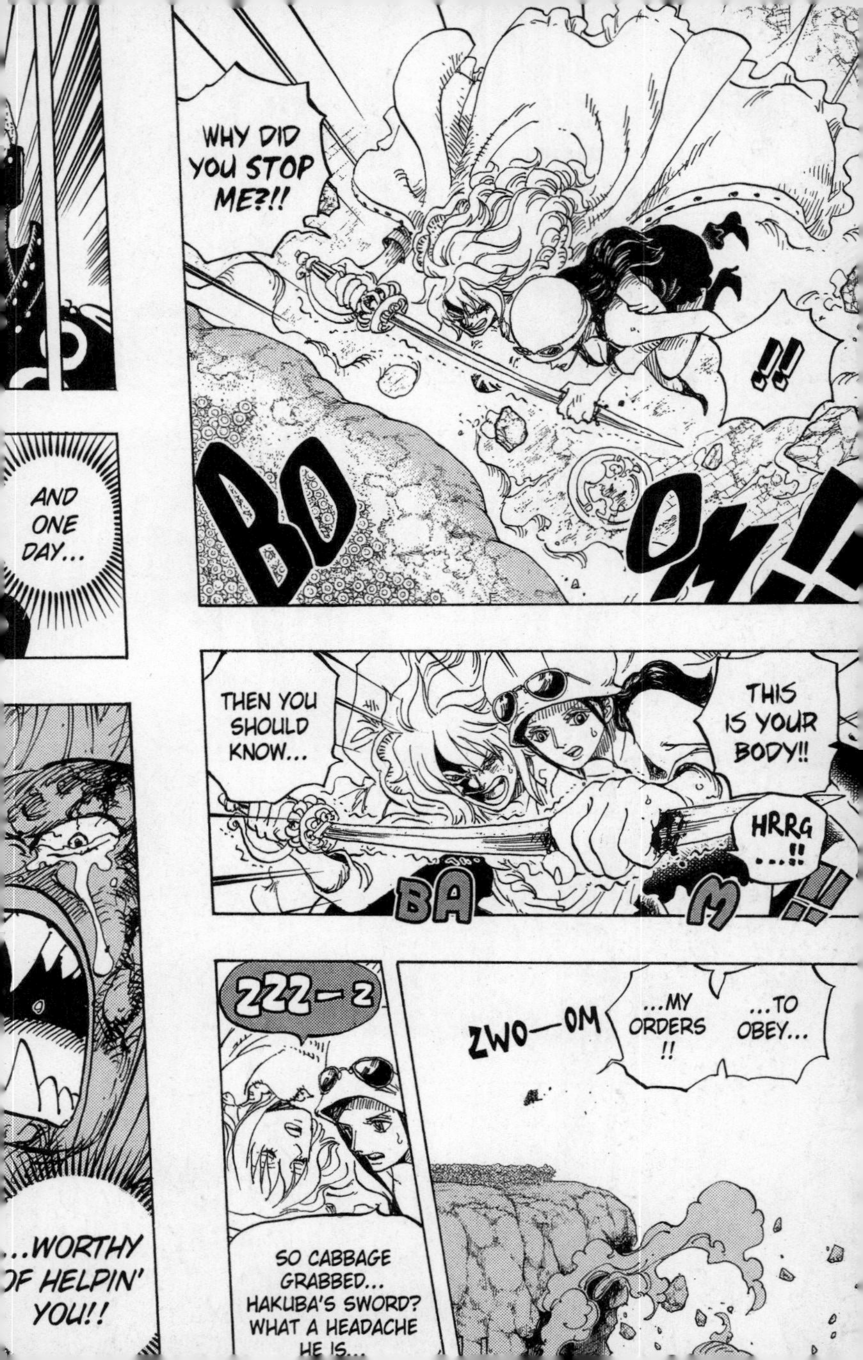
WHY DID YOU STOP ME?!!
!!
BOOM!!
THIS IS YOUR BODY!!
HRRG ...!!
THEN YOU SHOULD KNOW...
BAM!!
...TO OBEY...
...MY ORDERS !!
ZWO—OM
ZZZ-Z
SO CABBAGE GRABBED... HAKUBA'S SWORD? WHAT A HEADACHE HE IS...
AND ONE DAY...
...WORTHY OF HELPIN' YOU!!

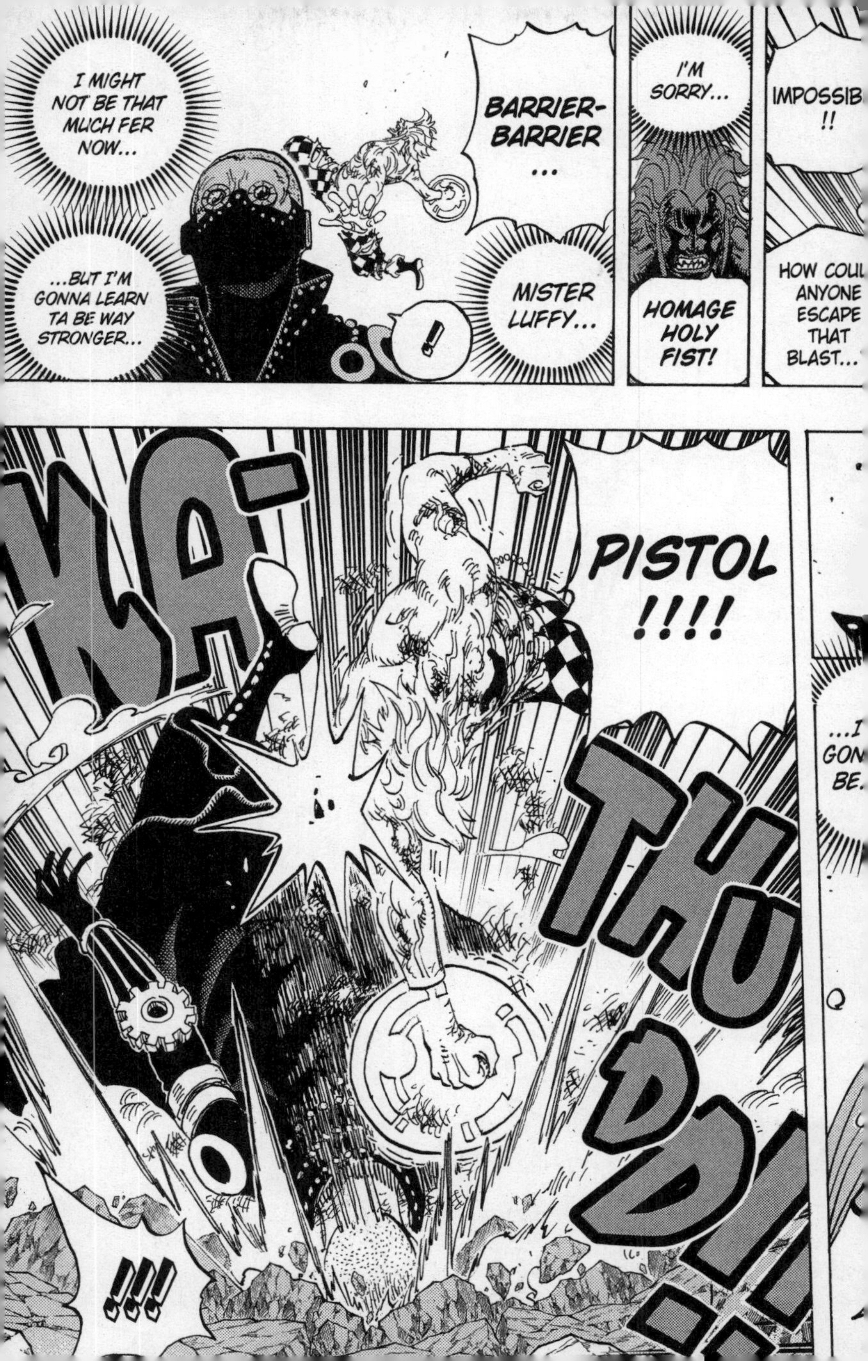
IMPOSSIB !!
HOW COUL ANYONE ESCAPE THAT BLAST...
I'M SORRY...
HOMAGE HOLY FIST!
BARRIER-BARRIER ...
MISTER LUFFY...
I MIGHT NOT BE THAT MUCH FER NOW...
...BUT I'M GONNA LEARN TA BE WAY STRONGER...
!
...I GON BE.
PISTOL !!!!
THUD
KA-
!!!

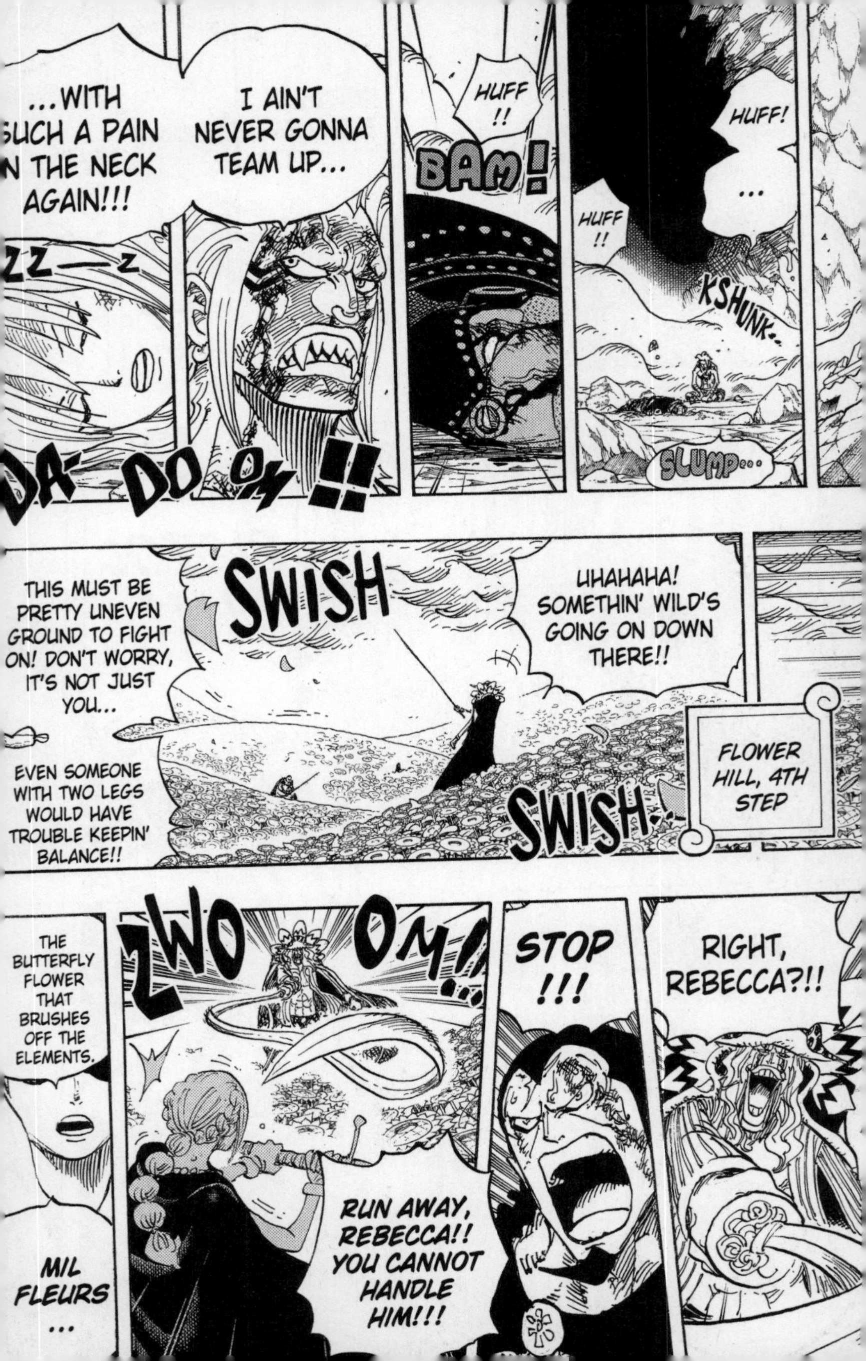
HUFF!
...
HUFF !!
KSHUNK...
SLUMP...
HUFF !!
BAM!
I AIN'T NEVER GONNA TEAM UP...
...WITH SUCH A PAIN N THE NECK AGAIN!!!
ZZ—Z
DA-DO-OM!!
FLOWER HILL, 4TH STEP
UHAHAHA! SOMETHIN' WILD'S GOING ON DOWN THERE!!
SWISH
SWISH...
THIS MUST BE PRETTY UNEVEN GROUND TO FIGHT ON! DON'T WORRY, IT'S NOT JUST YOU...
EVEN SOMEONE WITH TWO LEGS WOULD HAVE TROUBLE KEEPIN' BALANCE!!
RIGHT, REBECCA?!!
STOP !!!
RUN AWAY, REBECCA!! YOU CANNOT HANDLE HIM!!!
ZWO OM!!
THE BUTTERFLY FLOWER THAT BRUSHES OFF THE ELEMENTS.
MIL FLEURS ...

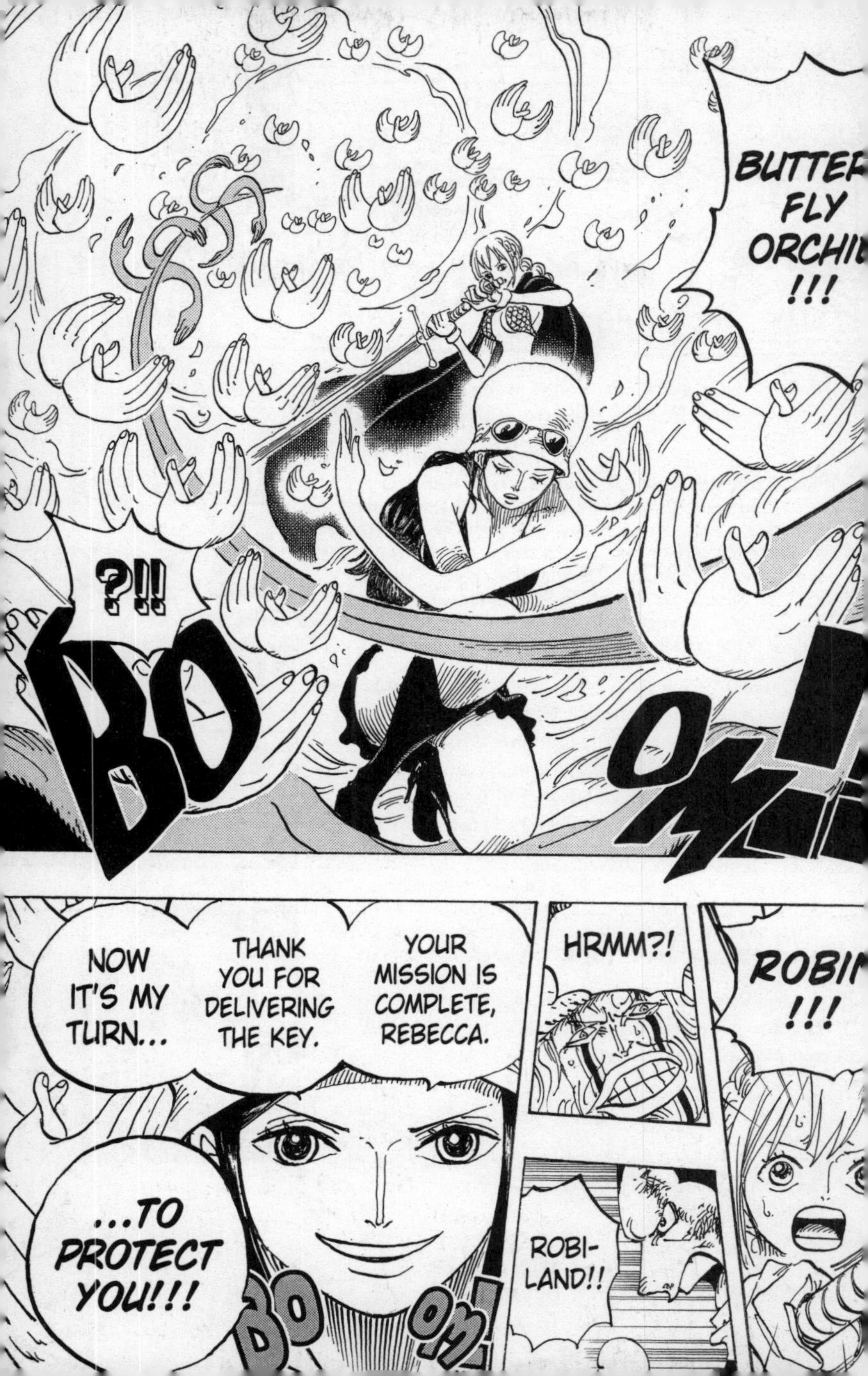
BUTTER
FLY
ORCHI
!!!
?!!
BOOM!
ROBI
!!!
HRMM?!
ROBI-
LAND!!
YOUR MISSION IS COMPLETE, REBECCA.
THANK YOU FOR DELIVERING THE KEY.
NOW IT'S MY TURN...
...TO PROTECT YOU!!!
BOOM!

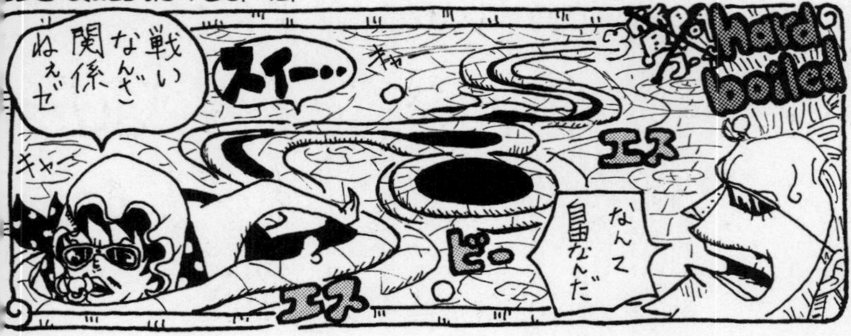
hard boiled
エス
なんて自由なんだ
スイー…
キャー
ぴっ
エス
戦いなんざ関係ねぇゼ
キャー

(Haru, Nagano)

Q: Hello, Mr. Oda. You mentioned in the story that Bartolomeo's barrier ability has its limits. How many Barri-Barris can he do, at maximum?

--Hoichael Jackson

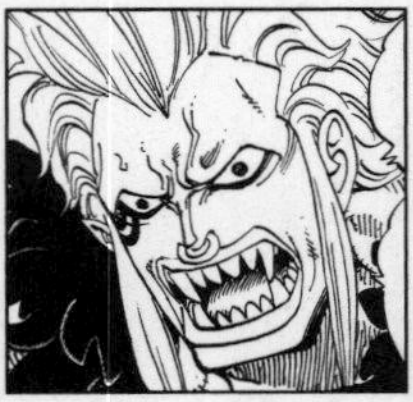

A: That's a very good question. There is a limit to how much surface area and how many barriers he can deploy at once. He can only create one barrier at a time, and its maximum surface is 50,000 Barri-Barris!! That's incredible! One Barri-Barri is equivalent to 100 Borri-Barri-Barris, which means his defense is as much as 500 Pickle-Porri-Porri-Barri-Barris.

Q: In Chapter 765, it really looks like Corazon and Law are on the island belonging to the Lvneel Kingdom that Noland was from, based on the look of the palace! Do you suppose that Corazon figured the country that conquered the skin-changing wood fever might also have a cure for white lead disease? I was crying about it, just thinking about that possibility. Handkerchief, please.

--Kamiki

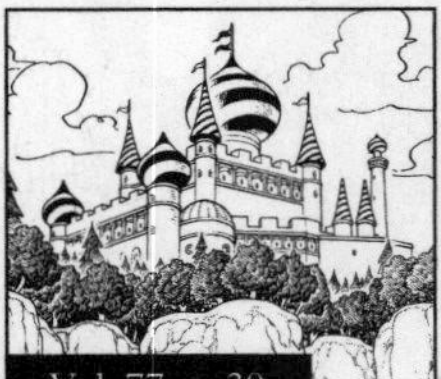

Vol. 77, p. 30

A: Yes, that's the place. It still has the same look as it did centuries ago. Was that really his thought process?! I'm crying too, now. What a great guy that Corazon was. (crying)

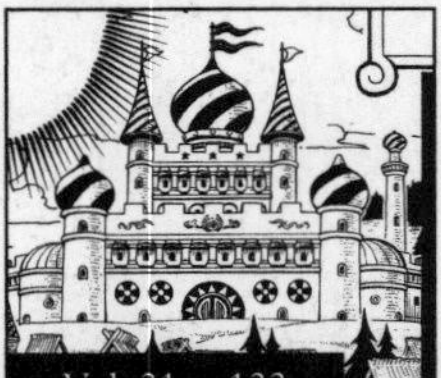

Vol. 31, p.133

Q: It turns out that Corazon's birthday was July 15… Because in Japanese, you can make the numbers 0715 sound like "silent Corazon"!!

--Yabu Smith

A: Oh, I get it. Well, there you go. That's the end of this SBS.
They've opened a One Piece exhibit at the Tokyo Tower! Come check it out! See you next volume!!

Chapter 774:
LEO, CAPTAIN OF THE TONTATTA WARRIORS

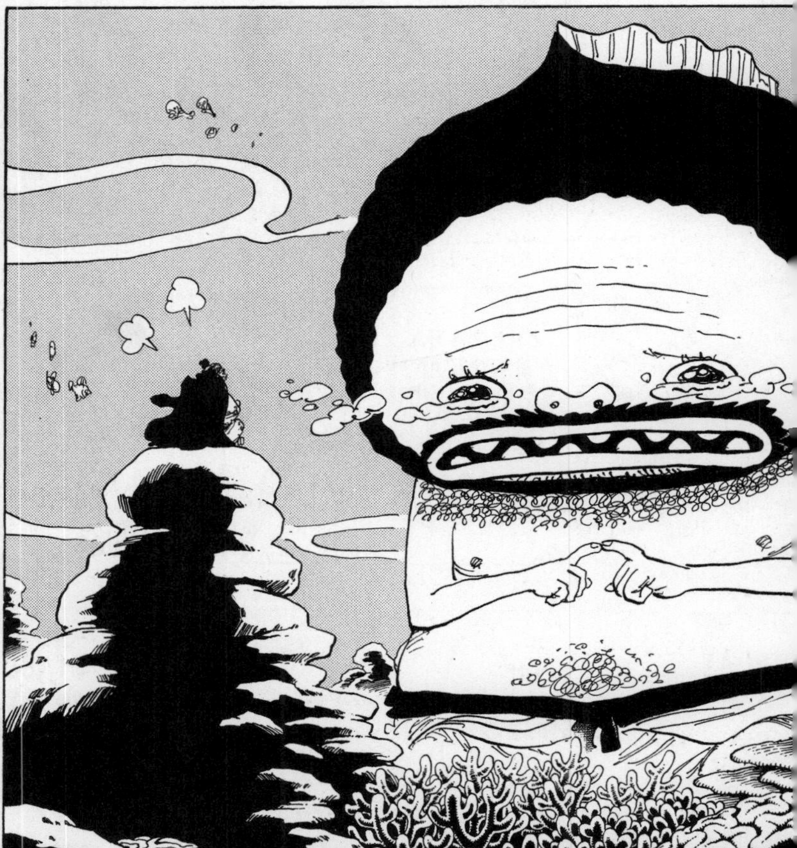

THE SOLITARY JOURNEY OF JIMBEI, FIRST SON OF THE SEA, VOL. 20: "JIMBEI LECTURES THE SEA GOD"

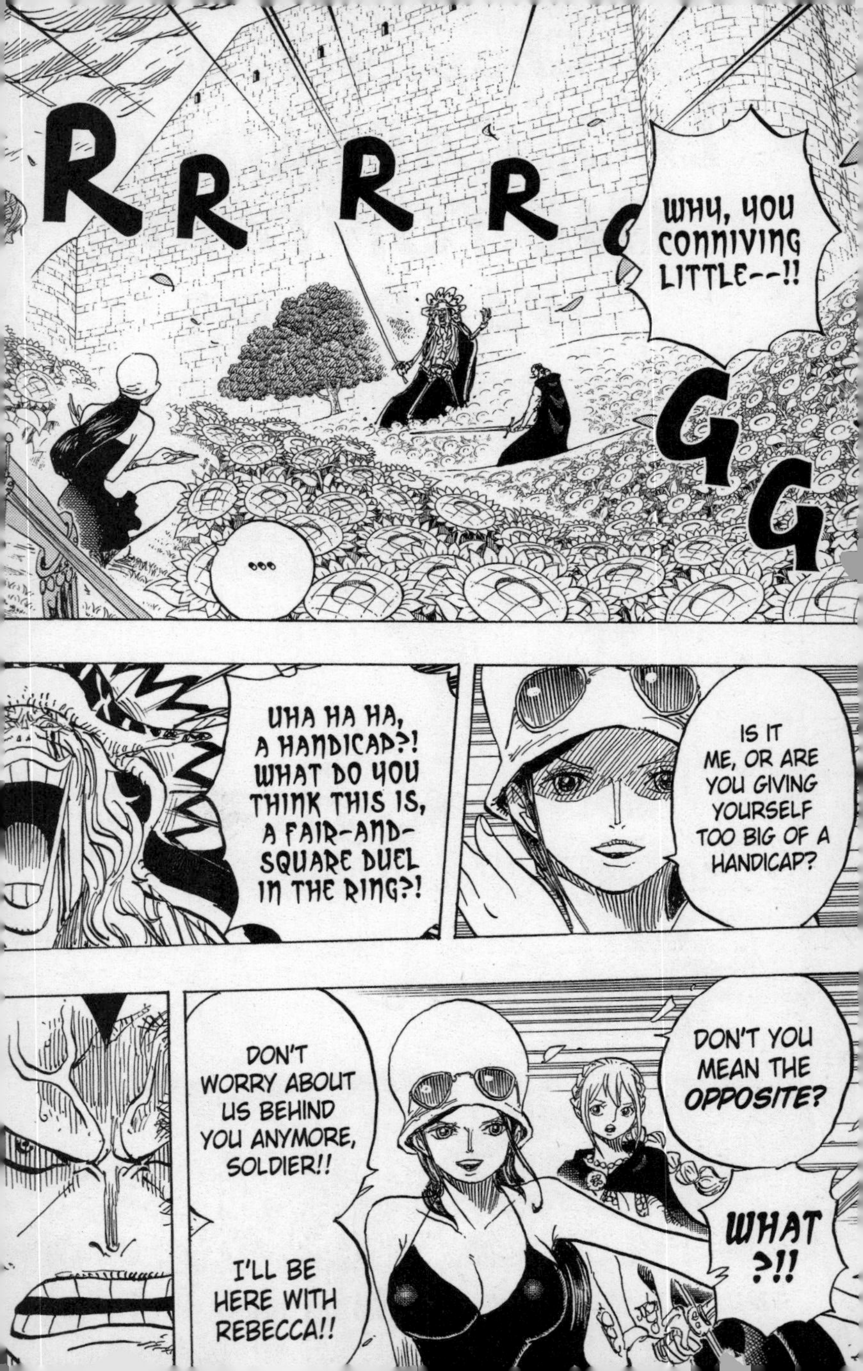
RRRRRGGG
WHY, YOU CONNIVING LITTLE--!!
...
IS IT ME, OR ARE YOU GIVING YOURSELF TOO BIG OF A HANDICAP?
UHA HA HA, A HANDICAP?! WHAT DO YOU THINK THIS IS, A FAIR-AND-SQUARE DUEL IN THE RING?!
DON'T YOU MEAN THE *OPPOSITE*?
DON'T WORRY ABOUT US BEHIND YOU ANYMORE, SOLDIER!!
WHAT?!!
I'LL BE HERE WITH REBECCA!!

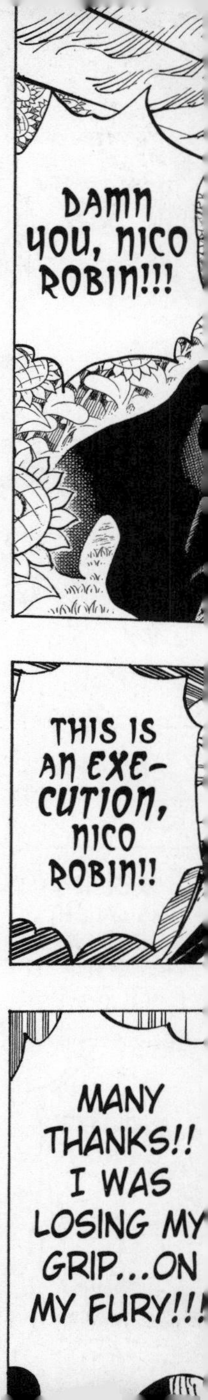
DAMN YOU, NICO ROBIN!!!
THIS IS AN EXE-CUTION, NICO ROBIN!!
MANY THANKS!! I WAS LOSING MY GRIP...ON MY FURY!!!

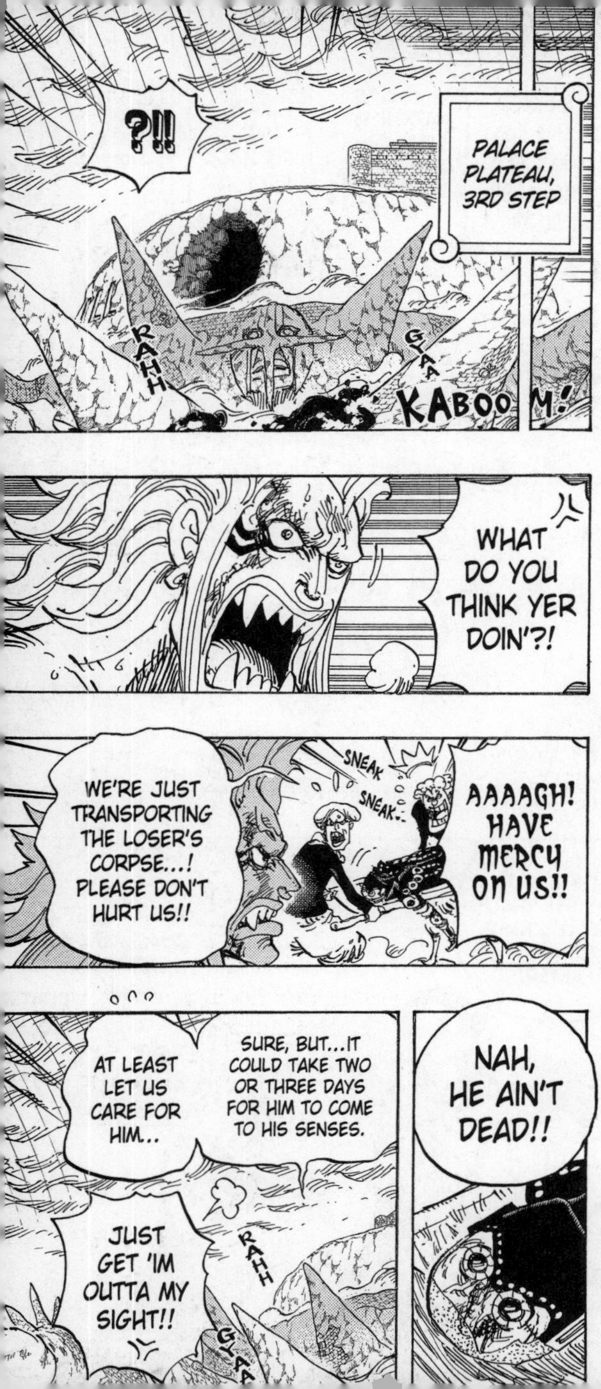
PALACE PLATEAU, 3RD STEP
?!!
GYAA
KABOOM!
RAHH
WHAT DO YOU THINK YER DOIN'?!
AAAAGH! HAVE MERCY ON US!!
SNEAK
SNEAK
WE'RE JUST TRANSPORTING THE LOSER'S CORPSE...! PLEASE DON'T HURT US!!
NAH, HE AIN'T DEAD!!
SURE, BUT...IT COULD TAKE TWO OR THREE DAYS FOR HIM TO COME TO HIS SENSES.
AT LEAST LET US CARE FOR HIM...
RAHH
JUST GET 'IM OUTTA MY SIGHT!!
GYAA

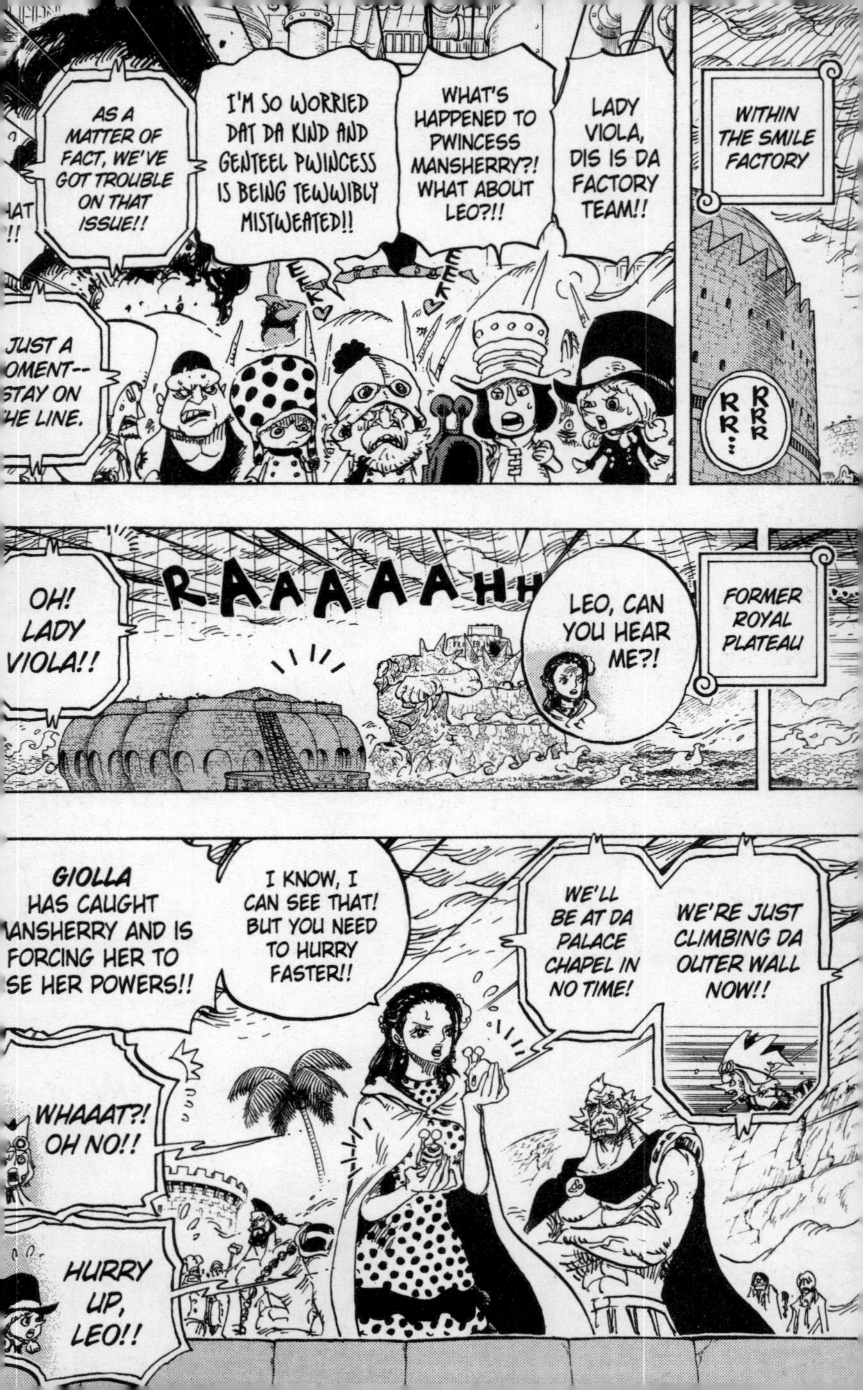

WITHIN THE SMILE FACTORY
RRRRR...
LADY VIOLA, DIS IS DA FACTORY TEAM!!
WHAT'S HAPPENED TO PWINCESS MANSHERRY?! WHAT ABOUT LEO?!!
I'M SO WORRIED DAT DA KIND AND GENTEEL PWINCESS IS BEING TEWWIBLY MISTWEATED!!
EEK
EEK
AS A MATTER OF FACT, WE'VE GOT TROUBLE ON THAT ISSUE!!
JUST A OMENT-- STAY ON HE LINE.
FORMER ROYAL PLATEAU
LEO, CAN YOU HEAR ME?!
RAAAAAHH
OH! LADY VIOLA!!
WE'RE JUST CLIMBING DA OUTER WALL NOW!!
WE'LL BE AT DA PALACE CHAPEL IN NO TIME!
I KNOW, I CAN SEE THAT! BUT YOU NEED TO HURRY FASTER!!
GIOLLA HAS CAUGHT ANSHERRY AND IS FORCING HER TO SE HER POWERS!!
WHAAAT?! OH NO!!
HURRY UP, LEO!!

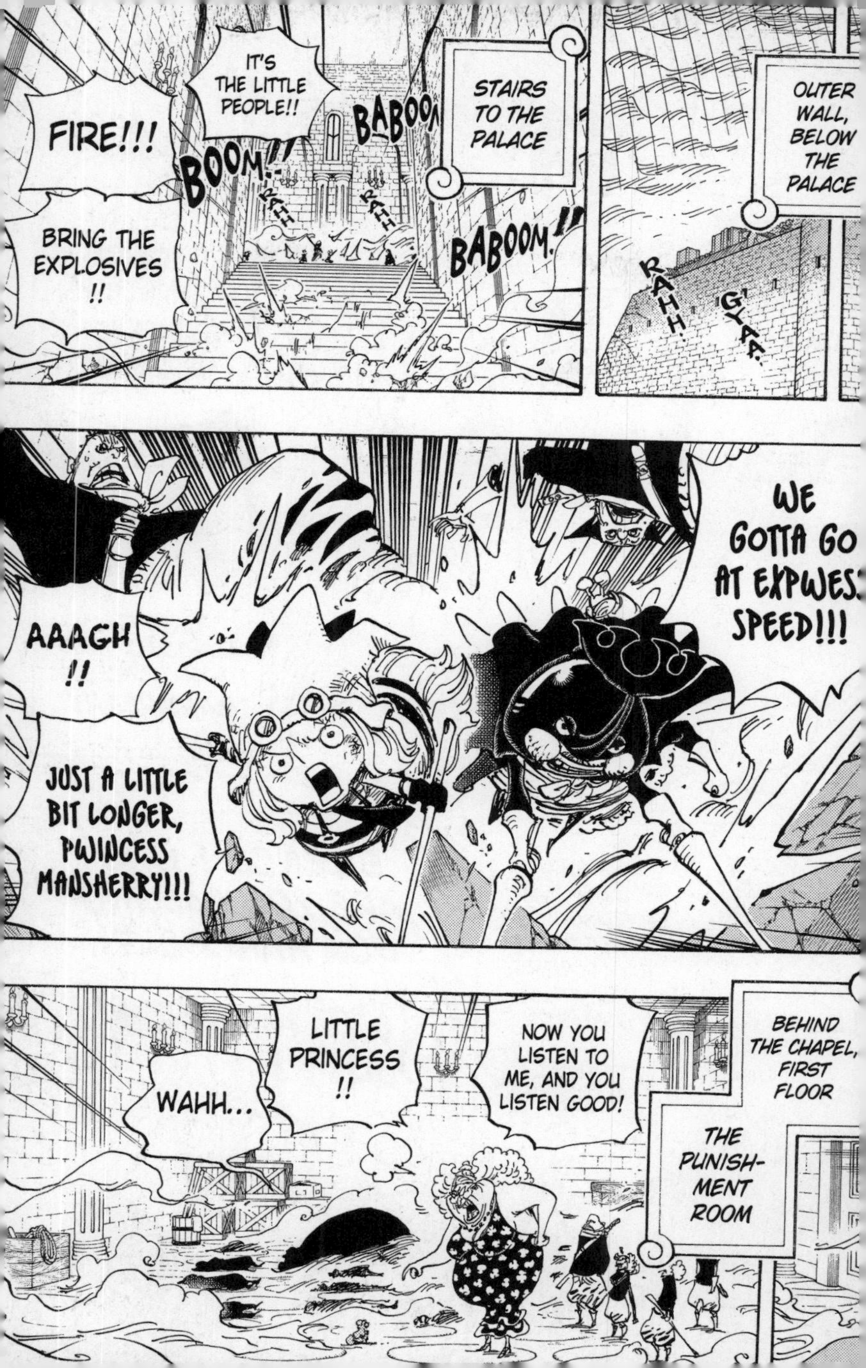

OUTER WALL, BELOW THE PALACE
RAHH...
GYAA...
STAIRS TO THE PALACE
IT'S THE LITTLE PEOPLE!!
BABOOM
BOOM!!
RAHH
RAHH
FIRE!!!
BRING THE EXPLOSIVES!!
BABOOM!!
WE GOTTA GO AT EXPWESS SPEED!!!
AAAGH!!
JUST A LITTLE BIT LONGER, PWINCESS MANSHERRY!!!
BEHIND THE CHAPEL, FIRST FLOOR
THE PUNISHMENT ROOM
NOW YOU LISTEN TO ME, AND YOU LISTEN GOOD!
LITTLE PRINCESS!!
WAHH...

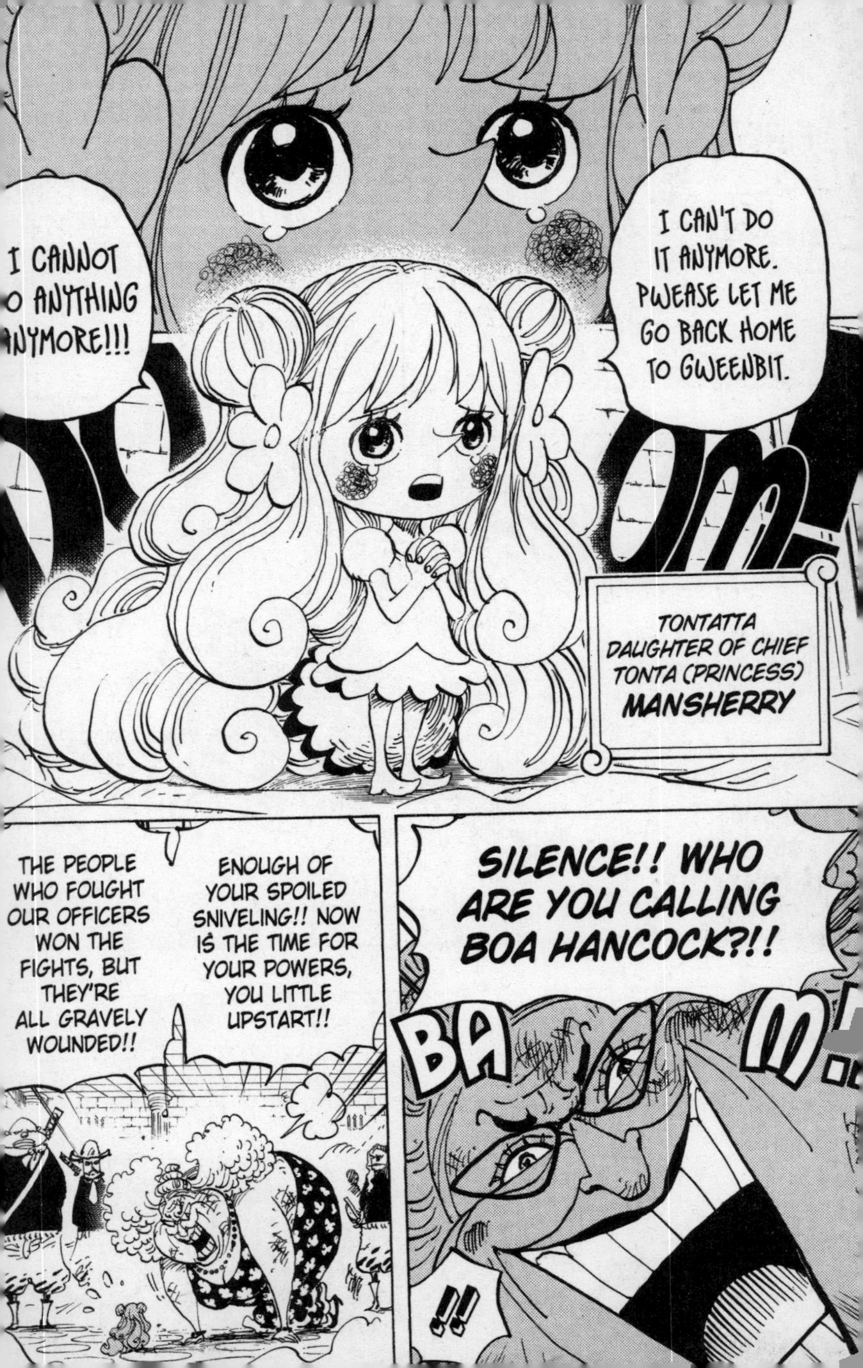
I CAN'T DO IT ANYMORE. PWEASE LET ME GO BACK HOME TO GWEENBIT.
I CANNOT O ANYTHING NYMORE!!!
TONTATTA DAUGHTER OF CHIEF TONTA (PRINCESS) MANSHERRY
SILENCE!! WHO ARE YOU CALLING BOA HANCOCK?!!
BAM..
!!
ENOUGH OF YOUR SPOILED SNIVELING!! NOW IS THE TIME FOR YOUR POWERS, YOU LITTLE UPSTART!!
THE PEOPLE WHO FOUGHT OUR OFFICERS WON THE FIGHTS, BUT THEY'RE ALL GRAVELY WOUNDED!!

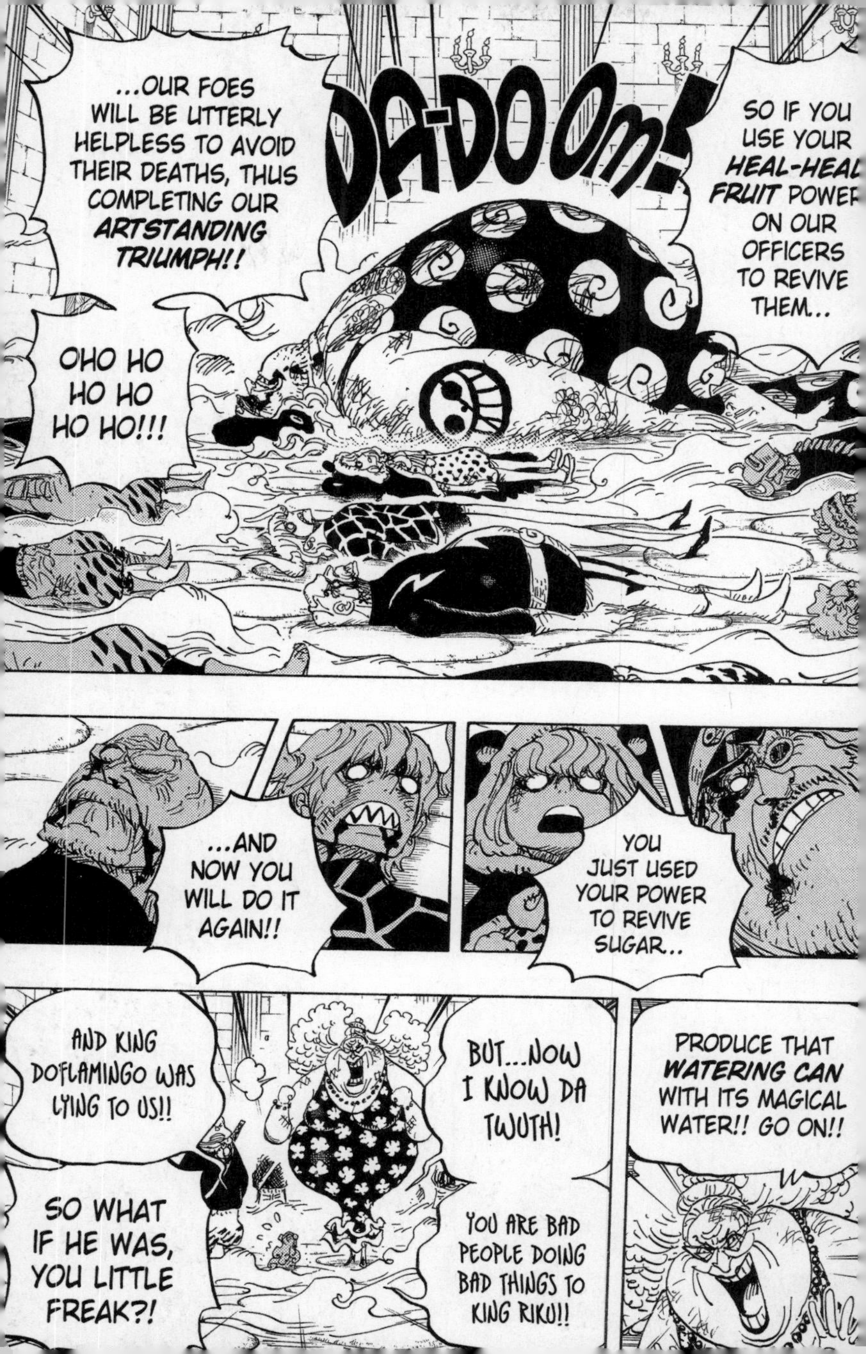
SO IF YOU USE YOUR HEAL-HEAL FRUIT POWER ON OUR OFFICERS TO REVIVE THEM...
DA-DOOM!
...OUR FOES WILL BE UTTERLY HELPLESS TO AVOID THEIR DEATHS, THUS COMPLETING OUR ARTSTANDING TRIUMPH!!
OHO HO HO HO HO HO!!!
YOU JUST USED YOUR POWER TO REVIVE SUGAR...
...AND NOW YOU WILL DO IT AGAIN!!
PRODUCE THAT WATERING CAN WITH ITS MAGICAL WATER!! GO ON!!
BUT...NOW I KNOW DA TWUTH!
AND KING DOFLAMINGO WAS LYING TO US!!
YOU ARE BAD PEOPLE DOING BAD THINGS TO KING RIKU!!
SO WHAT IF HE WAS, YOU LITTLE FREAK?!

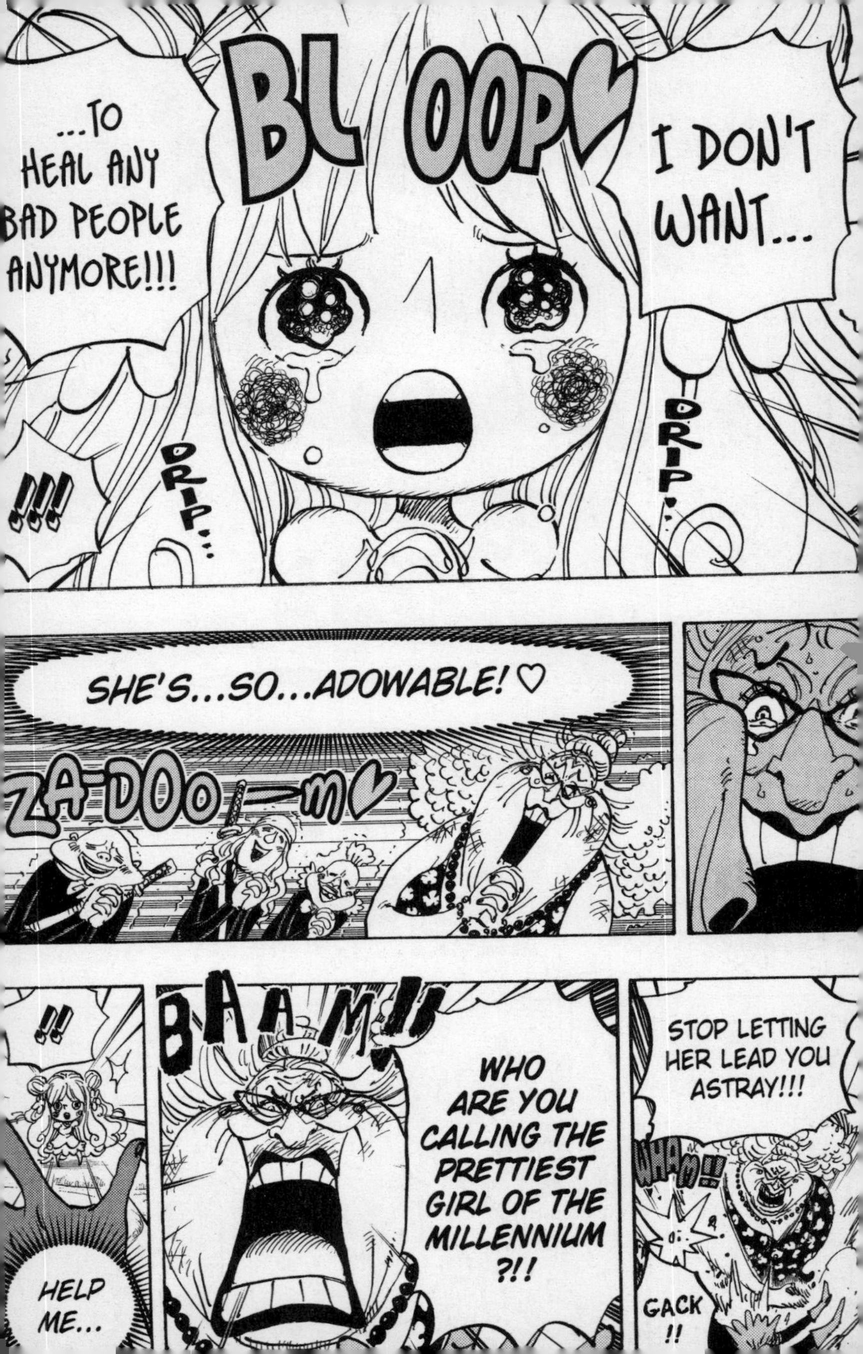
I DON'T WANT...
...TO HEAL ANY BAD PEOPLE ANYMORE!!!
BLOOP♡
DRIP...
DRIP...
!!!
SHE'S...SO...ADOWABLE! ♡
ZA-DOOO—M♡
STOP LETTING HER LEAD YOU ASTRAY!!!
WHAM!!
GACK!!
BAAM!!
WHO ARE YOU CALLING THE PRETTIEST GIRL OF THE MILLENNIUM ?!!
!!
HELP ME...

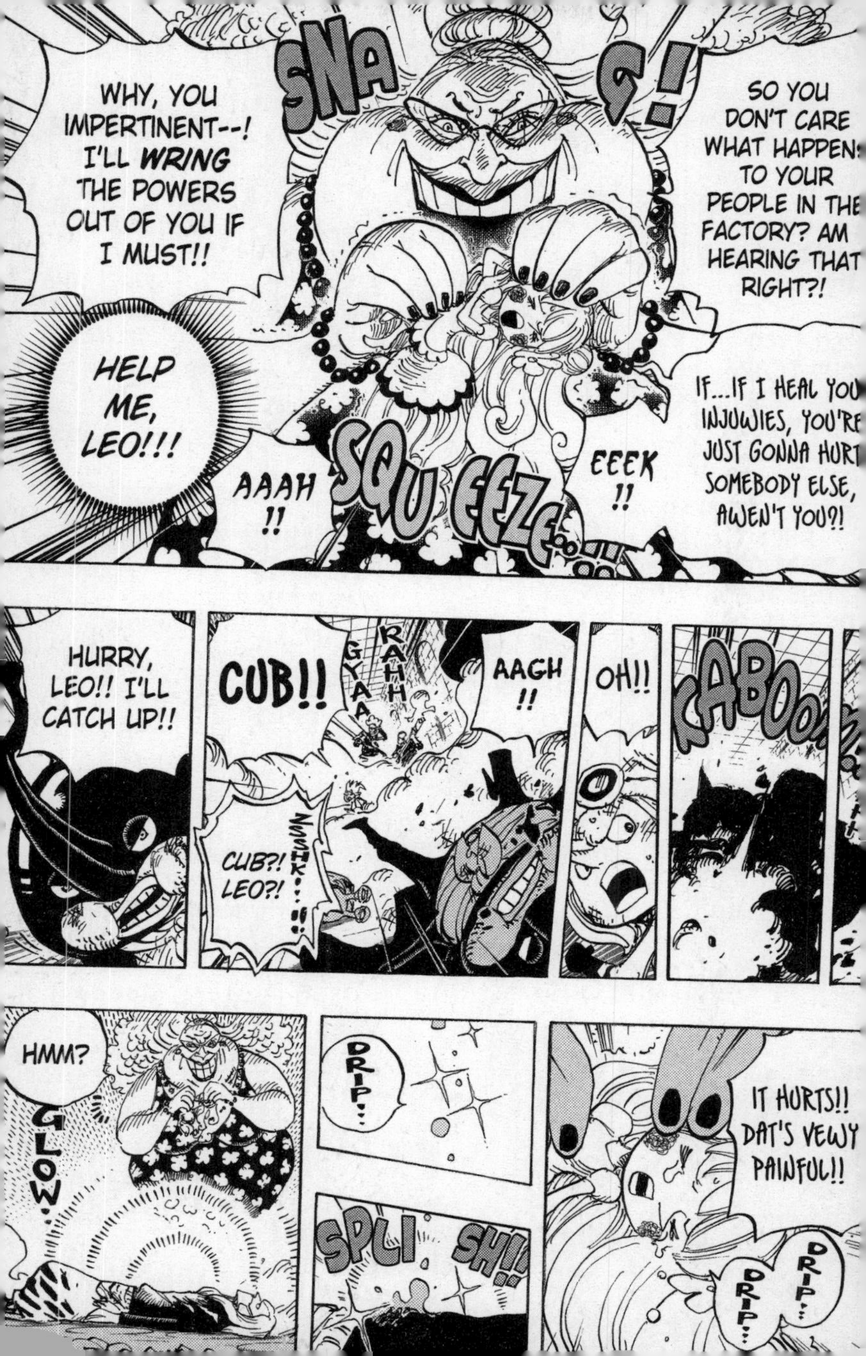
SO YOU DON'T CARE WHAT HAPPENS TO YOUR PEOPLE IN THE FACTORY? AM HEARING THAT RIGHT?!
SNAG!
WHY, YOU IMPERTINENT--! I'LL *WRING* THE POWERS OUT OF YOU IF I MUST!!
IF...IF I HEAL YOU INJUWIES, YOU'RE JUST GONNA HURT SOMEBODY ELSE, AWEN'T YOU?!
EEEK!!
SQUEEZE...!!
AAAH!!
HELP ME, LEO!!!
KABOOM!!
OH!!
AAGH!!
RAHH
GYAAA
CUB!!
CUB?! LEO?!
NSSHK...!!
HURRY, LEO!! I'LL CATCH UP!!
IT HURTS!! DAT'S VEWY PAINFUL!!
DRIP...
DRIP...
DRIP...
SPLISH!!
HMM?
GLOW...

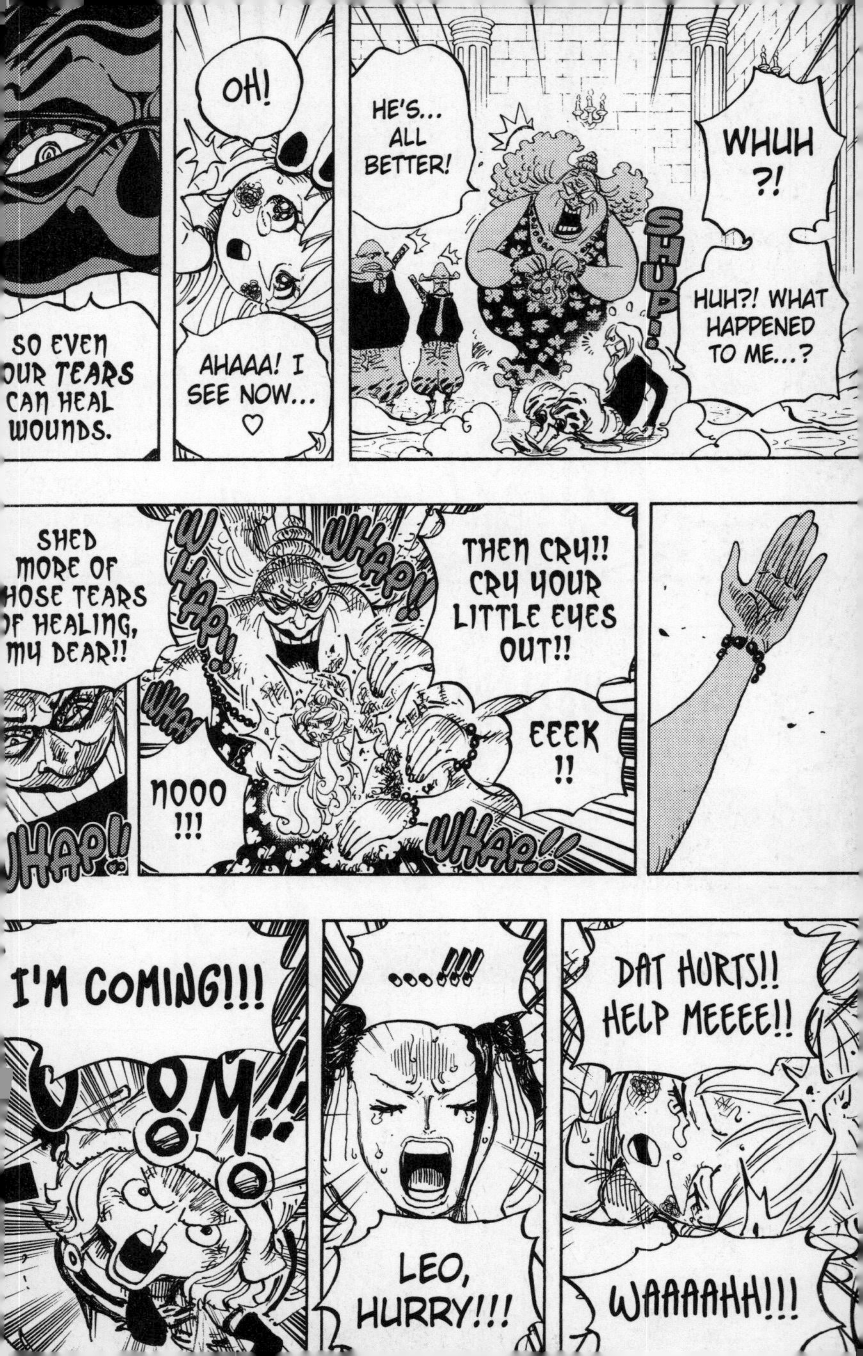
WHUH ?!
SHUP!!
HUH?! WHAT HAPPENED TO ME...?
HE'S... ALL BETTER!
OH!
AHAAA! I SEE NOW... ♡
SO EVEN OUR TEARS CAN HEAL WOUNDS.
THEN CRY!! CRY YOUR LITTLE EYES OUT!!
WHAP!!
WHAP!!
WHAP!!
EEEK !!
NOOO !!!
WHAP!!
SHED MORE OF HOSE TEARS OF HEALING, MY DEAR!!
HAP!!
DAT HURTS!! HELP MEEEE!!
WAAAAAHH!!!
...!!!
LEO, HURRY!!!
I'M COMING!!!
OM!!

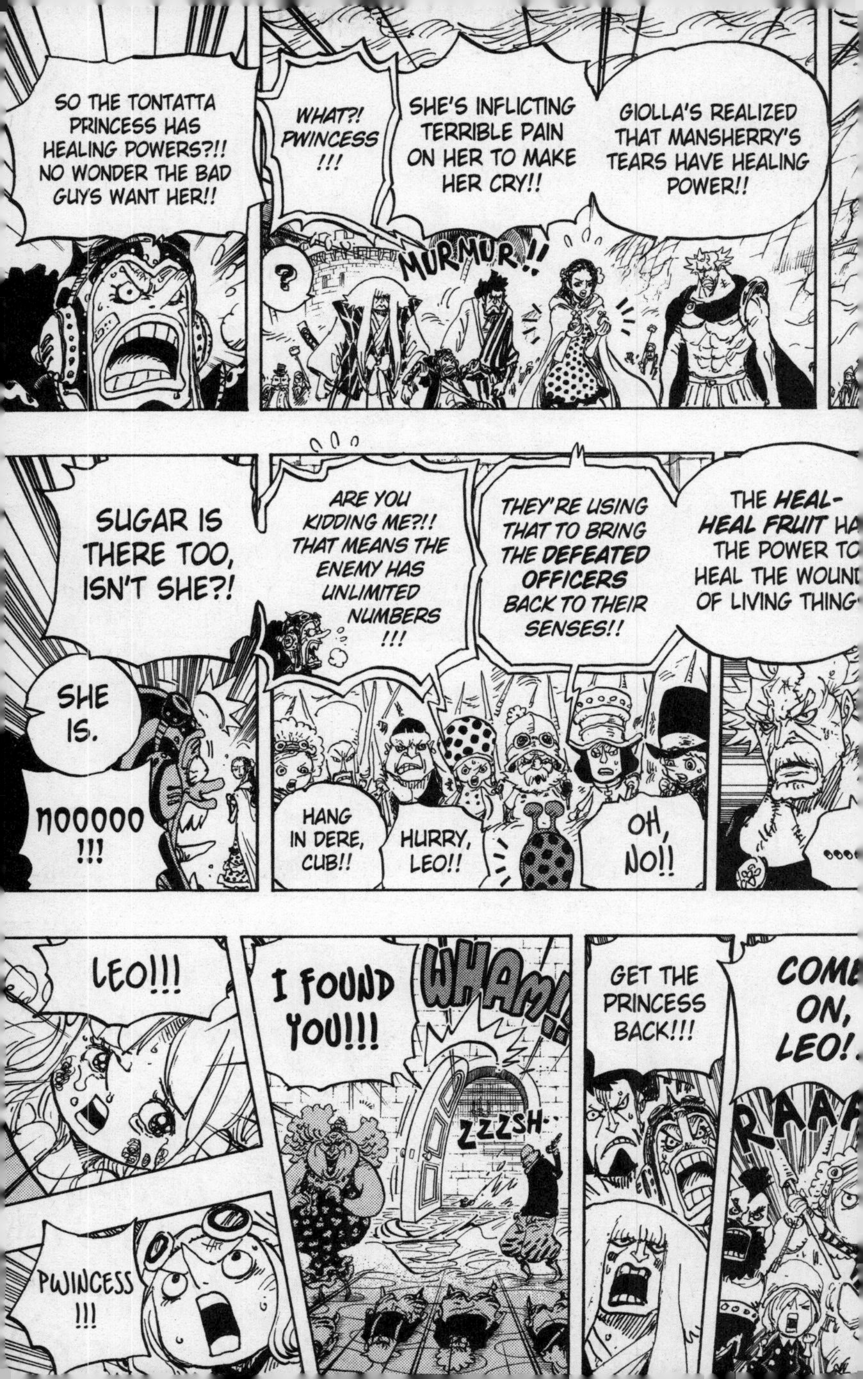
GIOLLA'S REALIZED THAT MANSHERRY'S TEARS HAVE HEALING POWER!!
SHE'S INFLICTING TERRIBLE PAIN ON HER TO MAKE HER CRY!!
MURMUR!!
WHAT?! PWINCESS !!!
?
SO THE TONTATTA PRINCESS HAS HEALING POWERS?!! NO WONDER THE BAD GUYS WANT HER!!
THE **HEAL-HEAL FRUIT** HA THE POWER TO HEAL THE WOUN OF LIVING THING
...
THEY'RE USING THAT TO BRING THE **DEFEATED OFFICERS** BACK TO THEIR SENSES!!
ARE YOU KIDDING ME?!! THAT MEANS THE ENEMY HAS UNLIMITED NUMBERS !!!
OH, NO!!
HURRY, LEO!!
HANG IN DERE, CUB!!
SUGAR IS THERE TOO, ISN'T SHE?!
SHE IS.
NOOOOO !!!
COM ON, LEO!
RAA
GET THE PRINCESS BACK!!!
WHAM!!
I FOUND YOU!!!
ZZZSH
LEO!!!
PWINCESS !!!

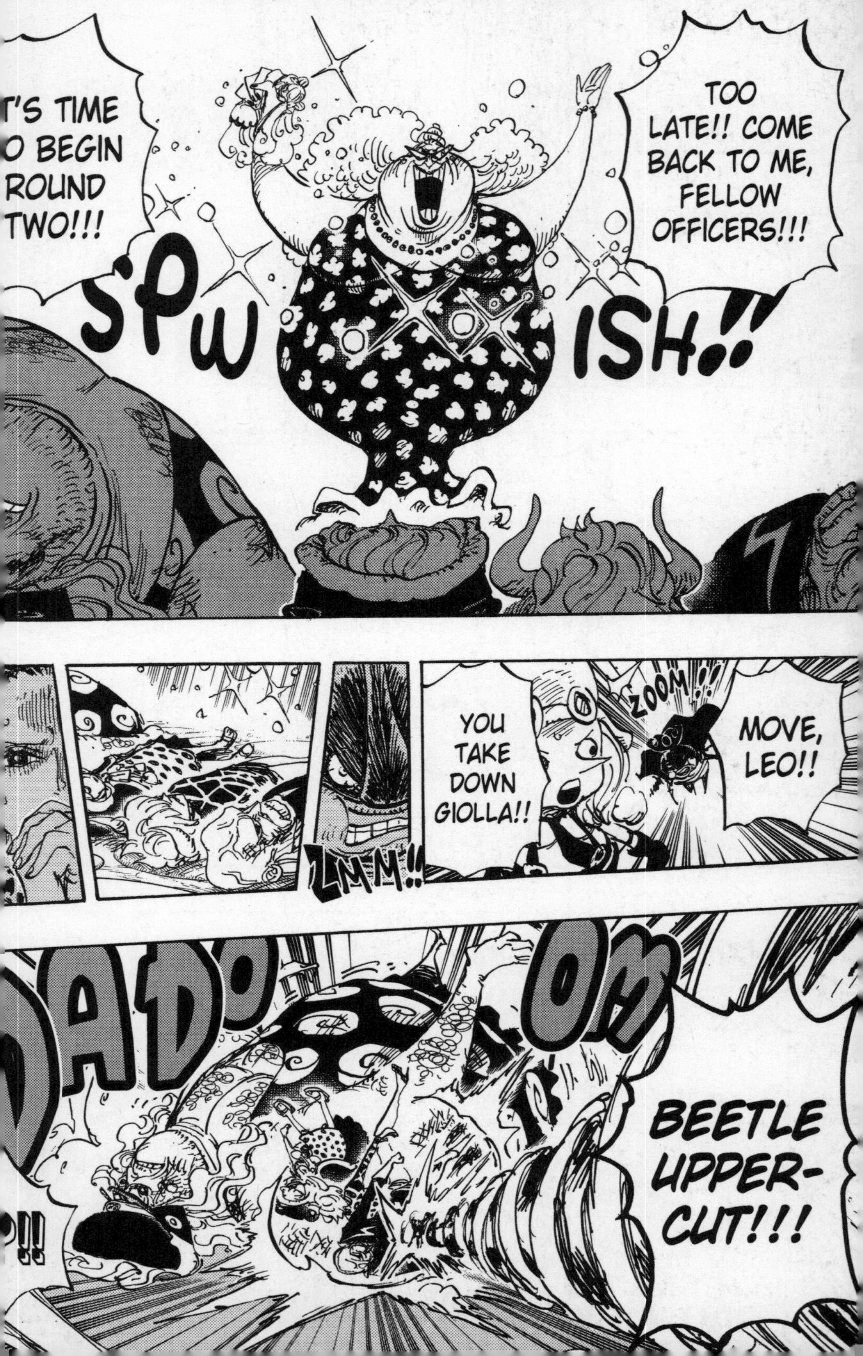
TOO LATE!! COME BACK TO ME, FELLOW OFFICERS!!!
SPWISH!!
T'S TIME O BEGIN ROUND TWO!!!
MOVE, LEO!!
ZOOM
YOU TAKE DOWN GIOLLA!!
ZMM!!
BEETLE UPPER-CUT!!!

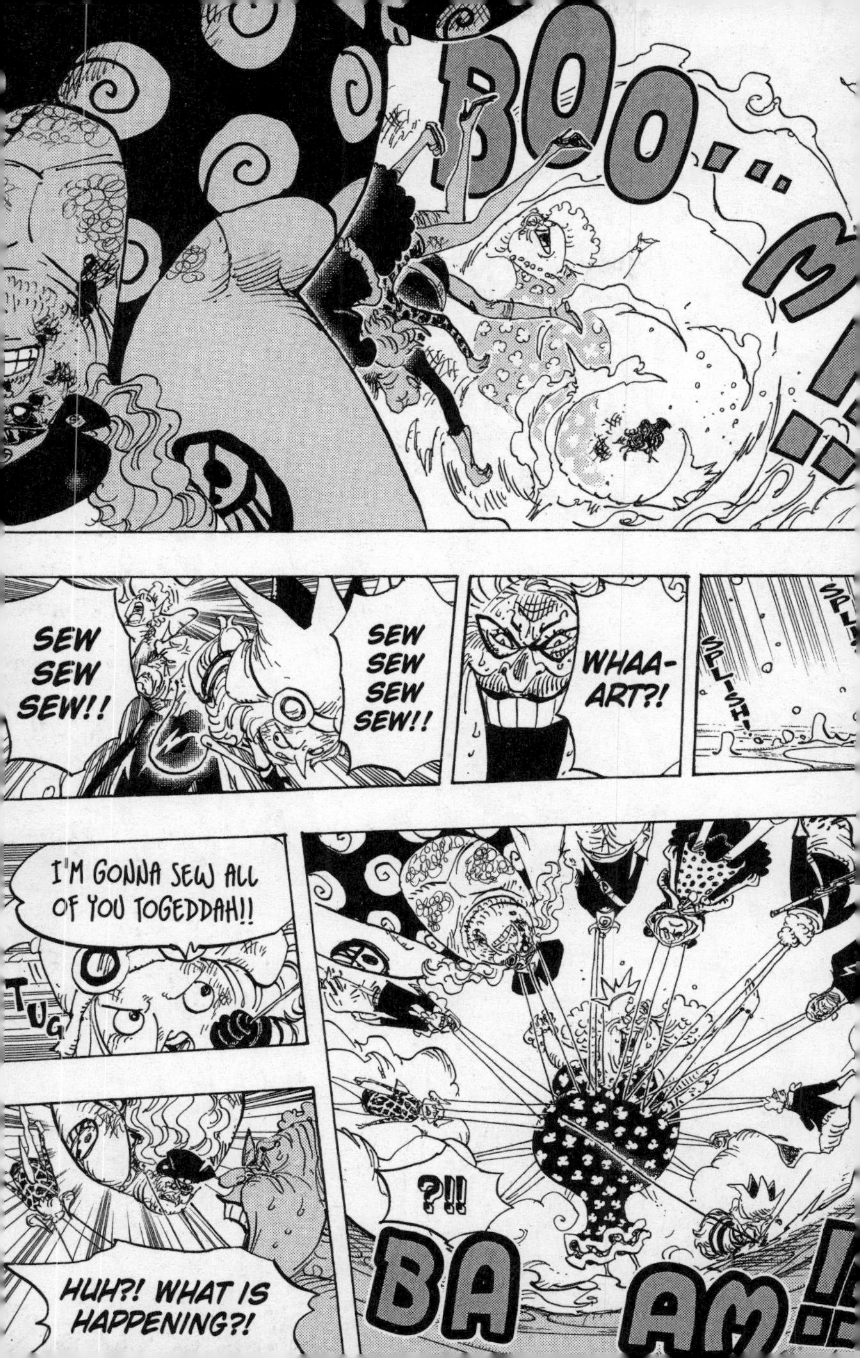
BOO...M!!
SPLISH!
WHAA-ART?!
SEW SEW SEW SEW!!
SEW SEW SEW!!
?!!
BAAM!!
I'M GONNA SEW ALL OF YOU TOGEDDAH!!
TUG
HUH?! WHAT IS HAPPENING?!

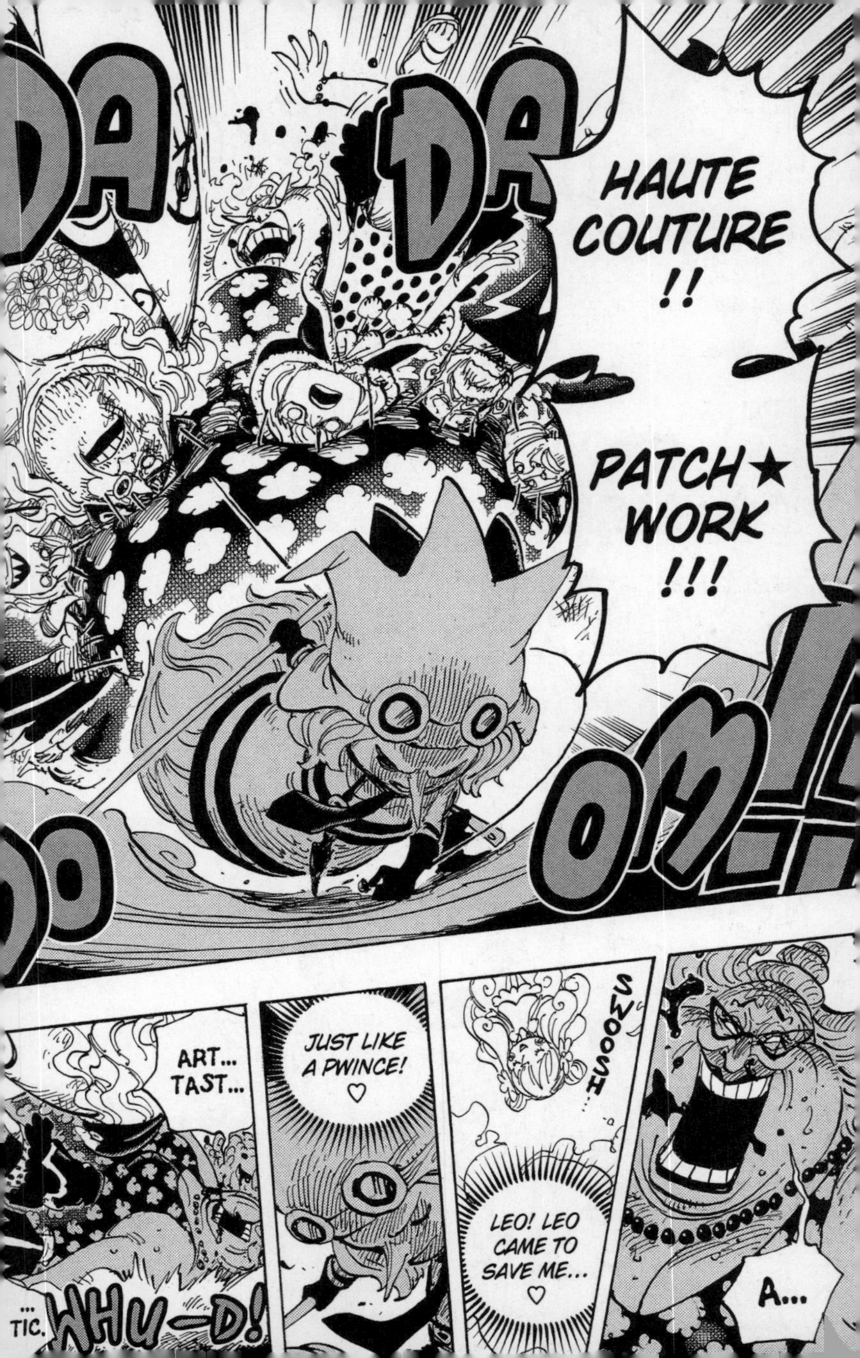
HAUTE COUTURE !!
PATCH★WORK !!!
DA
DA
OM!!
DO
A...
SWOOSH...
LEO! LEO CAME TO SAVE ME... ♡
JUST LIKE A PWINCE! ♡
ART... TAST...
...TIC.
WHU-D!

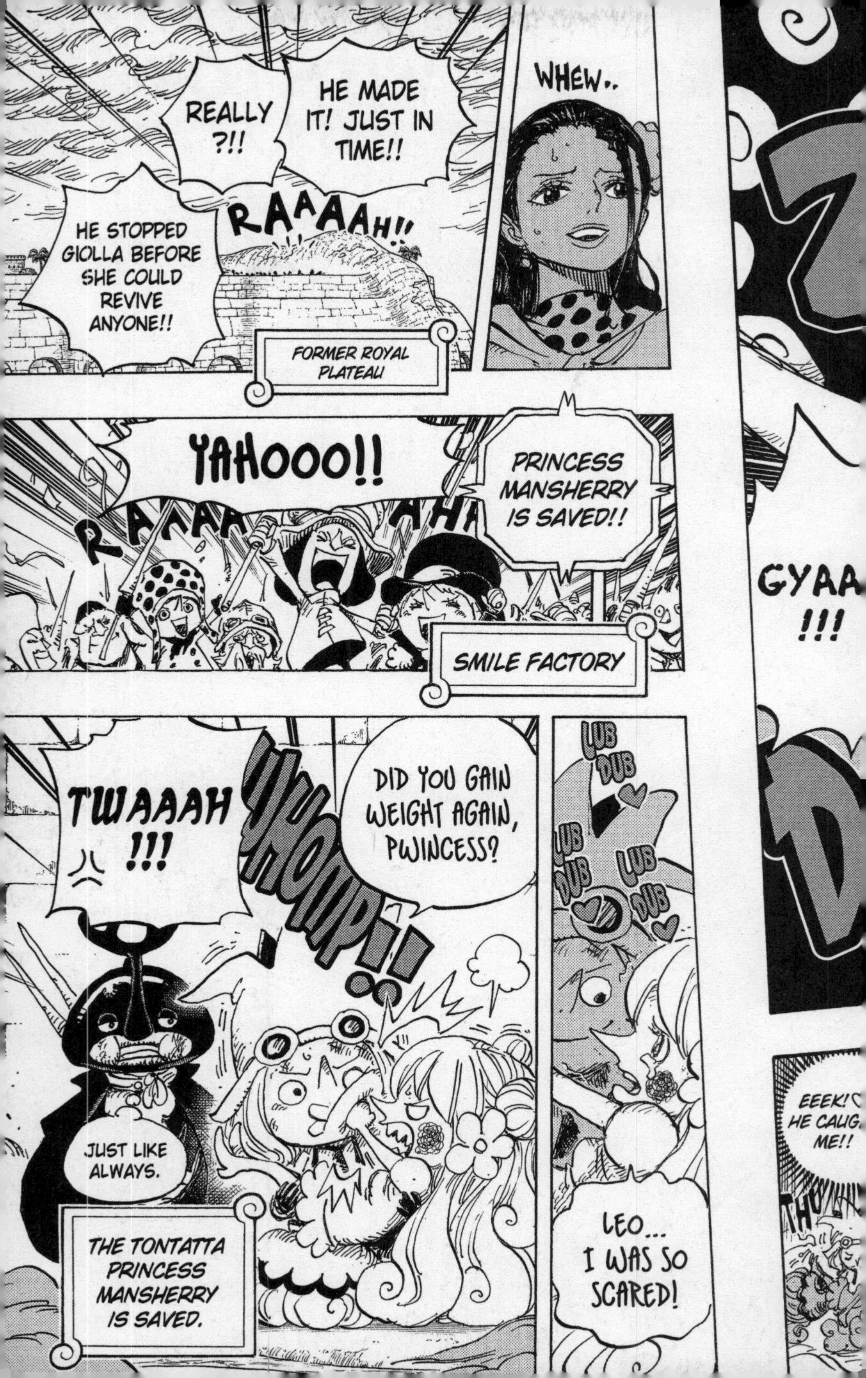
GYAA !!!
EEEK! HE CAUG ME!!
WHEW..
HE MADE IT! JUST IN TIME!!
REALLY ?!!
RAAAAH!!
HE STOPPED GIOLLA BEFORE SHE COULD REVIVE ANYONE!!
FORMER ROYAL PLATEAU
PRINCESS MANSHERRY IS SAVED!!
YAHOOO!!
SMILE FACTORY
LUB DUB
LUB DUB
LUB DUB
LUB DUB
LEO... I WAS SO SCARED!
DID YOU GAIN WEIGHT AGAIN, PWINCESS?
WHOMP!!
TWAAAH !!!
JUST LIKE ALWAYS.
THE TONTATTA PRINCESS MANSHERRY IS SAVED.

TO RUSSIAN WITH LOVE

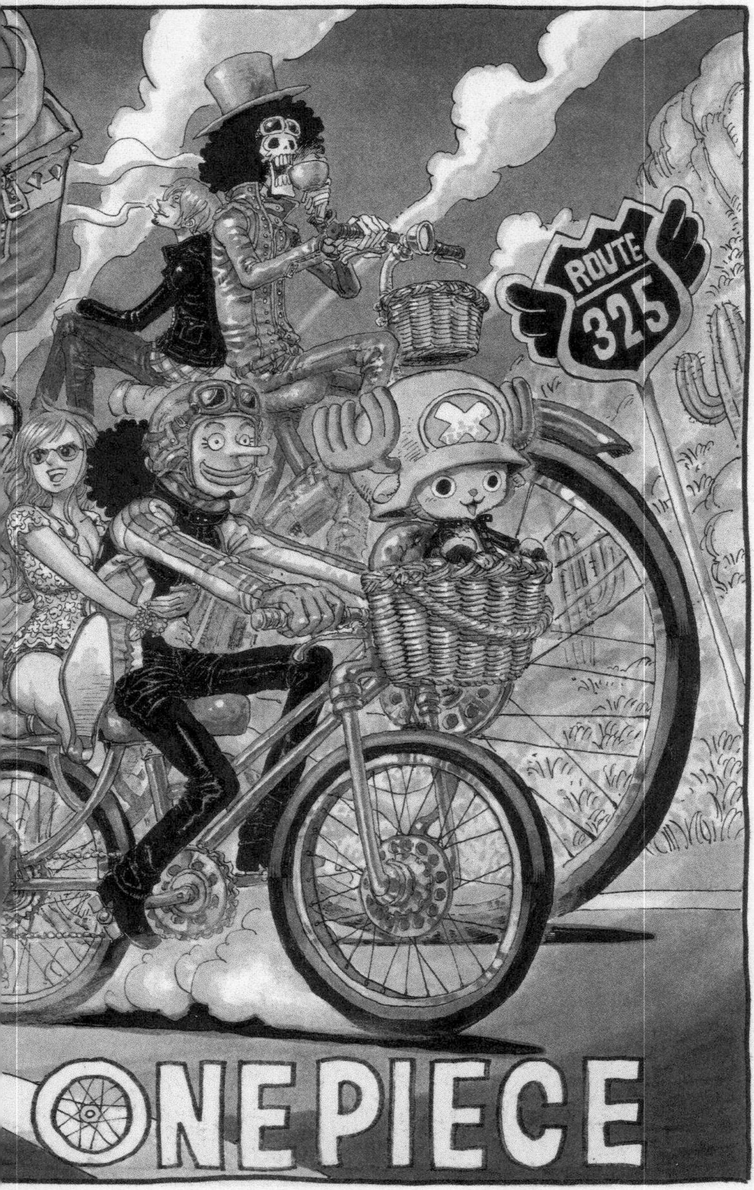
ROUTE
325
ONE PIECE

Chapter 775

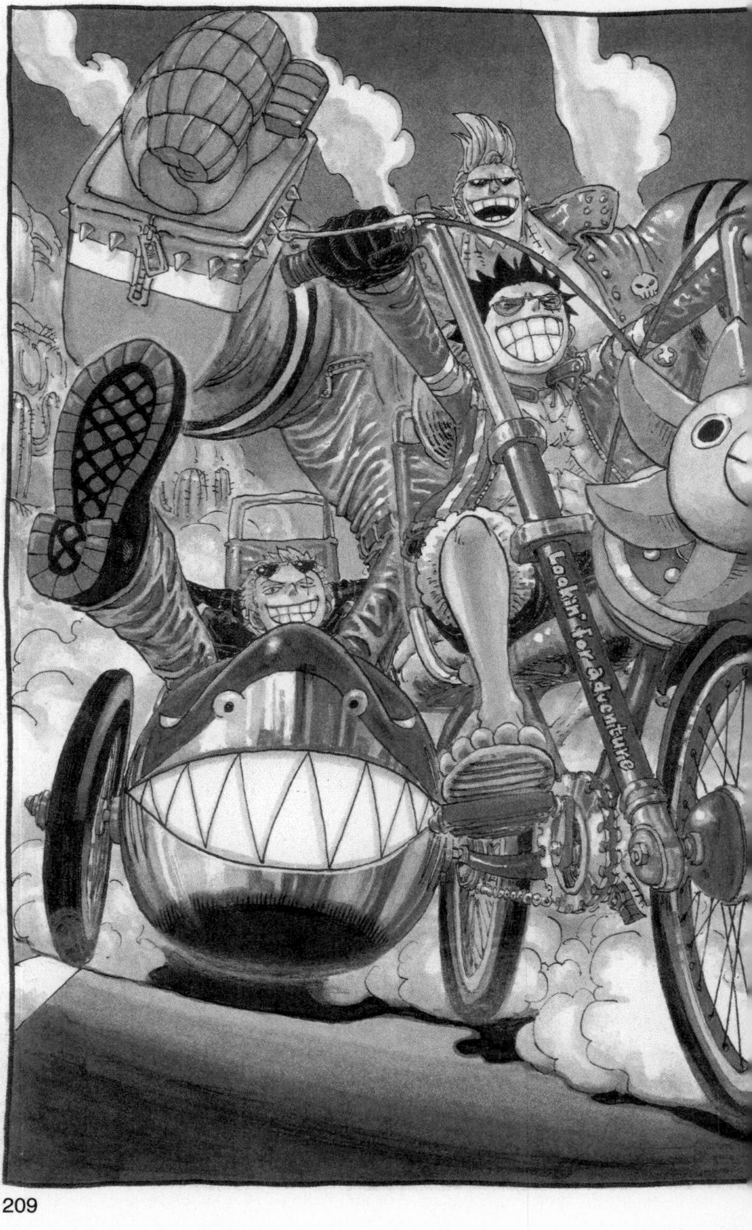

Lookin' for adventure

vol. 77
ONE PIECE

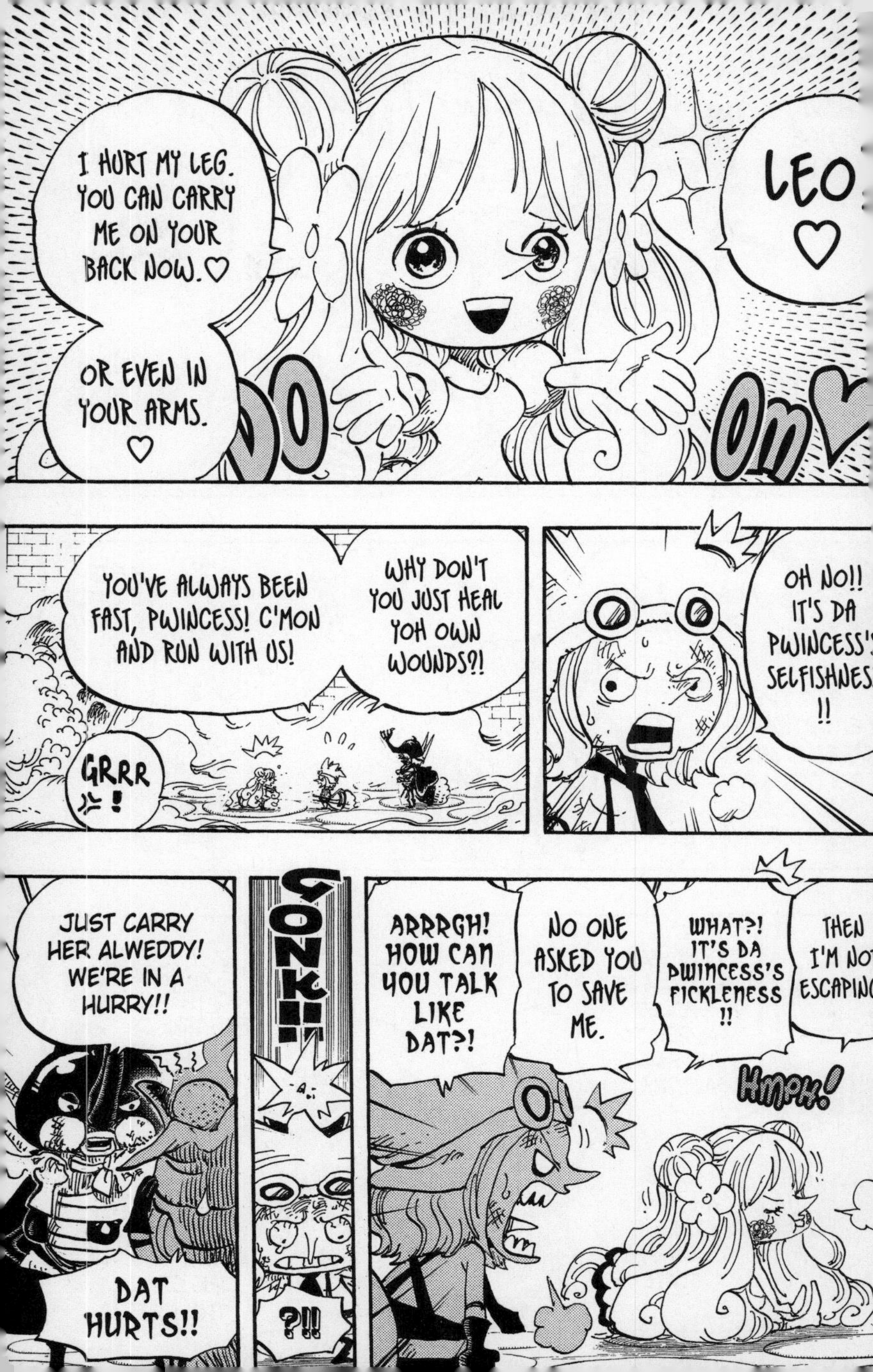
LEO ♡
I HURT MY LEG. YOU CAN CARRY ME ON YOUR BACK NOW. ♡
OR EVEN IN YOUR ARMS. ♡
OM♥
DO
OH NO!! IT'S DA PWINCESS'S SELFISHNES !!
WHY DON'T YOU JUST HEAL YOH OWN WOUNDS?!
YOU'VE ALWAYS BEEN FAST, PWINCESS! C'MON AND RUN WITH US!
GRRR !
THEN I'M NOT ESCAPING.
WHAT?! IT'S DA PWINCESS'S FICKLENESS !!
NO ONE ASKED YOU TO SAVE ME.
ARRRGH! HOW CAN YOU TALK LIKE DAT?!
HMPH!
GONK!!
?!!
JUST CARRY HER ALWEDDY! WE'RE IN A HURRY!!
DAT HURTS!!

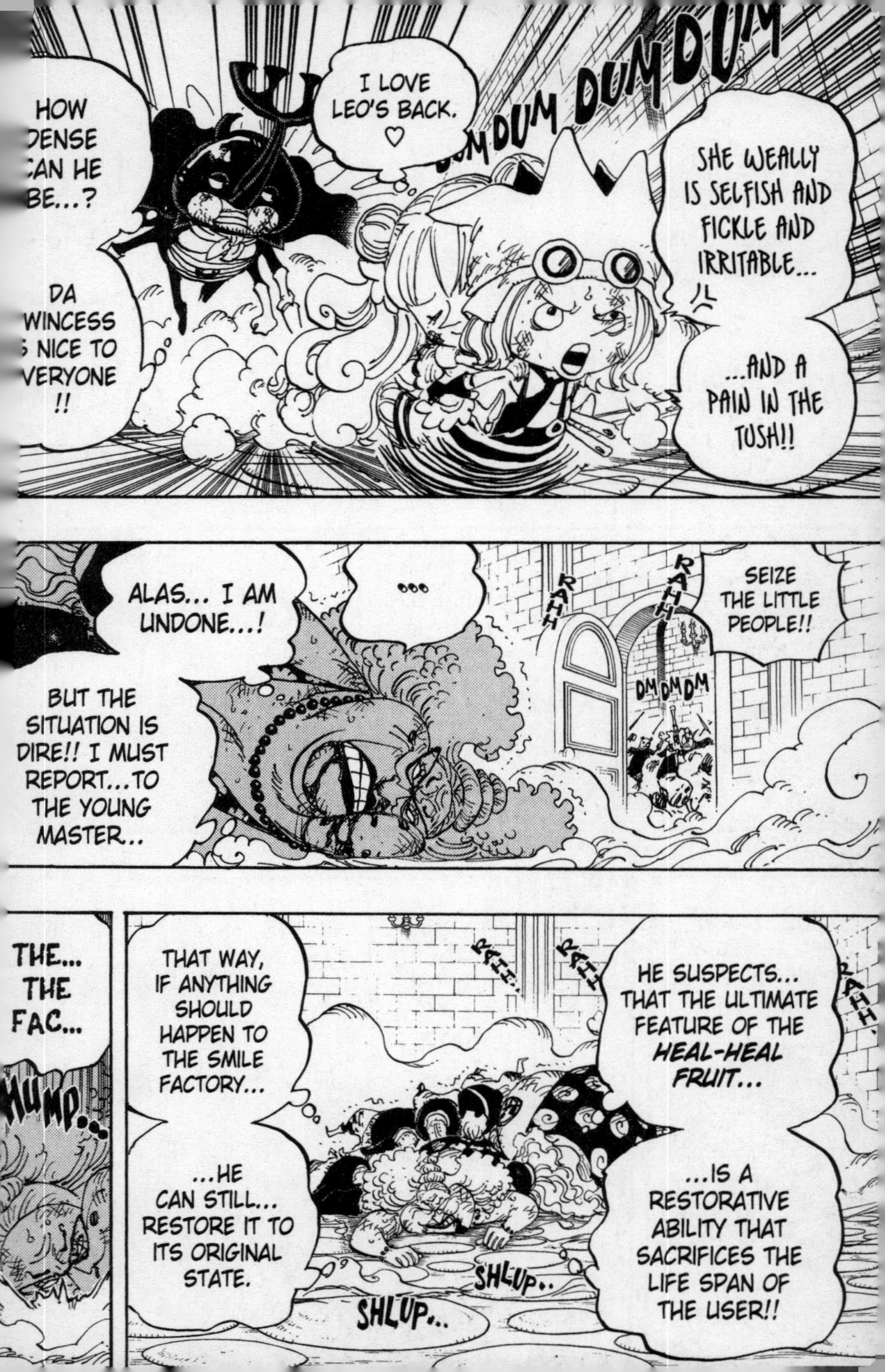

SHE WEALLY IS SELFISH AND FICKLE AND IRRITABLE...
...AND A PAIN IN THE TUSH!!
DUM DUM DUM DUM
I LOVE LEO'S BACK. ♡
HOW DENSE CAN HE BE...?
DA WINCESS S NICE TO VERYONE !!
SEIZE THE LITTLE PEOPLE!!
RAHH
RAHH
DM DM DM
...
ALAS... I AM UNDONE...!
BUT THE SITUATION IS DIRE!! I MUST REPORT...TO THE YOUNG MASTER...
RAHH.
HE SUSPECTS... THAT THE ULTIMATE FEATURE OF THE HEAL-HEAL FRUIT...
...IS A RESTORATIVE ABILITY THAT SACRIFICES THE LIFE SPAN OF THE USER!!
RAHH...
RAHH...
THAT WAY, IF ANYTHING SHOULD HAPPEN TO THE SMILE FACTORY...
...HE CAN STILL... RESTORE IT TO ITS ORIGINAL STATE.
SHLUP..
SHLUP...
THE... THE FAC...
HUMP...

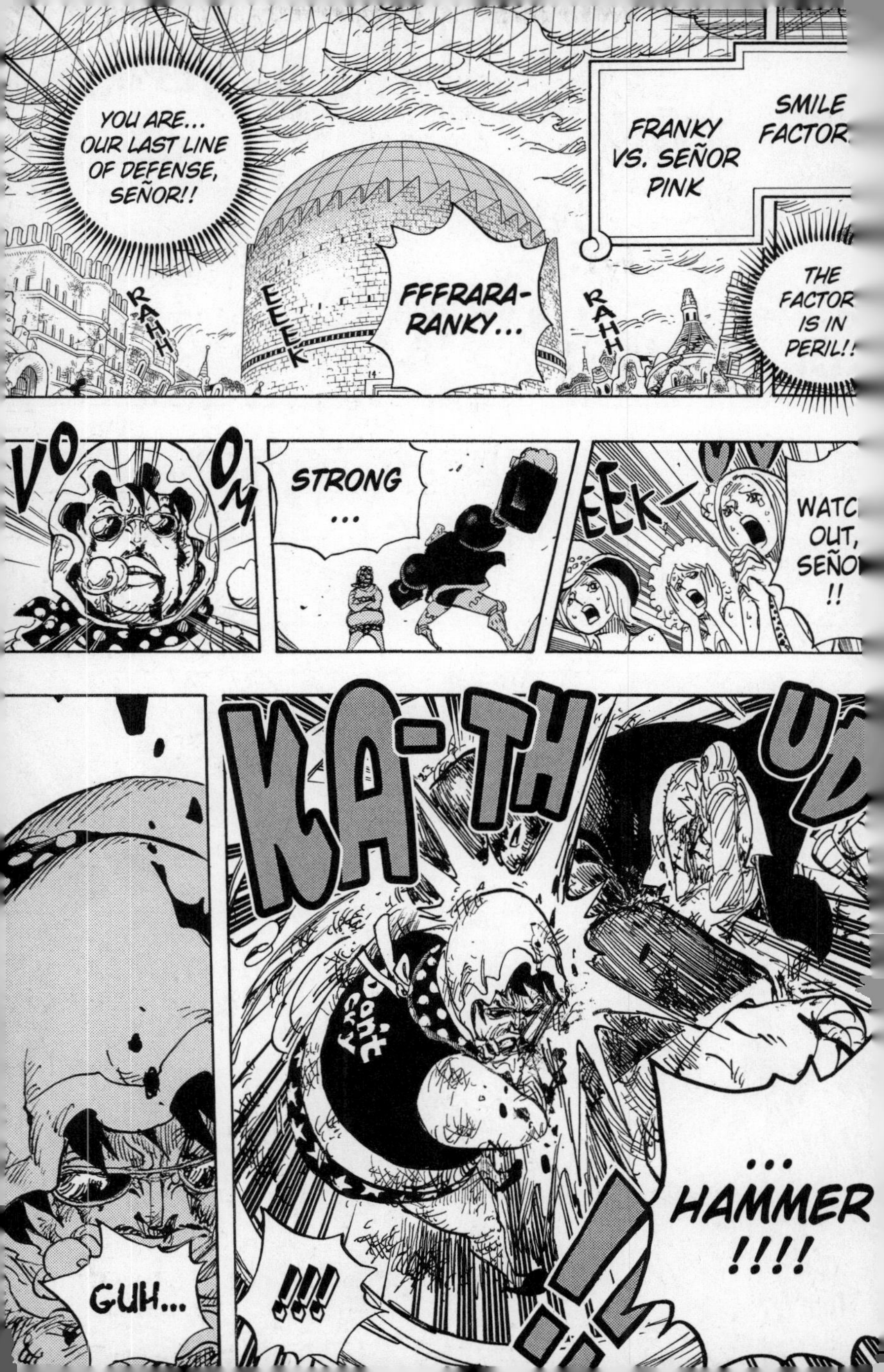
SMILE FACTOR
FRANKY VS. SEÑOR PINK
THE FACTOR IS IN PERIL!!
RAHHH
FFFRARA-RANKY...
EEEEK
RAHHH
YOU ARE... OUR LAST LINE OF DEFENSE, SEÑOR!!
WATC OUT, SEÑO !!
EEK
STRONG ...
VO OM
KA-TH UD
... HAMMER !!!!
!!
Don't cry
!!!
GUH...

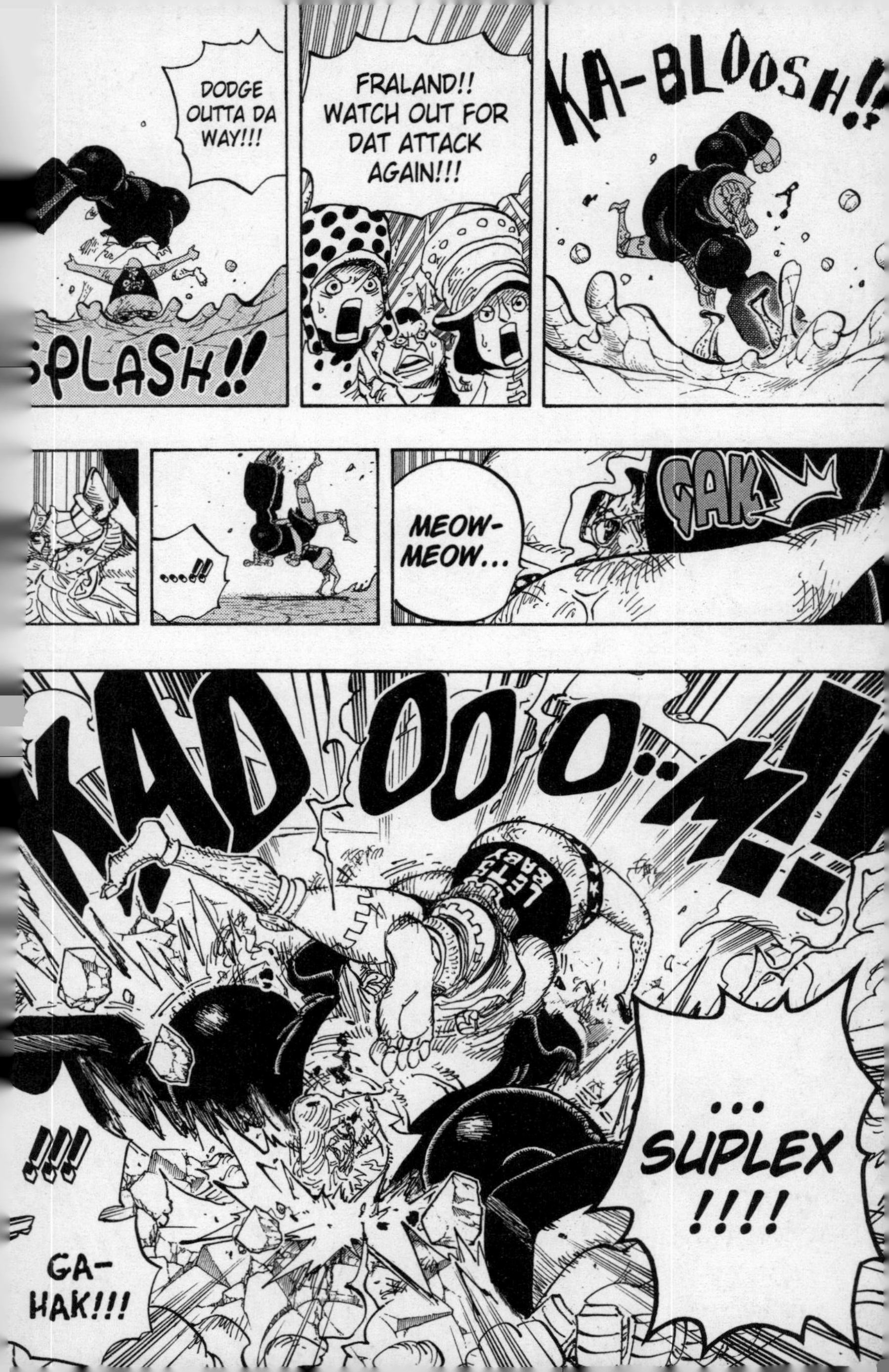
KA-BLOOSH!!
FRALAND!! WATCH OUT FOR DAT ATTACK AGAIN!!!
DODGE OUTTA DA WAY!!!
SPLASH!!
GAK
MEOW-MEOW...
....!!
KADOOOM!!
LET'S BABY
...SUPLEX!!!!
!!!
GA-HAK!!!

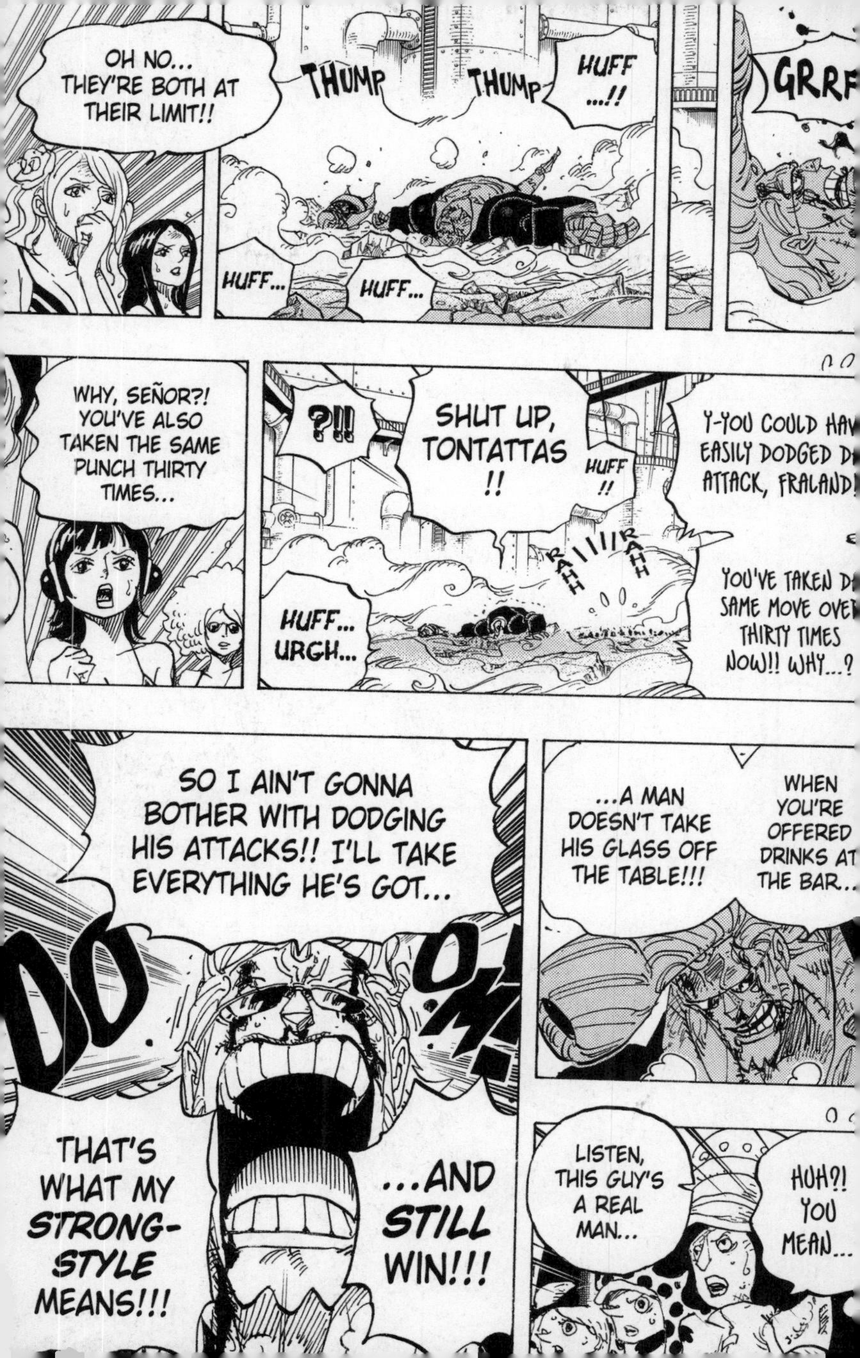
GRRF
HUFF ...!!
THUMP
THUMP
HUFF...
HUFF...
OH NO... THEY'RE BOTH AT THEIR LIMIT!!
Y-YOU COULD HAV EASILY DODGED D ATTACK, FRALAND!
YOU'VE TAKEN D SAME MOVE OVE THIRTY TIMES NOW!! WHY...?
HUFF !!
SHUT UP, TONTATTAS !!
?!!
RAHH
RAHH
HUFF... URGH...
WHY, SEÑOR?! YOU'VE ALSO TAKEN THE SAME PUNCH THIRTY TIMES...
WHEN YOU'RE OFFERED DRINKS AT THE BAR...
...A MAN DOESN'T TAKE HIS GLASS OFF THE TABLE!!!
HUH?! YOU MEAN...
LISTEN, THIS GUY'S A REAL MAN...
SO I AIN'T GONNA BOTHER WITH DODGING HIS ATTACKS!! I'LL TAKE EVERYTHING HE'S GOT...
OM
DO
...AND STILL WIN!!!
THAT'S WHAT MY STRONG-STYLE MEANS!!!

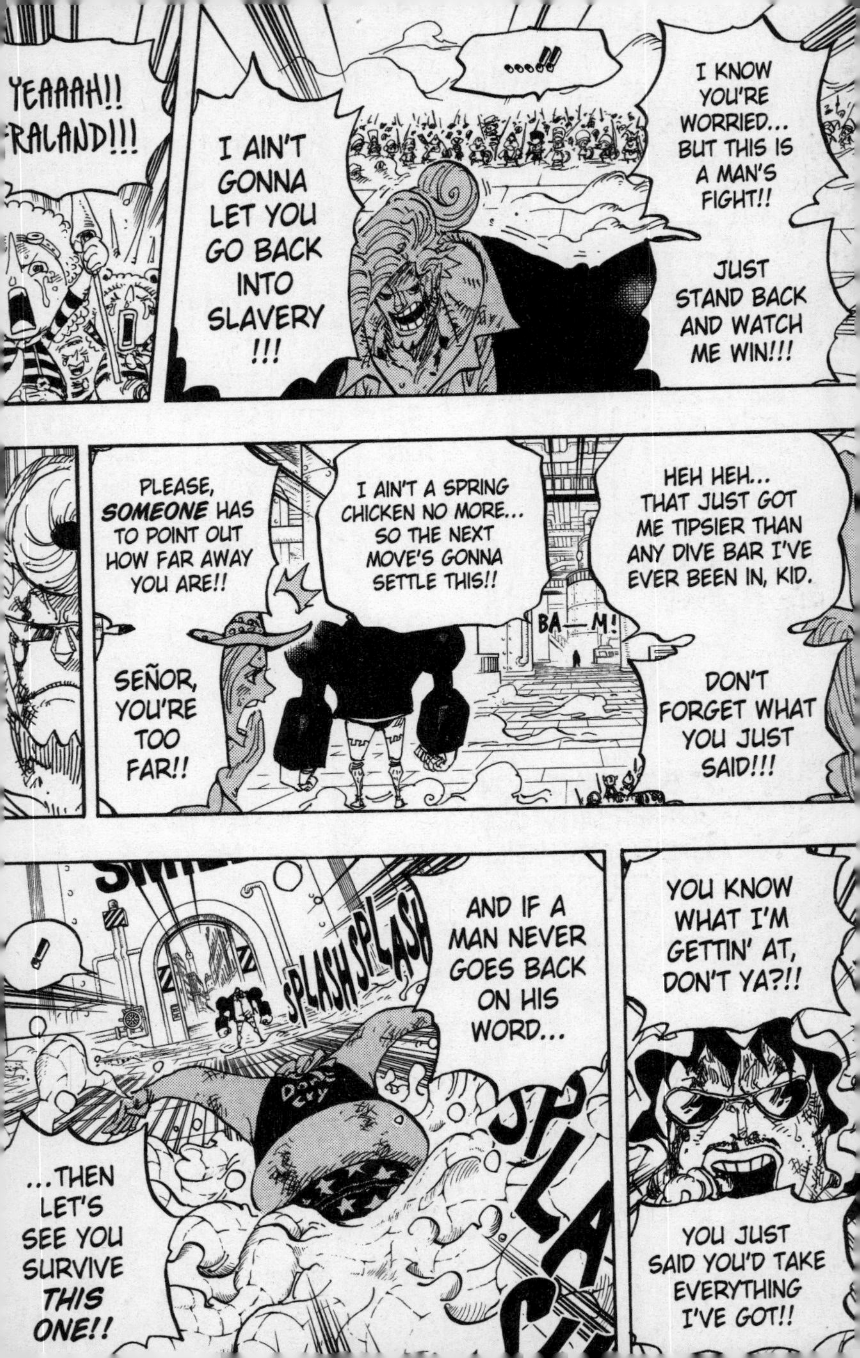
I KNOW YOU'RE WORRIED... BUT THIS IS A MAN'S FIGHT!!
JUST STAND BACK AND WATCH ME WIN!!!
....!!
I AIN'T GONNA LET YOU GO BACK INTO SLAVERY!!!
YEAAAH!!
RALAND!!!
HEH HEH... THAT JUST GOT ME TIPSIER THAN ANY DIVE BAR I'VE EVER BEEN IN, KID.
DON'T FORGET WHAT YOU JUST SAID!!!
I AIN'T A SPRING CHICKEN NO MORE... SO THE NEXT MOVE'S GONNA SETTLE THIS!!
BA—M!
PLEASE, ***SOMEONE*** HAS TO POINT OUT HOW FAR AWAY YOU ARE!!
SEÑOR, YOU'RE TOO FAR!!
YOU KNOW WHAT I'M GETTIN' AT, DON'T YA?!!
YOU JUST SAID YOU'D TAKE EVERYTHING I'VE GOT!!
AND IF A MAN NEVER GOES BACK ON HIS WORD...
SPLASH SPLASH
!
...THEN LET'S SEE YOU SURVIVE ***THIS ONE!!***

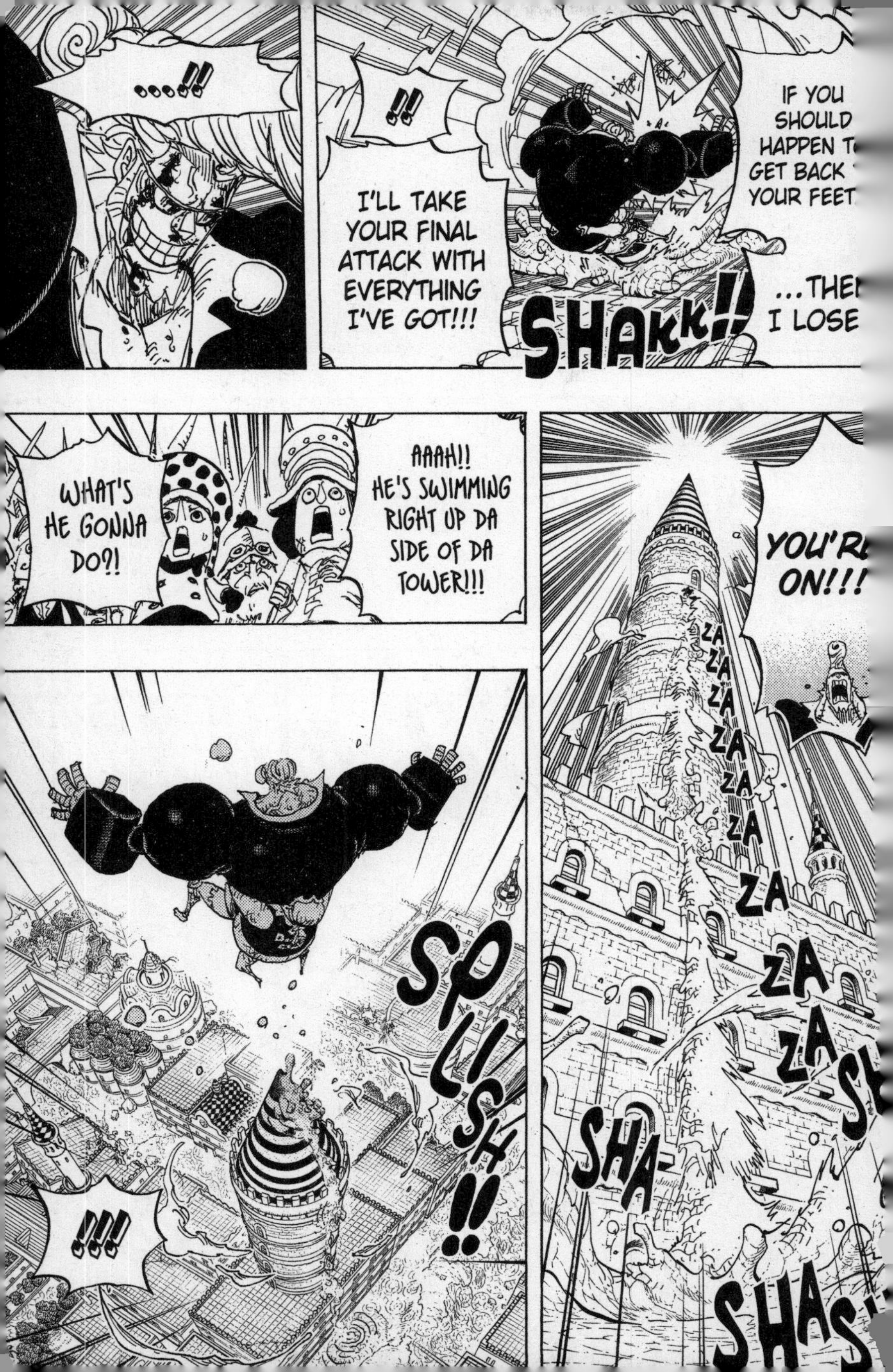
IF YOU SHOULD HAPPEN T GET BACK YOUR FEET
...THE I LOSE
SHAKK!!
!!
I'LL TAKE YOUR FINAL ATTACK WITH EVERYTHING I'VE GOT!!!
....!!
YOU'R ON!!!
ZA ZA ZA ZA ZA ZA ZA ZA ZA ZA
ZA
ZA
ZA
SHA-
SHASH
AAAH!! HE'S SWIMMING RIGHT UP DA SIDE OF DA TOWER!!!
WHAT'S HE GONNA DO?!
SPLUSH!!
!!!

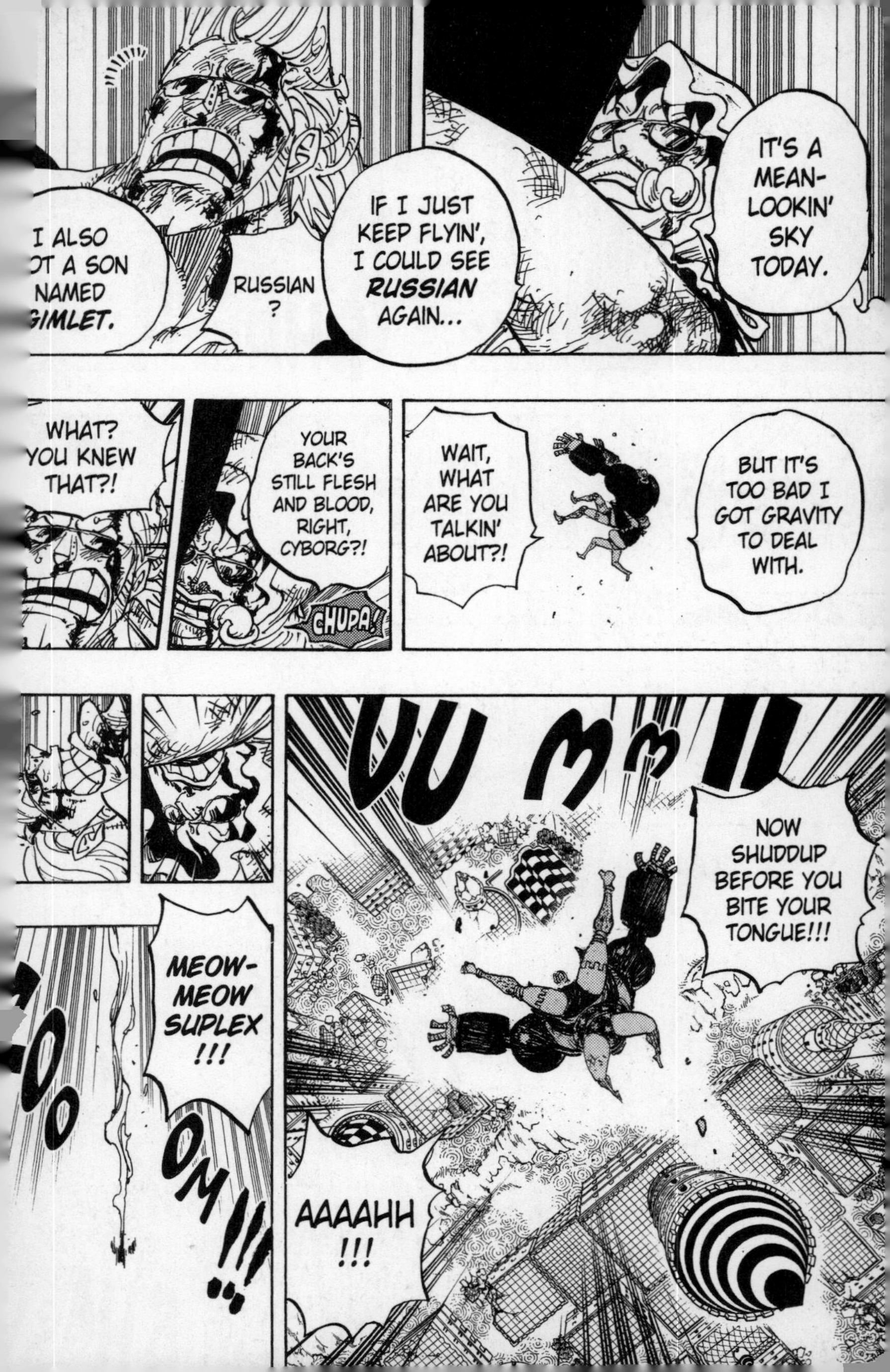
IT'S A MEAN-LOOKIN' SKY TODAY.
IF I JUST KEEP FLYIN', I COULD SEE RUSSIAN AGAIN...
RUSSIAN ?
I ALSO OT A SON NAMED GIMLET.
BUT IT'S TOO BAD I GOT GRAVITY TO DEAL WITH.
WAIT, WHAT ARE YOU TALKIN' ABOUT?!
YOUR BACK'S STILL FLESH AND BLOOD, RIGHT, CYBORG?!
CHUPA!
WHAT? YOU KNEW THAT?!
NOW SHUDDUP BEFORE YOU BITE YOUR TONGUE!!!
AAAAHH !!!
MEOW-MEOW SUPLEX !!!

FRALAAAND !!!

KABOOOM

BABY BUSTER !!!!

!!!

SPLISH! SH——HH

CLUNK KSHUNK...

KDOO...OM

...I LOSE.

WEEZ...

BZT!

WEEZ...

GRRM...

GRRK ▸...!!

?!!

?!!

MURMUR

SHH

●●●

CREAK... CRANK... HUFF... HUFF...

I'M SORRY, YOUNG MASTER!!

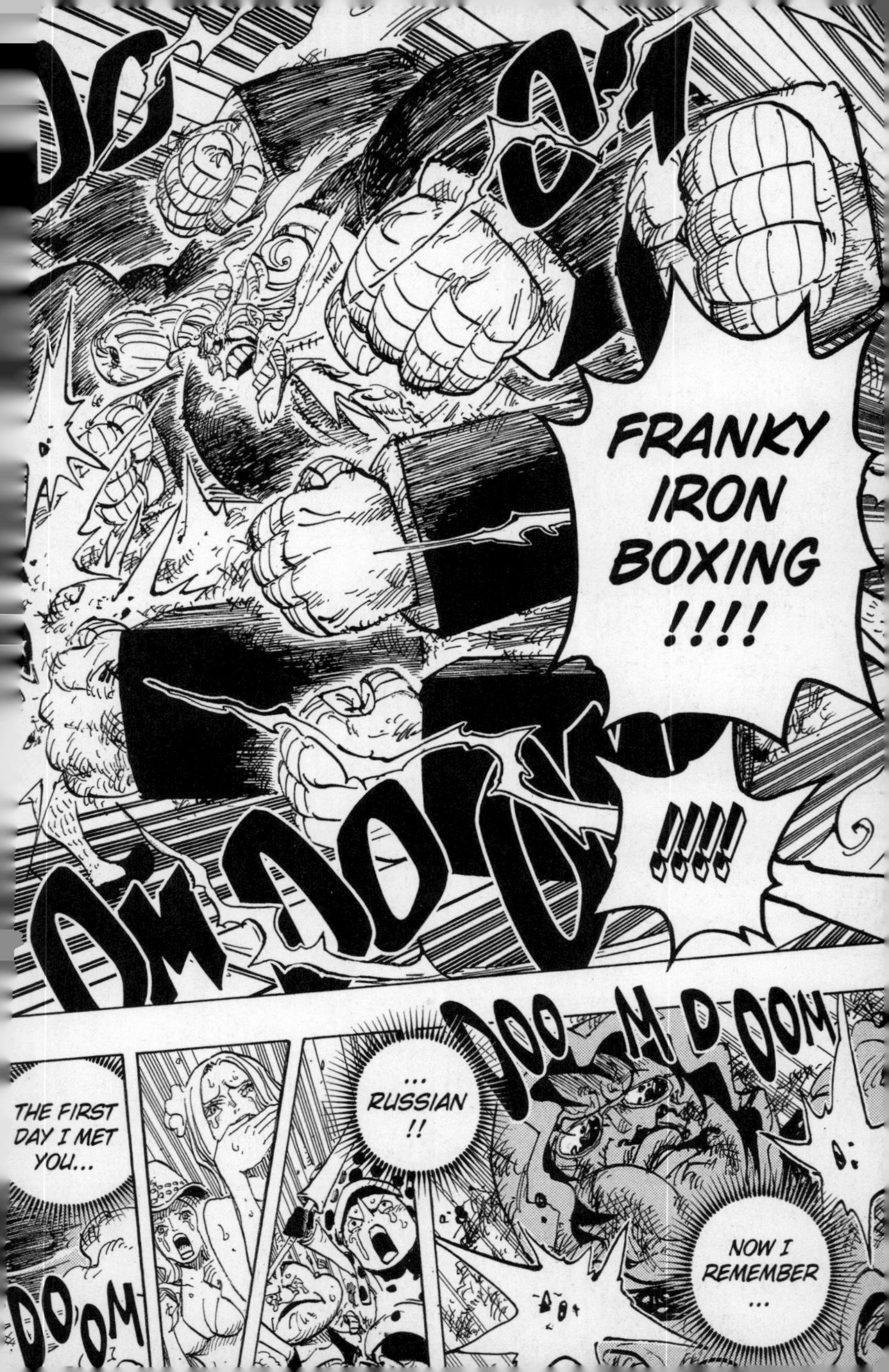
FRANKY IRON BOXING !!!!
NOW I REMEMBER ...
DOO M DOOM
... RUSSIAN !!
THE FIRST DAY I MET YOU...
DOOM

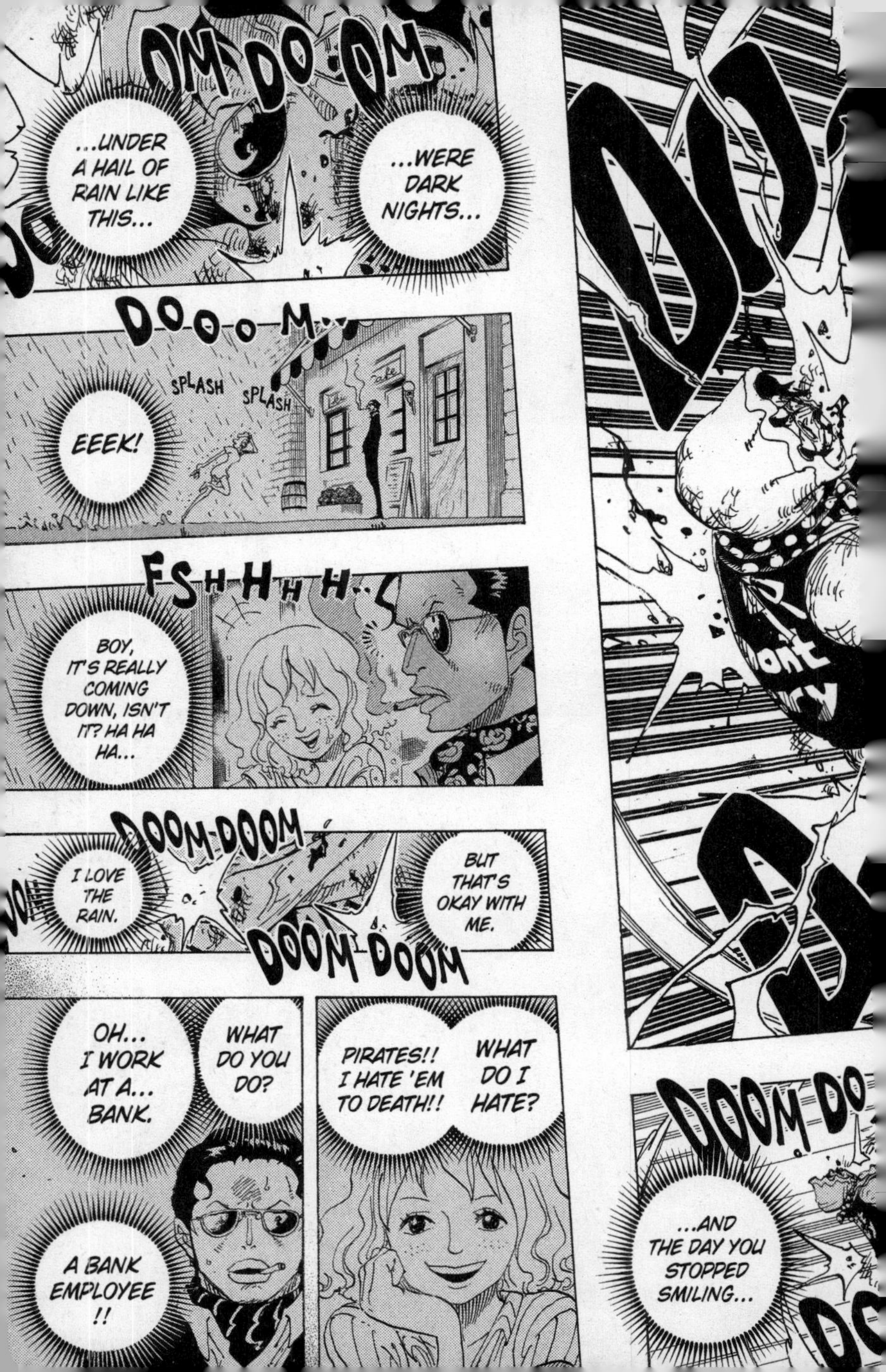
DOOM DO-DOM
...WERE DARK NIGHTS...
...UNDER A HAIL OF RAIN LIKE THIS...
DOOOOM...
SPLASH
SPLASH
EEEK!
FSHHHHH...
BOY, IT'S REALLY COMING DOWN, ISN'T IT? HA HA HA...
DOOM-DOOM
BUT THAT'S OKAY WITH ME.
I LOVE THE RAIN.
DOOM-DOOM
DOOM DO
...AND THE DAY YOU STOPPED SMILING...
WHAT DO I HATE?
PIRATES!! I HATE 'EM TO DEATH!!
WHAT DO YOU DO?
OH... I WORK AT A... BANK.
A BANK EMPLOYEE!!

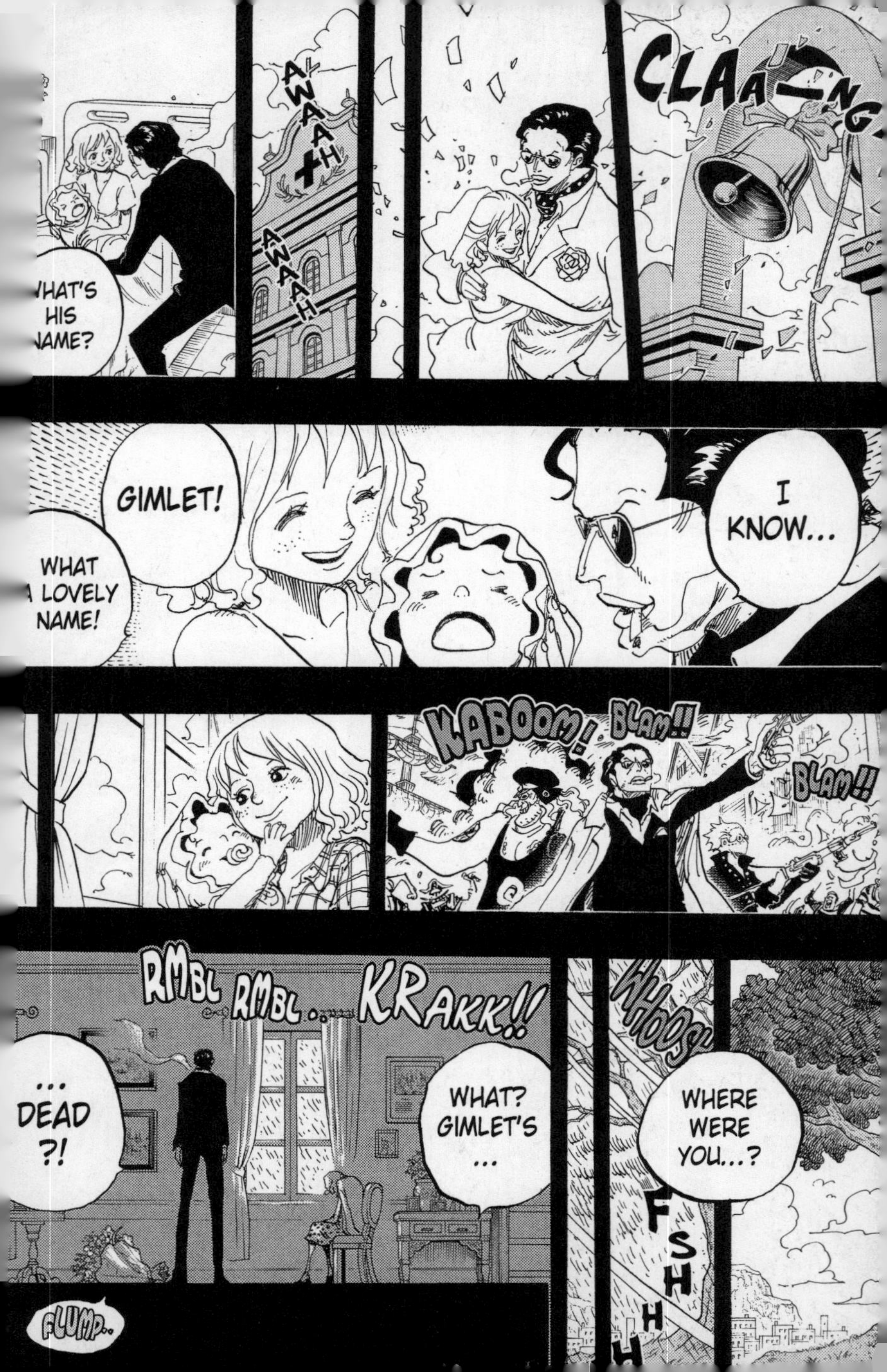
CLAA—NG
AWAAH
AWAAH
WHAT'S HIS NAME?
I KNOW...
GIMLET!
WHAT A LOVELY NAME!
KABOOM!
BLAM!!
BLAM!!
WHERE WERE YOU...?
FSHHH
RMBL RMBL...
KRAKK!!
WHAT? GIMLET'S ...
... DEAD?!
FLUMP..

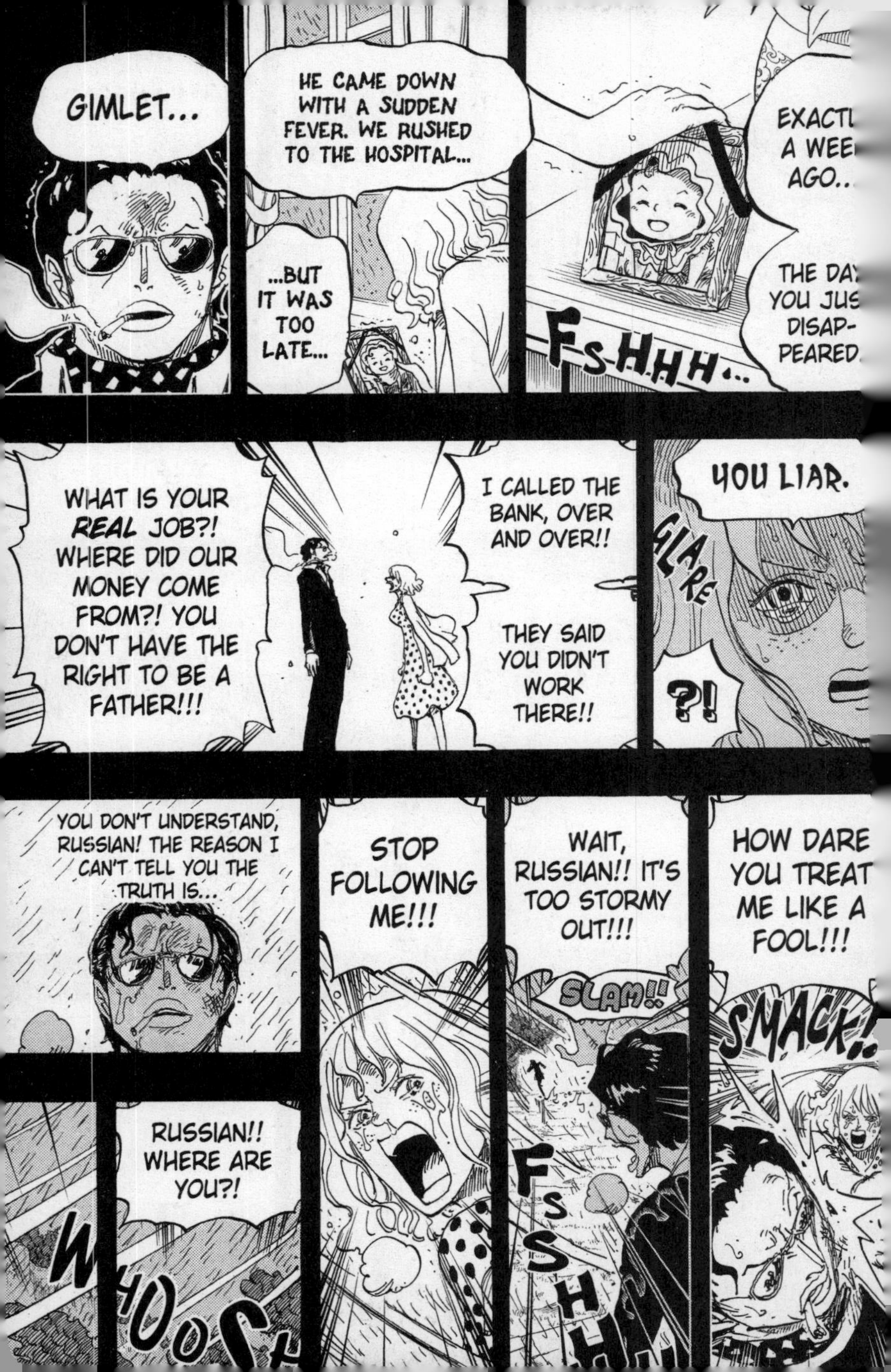
EXACTL A WEE AGO...
THE DAY YOU JUS DISAP-PEARED
FSHHH...
HE CAME DOWN WITH A SUDDEN FEVER. WE RUSHED TO THE HOSPITAL...
...BUT IT WAS TOO LATE...
GIMLET...
YOU LIAR.
GLARE
?!
I CALLED THE BANK, OVER AND OVER!!
THEY SAID YOU DIDN'T WORK THERE!!
WHAT IS YOUR *REAL* JOB?! WHERE DID OUR MONEY COME FROM?! YOU DON'T HAVE THE RIGHT TO BE A FATHER!!!
HOW DARE YOU TREAT ME LIKE A FOOL!!!
SMACK!!
WAIT, RUSSIAN!! IT'S TOO STORMY OUT!!!
SLAM!!
FSSH
STOP FOLLOWING ME!!!
YOU DON'T UNDERSTAND, RUSSIAN! THE REASON I CAN'T TELL YOU THE TRUTH IS...
RUSSIAN!! WHERE ARE YOU?!

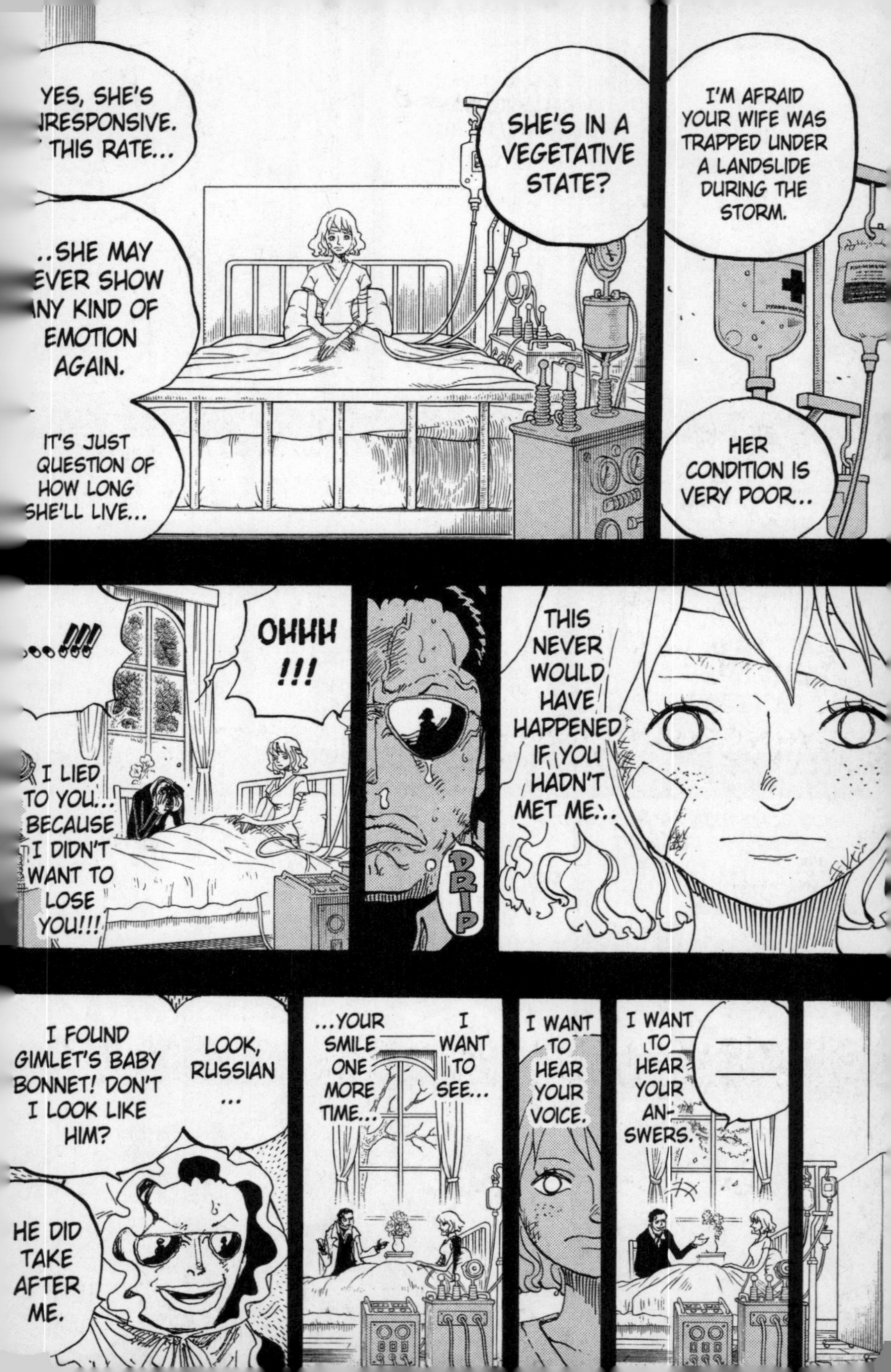
I'M AFRAID YOUR WIFE WAS TRAPPED UNDER A LANDSLIDE DURING THE STORM.
HER CONDITION IS VERY POOR...
SHE'S IN A VEGETATIVE STATE?
YES, SHE'S NRESPONSIVE. THIS RATE...
..SHE MAY EVER SHOW NY KIND OF EMOTION AGAIN.
IT'S JUST QUESTION OF HOW LONG SHE'LL LIVE...
THIS NEVER WOULD HAVE HAPPENED IF YOU HADN'T MET ME...
DRIP
OHHH !!!
...!!!
I LIED TO YOU... BECAUSE I DIDN'T WANT TO LOSE YOU!!!
I WANT TO HEAR YOUR ANSWERS.
I WANT TO HEAR YOUR VOICE.
I WANT TO SEE...
...YOUR SMILE ONE MORE TIME...
LOOK, RUSSIAN...
I FOUND GIMLET'S BABY BONNET! DON'T I LOOK LIKE HIM?
HE DID TAKE AFTER ME.

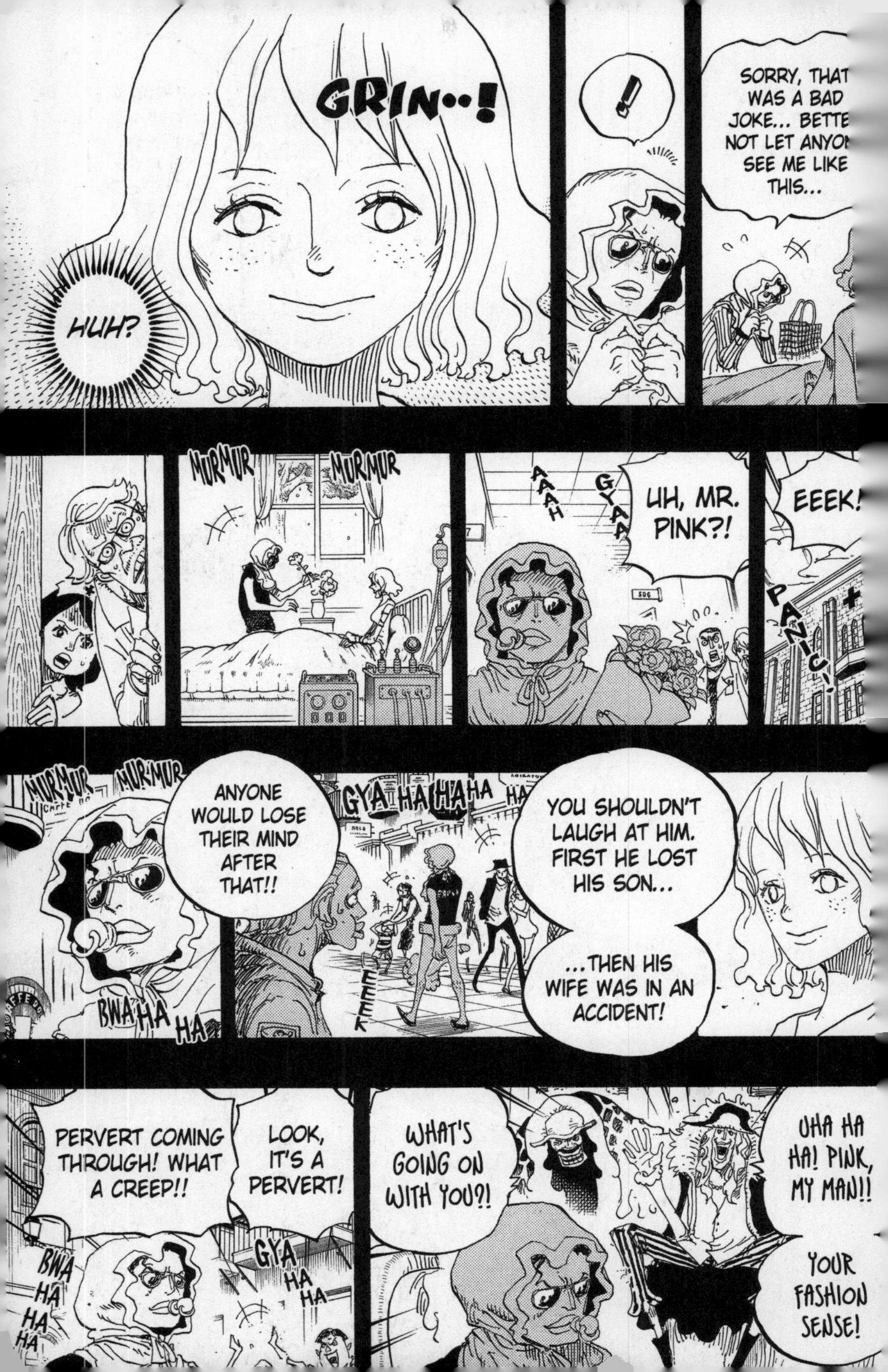

SORRY, THAT WAS A BAD JOKE... BETTE NOT LET ANYON SEE ME LIKE THIS...
!
GRIN..!
HUH?
EEEK!
PANIC!
AAAH
GYAA
UH, MR. PINK?!
MURMUR
MURMUR
YOU SHOULDN'T LAUGH AT HIM. FIRST HE LOST HIS SON...
...THEN HIS WIFE WAS IN AN ACCIDENT!
GYA HA HA HA HA
EEEK
ANYONE WOULD LOSE THEIR MIND AFTER THAT!!
MURMUR
MURMUR
BWA HA HA
UHA HA HA! PINK, MY MAN!!
YOUR FASHION SENSE!
WHAT'S GOING ON WITH YOU?!
LOOK, IT'S A PERVERT!
PERVERT COMING THROUGH! WHAT A CREEP!!
GYA HA HA
BWA HA HA HA HA

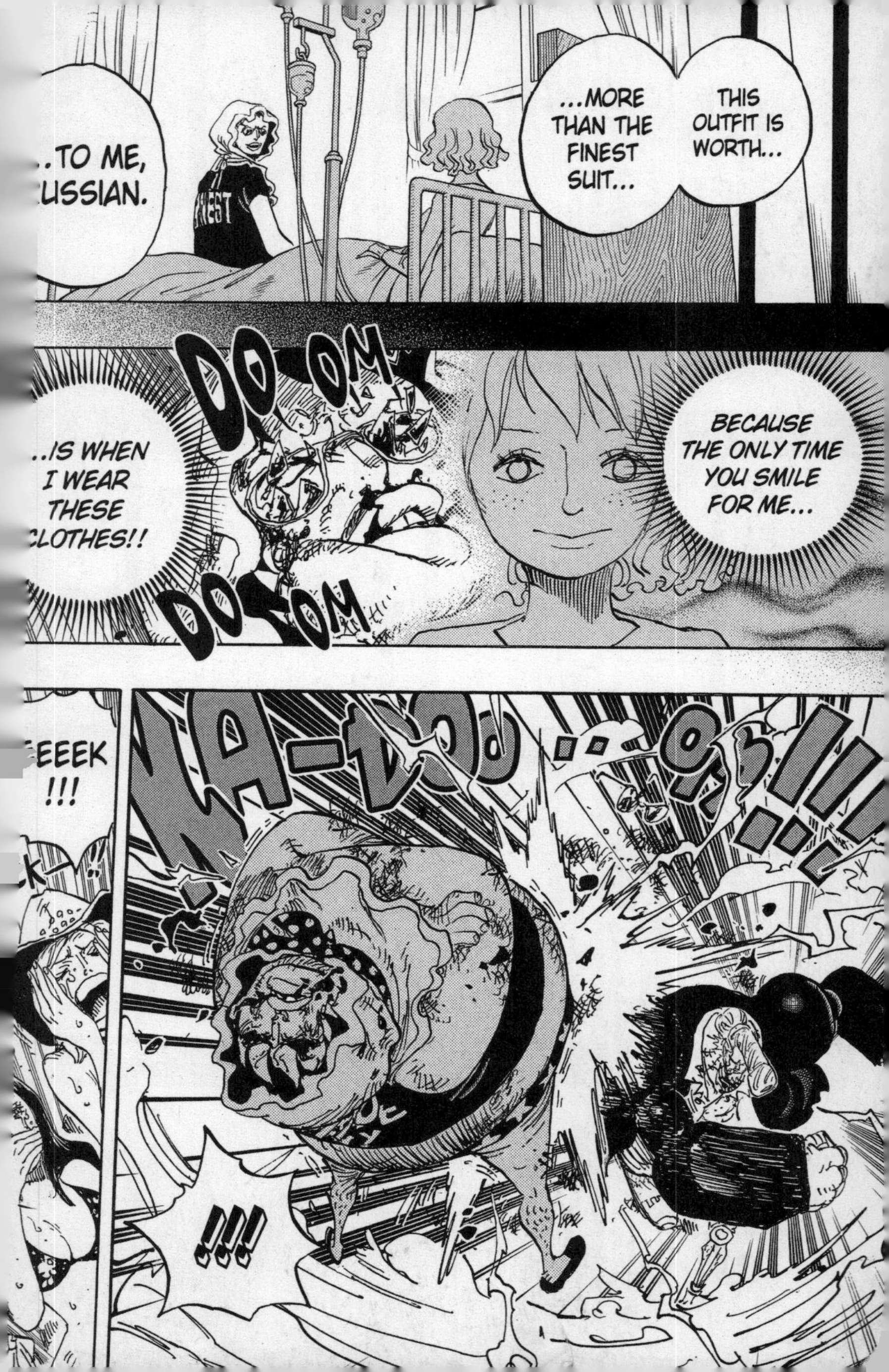
THIS OUTFIT IS WORTH...
...MORE THAN THE FINEST SUIT...
..TO ME, USSIAN.
DO-OM
DO-OM
BECAUSE THE ONLY TIME YOU SMILE FOR ME...
..IS WHEN I WEAR THESE LOTHES!!
EEEK !!!

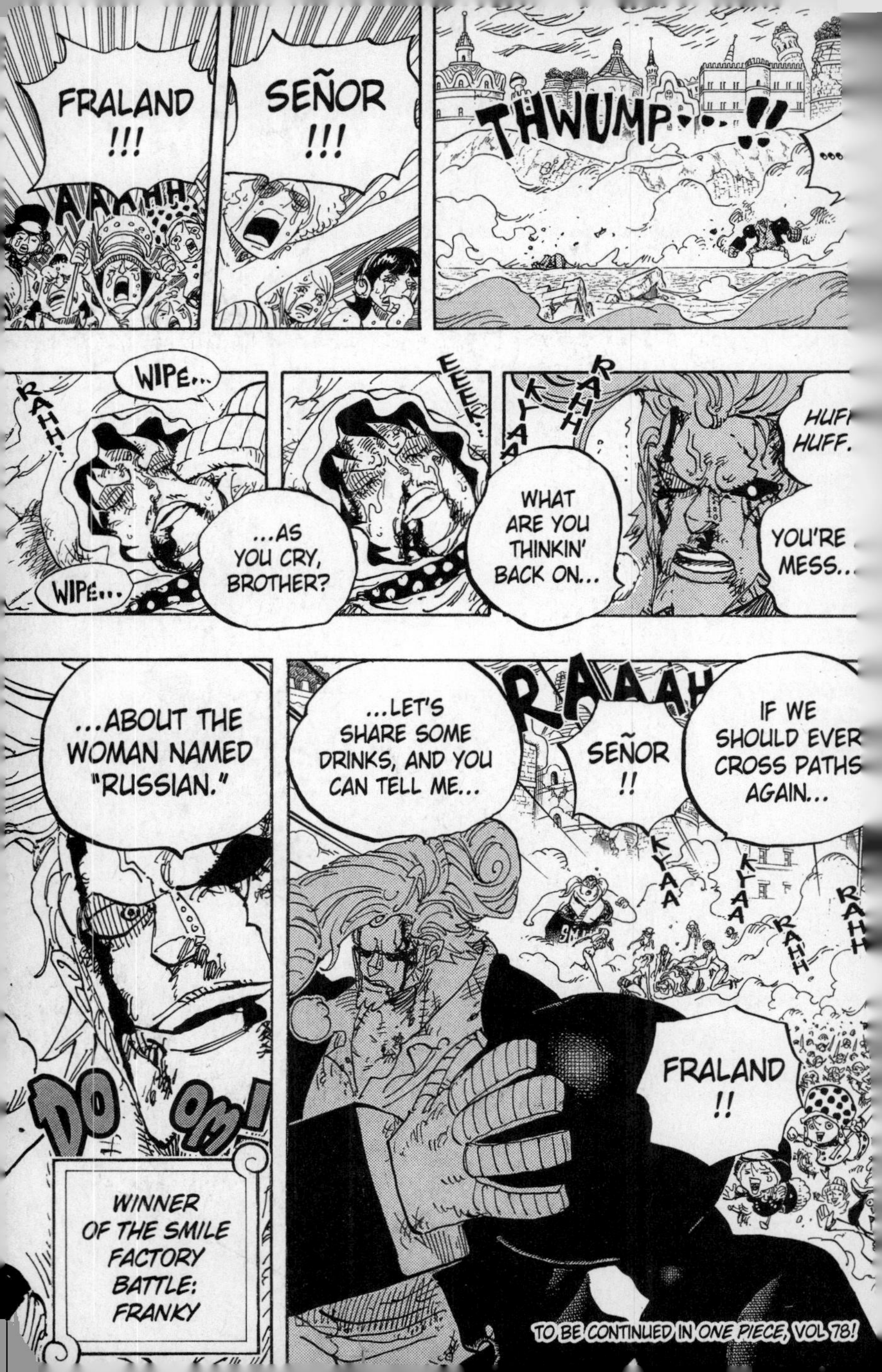
THWUMP...!!
...
SEÑOR !!!
FRALAND !!!
AAAHH
HUF HUFF.
YOU'RE MESS...
RAHH
KYAA
WHAT ARE YOU THINKIN' BACK ON...
EEEK...
...AS YOU CRY, BROTHER?
WIPE...
RAHH
WIPE...
IF WE SHOULD EVER CROSS PATHS AGAIN...
SEÑOR !!
RAAAH
...LET'S SHARE SOME DRINKS, AND YOU CAN TELL ME...
KYAA
KYAA
RAHH
RAHH
FRALAND !!
TO BE CONTINUED IN ONE PIECE, VOL 78!
...ABOUT THE WOMAN NAMED "RUSSIAN."
DOOM!
WINNER OF THE SMILE FACTORY BATTLE: FRANKY

COMING NEXT VOLUME:

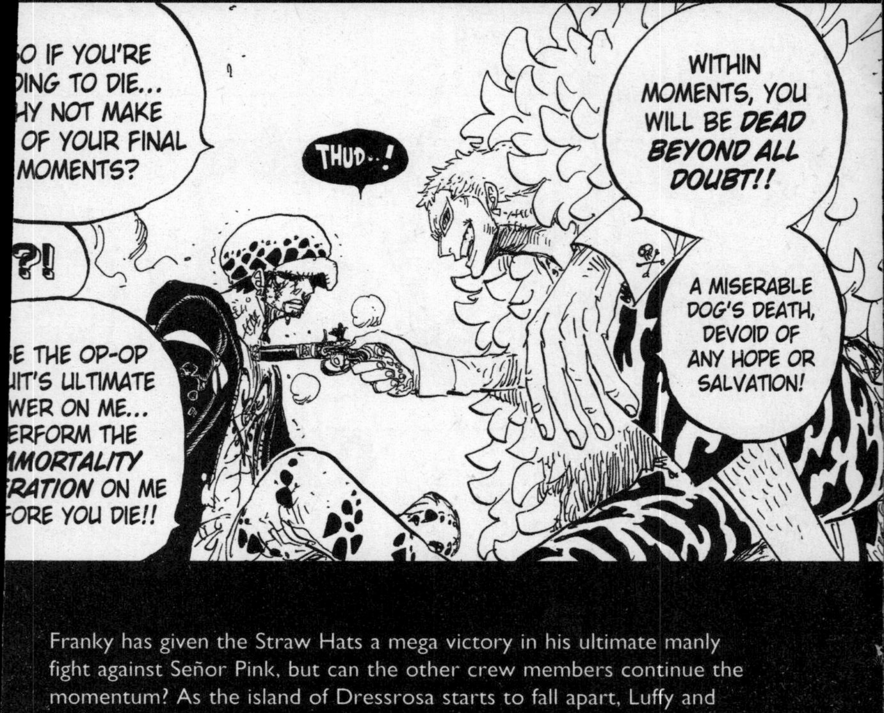
WITHIN MOMENTS, YOU WILL BE *DEAD BEYOND ALL DOUBT!!*
A MISERABLE DOG'S DEATH, DEVOID OF ANY HOPE OR SALVATION!
THUD..!
O IF YOU'RE DING TO DIE... HY NOT MAKE OF YOUR FINAL MOMENTS?
?!
E THE OP-OP UIT'S ULTIMATE WER ON ME... ERFORM THE *MMORTALITY RATION* ON ME FORE YOU DIE!!

Franky has given the Straw Hats a mega victory in his ultimate manly fight against Señor Pink, but can the other crew members continue the momentum? As the island of Dressrosa starts to fall apart, Luffy and Doflamingo finally begin their battle!

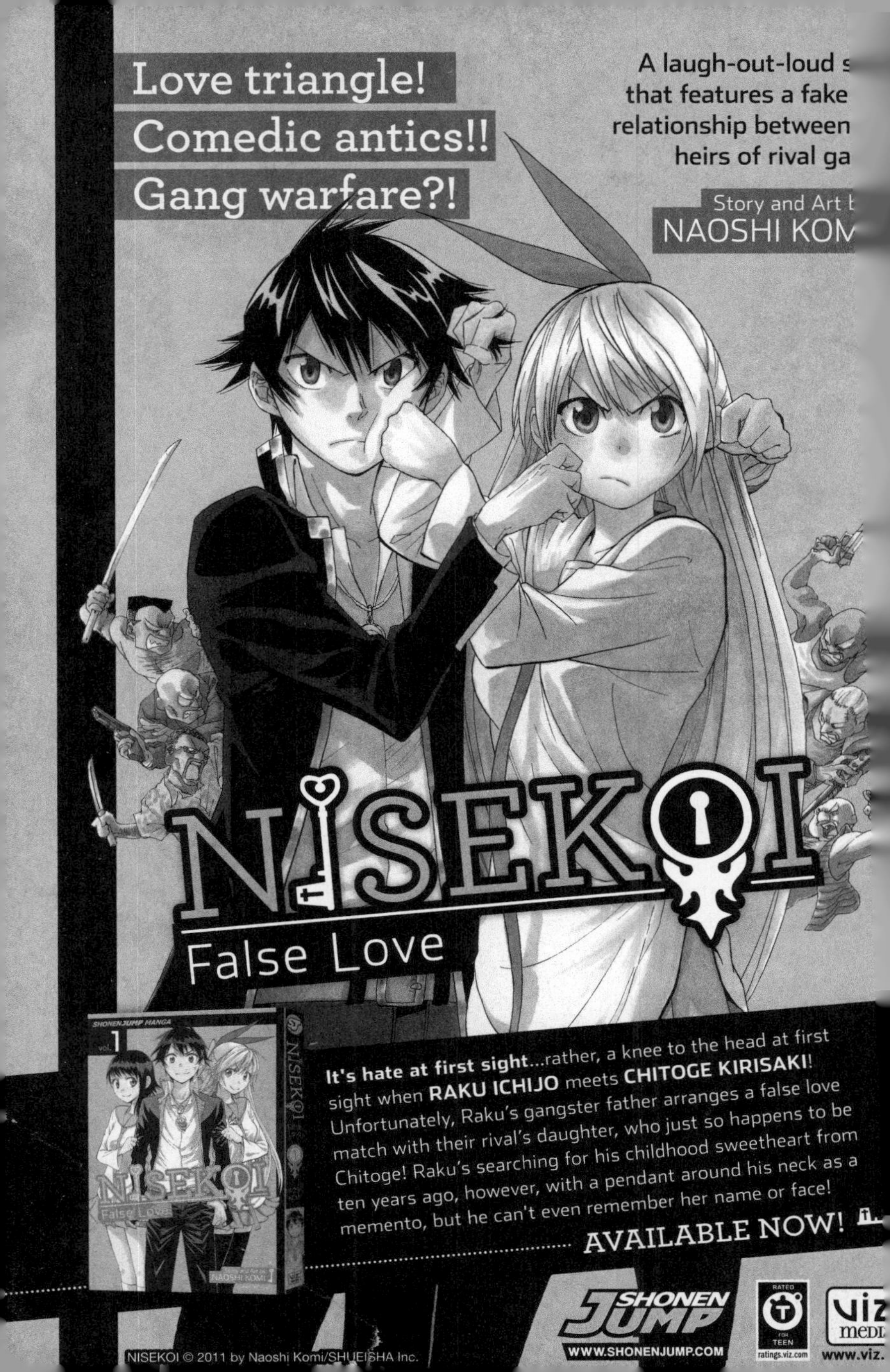

Love triangle!
Comedic antics!!
Gang warfare?!
A laugh-out-loud s
that features a fake
relationship between
heirs of rival ga
Story and Art b
NAOSHI KOM
NISEKOI
False Love
SHONEN JUMP MANGA
vol. 1
NISEKOI False Love
NAOSHI KOMI
It's hate at first sight...rather, a knee to the head at first
sight when RAKU ICHIJO meets CHITOGE KIRISAKI!
Unfortunately, Raku's gangster father arranges a false love
match with their rival's daughter, who just so happens to be
Chitoge! Raku's searching for his childhood sweetheart from
ten years ago, however, with a pendant around his neck as a
memento, but he can't even remember her name or face!
AVAILABLE NOW!
SHONEN JUMP
RATED T FOR TEEN
ratings.viz.com
VIZ MEDI
WWW.SHONENJUMP.COM
www.viz.
NISEKOI © 2011 by Naoshi Komi/SHUEISHA Inc.

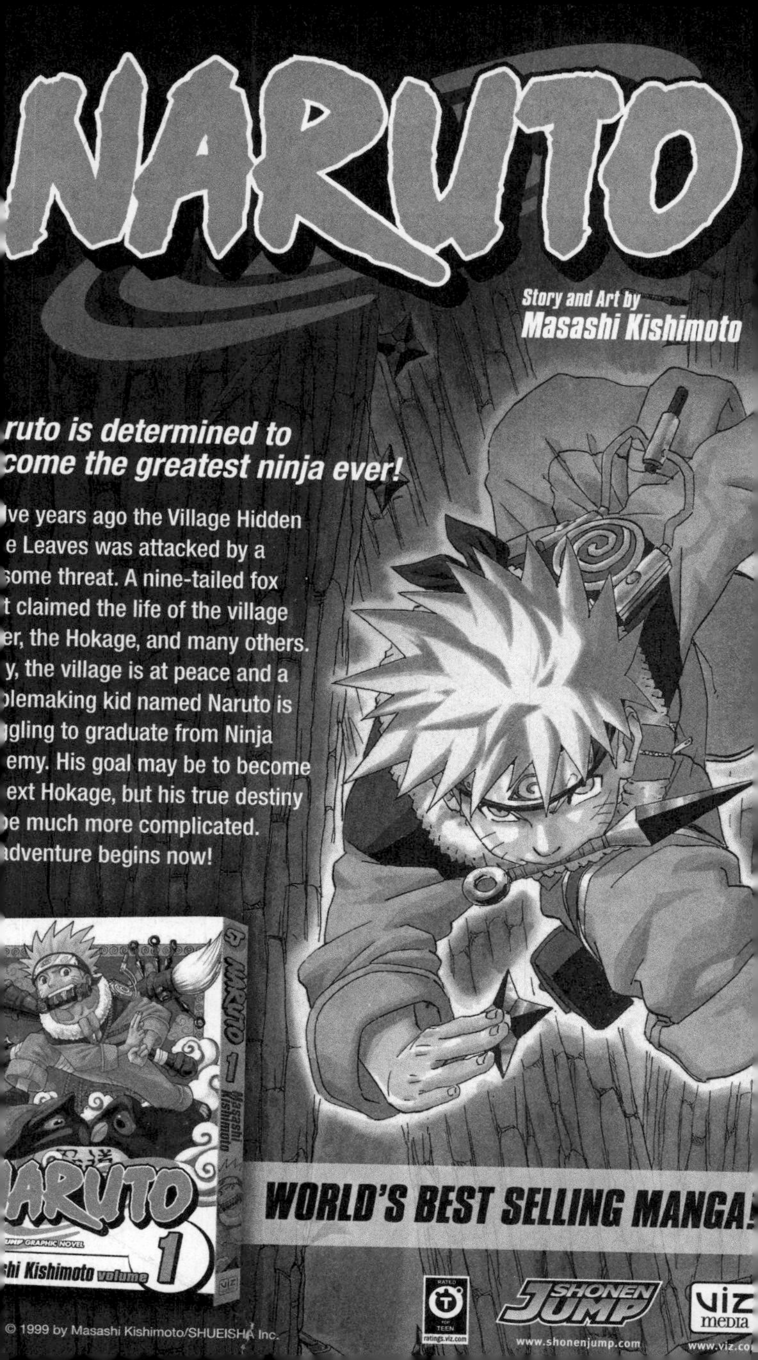
NARUTO
Story and Art by
Masashi Kishimoto
ruto is determined to
come the greatest ninja ever!
ve years ago the Village Hidden
e Leaves was attacked by a
some threat. A nine-tailed fox
t claimed the life of the village
er, the Hokage, and many others.
y, the village is at peace and a
blemaking kid named Naruto is
ggling to graduate from Ninja
emy. His goal may be to become
ext Hokage, but his true destiny
be much more complicated.
adventure begins now!
NARUTO 1 Masashi Kishimoto
NARUTO
GRAPHIC NOVEL
shi Kishimoto volume 1
WORLD'S BEST SELLING MANGA!
RATED T TEEN
ratings.viz.com
SHONEN JUMP
www.shonenjump.com
VIZ media
www.viz.co
© 1999 by Masashi Kishimoto/SHUEISHA Inc.

You're Reading in the Wrong Direction!!

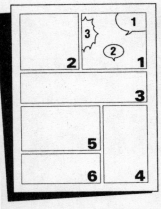

Whoops! Guess what? You're starting at the wrong end of the comic!

…It's true! In keeping with the original Japanese format, **One Piece** is meant to be read from right to left, starting in the upper-right corner.

Unlike English, which is read from left to right, Japanese is read from right to left, meaning that action, sound effects and word-balloon order are completely reversed…something which can make readers unfamiliar with Japanese feel pretty backwards themselves. For this reason, manga or Japanese comics published in the U.S. in English have sometimes been published "flopped"— that is, printed in exact reverse order, as though seen from the other side of a mirror.

By flopping pages, U.S. publishers can avoid confusing readers, but the compromise is not without its downside. For one thing, a character in a flopped manga series who once wore in the original Japanese version a T-shirt emblazoned with "M A Y" (as in "the merry month of") now wears one which reads "Y A M"! Additionally, many manga creators in Japan are themselves unhappy with the process, as some feel the mirror-imaging of their art skews their original intentions.

We are proud to bring you Eiichiro Oda's **One Piece** in the original unflopped format. For now, though, turn to the other side of the book and let the journey begin…!

—Editor